POLICE-COMMUNITY RELATIONS: BRIDGING THE GAP

POLICE-COMMUNITY RELATIONS: BRIDGING THE GAP

WAYNE L. DAVIS, PH.D.

ISBN:	Softcover	978-1-5035-3391-2
	eBook	978-1-5035-3392-9

This book was printed in the United States of America.

Rev. date: 02/12/2015

To order additional copies of this book, contact:
Xlibris
1-888-795-4274
www.Xlibris.com
Orders@Xlibris.com
657053

Table of Contents

List of Tables

List of Figures

Preface

This book provides an overview of police-community relations. First, this book examines elderly people and some of their concerns. To best serve the public, the police must understand the concerns of the public. Second, this book discusses various criminal theories and their limitations. Theories are effective for understanding problems and for solving the problems. However, every theory has a limitation. Third, this book discusses ethical systems and police department orientations, which are used to judge good police officer behavior. Fourth, this book discusses communication, deviance, and dealing with disadvantaged individuals. Fifth, this book discusses hot spots, crime prevention through environmental design, community policing, and community intervention. Finally, this book discusses how to estimate the implementation of a police-community relations program and provides several examples of how to evaluate a program via academic research.

Author

Wayne L. Davis

Wayne L. Davis holds a Bachelor of Science in Electrical Engineering from the University of Michigan-Dearborn, a Master of Science in Business Administration from Madonna University, and a Ph.D. in Criminal Justice from Capella University. In addition, Dr. Davis has earned a helicopter pilot license, an advanced open water scuba diving certification, a technician plus amateur radio license (N8ZFG), and a basic emergency medical technician certificate from the State of Michigan.

Dr. Davis has graduated from city, state, and federal law enforcement academies. He has over 20 years of law enforcement experience with city, state, and federal law enforcement agencies. He has served as a state police post commander and as a field training police officer. In addition, Dr. Davis has received the U.S. Customs & Border Protection Scholastic Award and the U.S. Customs & Border Protection Commissioner's Award.

While he worked as a product design engineer at Ford Motor Company, Dr. Davis introduced the electronic engine control module into the pleasure boat industry. This included writing a product specification manual and performing test-to-failure statistical research. As a result, Dr. Davis was nominated for the Ford Motor Company Electronics

Division Worldwide Leadership Excellence Award. Subsequently, this led to his research paper called, *A Study of Factors Affecting a Supply Decision by the Ford Motor Company International Division for Original Equipment*.

Dr. Davis has several other academic and textbook publications. He has also taught graduate and undergraduate college courses at several different colleges, including Trine University, South University, Waldorf College, and Aiken Technical College. Dr. Davis specializes in converting English logical statements (i.e., the law) into mathematical logical statements in order to determine the truth values of laws, police reports, and the actions of police officers and residents. In other words, Dr. Davis uses English and truth values (Boolean algebra) to articulate the legality of police actions.

Chapter 1

UNDERSTANDING PEOPLE & CONCERNS

Police-Community Relations

Community members went out on a limb,
And gave police the authority to rule over them.

However, in order for residents to feel free in the nation,
Police officers must have good community relations.

One way to minimize social conflict and not to get on their nerves
Is for officers to represent the community members that they serve.

For law and order, the police require public compliance;
Failure to serve residents will lead to defiance.

Furthermore, because residents well outnumber the police,
The public is responsible for maintaining social peace.

Laws & Rules

There are some laws, rules, and sayings that will explain why police officers should work hard to enhance police-community programs. First, according to Davis's Dictum, community problems that go away by themselves come back by themselves (Dickson, 1980). Hence, in order to effectively manage crime, the root causes of crime need to be addressed. Second, according to Wolf's Law, a police officer does not get a second chance to make a first impression. Thus, police officers should always put forth their best efforts. Third, Winston's Second Rule of Success states that a police department's greatest assets are the local residents, who provide valuable resources. Indeed, social peace depends on the assistance provided by residents. Fourth, according to the Woolsey-Swanson Rule of Problems, individuals would rather live with problems that they cannot solve than solutions they cannot understand. Therefore, officers need to effectively communicate with the public. One way to do this is for the police departments to represent the community members that they serve (e.g., same % sex and race). Finally, Vietinghoff's Precept indicates that the managers who control the police forms control the program, which impacts the police department culture. In short, officer performance reviews are dictated by upper management via forms. Thus, upper management can endorse the behaviors that promote good police-community relations by using forms that assess officer performance based on police-community efforts instead of using forms that assess officer performance based on quotas.

There are some laws, rules, and sayings that will explain why some police officers resist police-community programs. First, according to the Upward-Mobility Rule, police officers should not work so hard that they are irreplaceable (Dickson, 1980). If the officers cannot be replaced, they will not be promoted. Second, according to Rutherford's Rule, the less the officers know, the less work they will have to do. By investigating the community's concerns, the police department may be opening a can of worms. Third, according to Toomey's Rule, it is easy to make decisions on matters in which the officers have no responsibility. If the officers have high stakes in the community, they may not be able to make the tough decisions. Fourth, according to Vaughan's Rule of Corporate Life, the lower an officer is on the organizational chart, the more work that officer will have to do. Although police management may make a lot of promises to the community, it is the officers who will get stuck with all of the work. Fifth, according to Weiner's Wisdom, indecision is the key component to flexibility. Thus, if a police-community program is implemented and it is less than optimal, the department may be too invested and too committed to change its position. Finally, according to Rigsbee's Principle of Management, the brightest and best employees will be the first officers to leave the department when given the opportunity. In other words, if officers demonstrate superior skills in serving the public, other departments may seek to hire them and, if the officers leave the department, the department will lose much money that was invested in the officers' training.

Critical Thinking and Police Action

Critical thinking is the open-minded process of collecting, analyzing, and evaluating information in order to make best-practice decisions. For police officers, critical thinking is the process needed to establish probable cause. By applying intellectual standards to the elements of reasoning, police officers may be able to effectively articulate their actions (Paul & Elder, 2009). See Figure 1, Tables 1-2.

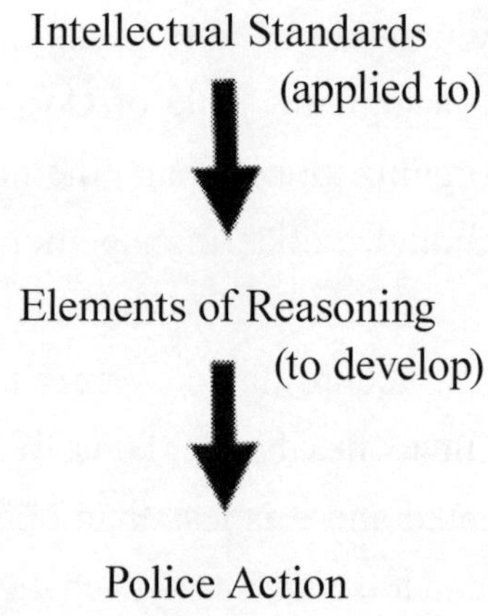

Figure 1. Determining proper police action.

Table 1

Intellectual Standards (Paul & Elder, 2009)

#	Intellectual Standard	Description
1	Clarity	A statement needs to be clear so that it can be determined to be accurate and relevant; elaborate; provide examples
2	Accuracy	A statement needs to be valid; a reliable statement may not necessarily be valid; seek confirmation
3	Precision	Continuous data are more detailed than categorical data; be more exact
4	Relevance	Statements need to be related to the subject of investigation; do not target diversionary flares (red herrings); contribute toward solution
5	Depth	A statement should be more than superficial and should address the most significant factors and complex issues under investigation; use open-ended questions; consider multiple and interacting variables
6	Breadth	All perspectives should be considered; multiple realities may exist; multiple truths may exist; consider various lenses of truth
7	Logic	Multiple statements should support one another; deductive and inductive reasoning should be applied to confirm the data
8	Completeness	Totality of circumstances will enhance the credibility of the evidence; all evidence should be evaluated cumulatively
9	Significance	The statements need to keep focused on the most important problems; the central ideas need to be addressed
10	Fairness	The evidence should be unadulterated; the evidence should be evaluated objectively and reported without bias

Table 2

Elements of Reasoning (Paul & Elder, 2009)

	Element of Reasoning	Description
1	Purpose	The reason needs to be clear and justifiable
2	Question	The subject or topic under investigation needs to be clearly expressed; the question must be unbiased and must address the complexity of the matter
3	Information	The data must be valid, must address the complexity of the issue, and must be supported by credible references
4	Concepts	The notions may need to be clarified; the concepts need to be justifiable
5	Assumptions	The investigator needs to consider assumptions and limitations of the data; human intelligence is limited
6	Inferences	Correlation does not equal causation; hypotheses cannot be proved true (need to demonstrate falsification); use deductive and inductive reasoning to make decisions based on confidence levels
7	Point of View	Different cultures, lenses of truth, ethical systems, and department orientations may influence perceptions and interpretations of data
8	Implications	The investigator needs to consider the consequences of an investigation; public safety is essential; actions that are punitive in nature are inappropriate

Community Policing

There is no one single definition of community policing (Miller, Hess, & Orthmann, 2011). Community policing may be defined as a philosophy that systematically uses partnerships for problem-solving techniques to proactively address problems of public safety, which include social disorder, crime, and the fear of crime. Community policing involves a collaborative effort between the police and local community members. Community policing engages local residents in the identification of problems, seeks input from local residents to prevent the problems, and utlilizes various social agencies to manage the problems. Community policing involves four general principles: organizational transformation (e.g., social interactions and structural dimensions), community engagement, problem solving, and crime prevention via police-citizen cooperation.

Minorities in Government

Minority groups perceive the police force as symbolic for white oppression (Carter, 2002). In order to build trust and a strong police-community bond, it is important that the police department be representative of the local community that it serves. Thus, the racial and ethnic makeup of the police department's officers should be in proportion to that of the community that the officers serve (a similar argument can be made about the percentage of females in the department). A good police-community bond will help promote a good police image and may enhance public participation in law enforcement activities. Police officers must not use excessive force and they must not abuse their authority; excessive force and abuse of authority will damage police-community relations. Because social order depends mostly on community members and not on police officers (as evidence by Prohibition), it is important to get the public involved with local law enforcement programs. Similar to medical HMO programs, it may be better and more cost effective to prevent crime rather than to treat it.

The Poor

The poor may perceive the police force as symbolic for oppression. It costs money to protect personal rights. If a person is abused by the police, the person may be required to hire a lawyer to protect self-interests. However, lawyers are very expensive. One technique that may be used by a police department to overcome the poor is to drag out a case for many years. The police department may hope that the plaintiff runs out of money, moves away, or dies. All three situations may result in a dismissal of the case and a victory for the police. If a police department does happen to lose a case, the cost may be incurred by the taxpayers. Either way, police departments have the upper hand.

Image of Police

Many police officers belong to police unions. Because unions are associated with blue collar workers, this stigmatizes police officers from being recognized as professionals (Carter, 2002). Unions also create the impression that there is conflict within the police agency between two opposing sides, management and officers. The shady appearance that the unions portray to the public negatively impacts the image of the police.

History of Communication and Persuasion Theories

Communication theory as it relates to persuasion theory started around the 5th century BCE (Schiappa, 1991). During this time, Protagoras (490-421 BCE), a philosophical thinker in Athens, became the pioneer of the study of language; he invented a new way of thinking and speaking. Protagoras, the father of debate and a promoter of democracy, organized dialogue and invented the lecture between teachers and students. Each side presented an argument in an informal discussion group and then had to defend it. About the same time, in 466 BCE, the Sicilian government was overthrown. That government, subsequently, changed from tyranny to democracy. As a result, there was a high demand for people to be able to speak their minds in assemblies and to be able to testify for themselves in court. There were few lawyers at that time. Meeting this demand, Corax and Tisias, two Sicilians, developed the argument from probability. Thus, persuasive arguments had begun.

In 1776, the American Revolution took place. During this era, the U.S. Constitution was written, which affords each person charged with a crime the right to a trial by jury. Like Great Britain, trials are based on an adversarial model, where debate is expected (Resnick & Knoll, 2007). Thus, the founding fathers have promoted communication theory and persuasive arguments within the courtroom. Indeed, persuasion has always been a part of the U.S. legal system.

Modes of Persuasion

Police departments, who have a history of corruption, need to persuade the public to trust them (Carter, 2002). In trying to convince individuals to change their opinions, there are three different modes of persuasion. The three modes of persuasion are **ethos, pathos, and logos** (Honeycutt, 2004). **Ethos** is based on credibility, which is the attitude or perception that the audience member has of the speaker; in other words, it is based on the speaker's reputation. **Pathos**, on the other hand, is based on emotional appeals. Referencing emotions in the heat of the moment, pathos is very effective and is commonly used, especially by salespeople. Indeed, a common technique by salespeople is to make emotional appeals to potential customers and then to close the deals before the customers have time to cool down and reason things out. Finally, **logos**, which maintains personal beliefs the longest, is based on critical thinking and reasoning. Although police officers may need to use all three modes of persuasion when they perform their duties, officers also need to understand when suspects are employing the techniques on them.

Communication & Persuasion

Each year about 23 million people within the U.S. become victims of crime (Truman & Planty, 2012). Since September 2001, federal resources, which were previously used to fund local law enforcement, have been redirected toward homeland security (Kingsbury, 2006). With a 45% cut in funds, many local law enforcement agencies have reduced their manpower, with some midsize cities reducing their manpower by about 25%. In addition, U.S. prisons are releasing about 630,000 inmates each year, and the recidivism rate from state prisons is about 67%. Thus, with fewer police officers on the streets and more criminals on the streets, this is a concern. So, it is not surprising that the FBI has indicated that violent crimes rates, such as murder, robberies, and aggravated assaults, are rising in the U.S. (Edwards, 2006). If more crimes occur, then more arrests will be made. Therefore, police officers may find themselves in the courtroom more often. Indeed, the public's safety depends upon police officers effectively testifying in the courtroom.

To effectively serve the public, a police officer must be a credible witness in the courtroom during a jury trial. Part of the job of police officers is to arrest criminals, to complete the proper paperwork, and then to testify in the courtroom. If police officers make arrests, complete the paperwork, but fail to effectively testify in the courtroom, then those police officers have failed to do their jobs and have failed to adequately protect the public. Because police officers are public servants and are expected to protect society, it is vital that police officers learn how to effectively present their arguments in the courtroom and how to persuade jurors.

Democracy and truth rely upon open debate within the courtroom. However, jurors select their own truths based on their perceptions of the credibility of the information that they receive. One way that this credibility is determined is through the jurors' assessment of the way police officers communicate, both verbally and nonverbally. Thus, police officers must communicate well, be credible, and learn to effectively persuade.

Communication Theory

U.S. democratic principles rely upon truth being discovered via open debates within the courtroom (Bank, 2001). Hence, communication theory is very important in law enforcement, especially within the courtroom. How police officers communicate within the courtroom will influence the jurors' decisions. The basic assumptions of communication theory indicate that jurors will perceive information that will affect their attitudes, allowing them to make decisions that could be significant (Tucker, Donovan, and Marlatt, 1999). For example, based on the information that they receive and perceive, the jurors may set a killer loose, or, on the other hand, they may convict an innocent person. Thus, police officers, who are the messengers of information, must use persuasion to affect the attitudes and opinions of the jurors in order to arrive at an appropriate verdict.

Although most police officers receive very little training in courtroom testimony, the jurors believe otherwise (Smith & Hilderbrand, n.d.). Indeed, the jurors already have a misconception about how police officers should testify. Thus, police officers must learn how to effectively communicate in the courtroom so that their testimonies will be credible. In short, credibility is directly related to persuasiveness.

Verbal Persuasion

A police officer's verbal communication in the courtroom will impact the officer's credibility as a witness. Verbal communication can be either written or spoken. If it is written, then it takes the form of police reports. If it is verbal, then it takes the form of oral testimony. Indeed, both types of verbal communication will impact the office's credibility as a witness. In all cases, any courtroom testimony that is less than truthful is illegal and unacceptable. This being said, it is assumed that the police officers have made justifiable arrests in which they are testifying.

A police officer's written report will impact the officer's credibility as a witness. First of all, a police report must have good content, and the officer must be familiar with its content ("Speaking", 2006, pp. 10). Because it is not uncommon for trials to take place years after the event, the police officer should review the report immediately prior to the court date. In other words, a police officer should never go onto the stand without knowing what is in his or her report. If the officer is unprepared, it will not take long for the jurors to find the officer less than credible. Furthermore, the police report must contain all pertinent information; if it is not written down in the report, then it cannot be used in court (Stewart, 2007). In other words, there is no pulling a rabbit out of a magic hat. Furthermore, the report must be objective, complete, accurate, and clear. For example, if a hockey team has played 10 games and is undefeated, this does not mean that the team has won all ten games; they could have tied some of the games. In addition, the report must be relevant and must focus on what was witnesses saw and not on what the witnesses did not see. For instance, the statements, "***I did not see*** *the driver look back before he backed into the other car*," is not equivalent to, "***I saw*** *the driver not look back before he backed into the other car*." The first statement is irrelevant because it indicates that the witness did not see the event (the witness may not have even been at the scene), but the second statement is valuable and describes what the witness actually saw.

The report must also be organized and structured (Navarro, 2004). In order to keep the jurors' attention and to help them understand the flow of events, the report must be presented like one complete television show (do not keep changing channels, which may frustrate the jurors). Furthermore, if there are grammar mistakes within the report, the jurors may view the officer as incompetent. Jurors may perceive that the police officer is unprofessional, uncaring, and/or a fool. If the officer is judged to be unprofessional or uncaring, then the jurors may perceive that the report is incomplete and less than accurate (if it is not important to the police officer to do a good job, then it is not important to the juror for a conviction). If the jurors perceive the officer as a fool, then they may feel that they will be bigger fools if they follow a fool. In both cases, weaknesses in a police officer's written report will be exposed and this may impact the police officer's credibility as a witness (Lewis, 2001).

A police officer's oral testimony will impact the officer's credibility as a witness. Although testifying on the stand can be intimidating and can cause anxiety, the police officer must be professional and objective (Klimon, 1985). When testifying, it is more important to make a lasting impression than to present a perfect testimony (Maxey & O'Connor, 2007). If the officer makes a mistake or cannot remember a particular event, then the officer must admit it; the officer must not weave a web of deceit (Lewis, 2001). First of all, lawyers set traps and look for contradictions. Indeed, lawyers are experts at finding deceit. Furthermore, once a police officer has been discovered to be untruthful, jurors will lose confidence in the officer, which may impact the jurors' final verdict.

When police officers are testifying, they should never start a sentence with, "*To be honest . . .*" or "*To tell the truth . . .*" because this will lead the jurors to believe that the rest of the testimony is untruthful. However, if an officer makes a mistake during a testimony, then the officer should admit it as soon as it is realized (Lewis, 2001; Navarro, 2004; Reynolds, 1990; Stewart, 2007). The jurors understand that not everyone is perfect and that mistakes are made. If the police officer admits to a mistake right away, then the jurors may perceive the officer as an honest person who will correct a mistake instead of trying to cover it up. In addition, when testifying, the officers need to use plain language. If police officers use slang or police lingo, the jurors may become confused or they may feel that the officers are trying to insult them by making them feel dumb. Just as an example, suppose an officer said, "*District 21, 21-43, 10-23, 7 south, signal 6, 10-0.*" Although this message is quite clear to an Indiana state police officer on the toll road, the message is meaningless to the average civilian or juror (the message is notifying the South Bend Indiana state police post that the trooper has arrived on I-80 at mile post 125 eastbound in Lagrange County, is in the service area, is requesting immediate backup, and that someone has been killed).

Testifying in the courtroom is an art and the police officer is a performer (Navarro, 2004). A good way to think about this is to consider the courtroom as an amusement park and the jurors as customers who love thrills. If the police officer rehearses and memorizes the testimony, the jurors will perceive the testimony as a boring and lame merry-go-round (Boccaccini, 2002). Also, if an officer continually pauses during the testimony, jurors will perceive this as a frustrating Ferris wheel, which keeps stopping every few seconds to let passengers on (Navarro). However, by speaking moderately fast with variations in pitch and volume, the jurors will perceive this as a roller coaster, something interesting and exciting. Moreover, the officers must project their voices with confidence, like a big screen television. This will eliminate any perception of doubt in their voices (Defoe, 2007). In short, just as in written communications, weaknesses in a police officer's oral testimony will be exposed. Thus, police officers must practice testifying so that they are perceived as credible witnesses.

Nonverbal Persuasion

In addition to communicating verbally, police officers communicate in many nonverbal manners (Carter, 2002). Similar to verbal communication, nonverbal communication in the courtroom will impact the police officer's credibility as a witness. First, a police officer's appearance sets the stage for the perception of his or her credibility as a witness. Because jurors make judgments on the outward appearances of police officers, the officers must dress appropriately and professionally (Navarro, 2004; Stewart, 2007). The jurors may make the analogy that a dirty yard equals a dirty house. In other words, if the officers do not even care enough to take care of themselves, then they probably also do not care about their work. Second, a police officer's body language impacts the officer's credibility as a witness. Indeed, police officers must have postures that show interest (Boccaccini, 2002; Lambert, 2008; Navarro). For instance, if a boy is interested in a girl and is about to kiss her, he will lean toward her and he will focus his eyes upon her. This is an example of a person showing interest, and it is obvious when it is observed. On the other hand, negative body language, such as fidgeting, crossing the arms, looking at one's watch, and looking at the ceiling, gives the impression that the officer has more important things to do than to be in court (Navarro; Tower, 2011). Thus, if the officers are perceived as being disinterested, the jurors will perceive the officers as less than sincere.

Implementing Communication Theories within the Courtroom

There are several landmark theories that involve communication theory and interpersonal persuasion (Reardon, 1981). These landmark theories include a) the Balance Theory, b) the Attribution Theory, c) the Congruity Principle Theory, d) the Cognitive Dissonance Theory, e) the Learning Theory, f) the Functional Theory, g) the Inoculation Theory, and h) the CounterAttitudinal Advocacy Theory. See Table 3. These theories may be applied in the courtroom by the prosecutor to manipulate the jurors' attitudes toward the defendant.

Because, according to the **Balance Theory**, people like consistency and they resist change, people must be motivated to change their attitudes (Reardon, 1981). In this case, a prosecutor can achieve persuasion by distancing the criminal from the jurors. For example, if a person was being tried for public intoxication, the jurors may be strongly resistant to convict the defendant. The jurors may feel that they have personally consumed too much alcohol, at one time or another, and that this could be one of them on the stand. However, to overcome this perception, the prosecutor must differentiate the criminal from the jurors. First, by drawing a target with concentric circles around it, the prosecutor could start at the outer most ring and state that this level represents the subject's bloodshot eyes. Second, the prosecutor could move to the next circle inward, which represents a person with bloodshot eyes and slurred speech. Third, the prosecutor could move to the next circle inward, which represents bloodshot eyes, slurred speech, and staggering. Fourth, the prosecutor could move to the next circle inward, which represents all of the previous symptoms plus the subject urinating upon the roadway. This process will continue until the center of the target is reached. In this way, the jurors can clearly distance themselves from the defendant and this may help persuade them to change their attitudes.

The **Attribution Theory** states that people seek reasons to justify someone else's behavior; they try to find a motive when a person commits a crime (Reardon, 1981). If a person commits a benevolent act but it is perceived by someone else to be a criminal act, then the motive may be the determining factor for whether a crime has been committed. Because the jurors do not want to convict an innocent person of a crime, and because they do not want themselves to be wrongly convicted of a crime, they desire to find reasons for the actions. Thus, with no motive for committing a crime, the jurors will be less likely to convict a person. As part of the criminal investigation, it is the police officer's job to determine a motive. Once the motive is determined, it will be included as part of the written case report. It is then up to the police officer to explain the motive, in simple language, to the jurors so that they will understand it.

The **Congruity Principle Theory** states that jurors will try to align two or more incompatible concepts (Reardon, 1981). The prosecutor and police officer can take advantage of this by aligning the criminal activity to a negative concept held by the jurors. For example, if the local county is dry and the jurors disapprove of alcoholic beverages, then a person who is being tried for possession of marijuana can be associated with being an alcoholic. In this case, the prosecutor can say that marijuana, like alcohol, causes intoxication and leads to car crashes, which kills innocent people. Furthermore, marijuana is an addictive habit, just like alcohol.

The **Cognitive Dissonance Theory** states that people behave in ways that reduce dissonance between two cognitive elements (Reardon, 1981). In this case, the prosecutor can associate the idea that if the defendant is set free, then one of the jurors may be the defendant's next victim. This stressful perception will persuade the jurors to convict the accused; they will associate the defendant's freedom to negative feelings. Furthermore, by persuading the jurors that justice and democracy demand fair payment for the defendant's actions, and that jail is the perfect place for the accused, the jurors will appropriately align the two cognitive elements.

The **Learning Theory** describes how people are conditioned to respond in particular ways (Reardon, 1981). The county prosecutor is an elected official and knows the local community issues. By associating the particular crime to something that the jurors, who are local community members, find upsetting, the prosecutor can direct their anger toward the accused. For example, if the jurors are upset about paying higher taxes, the prosecutor can illustrate how the accused could not care less about their money problems, as is evidenced by the commission of the criminal act, and that the accused is now mocking them by using their tax paying dollars to get away with it.

According to the **Functional Theory**, people refuse to humble themselves and tend to perform only those actions that they find favorable (Reardon, 1981). In this case, the prosecutor can use the jurors' pride against them by linking the conviction of the accused to the jurors' intelligence. This can be achieved by indicating to the jurors that they are too smart to be fooled by a common criminal (who was not too smart to get caught). By stating that the jurors are community pillars whom the local residents are relying upon to protect them, the jurors may find it beneficial to convict the accused.

The **Inoculation Theory** states that the best persuasion is one that supports one side of an argument and, at the same time, refutes the other side of the argument (Reardon, 1981). In this case, the prosecutor can argue that in order to reduce crime, the accused needs to be locked up. On the other hand, if the jurors fail to convict, their safety is at risk. Thus, the jurors can reduce crime and promote safety at the same time. In order to reinforce this argument and to make it as persuasive as possible, all submitted evidence related to the crime should be emphasized, including victim statements, witness statements, photographs, and laboratory reports (Tucker et al., 1999).

Finally, the **CounterAttitudinal Advocacy Theory** states that people will best construe their own beliefs and behaviors when rewards are not associated with their activities (Reardon, 1981). In this case, the prosecutor can remind the jurors that by serving on the jury, they are serving their community. Convicting the perpetrator is not for personal gain, but it is their patriotic duty as U.S. citizens. Democracy and freedom depend upon law and order. For without law and order, there can be no democracy.

In short, truth in the courtroom relies upon persuasion. Jurors determine their own truths based on the information that they receive (Peterson, 1954). By using multiple persuasion theories, and by simultaneously employing as many of them as possible, prosecutors can align information in ways that will be well received by the jurors.

Table 3

Persuasion Theories (Reardon, 1981)

Persuasion Theory	**Persuasion of Jurors**
Balance Theory	Jurors like consistency and they resist change; jurors must be motivated to change their attitudes
Attribution Theory	Jurors seek reasons to justify someone else's behavior; jurors try to find a motive when a person commits a crime
Congruity Principle Theory	Jurors will try to align two or more incompatible concepts
Cognitive Dissonance Theory	Jurors will behave in ways that reduce dissonance between two cognitive elements
Learning Theory	Jurors are conditioned to respond in particular ways
Functional Theory	Jurors refuse to humble themselves and tend to perform only those actions that they find favorable
Inoculation Theory	Jurors will need to be persuaded by supporting one side of an argument and, at the same time, refuting the other side of the argument
CounterAttitudinal Advocacy Theory	Jurors will best construe their own beliefs and behaviors when rewards are not associated with their activities

Crime Prevention

The job of police is to prevent crime. According to Barkan (2006), there are three levels of crime prevention: primary, secondary, and tertiary. In order to reduce crime, the root causes must be addressed.

First, the primary level of crime prevention indicates that the social and physical environments create the conditions for crime (Barkan, 2006). If crime is to be reduced at this level, poverty and racial tensions must be reduced. The following are examples of actions that may be taken to prevent crime at the primary level. The government can create decent paying jobs for all people; the government can provide aid to people who are under the poverty level; the government can take actions to end racial housing segregation; the government can create new housing where the housing population is not so dense; the government may employ strategies to eliminate gender inequality; and the government can create valued activities in which youths may participate. In addition, community residents can take pride in their neighborhoods by reducing dilapidation and parents may minimize male masculinity by controlling the amount of violence in which their sons are exposed (such as in television, music, toys, and movies).

Second, the secondary level of crime prevention involves addressing the situations and practices that place children at risk for disease, such as failing to provide them with adequate vaccines (Barkan, 2006). The following are examples of actions that may be taken to prevent crime at the secondary level. The government can provide early childhood intervention programs; the government can provide low income parents with affordable child day care so that the parents may work; the government can improve the school system by having smaller schools with fewer students; the government can provide prenatal and postnatal nutrition to the poor; and the government can provide adequate resources to battered women. By providing children and their caretakers with necessary resources, crime may be prevented later in life.

Finally, the tertiary level of crime prevention addresses criminal behavior after the crime has already occurred; it tries to minimize the long-term consequence through punishment (Barkan, 2006). The following are examples of actions that may be taken to prevent crime at the tertiary level. First, the U.S. prison system is very costly and is proving to be less than effective. Therefore, perhaps more emphasis should be placed on community corrections and less on prisons. Second, jails and prisons must be improved through smaller jails and less crowded prisons. These poor living conditions only promote deviance and do little in the area of rehabilitation. Third, because many crimes are committed by youths, the mandatory imprisonment of people who commit three felonies serves no purpose for those past their criminal careers (this is a cost with no real benefits). Fourth, many people are in prison due to nonviolent drug offenses. Indeed, legalizing some of these drugs will reduce the prison population, and, consequently, will allow more resources to be applied to other government programs. Finally, gun control efforts must be increased. Because guns are used during the commission of many crimes, it is important that only law-abiding people have them.

Factors Affecting Truth

Crime prevention requires an understanding of information. However, there are multiple factors that may influence how a police officer sees reality/truth. Some of the factors include morals, laws, education, and experience. See Table 4 and Figure 2. For legal and liability reasons, police officers must often justify their realities to various audiences. Some of the audiences may include judges, juries, police management, victims, third parties (e.g., insurance companies), the media, and community members.

Table 4

Factors that Influence Reality/Truth

#	Factor	Description
1	Lenses of Truth	Critical inquiry philosophy used to determine reality and truth.
2	Personal Ethical Systems	Morals used to assess good behavior.
3	Police Department Orientation	Philosophy used to determine the purpose of the police department and officer behavior.
4	Police Officer Discretion	There is less discretion for more serious crimes (cameras may influence decisions; sex of the offender may influence officer behavior).
5	Culture of Community	Complaints against the department may motivate police behaviors.
6	Political Power	The police superintendent may be directed by the governor to focus on certain activities; prosecutors may influence police behaviors.

7	Generational Clash	Different generations of people have different values.
8	Formal Education	Formal education of officers may help officers to be better problem solvers.
9	Police Rules & Regulations	Failure to comply with department rules and regulations may result in punishment.
10	Laws	Failure to comply with state and federal laws may result in punishment.
11	Research (Inferential Statistics/Themes)	Valid information is needed to solve the root cause of problems; however, research may expose weaknesses and may expose the department to liability.
12	Descriptive Statistics	Descriptive statistics are used to justify officer performance (quotas) and to control classes of people who have been identified as trouble makers.
13	Personal Experience	Social learning environments (e.g., prior police stops) may influence officer behaviors.

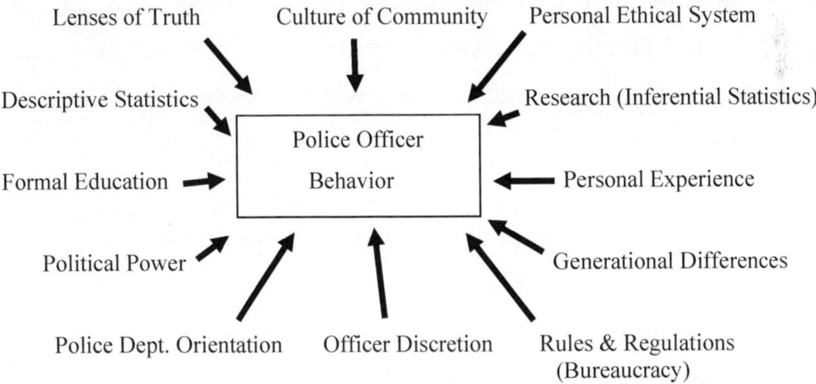

Figure 2. Factors that impact the behaviors of police officers.

Serving the Public by Understanding Generational Differences

Individuals who have grown up in different times have experienced different social learning environments. Indeed, there are several different generations of individuals who have learned different values. The following is a short description of select factors for generational differences. See Table 5.

Individuals in the generation called the **Traditionalists** were born from 1925 to 1945 (United Nations, n.d.). They experienced World War II, political uncertainty, and economic uncertainty. As a result, they have learned to be hard working, thrifty, and cautious. They do not like change and are not very tolerant of risk. Many of the rules today that exist in organizations were established by the Traditionalists.

Individuals in the generation called the **Baby Boomers** were born from 1946 to 1964 (United Nations, n.d.). They grew up in an abundant and healthy economy. Baby Boomers are egocentric and workaholics. They evaluate a person's worth based on his or her work accomplishments.

Individuals in the generation called the **Generation X** were born from 1965 to 1980 (United Nations, n.d.). They grew up and witnessed their parents' great sacrifice for their companies. As a result, they like their independence and to make their own decisions without consulting others. They witnessed the birth of the information age and are resilient and adaptable. Individuals in the Generation X challenge the rigidity of the rules that have been established by the Traditionalists and Baby Boomers.

Individuals in the generation called the **Millennials** were born from 1981 to 2000 (United Nations, n.d.). They grew up in a time of reward and empowerment. They have been encouraged to be opinionated, to make their own choices, and to challenge everything. They expect employers to treat them as consumers, which has resulted in a high employment turnover rate. The computer, Internet, and social media are very important to the Millennials. Consequently, the Millennials have developed news skills and new ways of working together, which confuse the Traditionalists and Baby Boomers. The Millennials challenge the rigidity of the rules that have been established by the Traditionalists and Baby Boomers.

Table 5

Generational Differences ("Generational difference chart", n.d.; Robey-Graham, 2008; United Nations, n.d.).

Name	**Traditionalists**	**Baby Boomers**	**Generation X**	**Millennials**
Birth Years	1900-1945	1946-1964	1965-1980	1981-2000
Dislikes	Technology; waste of resources	Laziness	Red tape	Negativity; anything slow
Preferred Communication	1-1, face-to-face; formal; memo	In person; team player; structured meetings; telephone	E-mail; causal; direct; entrepreneur	Texting; social media; fast; participative
Motivation	Self-motivated	Career driven	Time off	Public Praise
Feedback	No news is good news	Does not appreciate it	Wants to know if doing it right	When want it, will ask for it; wants it frequently and immediately

Rewards	Satisfaction is a job well done	Title recognition; money	Freedom	Meaningful work
Core Values	By the book; discipline; family focus; trust in government	Whatever it takes; loyal to children; equal rights; anti-government	Efficient; diversity; informality; pragmatism; suspicious of Baby Boomer values	Fun; social; diversity; tolerant; highly technical; civic duty
Leadership	Respect to authority	Respect to power	Collaboration	Freedom
Messages that Motivate	Your experience is respected	You are valued and needed	Forget the rules and do it your way	You will work with bright, creative individuals
Loyalty	To the company	To the profession	To the individual	To friends
Attributes	Hard work; sacrifice; work before pleasure; honor; task oriented; trust authority; loyal to company; conservative	Ambitious; competitive; live to work; workaholics; personal fulfillment; questions authority; seeks responsibility	Self-reliance; seeks direction; unimpressed with authority; adaptable; focus on results; loyal to manager; sense of entitlement	Ambitious but not focused; tolerant; goal oriented; innovative; independent; loyal to peers; self-absorbed; sense of entitlement
Preferred Learning Method	From expert	From expert	From each other	From interactive group; technology

Serving the Public

In addressing a community's needs, a police department must decentralize its power so that each officer has the flexibility to be creative in resolving the issues at hand (Miller et al., 2011). Police officers and community leaders must work together to determine how to best meet the community's needs. Instead of reacting to social problems, police departments and community members must work together to implement a proactive police strategy that best serves the public.

The job of police is to serve the public. This means serving the entire population in a fair manner, without discrimination. Being fair does not mean that all persons are treated in exactly the same manner (e.g., children are treated differently than adults). Police need to use common sense and to make best practice decisions that promote the desired outcomes, which are peace and the protection of personal rights. Serving the public includes enforcing laws to make a safer society and to provide services that meet the special needs of particular residents. However, before the police can best serve the public, the police must understand the public.

Intelligence

Howard Gardner, who is well known worldwide for his theory of multiple intelligences, argued that intelligence is not the same as logic, reason, or knowledge (Brualdi, 1998). Gardner argued that intelligence is defined as the ability to solve problems or to make products that are valued by society. One way that intelligence was measured, the psychometric approach, was to use standardized tests to measure performance. As a way to indicate intellectual abilities, interrelationships among performances on intelligence tests were determined. This eventually led to classifications of intelligence, which were labeled secondary mental abilities. Within the secondary mental abilities are crystallized and fluid intelligences (Cavanaugh & Blanchard-Fields, 2006).

Crystallized intelligence is knowledge accumulated through formal education and general life experiences. Crystallized intelligence is primarily language-based accumulated knowledge in a particular culture, which provides a bank of knowledge to organize and solve familiar problems (Bell, Matthews, Lassiter, & Leverett, 2002). Due to accumulated knowledge in a particular culture, a person with crystallized intelligence can effectively communicate, judge, and understand cultural conventions. Jobs utilizing crystallized intelligence involve writing, music, drama, accounting, and practicing law. Crystallized intelligence is learned and continues to increase until very late in life (Stoner, 1982).

Fluid intelligence is basically innate and independent of acquired knowledge and experience (Stoner, 1982). Fluid intelligence involves forming and recognizing concepts, recognizing relationships among patterns, and being adaptive and flexible, which means using deductive and inductive reasoning to solve novel problems. Jobs utilizing fluid intelligence include such jobs as mathematicians and scientists (Bell et al., 2002). Fluid intelligence increases until neural maturation, and then it continuously declines through adulthood along with the neurophysiology status of the individual (Cavanaugh & Blanchard-Fields, 2006; Stoner).

Adulthood

Adulthood is a specific moment in time during the later phase of the life-span perspective, which is based upon a chronological calendar (18 years of age as defined by many state laws). It is a time when a person is expected to have the psychological ability to adapt to the environment and the mental capability to be able to fit into society (Cavanaugh & Blanchard-Fields, 2006). In law enforcement, adulthood would be similar to using RADAR to clock a vehicle's speed because both, adulthood and RADAR, deal with a particular moment in time. However, RADAR may not be very representative of the vehicle's average speed, just as adulthood may not necessarily be representative of successful aging (being healthy and satisfied with life).

Aging is the continuous process of change during one's life. In law enforcement, aging would be similar to using VASCAR (a device that measures distance and time and calculates a vehicle's average speed) because both, aging and VACAR, do not consider a particular moment in time but considers a process over a time interval. Aging has tradeoffs, with some abilities diminishing over time and some abilities improving over time. For example, the physical ability to see may diminish over time but the ability to use new areas of the brain may improve over time (Cavanaugh & Blanchard-Fields, 2006). How a person ages will depend on many factors, which include genetics, social-economic class, geographical location, and consumption habits.

Myths

There are several myths about what is supposed to happen to attention and memory as people become elderly. Some of these myths include a) everyone over 60 years of age has Alzheimer's disease; b) an old dog cannot be taught new tricks; and c) most elderly people's earlier memories become clearer as time passes (Marshall, 2004; Plimpton, 1984; Smith & Eiben, 1995). Concerning the myth that everyone over 60 years of age has Alzheimer's disease, evidence indicates that only four percent of people between 65 to 74 years of age have it. The fact that a person will lose all of his or her memories due to the brain aging is not the norm (Brown University 1997; Harvard College, 2002). In fact, some memories can be recalled throughout one's life. The memories that are harder to recall are the explicit memories, which are the ones deliberately learned at a particular point in time (Cavanaugh & Blanchard-Fields, 2006). The problem is that the hippocampus part of the brain, where memories are created, experiences communication problems during the transfer of memories to other parts of the brain for storage (Smith & Eiben). Elderly adults show much less blood flow to the areas in the brain necessary for effective encoding of information. Thus, information is not being effectively stored into memory (Cavanaugh & Blanchard-Fields). Consequently, memories cannot be retrieved if they were not effectively stored.

For the second myth, it is commonly portrayed that elderly persons cannot learn. For example, the grandfather in the popular cartoon show is portrayed as an old man with little memory. When he is shown at the nursing home, he does little more than sit around. Because the myth that elderly people have bad memories is continually repeated, people start to believe it. The brain is like a muscle and needs to be exercised (Cavanaugh & Blanchard-Fields, 2006). By exercising the mind, it will get stronger. Although the elderly may have slower times encoding and retrieving information, they compensate in other ways, such as by using external memory aids. As a result, learning is still possible.

The third myth indicates that earlier memories become clearer as one ages. This is only true relatively speaking. The older memories may seem clearer but only when they are compared to newer ones, which have been weakly formed. Furthermore, because earlier memories are often accessed repeatedly, such as in storytelling, these memories are reinforced by the creation of a rich neural network (Smith & Eiben, 1995).

In short, there are myths about losing one's learning capabilities as one grows older. Furthermore, these myths are reinforced through television programs. However, the mind is like a muscle and needs to be exercised if it is to remain effective and efficient (Cavanaugh & Blanchard-Fields, 2006).

Changes

Three changes that are associated with attention, perception, and memory functions are a) hearing loss, b) strokes, and c) normal neurochemical changes within the brain (Cavanaugh & Blanchard-Fields, 2006). Hearing loss is a typical change that people often realize in their forties and this affects their mental health. Hearing is important in social interactions and in human communications; the lack of hearing leads to social isolation, paranoia, and depression. Diminished hearing causes people to experience sensory decline, thus reducing the amount of information received through hearing (Wingfield, 2005). Hearing loss makes it harder for people to distinguish information from noise; speech processing is inherently involved with cognitive abilities (Gordon-Salant & Fitzgibbons, 1997). If a person cannot effectively receive information, then the person will be unlikely to encode accurate information into memory.

Consequently, if the information is not received and stored into memory, it cannot be retrieved. Feeling helpless and isolated, this may lead to depression. Depression impairs memory and has a negative impact on a person's attention and ability to learn (Cavanaugh & Blanchard-Fields). In short, hearing loss has a negative impact on mental health.

A stroke may have a negative impact on mental health (Cavanaugh & Blanchard-Fields, 2006). A person who becomes paralyzed due to a stroke incurs brain damage and this directly affects the mental capacity of the person. Furthermore, a stroke victim may not be able to interact with other people in the same manner as before the stroke. This social isolation can lead to depression and may impair memory.

Finally, normal neurochemical changes occur within the brain, which may have a negative impact on mental health (Cavanaugh & Blanchard-Fields, 2006). The idea that memory loss is due to brain cells dying is the old way of thinking. By using sophisticated technology, such as magnetic resonance imaging, the anatomy and physiology of the brain is much more accurate than before. Current information indicates that small structures, called nuclei, within the brain change with age. The nuclei provide essential chemicals within the brain, which are necessary for the transmission of information. This means that memory loss is a physiological problem, specifically a chemical problem, versus an anatomical problem. On the positive side, this means that there is the potential for medical intervention via drugs, which could minimize mental impairment (Herbert, 1999).

What is considered normal mental health depends upon the circumstances surrounding an individual (Cavanaugh & Blanchard-Fields, 2006). For instance, a person who gets upset about going outside at night may be acting in self-preservation, especially if the area is dangerous. However, if the emotions are a change in behavior, then the new behavior is suspect. The best people to evaluate change in an individual's behavior are the ones who personally know the individual and who spend a good amount of time with the individual. Individuals are considered mental healthy as long as they have an accurate perception of reality, have a positive attitude toward self, and have everyday competency. If an individual starts displaying a lack of motor skills, starts losing coordination, starts using incomprehensible words, and starts showing both short-term and long-term memory loss, then the behaviors of that individual are not considered normal (Stein, 2003).

Concerns Involving the Elderly

People over 50 years of age make up about 57% of all victims of fraud and swindles nationwide ("Senior fraud initiative", n.d.). Society needs to pull together and to help defend the elderly from being scammed. One possible solution to help the elderly is to make it mandatory for bank tellers to monitor and report large suspicious financial transactions. Such transactions can be held until certain conditions are satisfied. However, banks do not support this idea because they feel that it is not their job to act like police officers ("Opinion", 2005). Perhaps by passing laws that hold banks financially responsible for failing to report suspicious financial transactions will motivate banks to change their position. Once the banks start feeling a financial sting, then perhaps they will start protecting the elderly.

Another concern for the elderly is end-of-life problems. In 1997, the United States Supreme Court ruled that people do not have a constitutional right to die (Cavanaugh & Blanchard-Fields, 2006). However, murder, or assisted suicide, is a state violation and not a federal violation, therefore it falls under state guidelines (although there is the possibility of civil rights violations under federal law). Although people do not have the right to die, they do have the right to refuse medical treatment and to accept care that they find suitable. The following websites provide information about the end-of-life process, which may be helpful to caregivers, family members, and patients.

The **endoflifejourney.com** is a website that represents a company called End of Life, Peaceful Journey (End of Life, n.d.). The company educates care providers on individual concepts of comfort, advanced care directives, spiritual concerns, and the end-of-life process. The company provides testimonials as a means of developing credibility and generating business.

The **www.acponline.org** is a website that represents the American College of Physicians (ACP), which is the largest medical specialty society (American College of Physicians, 2011). This society provides information that is devoted to policy development and implementation related to medical ethics. The Center for Ethics and Professionalism within the ACP develops policies on ethical dilemmas involving patients and physicians. The website is written from the doctor's point of view, which generally means to protect life at all costs. The website provides many references relating to professional research conducted by its members, who are doctors and experts in their fields. The ACP's activities include shaping legislative and administrative sectors of the government by testifying, as experts, before Congressional committees. The ACP also provides its annual report for the public to view.

The **http://www.painfoundation.org** website represents the American Pain Foundation (APF), founded in 1997, which is an independent nonprofit organization (American Pain Foundation, 2011). The APF serves people who are suffering from pain through information and support, hoping to improve their quality of life through pain management and by raising public awareness. The APF hopes to modify legislation through the combined voices of millions of people suffering from pain. The APF's website has been fully endorsed by Dorland Healthcare Information, who describes and rates websites that specialize in health information. The APF receives it funds through contributions from thousands of individuals and corporations. Many of these contributors include pharmaceuticals corporations, who are biased toward creating a market for drugs.

The **www.compassionandchoices.org** website represents Compassion & Choices (C&C), a nonprofit organization created in 2005 when Compassion in Dying and End-of-Life Choices unified (Compassion & Choices, n.d.). C&C is the oldest and largest choice-in-dying organization in the country with the most comprehensive resources available. Its goal is to improve laws that allow people to experience peaceful deaths, consistent with their wishes. C&C specializes in referring people who are near death, and in much pain, to specialists, hospice programs, social service agencies, and disease-specific support groups. Its philosophy champions the idea that knowledge is power. The society also helps with living wills and advanced directives. Its vision is to provide everyone with a full range of state-of-the-art care, which includes choices that involve dying in comfort and with dignity. It appears that the board members and advisors are mostly lawyers, doctors, insurance agents, and religious personnel. The C&C receives it funds through contributions and fundraising. However, the organization has a set policy on fundraising activities, which ensures that the activities meet C&C's standards.

Life-long Process of Development

Human development is a lifelong process. Furthermore, there are different areas of human development. For example, development involves personality, behavior, and morality. Following are tables that summarize a) Needs and Motives, b) Five Views of Behavior, c) Human Development and Stages, d) Kohlberg's Stages of Moral Development, e) Several Theories on Basic Human Development, f) Rational-Emotive Behavior Therapy, and g) Irrational Beliefs. See Figure 3 and Tables 6-10.

According to Maslow, people have certain needs and motives. The bottom two levels of his hierarchy represent basic and primary needs, and the higher levels represent secondary needs. As individuals grow and develop, they move upward from one level to the next.

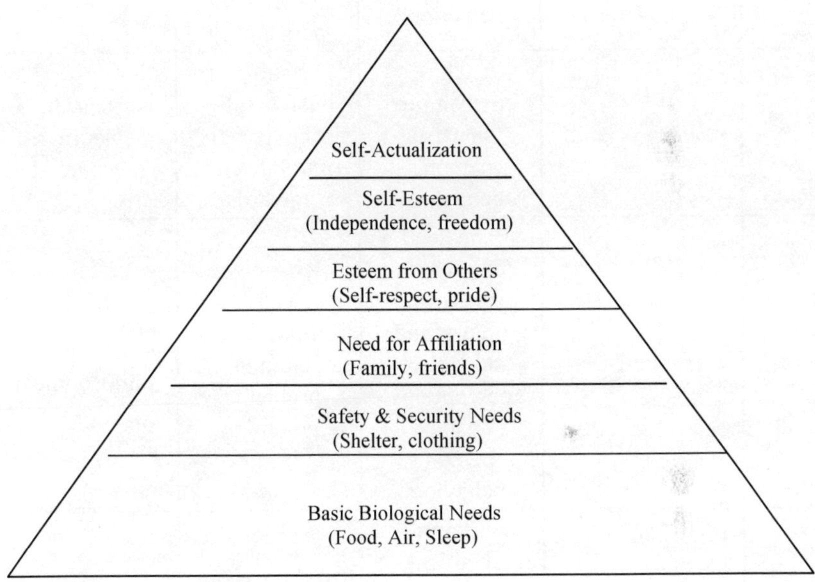

Figure 3. Maslow's hierarchy of needs and motives (Ryckman, 2013).

Table 6

Five Views of Behavior (Coon, 1998)

Item #	Behavioral View	Claim	Factors	View of Human Nature
1	Psychodynamic	Forces within a person's personality shape a person's behaviors.	Desires, internal impulses and conflicts, and clashing forces with personality	Negative, pessimistic
2	Behavioristic	The environment shapes a person's behaviors.	Learning as the result of external and internal rewards	Neutral, scientific, mechanistic
3	Humanistic	The need for personal growth, self-image, and subjective perceptions shape a person's behaviors.	Self-image, self-actualization, human problems, potential, ideals	Positive, philosophical
4	Biopsychological	Internal chemical, biological, and physical processes shape a person's behaviors.	Brain, nervous system, genetics, biochemistry, evolution	Neutral, reductionistic, mechanistic
5	Cognitive	Mental processing of information shapes a person's behaviors.	Perception, understanding, memory, critical thinking	Neutral, computer-like

Table 7

Human Development and Stages (Berk, 2007; Coon, 1998)

Age	Period of Human Development	Freud's Personality Development	Erikson's Psychosocial Stages	Piaget's Stages of Cognitive Development
Conception – birth	Prenatal			
0 < 3 years	Infancy / Toddlerhood	Oral Stage (infant interacts with world via the mouth)	Trust v. Mistrust (relationship to caretakers)	Sensorimotor (knowing by sensing & acting)
3 – 5 years	Preschool	Anal Stage (focus on bladder and bowel movements)	Self-reliance v. Self-doubt (toilet training)	Preoperational Thought (concept formation, symbolic reasoning)
		Phallic Stage (ID – genitals)	Initiative v. Guilt (role-playing and sense of competency)	
5 – 13 (onset of puberty)	Childhood	Latency Stage (Ego & Superego – social skills)	Industry v. Inferiority (develop competency)	Concrete Operations (logical operations, concrete objects)
13 (puberty) – early 20s	Adolescence	Genital Stage (Sexual maturity)	Identity v. Role Confusion (sense of gender and personal identity)	Formal Operations (abstracts, analogies, metaphors, hypothetical reasoning
Early 20s – mid 30s	Early Adulthood		Intimacy v. Isolation (develop and maintain close personal relationships)	
Mid 30s – mid 60s	Middle Adulthood		Generativity v. Self-Absorption (contribute to society)	
Mid 60s - death	Later Adulthood		Integrity v. Despair (sense of accomplishment)	

Table 8

Kohlberg's Stages of Moral Development (Coon, 1998)

Kohlberg's Stages of Moral Development
Pre-Conventional
Stage 1: punishment orientation. Obedience is obtained via potential punishment.
Stage 2: Pleasure-seeking orientation. Personal needs and personal gain determine behaviors.
Conventional
Stage 3: Good boy/good girl orientation. Good behavior is displayed in order to please significant others.
Stage 4: Authority orientation. Doing one's duty and obeying the law determine behaviors.
Post-Conventional
Stage 5: Social-contract orientation. Rational thought and mutual agreement result in the development of laws that determine behaviors.
Stage 6: Morality of individual principles. Self-chosen ethical principles that promote dignity, justice, and equality determine behaviors.

Table 9

Several Theories on Basic Human Development (Berk, 2007)

Theory	Development	Developmental Influence
Psychoanalytic perspective	Psychosexual and psychosocial	Development is determined by both nature and nurture. Innate impulses are controlled via child rearing.
Behavioral and social learning theory	Learned behaviors	Development is determined by conditioning and modeling.
Piaget's cognitive-developmental theory	Cognitive development	Development is determined by brain growth and the innate drive to discover reality in stimulating environments.
Information processing	Gradually improve perception, attention, memory, and problem-solving skills	Development is enhanced when the brain grows and active individuals are required to modify their thinking when they confront new situations.
Ethology and evolutionary developmental psychology	Develop a wider range of adaptive behaviors; distinct capacities emerge quickly	Heredity and evolution influence learning adaptiveness.

Vygotsky's sociocultural theory	Language and complex dialogue lead to change; varies from culture to culture	Heredity, brain growth, and evolution influence learning adaptiveness.
Ecological systems theory	Environmental factors impact biological dispositions to influence behaviors.	Development is bidirectional and is determined by personal characteristics and the reactions of other people.
Lifespan perspective	Gains and declines in development are influenced by biological, social, and psychological factors	Development occurs throughout life and is influenced by multidimensional factors, both heredity and environmental.

Rational-Emotive Behavior Therapy

The basic idea of the rational-emotive behavior therapy is that individuals develop faulty or unrealistic beliefs, which lead to self-defeating habits (Coon, 1998). As a result, individuals become unhappy. Thus, emotional problems can be reduced if irrational beliefs are replaced with rational beliefs. According to Ellis, there are 10 irrational beliefs that people often hold.

Table 10

Irrational Beliefs

Irrational Beliefs	
1	Some individuals feel that everyone important to them must love and approve of them; their happiness depends upon it.
2	Some individuals feel that they always need to be the best at everything that they do; their happiness depends upon accomplishments.
3	Some individuals believe that they are never wrong and that other people need to be punished.
4	Some individuals get upset when everything is not exactly that way that they want it.
5	Some individuals feel that someone else always causes their problems.
6	Some individuals are consumed with reliving bad experiences of the past.
7	Some individuals believe that it is better to avoid responsibilities than to deal with them.
8	Some individuals believe that their success depends on associating with others who are powerful.
9	Some individuals continually let bad experiences dictate future behaviors.
10	Some individuals believe that there is a perfect solution to human problems and that the failure to find that solution is horrific.

Psycho-Spiritual Development and Therapy

Educating clients is the business of the helping professions (Davis & Moldenhauer, 2012). From the perspective of psycho-spiritual development and therapy, all individuals are endowed with the innate ability to care for themselves. However, to maintain their mental, emotional, and physical health, individuals may need professional assistance from time-to-time. In other words, a person may need to call upon the helping professions during their time of need. However, although all individuals may benefit from occasional counseling and psychotherapy, a typical client, who may have unbearable concerns, does not generally contact a therapist prior to his or her *crisis of urgency.*

Many contemporary psychotherapists, physicians, and psychologists claim that unconditional positive regard and love are the best therapy - through openness, honesty, and acceptance (Davis & Moldenhauer, 2012). Professional therapists educate people to dispute their irrational thoughts, beliefs, and feelings. Individuals are taught through Maslow's Hierarch of Motives and Needs that the ultimate goal is to attain self-actualization and self-fulfillment (Coon, 1998). Hope is in the personal philosophy that humans are always in the process of improving - both in the temporal and spiritual domains.

Five-factor Model

The Five-Factor Model theory of personality indicates that people can be described with five independent dimensions when they encounter emotional, interpersonal, experiential, attitudinal, and motivational situations. The five dimensions of the Five-Factor Model include a) neuroticism, which is negative affectivity or nervousness, b) extraversion, which is energy or enthusiasm, c) openness to experience, which is originality, d) agreeableness, which is altruism, and e) conscientiousness, which is control or constraint (Cavanaugh & Blanchard-Fields, 2006; McCrae 1991). However, personality traits and adaptations alone cannot completely describe people's personalities because people desire purpose and meaning in their lives as organized through stories of lived experiences (Cavanaugh & Blanchard-Fields; McAdams, 2005). According to McAdam's theory, people's personal stories of where they came from, where they are, where they are going, and who they will become provide each person with a sense of identity (Cavanaugh & Blanchard-Fields).

References

American College of Physicians (2011). Retrieved from www.acponline.org

American Pain Foundation (2011). Retrieved from http://www.painfoundation.org

Bank, S. (2001). From mental health professional to expert witness: testifying in court. *New Directions for Mental health Services,* 91.

Barkan, S. (2006). *Criminology: A sociological understanding* (3rd ed.). Upper Saddle River, NJ: Pearson Prentice Hall.

Bell, N., Matthews, T., Lassiter, K., and Leverett, J. (2002). Validity of the wonderlic personnel test as a measure of fluid or crystallized intelligence: Implications for career assessment, *North American Journal of Psychology, 4*(1), 113.

Berk, L.E. (2007). *Development through lifespan* (4th ed.). Boston, MA: Pearson, Allyn and Bacon.

Boccaccini, M. (2002). What do we really know about witness preparation? *Behavioral Sciences and the Law, 20*(1/2), 161-189.

Brown University (1997). *Memory loss due to aging is not normal, 9* (16).

Brualdi, A. (November 1, 1998). Gardner's theory. *Teacher Librarian.*

Carter, D. (2002). *Issues in police-community relations: Taken from The Police and the community* (7th ed.). Boston, MA: Pearson Custom Publishing.

Cavanaugh, J. & Blanchard-Fields, F. (2006). *Adult development and aging* (5th ed.). Belmont, CA: Thomson Wadsworth.

Compassion & Choices (n.d.). Retrieved from www.compassionand choices.org

Coon, D. (1998). *Introduction to psychology: Exploration and application* (8th ed.). Pacific Grove, CA: Brooks/Cole.

Davis, W.L., & Moldenhauer, R.E. (2012). *Police-community relations: Different lenses & perceptions of truth.* Mason, OH: Cengage.

Defoe, T. (2007). The truth is, you gave a lousy talk. *Chronicle of Higher Education, 54*(17).

Dickson, P. (1980). *The official explanations.* New York, NY: Delacorte.

Edwards, S. (2006, June 13). Violent crime rates rising in U.S., FBI says: Murder, assault, robbery. *CanWest News Service.*

End of Life, Peaceful Journey (n.d.). Retrieved from www. endoflifejourney.com

Generational difference chart (n.d.). Retrieved from http://www.wmfc.org/uploads/GenerationalDifferencesChart.pdf

Gordon-Salant, S. and Fitzgibbons, P. (1997). Selected cognitive factors and speech recognition performance among young and elderly listeners. *Journal of Speech, Language, and hearing Research.*

Harvard College (2002). How memory changes with age. *Harvard Health Publications*, 11.

Herbert, W. (1999). Losing your mind? *U.S. News & World Report, 127* (4).

Honeycutt, L. (Ed.). (2004). *Aristotle's rhetoric*. Retrieved from http://rhetoric.eserver.org/aristotle/index.html

Kingsbury, K. (2006). The next crime wave. *Time, 168*(24), 70-77.

Klimon, E. (1985). "Do you swear to tell the truth?" *Nursing Economics, 3*(2), 98-102.

Lambert, D. (2008). *Body language 101: The ultimate guide to knowing when people are lying, how they are feeling, what they are thinking, and more.* New York, NY: Skyhorse.

Lewis, D. (2001). *The police officer in the courtroom*. Springfield, IL: Charles C Thomas Publisher, LTD.

Marshall, A. (2004). Gray matters: How to profit from an aging marketplace. *H&MM*, 8.

Maxey, C., and O'Connor, K. (2007). Dealing with blunders. *T+D, 61*(3), 78-79.

McAdams, D. (2005). Sexual lives: The development of traits, adaptations, and stories. *Human Development*, 298-302.

McCrae, R. (1991). The five-factor model and its assessment in clinical settings. *Journal of Personality Assessment*, 399-414.

Miller, L.S., Hess, K.M., & Orthmann, C.H. (2011). *Community policing: Partnerships for problem solving* (6th ed.). Clifton Park, NY: Delmar Cengage.

Navarro, J. (2004). Testifying in the theater of the courtroom. *FBI Law Enforcement Bulletin, 73*(9), 26-30.

Opinion: Stop scams on elderly (July 06, 2005). *Contra Costa Times.*

Paul, R. & Elder, L. (2009). *The miniature guide to critical thinking: Concepts and tools.* Dillon Beach, CA: Foundation for Critical Thinking.

Peterson, R. (1954). I swear to tell. *Saturday Evening Post, 227*(10), 88.

Plimpton, B. (1984). Senior careerists: Strategies for using their skills. *Public Administration Review*, Sept.-Oct., 448-452.

Reardon, K. (1981). *Persuasion: Theory and context*. Beverly Hills, CA: Sage Publications.

Resnick, P. and Knoll, J. (2007). Being an effective psychiatric expert witness. *Psychiatric Times*, *24*(6).

Reynolds, D. (1990). *The truth, the whole truth and nothing but . . .* Springfield, IL: Charles C Thomas Publisher, LTD.

Robey-Graham, A.K. (2008). *Generational Comparisons and Contrasts Chart*. Retrieved from http://www.napavalley.edu/people/jhall/Documents/Generational%20Chart.pdf

Ryckman, R.M. (2013). *Theories of personality* (10th ed.). Belmont, CA: Cengage.

Schiappa, E. (1991). *Protagoras and logos*. Columbia, SC: University of South Carolina Press.

Senior fraud initiative (n.d.). Retirement Industry Trust Association. Retrieved from http://www.ritaus.org/fraud-statistics

Smith, L. & Eiben, T. (April 17, 1995). Memory. *Fortune, 131* (7).

Smith, R., & Hilderbrand, D. (n.d.). *Courtroom testimony techniques: Success instead of survival*. Retrieved from http://www.ronsmithandassociates.com/

Speaking successfully (2006). *Techniques: Connecting Educations & Careers*, *81*(8), 10-11.

Stein, A. (2003). Aging is more than skin deep. *Nursing, 33* (2), 7-8.

Stewart, S. (2007). Effective courtroom performance by Indiana law enforcement. *Clark County Prosecuting Attorney for Police Officers*. Retrieved from http://www.clarkprosecutor.org/html/police/police2.htm

Stoner, S. (1982). Age differences in crystallized and fluid intellectual abilities. *The Journal of Psychology, 110*(1), 7-10.

Truman, J.L., & Planty, M. (2012). *Criminal victimization, 2011.* Retrieved from http://www.bjs.gov/content/pub/pdf/cv11.pdf

Tucker, J., Donovan, D., and Marlatt, G. (Eds.). (1999). *Changing additive behavior: Bridging clinical and public health strategies.* New York: Guilford Press.

United Nations Joint Staff Pension Fund (n.d.). *Traditionalists, Baby Boomers, Generation X, Generation Y (and Generation Z) Working Together*

Wingfield, A., Tun, P. and McCoy, S. (2005). Hearing loss in older Adulthood: What it is and how it interacts with cognitive performance. *American Psychological Society, 14*(3), 144-148.

Chapter 2

THEORIES OF CRIME

People commit crimes for a variety of reasons. For example, due to an electrical-chemical problem inside the brain, some people may not be able to distinguish right from wrong. Other people claim that conflict arises when goals are defined but barriers are created that inhibit the ability of individuals to lawfully reach those goals. Others claim that crimes are committed simply because they are profitable. Others believe that people commit crimes because they are influenced by significant others to be deviant. If people know the difference between right and wrong, are people naturally good and taught to violate the law or are they naturally bad and must be motivated to obey the law? In short, there are a great many beliefs for why people commit crimes.

Historically, the consensus theory, which is based on the assumption that laws represent the views of the greatest normative consensus, has played a major role in understanding law and human behavior (Akers & Sellers, 2009). During the 1960s, however, the conflict theory, which is based on the assumption that competing groups struggle for power, became the forefront of criminological theory. According to the conflict theory, the public disagrees on many social issues, which are usually due to differentials in wealth and power (Barkan, 2006). The most powerful groups gain control of the government and they adopt their values as the legal standards of behaviors. Instead of serving the public, those individuals in power pass laws and policies to protect their own self-interests (Vold et al., 2002). Consequently, the people with power are able to pursue their self-interests while the people with less power, usually minorities, are unable to pursue their self-interests because their actions are defined as criminal.

Some individuals argue that laws have been created to protect the interests of a small powerful group of white males (Carter, 2002; Liska & Messner, 1999). This is evidenced by the fact that there are often hidden underlying social forces in society that negatively affect women and minorities (Hatch, 2002). Both groups have long been discriminated against. Although law enforcement is dominated by Caucasians, who have their own perspectives, it is important that police departments understand the problems faced by minorities (Carter). In order to best serve local residents, police officers need to understand the residents, which requires effectively communication. Indeed, any system without feedback is unstable, which leads to chaos.

Conflict Theory

One theory that helps explain why some individuals commit crime is the conflict theory (Straus, 2002; Vold et al., 2002). First, the conflict theory indicates that the people who control the resources have power and they pass laws to protect their own self-interests at the cost of other people who have less economic power. In other words, the people with governmental authority discount the interests of the less powerful people; this prevents the poor from being successful. Because the people who are in power control the social relationships of other institutions (e.g., educational, political, religious, and mass media groups), many institutions support the interests of the ruling class. For example, anti-prostitution laws have been passed because they reflect the self-interests of the ruling class, based upon their personal religious and moral convictions. Thus, crime is the result of social conflict.

According to the conflict theory, differentials in wealth and power lead to crime (Barkan, 2006). If everyone in an area is poor, then there are fewer opportunities to commit crime and there is less resentment among the people; thus, crime levels will remain constant. However, when there is economic inequality in society, people's emotions and behaviors may be affected. In this case, the difference between the socioeconomic classes is like potential energy, which is converted into kinetic energy in the form of violence (Rifklin, 1980).

This process is very similar to the law of entropy (second law of thermodynamics) (Rifkin, 1980). The law of entropy states that all matter and energy moves from order to disorder or from structure to the lack of structure (to randomness). In other words, the universe will dissipate all potential gradients between two non-equilibrium distributions of energy ("All about", 2001). However, people create pockets of order in this disorderly universe as a means of promoting survival (Rifkin). Indeed, cultures and communities exist in a universe with laws, and there is no reason to believe that cultures and communities would be exempt from those laws. Cultures, in fact, serve as the mechanisms for the transference of energy from the wealthy to the poor. Thus, wealth is a gradient of potential power and, because the control of power is the foundation of human culture, cultures will work to minimize that difference. Hence, there is a nexus between poverty and violence, but the connection is indirect (Vold, Bernard, & Snipes, 2002). In short, violence is due to the inequality of wealth, not simply due to poverty.

From the feminist perspective, women face issues that may appear obscure to men (Hatch, 2002). This is important because law enforcement is a male dominated culture. Thus, before conflict can be managed, the root causes of the problems must first be identified. Female officers may be able to provide valuable insight into these feminist issues. If the situations cannot be changed, at least police officers will be able to empathize with the public. In short, for police officers to best serve the public, they must understand the public.

Strain Theory

The founding fathers believed that democracy depends upon economic freedom (Schramm, 2006). Indeed, the founding fathers wrote the U.S. Constitution so that a capitalistic economic system would persist to ensure political freedom. As a result, achieving financial success is fundamental to American society.

According to the Robert Merton's strain theory, when people in power pass laws that do not represent the common interests of the local residents, and which inhibit them from legitimately achieving their financial goals, the local residents start to experience stress and strain (Vold et al., 2002). The strain theory indicates that the social structure fails to provide the legitimate means to achieve what the local culture values (i.e., financial success) and that negative feelings (e.g., stress, frustration, anxiety, depression, and anger) are created because the poor perceive that their financial opportunities are being oppressed by the government (Vold et al., 2002). In short, the residents who have little power perceive society as unjust.

The Declaration of Independence encourages residents to pursue happiness and the U.S. Constitution promotes economic freedom (Hames, & Ekern, 2005). Although American culture defines financial success as the country's most important goal, the poor are not always given the opportunities to pursue happiness (DuBois & Berg, 2002). This may negatively affect their quality of life within the community. Thus, being unable to lawfully pursue their dreams, the poor may engage in criminal activities.

Biological

Physical brain injury and brain disease are some biological reasons why deviant behaviors may occur. The human being is a creature with a biological central processing unit called the brain. The human brain uses chemical neurotransmitters to transit electrical signals across junctions within the brain (Brainbox, 2006). Because the chemistry within the brain is significant in determining behavior, illicit drugs, for example, which are ingested into the human body, may negatively affect the brain, and thus, human behavior.

The chemistry within the brain may be impacted in two ways: 1) the brain may not receive the chemicals that it needs, and 2) the brain may receive chemicals that will negatively affect it. In the former case, omega-3 fatty acids, which can only be obtained from a person's diet, are critical in brain development (Hibbeln, Ferguson, & Blasbalg, 2006). Studies have shown that low levels of omega-3 fatty acids are linked high levels of aggression. In the latter case, studies have shown that high levels of linoleic acid, gained from consuming seed oils, are linked to deviant behaviors (Hibbeln, Nieminen, & Lands, 2004). Furthermore, because the most significant phase of growth is during fetal development, poor nutrition and the use of toxins by the mother-to-be may negatively impact the developmental of the fetus' brain (Barkan, 2006). Likewise, environmental pollutants may have a negative impact on the brain (Vold et al.). In short, what people consume may affect their behaviors.

One method of determining the health of the brain is to examine the image of the brain via positron emission tomography (Vold et al., 2002). Positron emission tomography has indicated that decreased blood flow and hypo-metabolism in the frontal and temporal lobes of the brain may be linked to aggressive behaviors (Wacker Foundation, 2007). Likewise, brain images have been used to link a particular gene dysfunction within the brain to violent behaviors. In short, a brain scan, which provides firsthand data, is more reliable than examining the skull, which provides secondhand data.

Hare's Theory

The human brain can be divided anatomically into two cerebral hemispheres: a left side and a right side, where each side has it specialized functions (Bartol and Bartol, 2008). Several areas that the left side of the brain specializes in include verbal communication, logical thinking, and detail recognition (Geske, 1992). Furthermore, the left side of the brain is linked to self-inhibition (Bartol & Bartol).

On the other hand, several areas that the right side of the brain specializes in include spatial perceptions, pattern recognition, and intuitive thinking (Geske). Furthermore, the right side of the brain is linked to understanding emotional communications (Bartol & Bartol). Thus, because the left side of the brain plays a major part in understanding verbal language, and because the right side of the brain plays a major part in understanding nonverbal language, both sides are needed for effective overall communication. If one side of the brain is deficient, then communication may be less than optimal. Consequently, if children cannot effectively express themselves, then they may become frustrated due to the fact that they are unable to resolve their conflicts. Being frustrated, the children may become aggressive and disruptive, and this may lead to peer rejection (their peers may simply not want to associate with aggressive individuals). If aggressive children are socially rejected, then they will "miss critical opportunities to develop normal interpersonal and social skills" (Bartol & Bartol, p. 57). If these skills are not adequately developed, then these children will meet their needs by acting more aggressive. Consequently, this may lead to further rejection by their peers. In sum, the effective use of language is essential in the self-regulation of behavior.

Children who do not mature at the same rate as their peers will not be able to effectively communicate with them (Bartol and Bartol, 2008). Being unable to communicate with peers, these children may be socially rejected. If these children are socially rejected, then they will not be able to effectively improve their communication skills. Instead, they will learn aggressive and inappropriate techniques to resolve their issues. Consequently, this may lead some children to develop antisocial personality disorder (ASPD).

Social Learning Theory

According to the social learning theory, behaviors are reinforced over time according to the intensity, duration, and frequency of social learning experiences; however, deviant and conforming behaviors are simultaneously learned and modified through the same cognitive and behavioral mechanisms (Akers & Sellers, 2009). As children grow up, they learn about the U.S. Constitution and capitalism (i.e., making money) and what they must do in order to achieve their goals. A way of learning this behavior is through rewards, punishment, and by watching what happens to other people (Liska & Messner, 1999; Vold et al., 2002). Hence, American children are constantly exposed to a capitalistic society and are taught that the goal in life is to make money.

Rational Choice Theory

According to the rational choice theory, which is based on Beccaria's classical school of criminology, people freely choose their behaviors (Siegel, 2003). When considering potential options, if benefits and pleasures are greater than the associated costs and punishments, then those behaviors become attractive. Indeed, when there is more gain than loss, the decision, which is based upon the economic theory, is academic (Akers & Sellers, 2009). This is because the rational choice theory is based on a benefit versus cost ratio. Not surprisingly, a decision can be influenced and made less attractive by either decreasing the benefits or by increasing the costs. Costs can either be direct, such as fines and incarceration, and indirect, such as stigmatic costs and humiliation.

Deterrence Theory

A special case of the rational choice theory is the deterrence theory, which emphasizes the costs of legal sanctions (Liska & Messner, 1999). While the rational choice theory was initially applied to the field of economics, and considered all costs, the deterrence theory was initially applied to the field of law and only considered legal costs. Accordingly, as a deterrent for committing crime, increasing the severity of punishment, increasing the certainty of punishment, and increasing the celerity of punishment will all increase the legal costs for committing crime and, consequently, decrease the benefits versus cost ratio. Furthermore, there is a specific deterrence and a general deterrence (Barkan, 2006). Specific deterrence discourages individuals from committing crimes because they have learned through personal experience (i.e., by being punished) that the cost for their criminal behaviors is too high (Akers & Sellers, 2009). General deterrence, on the other hand, discourages individuals from committing crimes because they have learned through observation (i.e., by observing the suffering of offenders who have been punished) that the cost of committing crime is too high. By using fear, the behaviors of would-be criminals can be modified.

Labeling Theory

The labeling theory indicates that once individuals are arrested and labeled deviant, then there is a stigma that is attached to them (Liska & Messner, 1999). This may have negative consequences on self-image, social relationships, and may limit future legitimate economic opportunities. Once economic opportunities are limited, people will experience strain and may again be motivated to engage in criminal activities.

Teachers have been known to perceive some students as low achievers, and, accordingly, to label them as such (Ryan & Cooper, 2007). Teachers do this by calling on them less, by requiring less of them, by failing to give them feedback, by criticizing their failures more often than other students, by praising them less often, and by rewarding them for inappropriate behaviors. These students perceive how they are being treated and they come to identify themselves as being low achievers with deviant attributes. This becomes a self-fulfilling prophecy. Furthermore, the students' reputations precede them in future classes. Thus, once the students become stigmatized and these labels become reinforced, self-images plummet and social relationships deteriorate (Liska & Messner, 1999). Hence, it is important for authorities not to stigmatize students who need help because this may discourage them from seeking the help that they need (Tucker et al., 1999).

There are two types of shaming that can be utilized in dealing with those who commit deviant acts: re-integrative shaming and disintegrative shaming (Liska & Messner, 1999). Re-integrative shaming is the disapproval of the deviant act without condemning the offender. In this way, the offender is not stigmatized and efforts are made to forgive and welcome the person back into the community. This process has been demonstrated to work well in Africa, and perhaps, at a more personal level, between many American parents and their children (Braithwaite, 2000). Re-integrative shaming has been shown to reduce deviance.

Disintegrative shaming, on the other hand, disapproves of the deviant act and stigmatizes the offender (Liska & Messner, 1999). The community does not work as a family, and, therefore, makes no effort to bring the person back into the community without first labeling and punishing the person. Consequently, this negative experience threatens the identity of the person, which leads the person to reject those who have rejected him or her. Disintegrative shaming has shown to enhance deviance (Braithwaite, 2000).

The Looking Glass Self Theory

Cooley states that self-concepts are formed early in childhood by what he calls the Looking Glass Self (Hensley, 1996). This theory states that people develop their individual identities by evaluating how they think that they appear to others, how they perceive that others judge their appearance, and by how they react to those judgments. This is critical during childhood times, when identities are most impressionable. Thus, parents, teachers, and peers can all have a strong influence on the behaviors of children. Therefore, parents and teachers must be positive role models. Furthermore, it is important that teachers and parents not label children as delinquents because this is how they will see themselves and they will act accordingly (Adams, Robertson, Gray-Ray, & Ray, 2003; Bowditch, 1993). Indeed, instead of using negative reinforcements, children's behaviors must be developed using positive reinforcements. Moreover, parents should monitor with whom their children associate. Just as positive role models can be beneficial, negative role models can be detrimental.

Social Bonding Theory

Role modeling occurs in early childhood, when humans are at their greatest developmental rate for learning. According to the social bonding theory, children look toward other people and, when children care about their expectations, bonds are created (Barkan, 2006). This is important because parents and teachers can have a strong lifelong influence on children's behaviors. In short, strong healthy bonds produce pro-social attitudes (because children do not want to hurt the ones that they care about). However, because of the high divorce rate and dysfunctional families, children may not develop these healthy bonds and they may be at higher risk for committing crimes. Thus, without a good foundation, deviant behavior is likely later in life.

Hirschi's Theory

According to Hirschi, a strong bond between an individual and society will promote pro-social behaviors (Kelley, 1996). Thus, teachers must get students to understand that they are stakeholders in society; all students have a personal stake in their own futures. Students should be encouraged to participate in a moderate number of extracurricular and civic activities, which will reduce crime (Vieno, Nation, Perkins, & Santinello, 2007). One reason for this is that busy children have less idle time to engage in crime. Furthermore, students need to be active and participate because about 20% of students are considering dropping out of school because they are bored ("Bored", 2007). Thus, teachers must accept the responsibility for the students' learning and they may have to adapt their teaching styles in order to maximize the learning process (Heritage, 2007). In other words, teachers must motivated children to learn so that they will be more successful in life. Being more successful, the students will have more opportunities in life, thus avoiding the self-fulfilling prophecy of failure (that leads to deviance). By effectively challenging and rewarding students for their hard work, the students will learn to associate hard work with success. This is the first step in giving credence to the American value system.

Durkheim's Mechanical Community

Durkheim claimed that residents in a mechanical community have uniform lives (Vold et al., 2002). Residents have similar work, similar beliefs, and they have allegiance to the community. In addition, mechanical communities are isolated from other groups, and law enforcement promotes the uniformity of social norms. Residents band together and focus their attention, and hate, on anyone that they perceive as different from themselves.

Theory of Collective Efficacy

The theory of collective efficacy indicates that crime rates depend on community structures and cultures (Vold et al., 2002). According to the theory of collective efficacy, the crime rate will increase due to several reasons. First, the lack of individual resources will increase the crime rate. Second, the lack of social knowledge will increase the crime rate. Third, the lack of a stable family unit will increase the crime rate. Fourth, the lack of community participation will increase the crime rate. Finally, the lack of juvenile supervision will increase the crime rate. Basically, the local neighbor is disorganized, residents do not know one another, and the community members fail to work as a unit to resolve their issues. Furthermore, when there is a large number of unsupervised juveniles in the streets, they are highly motivated to commit crimes due to their anonymity. Consequently, the conditions create an attractive environment for crime.

Various Criminal Theories Over Time

Individuals learn to value certain things at certain times of their lives, depending upon the circumstances involved. When individuals are faced with particular conditions, they will make choices based on the totality of the circumstances. However, circumstances change over time (and place) and there may be different reasons why different people make particular decisions at different points in their lives. Although many factors may be relevant in the decision to commit crime, some factors may be more relevant at a particular point in time. In other words, time is a variable and different factors may have different values at different points in times. See Figure 4.

It is very important that a crime preventative solution be in alignment with the assumptions of the problem. For example, if an individual cannot make a rational choice due to a biological problem, then crime preventative measures based on increasing costs may be ineffective. It must be noted that there are many theories for the causes of crime but every theory has a limitation. See Table 11.

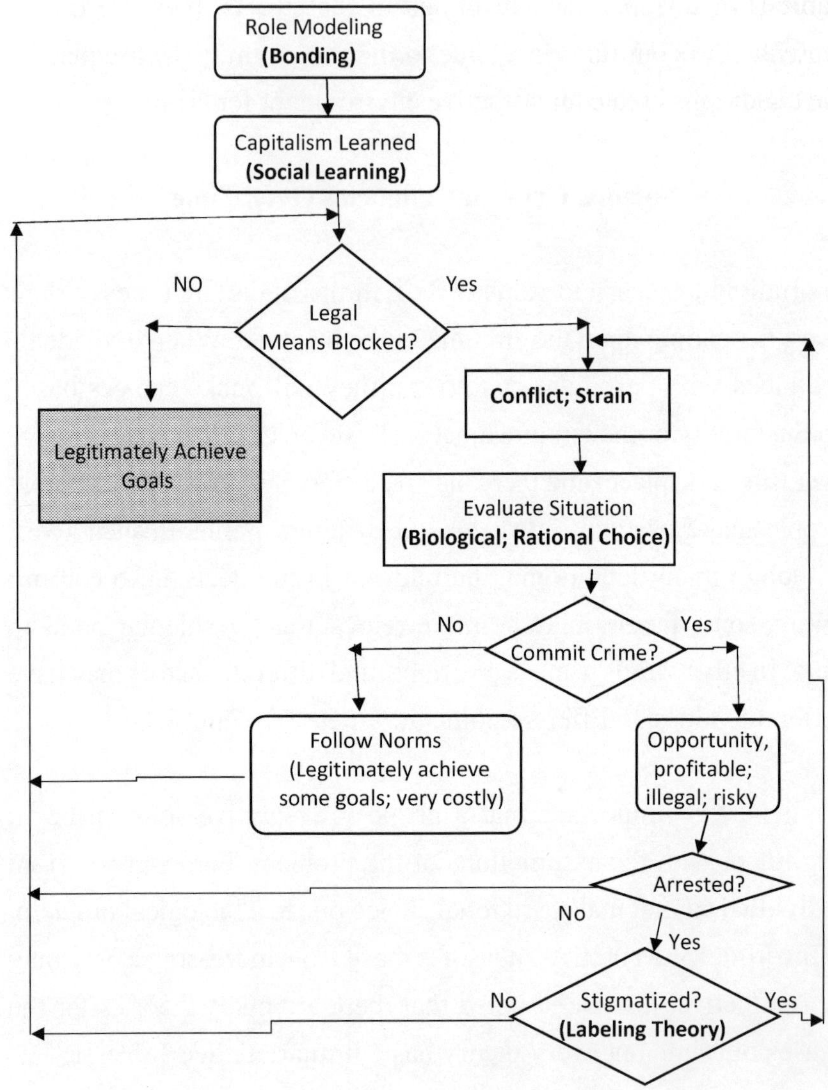

Figure 4. Impact of various criminal theories over time (bolded terms are criminal theories)

Table 11

Various Theories and their Limitations (Fay, 1987; Schmalleger, 2011; Sower, & Gist, 1994; Sower, Holland, Tiedke, & Freeman, 1957; Turvey & Petherick, 2009)

Theory	Description	Critique
Rational Choice Theory / Deterrence Theory	People freely choose their behaviors. Individuals evaluate the benefits versus costs ratio for each potential course of action. If the benefits are greater than costs, then the decision to perform that act is favorable. Rational choice theory focuses on benefits and on all costs. Deterrence theory focuses on legal costs. The deterrence theory relies on three factors: celerity, severity, and certainty of punishment.	Overemphasizes importance of individual choice; social factors, such as poverty, are dismissed; does not adequately consider emotions; target hardening causes displacement of crime; factors of deterrence may promote crime if all three factors are not effectively implemented simultaneously (certainty, severity, and celerity of punishment)
Routine Activities Theory	Crime occurs when three elements converge: motivated offenders, attractive targets, and the absence of capable guardians.	Level of motivation is not well defined; attractive targets and the absence of capable guardians are emphasized more than the motivated offender.
Durkheim's Mechanical Community	Social order and solidarity depend on the residents' reliance on each other to perform their specified tasks; interdependence is required.	Mechanical communities are isolated from other groups, and law enforcement promotes the uniformity of social norms in the local area; outsiders will be considered deviant.
Neoclassical Theory	Being tough on crime and retribution will curtail future crime.	Does not explain why crime decreases in areas without tough on crime policies; crime rate reductions may be due to demographic changes in the population.

Biological Theory	Human beings are biological creatures who are born with certain hardware, such as a brain, that controls thought and behavioral development. Because the brain uses a complex chemical-electrical process during the processing of information, any impairment in this process may interfere with the effective operation of the brain. Body shape, diet, hormones, environmental pollution, and chemical factors cause crime.	Denies role of free will; not everyone who is exposed to the same chemicals behave in the same way. Why is there no specific diet to cure crime? Increased exposure to pollution has not increased the crime rate; cannot explain crime in different parts of the country.
Sociobiology Theory	Behaviors are embedded in the process of natural selection and human survival; crime is the result of territorial struggles.	Fails to consider culture, social learning, and personal experiences; equates humans to animals.
Psychoanalytic Perspective Theory	Crime is the result of poorly developed superegos.	Lacks scientific support; elements of the theory were not applied to a wide context for society as a whole.
Social Learning Theory / Modeling Theory / Differential Association Theory	Criminal behaviors are learned through communications with intimate others; definitions favorable to crime exceed definitions unfavorable to crime; individuals learn behaviors by observing how others are rewarded and punished; frequency, duration, intensity, and importance of social learning experiences impact the learning of behaviors.	Pro-social and anti-social behaviors are simultaneously-learned through the same cognitive and behavioral mechanisms; does not consider free choice; does not explain why those surrounded by crime do not commit crime; only accounts for the communication of criminal values, not the emergence of criminal values.

Behavior Theory	The surrounding environment impacts behavior.	Dismisses cognition in human behavior; punishments may not deter martyrs; some groups believe that punishments are status-enhancing.
Theory of Collective Efficacy	The crime rate is increased due to the lack of individual resources, the lack of social knowledge, the lack of a stable family unit, the lack of community participation, and the lack of juvenile supervision.	Influence of the theory varies by crime type and does not address the number of years that the effects will last; paramilitary gangs located in economically disadvantaged neighborhoods deliver important economic and social resources that promote informal social control.
Looking Glass Theory	People see themselves as others see them; people develop their individual identities by evaluating how they think that they appear to others, how they perceive that others judge their appearance, and by how others react to those judgments.	How an individual appears to other people is subjective because the appearance relies on interpretations and assumptions.
Strain Theory	Crime is the result of frustration due to blocked opportunities, which prevent success.	The U.S. provides opportunities for all Americans to financially succeed; claims that wealth is the single most important goal in life; delinquent juveniles do not report being more stressed than law abiding juveniles; does not adequately explain the lack of crime for women, who may be stressed as a result of continual discrimination.

Conflict Theory	People in power pass laws to protect their own self-interests. There is a struggle for power and laws are passed that penalize the disadvantaged.	Can be tautological and may lack explanatory power; may be racist because minorities (who have little power) are labeled as criminals; overstresses social change and dismisses other well-developed theories of crime; fails to recognize that most people believe crime should be controlled.
Containment Theory	Crime results when internal (e.g., positive self-esteem) and external (e.g., social groups) control mechanisms fail to protect the individual.	May be feelings of the moment that have been conditioned through individual thought mechanisms; only some people who are exposed to social pressures commit crime.
Hirschi's Social Bond Theory	People commit delinquent acts when their bonds to society are weak; the four bonds in Hirschi's theory involve attachment, commitment, involvement, and beliefs.	Individuals commit crime even when they know that it is wrong; social bonds do not appear strong enough to negate criminal behavior.
Interactional Theory	Crime is the result of a weakened bond between an individual and society combined with the learning of anti-social behaviors that are rewarded.	Does not fully appreciate childhood maltreatment, which leads to crime.

Social Control Theory	Delinquent behavior occurs when social constraints on antisocial behaviors are weakened. Control ratio predicts criminal behavior; Control ratio = amount of control personally experienced versus amount of control exercised over others. Too much or too little self-control are equally dangerous.	Assumes that all individuals are automatically deviant unless socialized through control mechanisms; dismisses learned behaviors and human motivations.
Self-control Theory	Crime is the result of the lack of individual self-control; children who are ineffectually parented before the age of eight develop less self-control than children of approximately the same age who are raised with better parenting skills; individuals have low self-esteem and seek immediate gratification; individuals have little patience and are frustrated easily.	Dismisses external factors during different stages of life; oversimplifies the causes of crime; does not define self-control and the tendency toward criminal behavior separately; suggests that the concepts of low self-control and the propensity for criminal behavior are one and the same.
Social Disorganization / Zone Theory	Crime associated with urban transition zones; crime is higher in low income zones near city; crime is linked to high transition areas where people have anonymity.	Too much credence to spatial location; does not apply to all types of crime, just street crime at the neighborhood level; does not explain organized crime, corporate crime, or deviant behavior that takes place outside neighborhood settings.

Labeling Theory	If individuals are arrested, this may result in a negative stigma being attached to them. This may consequently disrupt their personal relationships and may block their future legitimate economic opportunities, which may lead to additional crime.	Does not explain the origin of crime; does not explain secret deviants.
Broken Window Theory	Broken windows, graffiti, litter, public drinking, and abandoned vehicles indicate disorder and a lack of caring. If people do not care about their neighborhood, then this attracts crime.	May be artifact of police decision-making practices; may bear little objective relationship to the actual degree of crime in the area; police may focus more efforts in poor areas. For example, if the department patrols a certain area with more officers, the police should make more arrests in that area. Does a higher arrest rate mean safer streets or more dangerous streets?
Normative Sponsorship Theory	Indicates that people who have a convergence of interest may cooperate with one another in order to satisfy their needs	Community members will only work together as long as the goals are within the normal limits of established standards

Critical Social Theory	Practical social science that encourages individuals to become socially and politically active in order to change and improve their current social conditions; endorses the enlightenment, empowerment, and emancipation of the people: people are enlightened when they obtain empirical knowledge about their states of oppression and their potential capacity to improve their situations, people are empowered when they are galvanized to engage in a socially transformation action, people are emancipated when they know who they are, what they genuinely want, and when they have collective autonomy and power to freely and rationally determine the nature and course of their collective existence.	Must raise the people's awareness of their current oppression; must demonstrate the possibility of a qualitatively different future; must hold community members responsible for actively getting involved and creating their own liberation.
Victim Precipitation	Victims unconsciously exhibit behaviors or characteristics that instigate or encourage the attackers; explains multiple victimizations	Relevant only to violent crimes or to particular forms of unlawful violence; assumes that victims and offenders interact prior to crime occurring.
Convict Criminology	Prisons are too big, hold too many people, and do not reduce crime; to control crime upon release from prison, prisons should focus more on treatment and less on security; based on the lived experiences of convicted felons and ex-inmates.	Most of the authors of the theory are white males, but not all are ex-convicts; authors are biased with agendas; non-convict feminists have been adding to the field, moving the theory from its roots.

Situational Crime Prevention (SCP) / Crime Prevention Through Environmental Design (CPTED)	SCP is a crime prevention strategy that attempts to eliminate or reduce the opportunities to commit specific crimes in specific locations by making crime more risky to attempt and more difficult to accomplish. Instead of relying upon law enforcers, the SCP strategy depends on public and private organizations. Furthermore, SCP and CPTED do not focus on the persons committing the crimes or the underlying causes of crime, such as unjust social and economic conditions, but focus instead on the settings for crime.	Only protects a limited geographical area; crime may be displaced.
Life Course Theory	Human lives are embedded in social relationships across the life span; the impact of various experiences depend on when they occur in life; each person makes choices, which impact each person's life course; a life course is shaped by historic times and places.	Many important life course determinants are experienced during childhood, which means adults may not be accountable for their crimes; individuals may select components of their life course and may influence their own trajectories.
Dual Taxonomic Theory	There are two types of offenders: life course persistent offenders (due to family dysfunction, poverty, neurophysiological deficits, and failure in school) and adolescence limited offenders (due to structural disadvantages).	Most antisocial children do not become criminals; family and psychological dysfunctions are not shown to be directly correlated to parent control or individual trajectories.

Developmental Pathways / Delinquent Development Theory	Anti-social behaviors are age dependent; as children age, they develop verbal coping skills, which help them manage conflict. Persistence in crime is influenced by many risk factors, such as broken homes, low family income, and harsh discipline. Desistance in crime has four factors: deceleration, specialization, de-escalation, and reaching a ceiling (plateau).	Aging causing desistance is meaningless because the theory fails to explain why desistance occurs; fails to explain free choice in human development.
Age-graded Theory	There is a positive relationship between social capital and pro-social behaviors; positive relationships are developed over time and lead to pro-social behaviors and reduced crime.	Positive relationships are subjective; some positive relationships may provide greater opportunities to commit crime; does not explain why social capital does not prevent everyone from committing crime.
Postmodern Criminology	Crime is an integral part of society.	Skeptical of science and scientific method; although it challenges other theories of crime prevention and control, it fails to offer feasible alternatives.
Peacemaking Criminology	Crime can be managed, not by stopping crime, but by making peace; citizens and social control agencies need to work together through education, social policies, human rights, and community involvement.	It is utopian and it fails to recognize the realities of law enforcement and crime control limitations.
Feminist Criminology	Men have dominated the field of criminal justice and have developed theories and written laws for the explanation and control of crime based on their own limited perspectives.	Inadequately accounts for crimes committed by females. Currently there is no single well-developed theory that explains female crime.

Why are Theories Important?

Theories help explain problems and they provide possible solutions to the problems. They also control the questions that are allowed to be asked on a survey (for validity) when collecting data during research. However, all theories rely on assumptions, which may impact the effectiveness of decisions based on those theories. Understanding criminal theories is important because police officers need to make best-practice decisions to solve social problems. Applying the wrong theory to solve the problem will be less than optimal. This is why Megan's Law is proving to be less than effective. According to research on Megan's Law, the deterrence theory and labeling theory are being used to solve a biological-based problem (Corrigan, 2006). Thus, the proposed solution is not in alignment with the theories used to explain the problem and, consequently, Megan's Law is not effectively working.

Example 1. Megan's Law

In 1994, a sex offender who had a history of violent crime against children was released from prison and moved into a residential area in New Jersey (Corrigan, 2006). Shortly thereafter, the sex offender lured a seven-year-old girl, named Megan, into his home to see a puppy. The sex offender then sexually assaulted and killed Megan.

Megan's parents were outraged that they were not notified that a violent sex predator was released from prison and resided in their neighborhood (Corrigan, 2006). Consequently, they organized a statewide movement to improve the laws regarding sex offenders. Due to the public outcry for reform, elected officials enacted Megan's law. The new law required states to provide information to the public about released sex offenders. In short, the purpose Megan's law is to deter sex offenders from committing additional crimes by requiring the authorities to provide the public with sex offenders' personal information so that community members can keep watch over them.

As far as the sex offenders are concerned, Megan's law applies to all sex offenders equally; the law does not differentiate between different types of sex offenders (Corrigan, 2006). However, not all sex offenders are alike. Indeed, what motivates one type of sex offender may be quite different than what motivates another type of sex offender. For example, what drives a pedophiliac to commit a sex crime may be quite different than what drives an exhibitionist to commit a sex crime. Furthermore, Megan's law assumes that most sex offenders are strangers to the victims. However, most sex predators are family members or friends of the victims. Thus, treating all sex offenders as though they are a homogenous group of sex predators and having a single community notification program designed to modify their behaviors may be less than optimal.

Theories Related to Community Notification

The effectiveness of the community notification process relies upon the assumptions of the labeling and deterrence theories. Tannenbaum argued that people learn to identify individuals in the way that they are labeled (Vold et al., 2002). Thus, the labeling theory indicates that sex offenders will be easily recognized if they are publically labeled and if their sex crimes are advertised. Consequently, community members will know who to protect themselves against sex offenders. In regards to Megan's law, it is assumed that all sex offenders are alike and they are all labeled as a homogenous group of sex predators (Corrigan, 2006).

The second theory that the community notification process depends upon is the deterrence theory. Beccaria proposed the idea that people choose to perform the acts that increase pleasure and reduce pain (Vold et al., 2002). In other words, personal decisions are based upon rational choice; people choose to do the activities in which the benefits outweigh the associated costs. Thus, according to the deterrence theory, authorities assume that by publically stigmatizing sex offenders, they will be deterred from committing additional sex crimes (Barkan, 2006).

Effects of Megan's Law

Because Megan's law is a principle that governs social action, it impacts the police, community members, and sex offenders. Indeed, the police have much discretion in how the law is implemented, community members rely upon the information provided by the police, and the sex offenders have to deal with the consequences of the law. Indeed, there are different perspectives involving the effectiveness of Megan's law.

Effects of Megan's Law on Police

Because Megan's law is a principle that governs social action, it requires police involvement. On the one hand, once sex offenders are released from prison, they have rights and the police need to protect them. On the other hand, the police also need to take preventative actions to protect the public. In short, the police must use their limited resources to provide protection to all community members, including sex offenders. The following studies will examine the effects of community notification on police departments, on police officers, and on probation and parole officers.

In order to examine the effects of community notification on police departments, Gaines (2006) conducted a qualitative study involving 21 police agencies, which used the Internet as the method for sex offender registration and community notification. The researcher collected data through telephone and Internet surveys. The findings indicated that police departments have mixed feelings about community notification. On the one hand, the police departments felt that the public appreciated the work that they did. For example, law enforcement departments that used community meetings to inform community members about sex offenders believed that educating the public regarding sex offenders was an important police function. On the other hand, the findings also indicated that the police departments felt that community notifications consumed limited police resources, such as manpower and money. Thus, community notification consumed valuable resources that could have been applied to other law enforcement areas.

In order to examine the effects of community notification on police officers, Redlich (2001) conducted a quantitative study and compared law officers to law students and community members. Redlich surveyed 78 law officers, 82 law students, and 109 community members. Data were collected through self-administered questionnaires. The findings indicated that law enforcement officers were more likely to support community notification than either law students or community members. Indeed, police officers felt that community notification was effective in protecting children. Furthermore, officers believed that community notification was not likely to violate the sex offenders' rights.

In order to examine the effects of community notification on probation and parole officers, Zevitz and Farkas (2000) conducted a study of 77 probation and parole officers. The researchers collected data via self-administered questionnaires and through field observations. The findings indicated that although probation and parole officers believed that community notification may have provided public awareness and community protection, the officers believed that the cost was high in terms of personnel, finances, and time. For example, each officer had to supervise an average of 25 sex offenders and, consequently, they felt that they did not have adequate time to supervise non-sex offenders.

In addition, in a survey of probation and parole officers in Wisconsin, researchers found that probation and parole officers perceived that they are being required to enforce community notification laws without being properly trained and funded (Cohen & Jeglic, 2007). Probation and parole officers were being required to create supervision networks, to monitor the offenders, to perform more home visits, to find housing and employment for the offenders, and to help the offenders with transportation. Consequently, the probation and parole officers felt that they were being overwhelmed and that their effectiveness in performing other functions was diminished (Sample & Bray, 2006).

Effects of Megan's Law on Community Members

Megan's law is a tool designed to protect community members, especially children who are the most vulnerable, against sex crimes (Corrigan, 2006). Megan's law views sex related violence as rare in society and assumes that sex crimes are committed by mentally disturbed individuals who attack without warning or reason. Consequently, community members believe that society does not need to change but that sex predators need to be better controlled. Thus, community members hope to gain peace of mind by believing that they will be able to better guard themselves and their children against sex offenders if they are provided with information about sex offenders via community notification. The following studies will examine the effects of community notification on community members.

Beck and Travis (2006) conducted a quantitative study and compared an aggressive sex offender community notification process in Hamilton County, Ohio to a passive sex offender community notification process in Jefferson County, Kentucky. For the aggressive notification process, the local Sheriff provided written notification to all community residents within the school district in which each sex offender resided. In the passive notification process, on the other hand, the state police required local residents to be proactive and to seek information through the state police website. The researchers received a total of 196 surveys from residents in both counties who were notified of sex offenders, and a total of 264 surveys from residents in both counties who were not notified of sex offenders. The findings indicated that participants who resided in the aggressive notification area were significantly more aware of sex offenders in their neighborhoods. However, the findings also indicated that the participants' fear of being victimized, the participants' perceived risk of being victimized, and the participants' engagement in protective behaviors were not significantly influenced by the variation in the notification process. In short, although aggressive community notification seemed to increase public awareness, it did not ease the public's fear.

Zevitz, Crim, and Farkas (2000a) conducted a study of 704 participants in order to determine the collective response of community members to community notification meetings. The researchers collected data from 22 different sex offender community meetings in 16 different locations across Wisconsin. Furthermore, the researchers collected data via self-administered questionnaires and recorded observations. The findings indicated that community members found the meetings both helpful and stressful. On the one hand, residents obtained what they perceived to be important information about neighbors whom they considered dangerous. On the other hand, the same information created anxiety and fear among the residents. Indeed, the amounts of anxiety and fear felt by community members were related to their perception of the governments' competence involving the meetings. In short, meetings that were more formal, more organized, and clearer in purpose generated less anxiety among the residents.

Levenson, Brannon, Fortney, and Baker (2007) conducted a study of 193 residents in Florida in order to understand their perception of sex offenders and to determine whether the residents supported community notification. The researchers collected data via self-administered surveys during a time when there was a considerable amount of media coverage on sex crimes against children. The findings indicated that residents perceived sex offenders as a homogeneous group of sex predators who were likely to reoffend. Consequently, they were in favor of public disclosure. However, the public's perception of sex offenders is problematic because not all types of sex offenders have the same risk of reoffending (Corrigan, 2006). Indeed, different types of sex offenders have different underlying motivations for their sex crimes. Therefore, treating all sex offenders in the same manner in order to reintegrate them into society may be less than optimal.

Malesky and Keim (2001) conducted a descriptive study of 133 mental health professionals and investigated their professional opinions on the effectiveness of community notification. The researchers collected data using self-administered questionnaires from licensed counselors, clinical social workers, and psychologists. The findings indicated that a majority of the mental health professionals felt that community notification was ineffective in reducing the number of children who were sexually assaulted each year and that community notification provided parents with a false sense of security. Thus, mental health professionals have indicated that community notification is ineffective.

Effects of Megan's Law on Sex Offenders

Megan's law does not differentiate between different types of sex offenders and the law applies to all sex offenders equally (Corrigan, 2006). Megan's law requires authorities to provide the personal information of sex offenders to the public. Consequently, because they are labeled a threat to society, sex offenders may have difficulty developing meaningful relationships, finding suitable housing, and securing employment (Levenson & Cotter, 2005; Levenson, D'Amora, & Hern, 2007; Tewksbury, 2005; Tewksbury & Lees, 2006). The following studies will examine the effects of community notification on sex offenders.

Zevitz, Crim, and Farkas (2000b) conducted a qualitative case study involving 30 sex offenders in Wisconsin in order to understand their perceptions of the community notification law. The researchers collected data through face-to-face interviews, the data were coded, and themes were identified. There were several findings of the study. First, sex offenders felt disturbed by the advertisement of their crimes. Indeed, they had feelings of worthlessness and hopelessness. Second, the sex offenders felt stigmatized and, consequently, they found that it was very difficult to obtain housing and employment. Third, although there was only one reported vigilante assault in the study, the sex offenders worried about being harassed by community members. Fourth, the sex offenders were concerned about their loss of supportive relationships. Because they were in prison and separated from family members for lengthy periods of time, because they lost personal resources, and because they were prevented from living in certain areas when they were released from prison, sex offenders felt that vital relationships that are necessary for effective reintegration into society had been lost. On the other hand, the sex offenders felt that community notification had forced them to accept responsibility for their past crimes. Furthermore, being forced to provide DNA samples, the sex offenders felt that they were somewhat protected against being wrongly accused by community members for other sex crimes.

Mustaine, Tewksbury, and Stengel (2006) conducted a quantitative study involving secondary data in order to determine the types of locations in which sex offenders resided. A list including a total of 1,504 registered sex offenders from two counties in Florida and two counties in Kentucky were used. Data were analyzed using differences between means tests. The findings indicated that registered sex offenders were likely to live in socially disorganized communities where crimes were more abundant. It appears that sex offenders resided in socially disorganized areas because they were shunned from more organized areas by local residents. Thus, sex offenders lived in social disorganized areas as a collateral consequence of community notification.

Indeed, there are numerous studies involving the negative consequences experienced by sex offenders as the result of community notification. For example, Levenson & Cotter (2005) conducted a quantitative study of 183 sex offenders in Florida and collected data via self-administered questionnaires; Tewksbury (2005) conducted a quantitative study of 121 sex offenders in Kentucky and collected data via self-administered questionnaires; Tewksbury and Lees (2006) conducted a qualitative study of 22 sex offenders in Kentucky and collected data via one-on-one interviews; and Levenson, D'Amora, and Hern (2007) conducted a quantitative study of 239 sex offenders in Connecticut and Indiana and collected data via self-administered questionnaires. The findings from all four studies indicated that sex offenders experienced negative consequences as the result of community notification. Some of the negative feelings experienced by the sex offenders in the studies include shame, stress, fear, depression, hopelessness, and vulnerability. Other negative experiences realized include loss of (a) employment, (b) relationships, (c) housing, and (d) property. However, the Levenson and Cotter study also indicated that some sex offenders experienced positive effects, such as the motivation to be honest with other people.

Evaluation of Community Notification on Recidivism

The whole purpose of Megan's law is to reduce the number of repeat sex crimes committed by sex offenders against community members. Hence, the effectiveness of community notification may be assessed by looking at recidivism. Therefore, the following studies will examine community notification and sex offender recidivism.

First, Langevin et al. (2004) conducted a quantitative study over a minimum period of 25 years, which retrospectively compared the lifetime recidivism rates of 320 sex offenders and 31 violent non-sex offenders who had been charged with various sex offender violations. Using Canadian police and hospital records, the researchers used the conviction rate, arrest rate, and the number of court appearances of 351 men who were required to undergo psychiatric assessment or treatment. The researchers employed analysis of variance and likelihood ratios to assess the data.

The findings of the Langevin et al. (2004) study indicated that recidivism rates were substantially greater for long-term studies than for short-term studies. In addition, although most sex offenders did not spend much time incarcerated, more than 80% of the convicted sex offenders committed additional sex offenses after they were released from prison. Indeed, because the criminal career of sex offenders is typically around 20 years, short-term studies may provide less than complete information. It appears that recidivism is a problem for a substantial part of the sex offenders' adult lives.

There are some limitations in the Langevin et al. (2004) study, which may impact the generalization of the study's findings to other populations. First, police officers have discretion in filing charges with the prosecutors. For example, some police officers may file multiple sex charges for a single offense, while other officers may file one charge for multiple sex offenses. Second, the sample was comprised of men who were mostly Caucasian Canadians. Thus, because the participants were primarily Caucasians who were processed under laws unique to Canada, the external validity of the findings is questionable. As a result, the findings may not be generalized to females and to individuals of other races, especially if they reside outside of Canada.

A detailed analysis of the Langevin et al. (2004) study was completed by Webster, Gartner and Doob (2006). Webster et al. reported that the findings from the Langevin et al. study are problematic and that the results are not interpretable. First, Webster et al. argued that the sample used by Langevin et al. was biased because the participants were drawn from a referral list of sex offenders who resided in Ontario and who were ordered to receive psychiatric assistance. Hence, the sample used by Langevin et al. may not be representative of the general population of sex offenders across Canada because sex offenders in other providences may not have been ordered to receive psychiatric assistance. Second, the definition of sex offender and the categories of sex offenses used by Langevin et al. were not identical to the categories used by the Canadian government. Third, Langevin et al. committed an error in defining the population of recidivists. For example, Langevin et al. considered individuals who committed first time sex offenses prior to the study and who reoffended during the study, but they failed to consider individuals who committed first time sex offenses prior to the study and who did not reoffend during the study. Thus, the recidivism rate in the study is inflated and less than accurate. In short, Webster et al. argued that the Langevin et al. study is methodologically weak and the findings are questionable.

Second, Zevitz (2006) conducted a quantitative study in order to evaluate the effectiveness of community notification in reducing recidivism for sex offenders who display similar characteristics. The population was comprised of adult male sex offenders in Wisconsin who were sent to prison in 1993 and who were released from prison from 1997 to 1999. The sample consisted of two groups. One group, which consisted of 47 sex offenders, was released into areas where extensive notification existed. Extensive notification included media releases, door-to-door notification, the posting of flyers, and community meetings. A second group, which consisted of 166 sex offenders, was released into areas were limited notification existed. In limited notification areas, the police required residents to be proactive in seeking sex offender information.

The researcher collected data via the Wisconsin Department of Correction and the U.S. Department of Justice National Crime Information Center computerized record systems (Zevitz, 2006). Each sex offender was tracked for 54 months following the date of release from prison. The researcher defined recidivism as all new arrests that resulted in convictions and incarceration. The researcher used Chi square and t-tests in order to determine if there was a difference between the type of community notification (i.e., extensive or limited) and sex offender recidivism.

The findings of the Zevitz (2006) study indicated that the type of community notification had no significant effect on sex offender recidivism. In other words, extensive and limited notification had the same result for sex offender recidivism. Furthermore, the findings also suggested that the type of community notification had no impact on the amount of time before sex offenders reoffend. In short, community notification appeared to be ineffective in sex offender recidivism.

There are some limitations in the Zevitz (2006) study, which may impact the validity of the study's findings. First, the researcher relied on official data, which is problematic because it is estimated that about half of all sex offenses are not reported. Thus, a great deal of information may be missing in the study. Second, because the definition of recidivism varies from state to state, the study's findings may not be generalized to other jurisdictions that define recidivism differently.

Third, Radkowski (2008) conducted a casual-comparative quantitative study of 4,000 sex offenders in order to determine if community notification was effective in reducing sex offender recidivism. The researcher used the sex offender database for one Midwestern state and compiled 2,000 cases prior to community notification requirements and 2,000 cases following community notification requirements. The researcher collected data from clerk of court records and performed chi-square analysis to determine if there was a significant difference between notifying and not notifying the public and recidivism.

The findings indicated that there was a significant relationship between community notification and sex offender recidivism (Radkowski, 2008). Indeed, sex offender recidivism was greater in communities where authorities employed community notification. In short, community notification had failed to deter sex offenders from committing additional sex crimes.

There are some limitations in the Radkowski (2008) study, which may impact the generalization of the study's findings to the other populations. First, the researcher used a non-probability sample. Indeed, the researcher only studied the sex offenders that he believed would likely reoffend. Second, the court restricted access to some of the data. Third, the researcher's definition of recidivism was unique because it placed a six year time limit on recidivism and it only included sex crime convictions. In other words, the researcher did not consider plea bargain results. Consequently, the study's findings are limited and may not be applicable to other sex offenders.

Finally, Meloy, Saleh, and Wolff (2007) conducted a critical analysis study of research literature in order to determine if community notification was related to sex offender recidivism. First, Meloy et al. reported that community notification has not been effective in deterring convicted sex offenders from committing additional sex crimes because the public misunderstands the data and ineffectively uses the data. For example, the residents believed that they were notified of all sex offenders. However, some sex offenders avoided registration requirements as a result of plea bargaining.

Thus, community members did not adequately protect themselves from all sex offenders. Second, community members misdirected their efforts to protect themselves against sex offenders because they believed that sex offenders were strangers. However, many sex crimes against children were committed by relatives and friends. Third, sex offenders were publically stigmatized and, as a result, they had a difficult time developing meaningful relationships and securing jobs. Thus, community notification has led some sex offenders to commit additional crimes. Finally, because there was no single definition of recidivism, some sex offenders who were arrested for non-sex crimes were not always included as part of the recidivism rate. Thus, the recidivism rate was undervalued.

In sum, it appears that the community notification program is ineffective. Indeed, the research has indicated that repeat sex offenses are not being reduced by aggressive community notification efforts (Beck & Travis, 2006). On the other hand, the fact that sex crimes have not decreased could be due to the community notification efforts making it easier to catch and record sex violations. Part of the problem in evaluating sex offender recidivism is that the definition of recidivism, along with the sex offender classifications, vary among state jurisdictions, making comparisons among states difficult.

Thoughts for Community Notification Improvement

There are several ways to improve the community notification system as it relates to sex offender recidivism. One way to improve the community notification system is to develop a national definition of recidivism. Indeed, it is difficult to compare recidivism rates among the states if there is no single definition of what constitutes recidivism (Webster et al., 2006).

Another way to improve the community notification system is to develop national classifications of sex offenders and national standards of who qualifies to be registered (Radkowski, 2008). Because state laws differ from one another, there is a lack of consistency from state to state of who qualifies to be registered as a sex offender. Thus, it is difficult to compare sex offender recidivism rates among the states if there are no standard classifications of sex offenders.

Finally, another way to improve the community notification system is to develop a national sex offender database (Radkowski, 2008). The federal government has more resources than each of the state governments, and, consequently, can operate and maintain an electronic sex offender database more efficiently and effectively. In addition, by having a centralized database, the communication gap between the state governments can be eliminated, which will make it easier to track sex offenders.

Megan's Law Summary

Today, all 50 states have sex offender registries and statutory provisions for notifying local residents when sex offenders reside in their neighborhoods (Tewksbury, 2002). Although the goals of community notification may be socially desirable, community notification efforts have not shown to be effective. This is not surprising because the underlying assumptions relied upon to prevent sex offenders from committing additional sex crimes are not in alignment with the assumptions of Megan's law. Indeed, authorities rely upon labeling and deterrence in order to get sex predators to rationally decide not to commit additional sex crimes. However, Megan's law assumes that sex offenders are mentally disturbed predators who attack without warning or reason (Corrigan, 2006). Because the research findings do not support the argument that community notification deters stigmatized sex offenders from committing repeat sex offenses, then perhaps programs that rely upon theories that support the argument that sex offenders are mentally disturbed need to be investigated (Zevitz, 2006). In other words, limited resources may be better spent on programs that address mental illnesses instead of labeling.

Another reason why community notification is less than effective is because sex offenders are treated as a homogenous group of strangers (Corrigan, 2006). However, because different types of sex offenders are not all motivated by the same reasons, a single program designed to modify their various behaviors will not work. Furthermore, most sex crimes against children are committed by friends or family members and not by strangers. Thus, community notification efforts are ineffective because they are not in alignment with the problem. In short, sex offenders need to be individually evaluated and properly treated for their effective reintegration into society.

Example 2. Sex Offenders

Psychological definitions of misbehavior may include terms like conduct disorder and antisocial behavior (Bartol & Bartol, 2014). These terms can be defined in the *American Psychiatric Association's Diagnostic and Statistical Manual,* fourth edition, revised. Similar to the elements of a law, a diagnostic checklist is used to determine the classification of behavior. See below for an example of a behavioral classification, its corresponding behavioral checklist, and possible theories that may be used to explain the behavior.

Pedophilia

Pedophilia is the intense sexual urges and fantasies of persons over 16 years of age who engage in sexual misconduct with prepubescent children who are usually less than 13 years of age (American Psychiatric Association, 2000). Individuals tend to have an attraction to a particular age range and this attraction may be toward either sex. Some of the behaviors that these individuals engage in may include undressing the children, exposing themselves to the children, masturbating in front of the children, performing oral sex on the children, and penetrating the orifices of the children. This is a chronic disorder and the recidivism rate for individuals who desire boys is about twice that of those who prefer girls.

Pedophilia Behavioral Checklist

- Sexual activity with prepubescent children (children usually less than 13 years of age)
- Activities may include fondling, oral sex, and masturbation in front of the children
- May threaten children to prevent the children from disclosing the events
- Sexually attracted to children of particular age range
- May be sexually attracted to males, females, or to both males and females

- May defend actions based upon the educational value provided to the children
- Signs of significant distress are not required for disorder
- Individuals develop complicated strategies in order to access children

Pedophilia Diagnostic Checklist

- Duration greater than 6 months
- Recurrent
- Intense sexual urges and fantasies involving prepubescent children, usually less than 13 years of age
- Failure to act on urges may cause clinical distress in important areas of functioning
- Perpetrator "is at least 16 years old and at least 5 years older than the child" (American Psychiatric Association, 2000, p. 572)
- Individuals need to be identified as to whether they are sexually attracted to males, females, or to both
- Individuals need to be identified as to whether their sexual activity is limited to incest
- Individuals need to be identified as to whether they are sexually attracted only to children

Theories for Behavior

There are several theories that can explain the etiology of pedophilia, which are 1) the emotional congruence theory, 2) the sexual arousal theory, 3) the blockage theory, and 4) the disinhibition theory (Bartol & Bartol, 2008). First, the emotional congruence theory indicates that "pedophiles see themselves as children with childish emotional needs and interests, and therefore feel most comfortable with children" (Bartol & Bartol, p. 440). Second, the sexual arousal theory indicates that some men are sexually stimulated by some particular characteristics that children possess, but these characteristics do not sexually stimulate the typical male. Third, the blockage theory indicates that some men are unable to develop normal social and sexual relations with other adults so they decide to develop relations with children, who they feel more comfortable with. Finally, the disinhibition theory indicates that some men are unable to regulate themselves and they fail to control their behaviors involving sexual activities with children.

In addition, there are several other theories that may contribute toward the explanation of pedophilia. First, America is a capitalistic society and Americans are willing to pay a lot of money for sexual items. In response to this demand, companies are making sexual products readily available. Consequently, sexual products are all around and they may be conditioning some men toward sexual addiction. In this sense, Americans may be engaging in social learning and may be learning to engage in a variety of sexual activities (Bartol & Bartol, 2008). Second, sexual pleasures are realized by chemical changes within the body. Thus, biological factors may influence sexual decisions. Finally, by perceiving that the benefits gained from engaging in pedophilia outweigh the potential costs involved, including that of being arrested and prosecuted, deviant sexual behaviors may be a rational choice (based on a benefit versus cost ratio) (Liska & Messner, 1999).

Treatment for Behavior

Although group therapy and cognitive learning theory based approaches are common treatment programs for pedophiles, there is no evidence that these programs are effective. On the other hand, individually tailored cognitive behavioral treatment programs, which include aversion conditioning, cognitive restructuring, covert sensitization, modeling, role playing, satiation, covert reinforcement, social skills training, and relax training, seem to be the most effective for relapse prevention. (Wakefield, & Underwager, 2007). However, motivating pedophiles to complete treatment programs requires therapists to develop therapeutic relationships with the pedophiles through complementary interpersonal dynamics (Drapeau, Korner, Granger, Brunet, & Caspar, 2005). Indeed, the pedophiles will test the therapists to make sure that they are trustworthy, reliable, and strong. If the therapists can demonstrate these qualities, then the pedophiles will be more likely to complete their training.

Civil Commitment for Violent Sexual Offenders

Each year in the U.S. more than one million individuals are civilly committed, with about one-third of them being involuntary (Falk, 1999). Opponents of civil commitment have argued that civil commitment violates the double jeopardy law and the constitutional prohibition against enforcing ex post facto laws (Johns, n.d.). However, in *Kansas v. Hendricks*, the U.S. Supreme Court has ruled that civil commitment does not violate these two laws (Falk). This is because civil commitment does not establish criminal proceedings and, therefore, is not considered punishment. Thus, because civil commitment is not punitive in nature, the federal laws that are designed to protect citizens against the government are not violated.

It is important to note that prisons are not designed to provide effective treatment to sex predators (Ryan, 2008). Thus, punishment must be considered separate than treatment. Therefore, once the punishment phase is over, the "inmate" should be relabeled as "patient" and then treated as such. Indeed, the civil commitment program has an ambience of treatment and not of punishment (Ryan). Even though the person is still confined, the goal is different. Furthermore, civil confinement requires that the patient take responsibility to change or else the patient is not released (Johns, n.d.).

Under the current conditions, civil commitment programs are the current solution to deal with sex predators. It forces the offenders to change their ways or else they will not be released (Johns, n.d.). Being in an atmosphere of treatment and not having a release date in sight, the focus will be on curing the patient (Ryan, 2008). This is important because the patient will not simple conform to expectations in order to reach a predetermined release date. Thus, the patient will receive the necessary help. In addition, the polygraph and penile plethysmographic exams can provide some validity for treatment. Indeed, according to the Indiana Court of Appeals, the lack of treatment may be more damaging than the patient's loss of liberty ("In the Matter of the Commitment of A.W.D.", 2007).

The existing civil commitment treatment programs involving sex predators have not proven to be effective (Ryan, 2008; Johns, n.d.). However, even if the current treatments do not cure the patients, they do at least protect the public, thus reducing the danger to society (Ryan, 2008). Furthermore, these patients are not committed randomly. They have a history of sexual violence, they are screened by mental health professionals, and they are evaluated by fact-finders. Like anyone else who has a sickness that may harm other people, sex predators need to be quarantined. However, the atmosphere is one of treatment and not one of punishment.

Example 3. Juveniles & Drugs

The U.S. government has declared a war on drugs and has targeted drug dealers (i.e., the supply side) (Gahlinger, 2004). However, the war on drugs cannot be won (Tucker, Donovan, and Marlatt, 1999). This is because many Americans demand illegal drugs and they are willing to pay a lot of money for them. Consequently, in a capitalistic society, there will always be someone there to meet the drug demand. If drug dealers are arrested, then other drug dealers will simply replace them. Thus, as learned during Prohibition (1920-1933), when the government tries to force its will upon a reluctant people, black markets will be created and the crime rate will soar. Because attacking the supply side of the drug war has proven to be ineffective, then economics dictate that the government attack on the demand side. Thus, in order to reduce the demand for drugs, the resolution may rest with educating the young.

Social Bonding Theory

Childhood is the time when people learn the most. Thus, this is the time when role modeling is most important. According to Hirschi's social bonding theory, people commit delinquent acts when their bonds to society are weak (Akers & Sellers, 2009). The four bonds in Hirschi's theory involve attachment, commitment, involvement, and beliefs. Attachment is the degree to which an individual identifies with other people. Commitment is the personal stake that an individual has in society. Involvement is the level of participation that an individual engages in within society. Belief is the credence that an individual gives to social norms. Thus, in order to reduce the youth drug problem, these four variables need to be targeted and strengthened.

Intervention Plan

A plan may be to strengthen the children's pro-social bonds through the development of positive relationships and by providing the children with worthwhile activities that they like to do. About 22% of American children live in poverty and are surrounded by drugs (McLoyd, 1998). These unfortunate children are not capable of removing themselves from the drug environment. Thus, in order to counter the negative effects of the drug environment, the local government must provide the children with worthwhile activities of interest. Otherwise, the children may be tempted to get involved with the only available activity in the area, which is drug use. In other words, if the children say "no" to drugs, then they must be given an alternative in which to say "yes" (DuBois & Berg, 2002).

The local government must get involved and spend some resources on providing activities for children. For example, the government could sponsor programs like the Midnight Basketball program (Tucker et al., 1999). As long as the children find these activities worthwhile, they will participate in them, and, thus, they will be less motivated to use drugs. Furthermore, by making participation in these activities contingent upon attending problem-solving workshops, the children may learn conflict resolution, cooperation, and, at the same time, develop self-esteem (DuBois & Berg).

Positive Peer Culture

Positive peer culture (PPC) is a staff guided peer-helping therapeutic community, which is designed to improve pro-social values by cultivating strengths in delinquent youths (California Evidence-Based Clearinghouse, n.d.; Tarolla, Wagner, Rabinowitz, & Tubman, 2002). Instead of demanding obedience to staff or peers, PPC empowers and encourages youths to build group responsibility by trusting and respecting one another during the development of pro-social values. By caring for and by being concerned about other youths, troubled youths will modify their behaviors, improve their self-worth, and minimize their engagement in delinquent activities.

However, although the goal of PPC is well intended, there are some disadvantages to the program. First, the participants in the PPC are trouble youths with criminal histories. Because the social learning theory indicates that behaviors are learned in proportion to the frequency, duration, and intensity of the social interactions, association with these deviant peers may have negative consequences (Akers & Sellers, 2009). These peer influences may undermine and offset the positive pro-social influences that family members and non-delinquent friends have had on them. Indeed, if positive peer group members develop a common social identity, and because they all are delinquents, then it may be unreasonable to expect these children to have pro-social influences upon one another (Blueprints for Violence Prevention, n.d.). In other words, because it is often easier to destroy than to create, these youths may be dragging each other down instead of raising each other up. Second, positive peer groups may be undervaluing the positive influence that parents have in creating pro-social values for their children. Parents and guardians often promote pro-social values and children learn these values through exposure with their parents and guardians. It is a question of which is more important, being exposed to positive peer group members who share similar delinquent backgrounds or being exposed to parents who may not share such similar backgrounds but who do promote pro-social values. Consequently, the positive peer group may promote antisocial behaviors, which may alienate these youths from adult influence, leading to conflict between these children and authorities. Third, ties between these youths and their parents and pro-social friends may be severed (Ryan, Marshall, Herz, & Hernandez, 2008). Not only are these youths being exposed to delinquent peers, but they are also being removed from pro-social peers. In other words, good environmental elements are being removed while bad ones are being introduced. Fourth, if youths' antisocial behaviors are being reinforced by the positive peer culture, then this may compromise public safety, this may require the authorities to engage the youths, and this may demoralize the parents. Because this is still a critical time when children are developing their values, and because parents' influence is still essential in the development of pro-social values, demoralizing the parents' during this time may neutralize essential positive interactions.

Although the PPC has been widely implemented due to its low cost, there are program limitations (Tarolla et al., 2002). These limitations include 1) a lack of empirical evidence to support the effectiveness of the program, 2) methodological flaws in the research studies, and 3) a lack of effective outcome measures. Thus, additional research studies are needed to determine the significance of these programs.

Cohen's Philosophy

Cohen found that most juvenile delinquency occurs in group environments rather than at the individual level (Vold et al., 2002). Unlike adult crime, which usually occurs for some obvious reason, many of the crimes committed by juveniles seem to be senseless and without purpose. However, upon closer examination, the rewards sought by juveniles are intrinsic (i.e., internal rewards, such as personal satisfaction) rather than extrinsic (i.e., external rewards, such as money). For example, juvenile gang members may seek status and prestige as defined by peers. Children who have no ascribed status within their families and who are unable to effectively compete with more capable children at school may decide to address their problems by banding together. Indeed, there is strength in numbers and gang members reinforce one another as they rebel against typical middle-class values.

Example 4. Etiology of Violence

Timothy McVeigh grew up in Pendleton, New York, a predominantly white neighborhood (Nichols, 2003). Although very bright, McVeigh was considered a loner and an underachiever in school. After high school, he developed an obsession with guns and began to stockpile weapons and supplies. In 1988, McVeigh enlisted in the U.S. Army. While in the Army, he became obsessed with the Turner Diaries, a book full of violent racist and anti-Semitic fantasies. Moreover, while in the U.S. Army, McVeigh had a race problem. For example, he had been known to assign undesirable work to African Americans and to use derogatory remarks against them. After McVeigh failed to make the Green Berets, he left the military. Without the discipline of the military, and being unable to secure a job, McVeigh lost his self-identity (Ottley, 2007). He soon gravitated toward the right-wing militia and began traveling around the country selling military type items at guns shows (Nichols). McVeigh developed an anti-government philosophy, joined the Ku Klux Klan, distributed hate literature, and believed an army of civilians had to stand against the corrupt U.S. government. William Cooper, a short wave radio announcer, soon caught McVeigh's attention. Cooper was a member of the Second Continental Army of the Republic (a secretive militia arm), and a member of the Citizens Agency for Joint Intelligence (an information acquisition and dissemination organization). Influenced by Cooper, McVeigh came to believe in a government conspiracy theory.

During the Waco incident with the Branch Davidians, McVeigh went to Waco in order to pass out pamphlets supporting the citizens' right to own firearms (Nichols, 2003). However, the ATF turned him around. During this time, McVeigh made it known that he disapproved of the government's attempt to control citizens' possession of firearms. After the Waco stand-off, McVeigh came to believe that the government had to pay for its actions. McVeigh began to attend the Michigan Militia, but due to a lack of action, he decided to form his own paramilitary group called *The Patriots.*

McVeigh believed that it was time for him to take action so he met with neo-Nazi Dennis Mahon, who was involved with the White Aryan Resistance, and neo-Nazi Andreas Strassmeir, Chief of

Security for Elohim City (a white supremacist compound for terrorists fronted by the Christian Identity) (Nichols, 2003). Both individuals supported small cell violence. The Aryan Republican Army, which raises money in order to commit acts of terrorism, was at the Elohim City compound. Because McVeigh needed to raise money for his mission, he made friends with members of the Aryan Republic Army. These individuals reinforced McVeigh's distorted perceptions and provided him with the means to carry out his mission.

It seems as though McVeigh felt that the government blocked his opportunity to become a Green Beret. This may have resulted in frustration-aggression (Bartol & Bartol, 2008). Because he was awarded the Bronze Medal in the U.S. Army, and because he was a dedicated solider who was good at his job, he may have expected to make the Green Berets (Ottley, 2007). Not making the Green Berets may have caused him to question the integrity of the government and to become aggressive toward the government. McVeigh appeared to be suffering from a) paranoid personality disorder, which is "a pattern of distrust and suspiciousness such that others' motives are interpreted as malevolent", b) schizoid personality disorder, which is "a pattern of detachment from social relationships and a restricted range of emotional expression", and c) antisocial personality disorder, which is "a pattern of disregard for, and violation of, the rights of others" (American Psychiatric Association, 2000, p. 685). First, McVeigh believed that the government exploits people and is untrustworthy; he associated with secretive organizations; he interpreted gun control laws as malicious attacks against citizens; and his frustrations against the government continued to build over the years as the government continually assaulted various organizations, such as the Branch Davidians (Nichols, 2003). Second, McVeigh did not seek close relationships; he had few friends; he did not seek sexual relations with other people; he liked solitary activities; and he showed a lack of remorse for the bombing. Finally, McVeigh failed to conform to social norms; he recklessly disregarded the safety of others; and he was consistently irresponsible, as he failed to sustain consistent work. In short, McVeigh has met the criterion for paranoid personality disorder, schizoid personality disorder, and antisocial personality disorder.

Because McVeigh's parents divorced when he was 10 years old, he may not have received the parental support that he needed (Nichols, 2003). Furthermore, when he had failed to make the Green Berets, he may have become frustrated. Finally, in an attempt to release his aggression, McVeigh acted in revenge.

Predicting Violent Behavior

Research of more than 200 cases of workplace violence indicates that there are characteristics and behaviors that may help identify potentially violent offenders (Mattman, 2001). Commonalities identified in offenders include 1) person is usually white male, 35 to 45 years of age, 2) person has a keen interest in firearms, 3) person identifies with violence, 4) person is chronically disgruntled, 5) person has a migratory job history, 6) person rarely takes responsibility for his or her own actions, 7) person is loner with little social support, 8) person takes criticism poorly, and 9) person is more than a casual user of alcohol and drugs. Furthermore, there are pre-incident factors that individuals display, which can help predict violence at the workplace. Persons having these factors will display 1) an increase in the use of alcohol or drugs, 2) an excess amount of tardiness and absences,

3) a decrease in attention to personal hygiene, 4) depression or withdrawal, 5) outbursts of anger and rage, 6) threats or verbal abuses to colleagues, 7) continual comments about suicide, 8) unstable emotional responses, 9) frequent complaints about personal health, 10) feelings of paranoia, 11) obsession with prior acts of violence, 12) an increase in mood swings, 13) an increase in domestic problems, 14) large money withdrawals from bank accounts, 15) empathy with persons who commit violence, 16) resistance to change in procedures, 17) continual violations of company policies, 18) an increase in the number of unsolicited comments about firearms, 19) an increase in interest in violent or sexually explicit material, and 20) a self-made plan to solve the world's problems.

There are ways to help identify employees who may commit acts of violence in the workplace. First, because the traits of "psychopathy correspond to the elemental characteristics of crime itself" (DeLisi & Vaughn, 2008, p. 164), a psychological test can be administered to each applicant. The results may help classify each person's personality with validity (depending upon the instrument). Second, interview questions, background investigations, and drug testing consistent with federal laws and regulations can be implemented to detect those who may be potentially dangerous employees (Mattman, 2001; U.S. Department of Agriculture, 1998). Third, by examining workers' compensation claims, injury and illness records, and employee reprimands, patterns of violence can be identified (U.S. Department of Labor, n.d.). Long track records may identify chronic offenders who may be set in their ways due to years of conditioning (Schmalleger, 2011). Indeed, they must be getting some intrinsic rewards out of offending or else they would stop doing it. Finally, employees need to be involved in the design, implementation, and evaluation of violence prevention programs (U.S. Department of Labor). By evaluating what each employee has to say, this may provide clues about their attitudes. Thus, by implementing a variety of techniques, triangulation of the data will help validate the information about who may be dangerous (Creswell, 2003).

Credibility of Theory and Best Practice Decisions

Whenever a theory is used to describe a problem and to provide possible solutions to the problem, the researcher has the responsibility to articulate the credibility of the theory to decision-makers. For example, if a researcher uses the social leaning theory to describe a police-community relations problem, and if the police department plans to implement social learning activities to address the problem, then the success of the activities will depend on the accuracy of the theory used to describe the problem. In order to make best-practice decisions, based on the totality of circumstances, decision-makers will need both the pros and the cons of the theory. Making decisions on incomplete data may be very costly. Below is an example of how to evaluate the social learning theory.

Evaluating Akers' Social Learning Theory

According to Akers' social learning theory, pro-social and anti-social behaviors are simultaneously-learned through the same cognitive and behavioral mechanisms (Hwang & Akers, 2003). Behaviors are learned through four learning mechanisms, which are a) differential association, b) definitions, c) differential reinforcement, and d) imitation (Akers & Seller, 2009; Hwang & Akers, 2003). First, differential association indicates that an individual selects the persons with whom he or she wants to associate. Consequently, the individual is exposed to their behaviors and the individual's behaviors are influenced according to which ones the group rewards and which ones the group punishes. Second, an individual learns the attitudes and orientations of individuals whom the person considers significant. Thus, individuals "learn to evaluate their own behaviors through their interactions with significant others and groups in their lives" (Siegel, 2003, p. 224); the content of learning is achieved through definitions (Akers, 2009). Consequently, a person learns which behaviors the significant persons define as favorable and which ones they define as unfavorable and the individual adapts their same definitions. Third, differential reinforcement indicates that behaviors are modified according to the rewards and punishments associated with specific behaviors. Indeed, behaviors can be manipulated through both positive reinforcement (e.g., by providing rewards), negative reinforcement (e.g., by not requiring extra work), direct punishment (e.g., by requiring extra work), and indirect punishment (e.g., by removing rewards) (Akers & Sellers). Also, learning occurs through direct experience and by observing the behaviors and consequences of other people (Akers). In other words, individuals model the behaviors that have demonstrated to be beneficial either to themselves or to other people.

Social Learning Theoretical Criticisms

The social learning theory has several criticisms. First, the social learning theory states that same learning process produces both conforming and nonconforming behaviors (Akers & Sellers, 2009). Thus, what is actually learned in any given situation depends upon the learning process within each individual. For example, because pro-social behaviors are culturally determined, whether a person perceives a role model to be positive or negative is relative. Therefore, the researcher must understand the background of the person under investigation in order to properly understand what that person is learning. Because America is a mosaic of different cultures, the actual behaviors learned by different individuals in any given situation are questionable.

Second, although social learning theorists believe that exterior forces influence interior behavior, they fail to consider cognitive development (Durkin, 1995). Indeed, social learning theorists emphasize internal cognitive processes and assume that the information processing capacities of individuals change with experience and maturity. However, they resist "the notion of general structural reorganizations as a response to conflicts between developing understanding and empirical discovers" (Durkin, p. 25).

Third, social learning theorists dismiss biological factors and they place too much emphasis on situational factors (Durkin, 1995). For example, social learning theorists fail to address the nature of human emotions. Indeed, they dismiss the notion that personality traits may be a major feature of social behavior.

Fourth, rewards, punishments, and reinforcement, which are central to the social learning theory, are poorly defined (Durkin, 1995). In fact, they are tautological. For example, a person may define something as reinforcing simply because the person finds it reinforcing. Thus, the social learning theory does not provide a true explanation of behavior (Bordens & Abbott, 2008).

Finally, the social learning theory is "limited in its conception of social context and social influences" (Durkin, 1995, p. 26). Specifically, aside from modeling and reinforcement, the social learning theory fails to adequately consider a) how other people help an individual construct the social world, b) how the individual acquires shared representations of social and interpersonal phenomena, and c) how some developmental routes are encouraged and some are inhibited as a result of particular social arrangements.

Validation of Akers' Social Learning Theory

Although the social learning theory has several criticisms, there is a large body of evidence that provides strong and consistent support for Akers' social learning theory (Akers, 2009; Hwang & Akers, 2003). Indeed, primary data have been used to assess the validity of Akers' social learning theory and to compare it to other theories (Sellers, Cochran, and Winfree, 2003). As part of the process, more than 100 empirical tests have been conducted, which have produced "high levels of explained variance, much more than other theoretical models with which it is compared" (Sellers et al., p. 53). Some of these studies include research on drug abuse, teenage smoking, problem drinking, rape and sexual coercion, serious delinquency, cross-national homicide rates, and terrorist violence.

In an effort to personally validate the social learning theory, Akers surveyed 3,065 adolescents in order to determine the relationship between drug and alcohol abuse and the social learning variables (Siegel, 2003). The findings indicated that there is a strong association between individuals who believed that they would be rewarded by someone that they respected for their deviant acts and the likelihood that they would perform those deviant acts. Furthermore, the findings indicated that individuals who commit deviant acts seek out other individuals who also commit deviant acts as a means for support and companionship. In short, Akers (2009) demonstrated that the findings of the study strongly supported the variables of his social learning theory.

References

Adams, M., Robertson, C., Gray-Ray, P., and Ray, M. (2003). Labeling and delinquency. *Adolescence, 38* (149), 171-186.

Akers, R.L. (2009). *Social learning and social structure: A general theory of crime and deviance*. New Brunswick, NJ: Transaction.

Akers, R.L., & Sellers, C. (2009). *Criminological theories: Introduction, evaluation, and application* (5th ed.). New York, NY: Oxford University Press.

All about entropy, the laws of thermodynamics, and order from disorder (2001). *Archives of Science*. Retrieved from http://www.entropylaw.com/

American Psychiatric Association. (2000). *Diagnostic and statistical manual of mental disorders* (4th text revision ed.). Washington, DC: Author.

Barkan, S. (2006). *Criminology: A sociological understanding* (3rd ed.). Upper Saddle River, NJ: Pearson Prentice Hall.

Bartol, C.R., and Bartol, A.M. (2008). *Criminal behavior: A psychosocial approach* (8th ed.). Upper Saddle River, NJ: Prentice Hall.

Bartol, C.R., and Bartol, A.M. (2014). *Criminal behavior: A psychosocial approach* (10th ed.). Upper Saddle River, NJ: Prentice Hall.

Beck, V.S., & Travis, L.F. (2006). Sex offender notification: A cross-state comparison. *Police Practice and Research*, *7*(4), 293-307.

Blueprints for Violence Prevention (n.d.). *Blueprints model programs: Multidimensional treatment foster care (MTFC).*

Bordens, K., & Abbott, B. (2008). *Research design and methods: A process approach* (7th ed.). Boston, MA: McGraw Hill.

Bored high school students (2007). *American School Board Journal, 194* (5), 7.

Bowditch, C. (1993). Getting rid of troublemakers: High school disciplinary procedures and the production of dropouts. *Social Problems*, *40*(4).

Brainbox (2006). *Economist, 381* (8509).

Braithwaite, J. (2000). Shame and criminal justice. *Canadian Journal of Criminology*, *42*(3), 281-298.

California Evidence-Based Clearinghouse (n.d.). *Positive peer culture (PPC) – detailed report.*

Carter, D. (2002). *Issues in police-community relations: Taken from The Police and the community* (7th ed.). Boston, MA: Pearson Custom.

Cohen, M., & Jeglic, E.L. (2007). Sex offender legislation in the United States: What do we know? *International Journal of Offender Therapy and Comparative Criminology, 51*(4), 369-383.

Corrigan, R. (2006). Making meaning of Megan's law. *Law & Social Inquiry, 31*(2), 267-312.

Creswell, J. (2003). *Research design: Qualitative, quantitative, and mixed methods approaches* (2nd ed.). Thousand Oaks, CA: Sage Publications.

DeLisi, M., and Vaughn, M. (2008). Still psychopathic after all these years. In M. Delisi, and P. Conis (Eds.), *Violent offenders: Theory, research, public policy, and practice* (p. 155-168). Boston, MA: Jones and Barlett Publishers.

Drapeau, M., Korner, A., Granger, L., Brunet, L., and Caspar, F. (2005). A plan analysis of pedophile sexual abusers' motivations for treatment: A qualitative pilot study. *International Journal of Offending Therapy and Comparative Criminology, 49*(3), 308-324.

DuBois, W.D., and Berg, B.L. (2002). Crime in society: Sociological understandings and society implications. In R. Straus (Ed.), *Using sociology: An introduction from the applied and clinical perspectives* (3rd ed.) (p. 199-233). New York, NY: Rowman & Litterfield.

Durkin, K. (1995). *Developmental social psychology: From infancy to old age*. Boston, MA: Blackwell.

Falk, A. (1999). Sex offenders, mental illness and criminal responsibility: The constitutional boundaries of civil commitment after Kansas v. Hendricks. *American Journal of Law & Medicine*, *25*(1), 117-157.

Fay, B. (1987). *Critical social science*. Ithaca, NY: Cornell University Press.

Gaines, J.S. (2006). Law enforcement reactions to sex offender registration and community notification. *Police Practice and Research*, *7*(3), 249-267.

Gahlinger, P. (2004). *Illegal Drugs: A complete guide to their history, chemistry, use, and abuse*. New York: Plume.

Geske, J. (1992). *Teaching creativity for right and left brain thinkers.* Quebec, Canada: Annual Meeting of the Association for Education in Journalism and Mass Communication.

Hames, J., and Ekern, Y. (2005). *Constitutional law: principles and practice*. Clifton Park, NY: Thomson Delmar.

Hatch, J. (2002). *Doing qualitative research in education settings.* Albany, NY: State University of New York Press.

Hensley, W. (1996). A theory of the valenced other: The intersection of the looking-glass-self and social penetration. *Social Behavior and Personality, 24*(3), 293-308.

Heritage, M. (2007). Formative assessment: What do teachers need to know and do? *Phi Delta Kappan, 89* (2), 140-145.

Hibbeln, J., Ferguson, T., and Blasbalg, T. (2006). Omega-3 fatty acid deficiencies in neurodevelopment, aggression and autonomic deregulation: Opportunities for intervention. *International Review of Psychiatry, 18* (2), 107-188.

Hibbeln, J., Nieminen, L., and Lands, W. (2004). Increasing homicide rates and linoleic acid consumption among five western countries, 1961-2000. *Lipids, 39* (12), 1207-1213.

Hwang, S., & Akers, R.L. (2003). Substance use by Korean adolescents: A cross-cultural test of the social learning, social bonding, and self-control theories. In R. Akers & G. Jensen (Eds.), *Social learning theory and the explanation of crime* (p. 39-63). New Brunswick, NJ: Transaction.

In the Matter of the Commitment of A.W.D. (Ind. Ct. App. 2007). Retrieved from http://www.in.gov/judiciary/opinions/pdf/02280705msm.pdf

Johns, C. (n.d.). *Civil commitment for sexual predators.* Retrieved from http://www.angelfire.com/fl4/fci/civilcommitment.html

Kelley, TM (1996). A critique of social bonding and control theory of delinquency using the principles of psychology of mind. *Adolescence*, *31*(122).

Langevin, R., Curnoe, S., Federoff, P., Bennett, R., Langevin, M., Peever, C., et al. (2004). Lifetime sex offender recidivism: A 25-year follow-up study. *Canadian Journal of Criminology and Criminal Justice*, *46*(5), 531-552.

Levenson, J.S., Brannon, Y.N., Fortney, T., & Baker, J. (2007). Public perceptions about sex offenders and community protection policies. *Analyses of Social Issues and Public Policy*, *7*(1), 137-161.

Levenson, J.S., & Cotter, L.P. (2005). The effect of Megan's law on sex offender reintegration. *Journal of Contemporary Justice*, *21*(1), 49-66.

Levenson, J.S., D'Amora, D.A., & Hern, A.L. (2007). Megan's law and its impact on community re-entry for sex offenders. *Behavioral Sciences and the Law*, *25*(4), 587-602.

Liska, A. and Messner, S. (1999). *Perspectives on crime and deviance* (3rd ed.). Upper Saddle River, NJ: Prentice Hall.

Malesky, A., & Keim, J. (2001). Mental health professionals' perspectives on sex offender registry Web sites. *Sexual Abuse: A Journal of Research and Treatment, 13*(1), 53-63.

Mattman, J. (2001). Preventing violence in the workplace. *Workplace Violence Research Institute*. Retrieved from http://www.workviolence.com/

McLoyd, V. (1998). Socioeconomic disadvantage and child development. *American Psychologist, 53*(2), 185-204.

Meloy, M.L., Saleh, Y., & Wolff, N. (2007). Sex offender laws in America: Can panic-driven legislation ever create safer societies? *Criminal Justice Studies, 20*(4), 423-443.

Mustaine, E.E., Tewksbury, R., & Stengel, K.M. (2006). Social disorganization and residential locations of registered sex offenders: Is this a collateral consequence? *Deviant Behavior, 27*(3), 329-350.

Nichols, N. (2003). *Domestic terrorism 101: Timothy James McVeigh (The boy next door).*

Ottley, T. (2007). The Oklahoma City bombing: Bad day dawning. *The Crime Library: Criminal Minds and Methods*. Retrieved from http://www.crimelibrary.com/serial_killers/notorious/mcveigh/dawning_1.html

Radkowski, M.E. (2008). Adult sex offenders, community notifications, and recidivism. *Dissertations & Theses*. (UMI No. 3330944).

Redlich, A.D. (2001). Community notification: Perceptions of its effectiveness in preventing child sexual abuse. *Journal of Child Sexual Abuse*, *10*(3), 91-116.

Rifkin, J. (1980). *Entropy*. New York, NY: The Viking Press.

Ryan, R. (2008). Civil commitment laws for sexual predators. In M. Delisi, and P. Conis (Eds.), *Violent offenders: Theory, research, public policy, and practice* (p. 205-220). Boston, MA: Jones and Barlett Publishers.

Ryan, J., Marshall, J., Herz, D., & Hernandez, P. (2008). Juvenile delinquency in child welfare: Investigating group home effects. *Children and Youth Services Review*, *30*(9), 1-12.

Ryan, K., & Cooper, J. (2007). *Those who can, teach* (11th ed.). Boston, MA: Houghton Mifflin.

Sample, L.L., & Bray, T.M. (2006). Are sex offenders different? An examination of rearrest patterns. *Criminal Justice Policy Review*, *17*(1), 83-102.

Schmalleger, F. (2011). *Criminology: A brief introduction*. Boston, MA: Prentice Hall

Schramm, C. (2006, June 28). Capitalism spreads freedom even as democracy falters. *USA Today*, 13a.

Sellers, C.S., Cochran, J.K, & Winfree, L.T. (2003). Social learning theory and courtship violence: An empirical test. In R. Akers & G. Jensen (Eds.), *Social learning theory and the explanation of crime* (p. 109-127). New Brunswick, NJ: Transaction.

Siegel, L. (2003). *Criminology* (8th ed.). Belmont, CA: Wadsworth – Thomson.

Sower, C., & Gist, G.T. (1994). *Formula for change: Using the urban experiment station methods and the normative sponsorship theory.* East Lansing, MI: Michigan State University Press.

Sower, C., Holland, J., Tiedke, K., & Freeman, W. (1957). *Community Involvement: The webs of formal and informal ties that make for action.* Glencoe, IL: The Free Press.

Straus, R. (2002). Using sociological theory to make practical sense out of social life. In R. Straus (Ed.), *Using sociology: An introduction from the applied and clinical perspectives* (3rd ed.) (p. 21-43). New York, NY: Rowman & Litterfield.

Tarolla, S., Wagner, E., Rabinowitz, J., and Tubman, J. (2002). Understanding and treating juvenile offenders: A review of current knowledge and future directions. *Aggression and Violent Behavior,* 7(2), 125-143.

Tewksbury, R. (2002). Validity and utility of the Kentucky sex offender registry. *Federal Probation*, 66(1), 21-26.

Tewksbury, R. (2005). Collateral consequences of sex offender registration. *Journal of Contemporary Criminal Justice, 21*(1), 67-81.

Tewksbury, R., & Lees, M. (2006). Perceptions of sex offender registration: Collateral consequences and community experiences. *Sociological Spectrum*, *26*(3), 309-334.

Tucker, J., Donovan, D., and Marlatt, G. (Eds.). (1999). *Changing additive behavior: Bridging clinical and public health strategies*. New York: Guilford Press.

Turvey, B. E., & Petherick, W. (2009). *Forensic victimology: Examining violent crime victims in investigative and legal contexts*. Burlington, MA: Academic Press.

U.S. Department of Agriculture (1998). *The USDA handbook on workplace violence: Prevention and response*. Retrieved from http://www.usda.gov/

U.S. Department of Labor, Occupational Safety & Health Administration (n.d.). *Guidelines for preventing workplace violence for health care & social service workers*. Retrieved from http://www.osha.gov/

Vieno, A., Nation, M., Perkins, D.D., & Santinello, M. (2007). Civic participation and the development of adolescent behavior problems. *Journal of Community Psychology, 35*(6), 761-777.

Vold, G., Bernard, T., and Snipes, J. (2002). *Theoretical criminology* (5th ed.). New York, NY: Oxford University Press.

Wacker Foundation (2007). [Review of the book Hardwired behavior: What neuroscience reveals about morality]. *Crime Times.* Retrieved from http://www.crimetimes.org/06a/w06ap9.htm

Wakefield, H., and Underwager, R. (2007). Sex offender treatment. *Institute for Psychological Therapies.* Retrieved from http://www.ipt-forensics.com/journal/volume3/j3_1_2.htm

Webster, C.M., Gartner, R., & Doob, A. (2006). Results by design: The artefactual construction of high recidivism rates for sex offenders. *Canadian Journal of Criminology and Criminal Justice*, *48*(1), 79-93.

Zevitz, R.G. (2006). Sex offender community notification: Its role in recidivism and offender reintegration. *Criminal Justice Studies*, *19*(2), 193-208.

Zevitz, R.G., Crim, D., & Farkas, M.A. (2000a). Sex offender community notification: Examining the importance of neighborhood meetings. *Behavioral Sciences and the Law*, *18*(2/3), 393-408.

Zevitz, R.G., Crim, D., & Farkas, M.A. (2000b). Sex offender community notification: Managing high risk criminals or exacting further vengeance? *Behavioral Sciences and the Law, 18*(2/3), 375-391.

Zevitz, R.G., & Farkas, M.A. (2000). The impact of sex-offender community notification on probation/parole in Wisconsin. *International Journal of Offender Therapy and Comparative Criminology, 44*(1), 8-21.

Chapter 3

ETHICAL SYSTEMS & POLICE DEPARTMENT ORIENTATIONS

Residents are Stakeholders

According to the Declaration of Independence, the U.S. government derives its power from the individuals that it governs (Hames & Ekern, 2005). Indeed, because there are about 400 U.S. residents for every full-time sworn police officer, law enforcement requires that people voluntarily comply with the law and assist with law enforcement efforts (Reaves, 2007; U.S. Department of Labor, 2009). Furthermore, because the Posse Comitatus Act of 1878 generally prohibits the U.S. military from engaging in domestic law enforcement, and because the U.S. Constitution protects the public against unreasonable searches and seizures (i.e., protects privacy), local police are ill equipped to handle the crime problem alone (Brinkerhoff, 2009). Residents are stakeholders in maintaining a peaceful society and they must take an active part in promoting pro-social behaviors (Carter, 2002). However, the definition of good behaviors is relative. In short, before individuals can promote pro-social behaviors, a reference point is needed to define good behavior.

Test of Ethics

There is a test of ethics. First, the end must be justified as good (e.g., the conviction of criminals) (Pollock, 2004). Second, the means must be a plausible way to achieve the ends (e.g., police officers must articulate their actions). Third, there is no less intrusive method to achieve the same end (e.g., instead of strip searching drug smugglers, U.S. Customs officers could X-ray the suspects). Finally, the means must not undermine some other equal or greater end (e.g., community members must not lose faith in the legal system).

Table 12

Canons of Ethics (Christian Police & Prison Association, n.d.).

Canons of Ethics

- Officers shall uphold the Constitution
- Officers shall use ethical procedures
- Officers shall discharge duties as a public trust
- Officers shall conduct their private lives with integrity
- Officers shall hold freedom as a paramount precept
- Officers shall maintain the integrity and competence of the profession
- Officers shall cooperate with other officials to achieve law enforcement objectives
- Officers shall observe confidentiality
- Officers shall not compromise their integrity by accepting gratuities

Ethical Dilemmas

Ethical dilemmas arise as a result of conflicting core ethical values and may be inherent in some situations (Perez & Moore, 2002). Situations that involve unfair advantage, conflicts between personal values and institutional goals, power differentials, abuse of power, breaches of confidentiality, hidden agendas, impropriety or boundary violations, multiple roles, and differences in perceptions may generate ethical dilemmas. Ethical dilemmas can sometimes be foreseen by evaluating if particular signals exist. These signals may involve whether laws or professional standards are violated, whether there is internal conflict and doubt about the issue, whether anyone can be harmed as a result of the decision, whether the decision is objective, whether there is strong opposition to the decision, whether the decision can be revealed without hesitation, and whether anyone else would be willing to make the decision. When conflict arises, professional, social, and economic pressures can make ethical decision-making difficult.

Integrity has many gray areas and is a complex subject that is not always easily defined. Generally, however, integrity is a positive, proactive system of values that is constant over time and consists of fairness, honesty, sincerity, and doing what seems to be the proper thing (Dreisbach, 2008; Harberfeld, 2006; Hess & Bennett, 2007). Several standards that may be used to evaluate the integrity of police conduct are a) fair access, b) public trust, c) safety and security versus enforcement, d) teamwork, and e) objectivity. Fair access relates to fair and open access of police services to all citizens. Public trust relates to the trust that the civilians give to the police officers in exchange for their right to enforce laws. Safety and security versus enforcement relates to police officers using discretion in balancing the goal of maintaining order with the goal of enforcing the law. Teamwork relates to police officers who are expected to coordinate, communicate, and cooperate with others in the law enforcement system. Objectivity relates to police officers who are expected to be impartial and a disinterested party.

Ethical Systems – What is Good Behavior?

Ethics is the study of human conduct in the light of set ideas of right and wrong (i.e., morals) (Pollock, 2004). However, there are different ideas of right and wrong in which to judge good behavior. Consequently, different ethical systems answer the question, "*What is good?*" in different manners. **Moral principles** are set ideas of right and wrong that form the basis of ethical behaviors.

Deontological ethical system is concerned with the intent of the actor or goodwill as the element of morality (Pollock, 2004). The consequence of the action is unimportant. For example, the assassination of Hitler might be unethical under a deontological system because killing is always wrong. For police officers, shooting a murderer who is about to kill again is unethical.

Teleological ethical system is concerned with the consequences of an action to determine goodness (Pollock, 2004). For example, the assassination of Hitler might be ethical under a teleological system because the consequence may save many lives. For police officers, shooting a murderer who is about to kill again is ethical because it may save innocent lives.

Each ethical system answers the question, "What is good?" (Pollock, 2004). In other words, good behavior is relative and depends on the reference system (i.e., morals) used to judge behavior. For example, a behavior may be considered good according to one ethical system and bad according to another ethical system. However, not all behaviors are subject to ethical judgment; only those behaviors that are performed by humans acting with free will and that impact other people are subject to ethical judgment. In addition, a particular act may be defined as bad behavior for one person but not bad behavior for another person. For example, a child under the age of reason and a person that is mentally incapacitated may lack the knowledge and intent of wrong doing. Therefore, good behavior is relative. In addition, although personal values may influence individual moral beliefs and behaviors, not all personal values have ethical components. For example, the act of valuing one color automobile over another is ethically neutral and is based solely on personal opinion.

Criteria are used to decide what is right or wrong (Pollock, 2004). There are various ethical systems that use different criteria to evaluate the morality of an action. Some of the basic ethical systems that shape moral and ethical principles include 1) ethical formalism, 2) utilitarianism, 3) act utilitarianism, 4) rule utilitarianism, 5) religious ethics, 6) natural law, 7) ethics of virtue, 8) ethics of care, 9) egoism, 10) enlightened egoism, 11) ethical relativism, 12) cultural relativism, and 13) situational ethics.

Ethical formalism ethical system states that good is defined by a person's goodwill and by doing one's duty (Pollock, 2004). Good actions are based on categorical imperatives: (a) act as if the behavior will become a universal law, (b) do not use people for one's own purposes, and (c) act consistent with universal laws. For example, a lie is only a lie if the recipient is led to believe or has a right to believe that he or she is being told the truth. For instance, not telling a car thief that a bait car is being used to capture car thieves is not unethical. However, ethical formalism is problematic when there are conflicting duties (e.g., judge's order versus department policy).

Utilitarianism ethical system determines the goodness of an act by a benefit-to-cost ratio (Kraska, 2004; Pollock, 2004). The needs of the many outweigh the needs of the few. In other words, as the benefit-to-cost ratio increases, the better the act will be perceived. For example, it is okay to arrest innocent people by mistake if it solves a bigger problem.

Act Utilitarianism ethical system determines the goodness of a particular act by measuring the utility of the specific act without regard for future acts (Pollock, 2004). For example, it is not unethical to steal food when a person is hungry and has no other way to get food.

Rule Utilitarianism ethical system determines the goodness of an act by measuring the utility of the act when made into a rule for behavior (Pollock, 2004). For example, it is unethical to steal food when a person is hungry and has no other way to get food because this will result in lawlessness if people are allowed to steal food anytime that they are hungry and cannot afford food. Likewise, it may be unethical not to engage in high speed chases because this may encourage people to flee.

Religious ethics ethical system determines the goodness of an act based on the concepts of good and evil and what is good is based on God's will (Pollock, 2004). Ethics are determined by individual conscious, religious authorities, and Holy Scripture. However, problems with religious ethics are that no one may ever know exactly what the will of God is and there are current controversies within and between religions. For example, it may not be unethical or illegal for Native Americans to consume contraband mushrooms for religious practices.

An example of a controversy within religion is the use of deceit to save a life. For example, should a person lie to save an innocent child who is being sought by a gunman? Some Christian thinkers may argue for the existence of a higher ethic, namely love, and that lying to save a life is okay because it is based on good intent and love (Father F. Rogers, personal communication on 6/26/2014). If one looks at this situation as the *lesser of two evils*, then the greatest evil would be to contribute to the intended victim's death. In this case, if a lie allows the intended victim to get away safely, or if the gunman's threat can be neutralized, then a lie would be the *lesser of two evils*. The lie would have the effect of preserving life, which is a greater good and, therefore, justified.

However, from a biblical perspective, one does not have to answer the gunman's question at all (Father F. Rogers, personal communication on 6/26/2014). A person can choose to remain silent and to face the consequences. In this case, a person may choose to die rather than to sin by lying or by contributing to the harm of another person. Hence, one need not lie. In Christian ethics, self-preservation is not the ultimate good. Indeed, death is preferable to sin.

Natural law ethical system states that there is a universal set of rights and wrongs but without reference to specific supernatural beings (Pollock, 2004). What is good is determined by what is natural to humans (e.g., socialization and the right to life) and is free of passion. Indeed, the founding fathers might be described as natural law practitioners. However, identifying what is consistent and congruent with natural inclinations of humankind is a fundamental problem of this ethical system. This is evidenced by the changing of laws (e.g., marijuana use) and the development of new laws.

Ethics of virtue ethical system determines the goodness of an act based on the attempt to achieve happiness, such as living a good life and achieving life's goals (Pollock, 2004). Good behavior is based on the golden mean, which is the median between extreme states of character. For example, absolute police powers and civil liberties oppose one another. Effective law enforcement must compromise between the two. It is based on a person's character and includes factors such as honesty, humility, and temperance.

Ethics of care ethical system determines the goodness of an act based on meeting needs and preserving and enriching relationships (Pollock, 2004). Actions are taken based on connecting with other people, caring for the needs of other people, and being aware of other people. For example, involving a single event in which battery threats are made, instead of arresting the offender for intimidation (a felony), the police officer may arrest the offender for disorderly conduct (a misdemeanor), provocation (a civil infraction), or simply separate the parties (a warning). By taking the minimum enforcement action necessary in order to achieve peace, relationships will be enhanced and labeling may be prevented.

Egoism ethical system claims that good results from pursuing self-interests (Pollock, 2004). However, every person acting in his or her own best interests is not logical or feasible and this will result in great conflict. An example of egoism in law enforcement is when police officers write unnecessary tickets in order to meet quotas for good performance reviews.

Enlightened egoism claims that it is in one's long-term best interest to help others so that they will learn to help themselves (Pollock, 2004). For example, a police officer may refuse to change a flat tire on a car occupied with capable adults and may instead instruct them on how to change the tire themselves. Having the occupants change the tire themselves may prove valuable in the future if they get another flat tire and no assistance is available.

However, community members may expect the police to provide full and immediate service and this may result in complaints. As a way to comply with departmental policy, police officers in the field may offer full service in terms of providing a wrecker service. If drivers are dissatisfied with that response due to time and cost, this may damage police-community relations.

Ethical relativism ethical system determines what is good or bad based on the individual or group (Pollock, 2004). For example, community members in a poor region may hunt and fish without purchasing the proper licenses. Likewise, prostitution may be encouraged and institutionalized in certain communities.

Cultural relativism defines good as that which contributes to the health and survival of society (Pollock, 2004). For example, men in certain cultures may kill their spouses if their wives expose their faces to strangers. However, U.S. law enforcers may sometimes need to identify these females. This conflict of interest is often encountered at the U.S. borders.

Situational ethics ethical system states that there are few universal truths and that different situations call for different responses (Pollock, 2004). Thus, the same action may be right in some situations and wrong in other situations. For example, it may be ethical for a person to violate the speed laws if he or she is racing an injured person to the hospital. However, the same action may be unethical if no such emergency exists.

Deceiving Suspects:

Is it ethical for police officers to lie to suspects in the field?

Ethical Formalism: condemned, due to violation of categorical imperative; lying would become rule for all people

Religious: condemned, God is truth; possibly justified, if person can argue that it is the lesser of two evils

Rule Utilitarianism: condemned, because it may undermine long-term system of laws

Utilitarianism: justified, if benefits outweigh costs to society as a whole

Natural Law: justified, as long as civil rights are not violated

Ethics of Virtue: justified, if crimes are severe and if methods are moderate

Ethics of Care: justified, if it protects victims

Egoism: justified, if it is profitable to the police officer

Cultural Relativism: justified, as long as accepted by culture

Situational Ethics: justified, if police officer can effectively articulate reasons for deception in this particular case (evaluated on a case-by-case basis)

<table>
<tr><th colspan="3">Ethics in Law Enforcement</th></tr>
<tr>
<td>Utilitarianism

Good is based on a benefit-cost ratio. Example of good behavior: arresting an innocent person in order to deter crime in general. </td>
<td>Types of Ethical Systems

• Ethical Formalism
• Utilitarianism
• Religious
• Natural Law
• Ethics of Virtue
• Ethics of Care
• Egoism
• Cultural Relativism
• Situational Ethics</td>
<td rowspan="2">Ethics in Law Enforcement

What is good behavior?

Ethics is the study of set ideas of right and wrong. However, there are different ideas of right and wrong in which to judge good behavior. Consequently, different ethical systems answer the question, “What is good?” in different manners.</td>
</tr>
<tr>
<td>Religious

Good is based on God’s will. Example of good behavior: always providing complete and truthful information, regardless of the cost. </td>
<td>Ethical Formalism

Good is based on goodwill and intent. Example of good behavior: catching a fleeing felon, even if the violator gets hurt. </td>
</tr>
</table>

Figure 5. Types of ethical systems.

<table>
<tr><th colspan="3">Ethics in Law Enforcement</th></tr>
<tr>
<td>Natural Law

Good is based on a universal set of rights (i.e., what is natural). Example of good behavior: acting in accordance with the U.S. Constitution.

</td>
<td>Ethics of Care

Good is based on the needs of those concerned. Example of good behavior: always arresting males who are involved in domestic violence in order to protect female victims.
</td>
<td>Cultural Relativism

Good is based on what promotes the health and survival of society. Example of good behavior: Middle Eastern women refusing to show their faces in public.
</td>
</tr>
<tr>
<td>Ethics of Virtue

Good is based on compromise. Example of good behavior: using non-intrusive X-Ray machines to search for contraband.
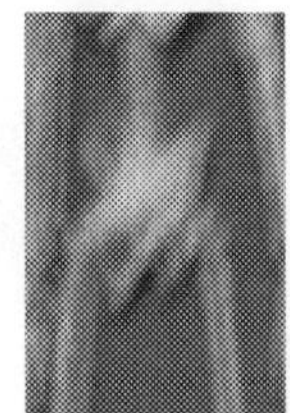 X-Ray</td>
<td>Egoism

Good is based on what benefits the actor. Example of good behavior: writing a lot of tickets to meet the monthly quota for a good performance review.

</td>
<td>Situational Ethics

Good is based on the particular situation at a particular time. Example of good behavior: speeding in order to get to the hospital to save a life.

</td>
</tr>
</table>

Figure 5 (continued). Types of ethical systems.

Ethics in Action: Gratuities

The formal law enforcement code of ethics disapproves of a police officer accepting gratuities if they negatively influence a police officer's actions (Hess & Wrobleski, 1997). Even though the formal law enforcement code of ethics generally disapproves of police officers accepting gratuities, accepting gratuities is a debatable issue. The reason for this is that there are both costs and benefits for both the police and the public when police officers accept gratuities. Furthermore, there is disagreement on what constitutes a gratuity. In short, police officers should not use their public office for personal gain and that they should not accept gratuities from people with whom they do official business.

One problem with police officers accepting gratuities is that there is no clear definition of a gratuity. According to Prenzler and Mackay (1995), a gratuity is a gift, reward, or discount that is given freely and that does not influence the police officer's performance. According to Coleman (2004), a gratuity can even be a glass of water because it has value. On the other hand, Corley (2005) states that a gratuity is something given freely in order to honor someone. Corley states that a gift, given in kindness, such as a cup of coffee, is not a gratuity. He also stresses that gratuities and gifts must not be confused with one another, and that officers must use common sense to distinguish them. However, this can only be achieved through proper training. If the officers have doubt, then to play it safe, they must refuse all gifts and gratuities.

Cons of Police Officers Accepting Gratuities

There are several arguments against police officers accepting gratuities. Because police officers strive at improving police-community relations, it is important to consider the image that the officers are portraying to the public. Below are eight cons for police officers accepting gratuities.

The first con with police officers accepting gratuities is the potential that this may lead to corruption (Coleman, 2004; Prenzler & Mackay, 1995). However, while some of those who oppose gratuities equate gratuities with corruption, others disagree, stating that most gratuities are given with no strings attached. To complicate the matter, legal opinions do not clearly define what is considered acceptable behavior; for example, how much is too much? Thus, with all this confusion, the actual acceptance of gratuities is considered to be a gray area.

A second con with police officers accepting gratuities is that this actually does lead to corruption (Prenzler & Mackay, 1995). There is a chance that police officers will come to expect gratuities. When this is not realized, police officers have been known to teach business owners a lesson (Ruiz & Bono, 2004). Furthermore, because there is no clear-cut guideline between simple gratuities and huge payoffs, some officers may unknowingly cross that ill-defined line.

A third con with police officers accepting gratuities is that the public may perceive that the officer is willing to become corrupt (Coleman, 2004). If a police officer accepts gratuities, this establishes a history of the police accepting things without paying for them.

Because the officer has not established what his or her limits are for accepting gratuities, the public will be doubtful about those limits.

The fourth con with police officers accepting gratuities is that it may give the impression of favoritism (Hess & Bennett, 2007; Prenzler & Mackay, 1995). If the public sees officers receiving free gifts, such as food and beverages, then the public may perceive that the provider will expect something in return. As stated earlier, America is a capitalistic society and people understand that nothing is free. Thus, by the officer accepting gratuities, capitalism dictates that the officer will have to return that payment in one way or another. Even though accepting the gratuities is not wrong in itself, the image that it portrays may be unethical (Pozo, 2005).

The fifth con with police officers accepting gratuities is that favoritism may actually take place (Coleman, 2004). The provider may expect preferential treatment and may demand that an officer overlooks minor violations of the law, such as speeding, and the officer may feel obligated to comply (Pozo, 2005). Although most business employees offer gratuities with no strings attached, there are some who do expect favors (Corley, 2005). In fact, after not receiving special treatment, an owner billed the local police department for all of the food that was given to the officers as gratuities (White, 2002). This business owner then went to the local media and provided the police officers' names and the dollar amounts for the food that they consumed as a means of extortion (the officers signed receipts). Thus, even if the police officers believe that gratuities are free, they never know if the business owners feel the same way.

A sixth con with police officers accepting gratuities is that the public is paying for services already bought (Hess & Bennett, 2007; Prenzler & Mackay, 1995; Ruiz & Bono, 2004). Police officers are paid out of a budget that has been collected from the taxpayers. Because all taxpayers have contributed toward this budget, the police services for the entire community have already been purchased. By business owners providing gratuities, this is considered an additional payment in order to receive personalized police services. Thus, by accepting gratuities, police officers are double charging the public.

A seventh con with police officers accepting gratuities is that if the gratuity is offered by a person who is unauthorized to offer gratuities, then the police officer is condoning theft (Coleman, 2004). For example, if only managers in a restaurant can offer gratuities, but the cashier offers them instead, then the cashier is giving away items that do not belong to her. By accepting these gratuities, the officers are participating in theft.

Finally, an eighth con with police officers accepting gratuities is the unfair social distribution of police services (Pozo, 2005). When police officers take their lunches at particular locations, those officers provide two services: deterrence of crime, and the rapid response to emergencies. Thus, by simply being there, that location receives additional services not being offered to other locations. Other restaurant owners may not be too happy with this situation and they may file complaints.

Pros of Police Officers Accepting Gratuities

There are several arguments that advocate police officers accepting gratuities. Because police officers strive at improving police-community relations, it is important to consider the relationships that the officers are building with the public. Below are seven pros for police officers accepting gratuities.

First, accepting gratuities may reduce uncomfortable public situations faced by police officers. Some business owners insist on giving gratuities out of civic friendship (Hess & Bennett, 2007; Pozo, 2005). If an officer refuses to accept the gratuity, a business owner may become upset and vocal. This may attract unwelcome attention. Arguing with the public may give the perception that the officer is unfriendly and aggressive. This may create an uncomfortable situation for the police officer and may weaken social bonds.

Second, accepting gratuities will enhance social bonds and police performance, which may promote a safer society (Coleman, 2004; Hess & Bennett, 2007). For instance, if a female rape victim offers the investigating officer a cup of coffee, failing to accept the coffee may damage the working relationship and impede the officer's job. Furthermore, because it is an American custom to leave a tip for good service, some people may feel that they need to tip police officers for good service. However, as stated earlier, when a police officer provides service to the public, that service has already been purchased. Therefore, if the gratuity is offered to the officer as a tip, then it must be rejected. However, if the gratuity is offered to the officer out of friendship, then accepting that gratuity may be beneficial. This is especially true if the gratuities are given after the fact, when they cannot influence any police actions. For instance, if a police officer protects a woman from being raped, she may later offer him a small gift of appreciation. Because this gift is presented after the fact, it will have no impact on the case. If, on the other hand, the officer refuses to accept the gift, the woman may come to believe that the officer never really cared about her. This may damage police-community relations.

Third, accepting gratuities improves police response time (Sewell, 2007). For example, if a restaurant owner provides a discount on food, then a police officer may be motivated to eat there. By being there, the police officer is capable of responding to emergencies rather quickly. If, on the other hand, the police officer is not motivated to eat at the restaurant, and instead goes home to eat because the food is better and cheaper, then the response time may be slower. To make things worse, the response time may be significantly slower in poor weather conditions.

Fourth, accepting gratuities promotes public safety. When officers go home to eat, they are not in the public's sight. Just by being on the road, police officers deter crime. Thus, police officers have presence when they eat their meals in the field. The police department may set a fixed dollar amount per month at each restaurant in order to discourage an officer from eating at the same restaurant too often.

Fifth, accepting gratuities prevents officers from being self-stigmatized (Coleman, 2004). If police officers are labeled as corrupt because they have already accepted a gratuity, then some may come to believe that are already deviant and corrupt. If they self-stigmatize themselves as deviant, then they may come to realize a self-fulfilling prophecy, thereby leading to additional deeds of deviance (Ryan & Cooper, 2007).

Sixth, the practice of accepting gratuities is so deeply entrenched in American culture that banning gratuities will be ineffective (White, 2002). Furthermore, most gratuities have only nominal value and are not significant enough to influence a police officer's actions. Banning gratuities will only result in unnecessary violations of department policy.

Finally, the seventh reason for allowing police officers to accept gratuities is that this will reduce departmental workload, if officers use discretion. If the department has a no tolerance gratuity policy, then this will increase the amount of work for the department. Every time that there is a complaint, the department will have to investigate. However, if the officers use their common sense and have some discretion, then the post commander could resolve any potential problem over the telephone. The post commander could tell the caller, for example, that officers are professionals who are well trained in ethics, and that a harsh judgment of them accepting a gratuity out of civic friendship cannot be justified within such a brief encounter (Pozo, 2005).

Theoretical Concepts and Research

There are several theories that may explain why police officers accept gratuities. The Rational Choice theory states that a police officer will perform an act when the benefits for the act outweigh the associated costs for the act (Liska & Messner, 1999). The Looking Glass Self theory indicates that people will react to how they perceive that others judge them (Hensley, 1996). Finally, the Behavioral Economics theory indicates that choices are influenced by available alternatives and environmental constraints (Tucker et al., 1999).

Rational Choice Theory

The Rational Choice theory states that people will perform acts when they are profitable (Barkan, 2006; Liska & Messner, 1999). There are two ways to enhance the benefit-cost ratio: by increasing the benefits so that they are greater than the costs, or by reducing the costs so that they are less than the benefits. Both cases will increase profitability.

The Rational Choice theory involves extrinsic and intrinsic rewards (Ryan & Cooper, 2007). The extrinsic rewards involve the actual receiving of the gratuities, which is something of value. Every time that the officer accepts a $5.00 free meal, that is $5.00 cash still in the officer's pocket. Intrinsic rewards, on the other hand, are the internal feelings that make an officer feel good. When an officer receives a gratuity, even if the officer does not need it, this may give the officer a feeling of superiority over the giver. This feeling of power is a reward that comes from within, providing the officer with personal satisfaction (Ryan & Cooper).

Costs, in the form of deterrence, can be measured in three ways: 1) the severity of punishment, 2) the certainty of punishment, and 3) the celerity of punishment (Akers & Sellers, 2009). Deterrence works best when officers perceive that the severity of punishment is great, the certainty of punishment is high, and the celerity of punishment is swift. For instance, if immediate suspensions are associated with accepting inappropriate gratuities, then an officer will compare the benefits of a free meal to the cost of a suspension. Furthermore, once a policy is established, the policy must be strictly enforced. If the officers perceive that the policy is not enforced, then they will not follow it; if an officer is caught violating the policy, then disciplinary action must be taken. If disciplinary action is not guaranteed, then the policy will have minimal influence upon the officers. By posting disciplinary actions taken against officers for their indiscretions, the word will spread that the issue is serious. Thus, officers will come to realize that the punishment is severe, certain, and immediate.

The Looking Glass Self Theory

Cooley states that people develop their self-concepts by evaluating how they believe that they appear to others, how they believe that others judge their appearance, and then by how they react to those judgments (Hensley, 1996). This is what Cooley calls the Looking Glass Self. By accepting gratuities on a regular basis, police officers may come to believe that the public expects it. Some officers may believe that gratuities are a perk that comes with the job. However, in order to redefine their self-concepts, the officers must be persuaded to change their attitudes.

Behavioral Economics Theory

Self-image is important to police departments and unethical behaviors will not be tolerated. However, the formal law enforcement code of ethics only disapproves a police officer accepting gratuities if they negatively influence a police officer's actions (Hess & Wrobleski, 1997). Thus, accepting gratuities is not always unethical (Prenzler

& Mackay, 1995). As in solving any problem, the root causes of the gratuity problem must be identified. Some of the variables that are associated with the problem include a) officer's preference, b) assignment location, c) restaurant availability, and d) social environment (Sewell, 2007). Once the issues have been determined, change must come from above and officers must be persuaded to modify their behaviors.

One possible idea is to require the officers to eat at randomly designated restaurants (Pozo, 2005). However, officers may only have few restaurants to choose from when they are working. Therefore, this action may be ineffective. A second idea would be to request that the officers bring their meals from home and to eat their meals within their police cars. However, a problem with eating meals in the police car is that is it very common to witness violations from within the vehicle. If the police officer is trying to eat lunch and does nothing, citizens will complain. If the officer chases the vehicle, then the officer will not have much of an opportunity to eat. Therefore, this suggestion may not be well received among the officers. A third idea is to have the officers bring their meals from home and to ask that they eat their meals inside a squad room. The problem with that idea is that there is no incentive to eat within the squad room; officers may prefer to go home where they can watch television and spend some time with the family. If an officer does goes home for a meal, then the response time for a detail may be longer.

Conclusion

The government derives its powers with the consent of the people (Cain, 2003). Indeed, the police can only govern the people if the people agree to be governed. Thus, the police must have a good relationship with the public. It is important that the community members respect the police. When police officers accept gratuities, this makes a statement and forms an image of the officers. Although there are both pros and cons for police officers accepting gratuities, and because there is no clear cut guideline of how much is too much, officers need to be adequately trained in this area and taught to use proper discretion. Furthermore, officers need to be persuaded to follow the department's gratuity policy. If a negative image is created by officers accepting gratuities, then this will weaken the bond between the police and the public. Indeed, the officers must have integrity and the public must perceive that the officers have integrity. In this way, police-community relations will be enhanced and this will promote public safety.

Police Department Orientations

Eight theoretical orientations have been identified that describe the lenses in which police department administrators perceive crime and the criminal justice system (Kraska, 2004). See Figure 6. The orientation that a police department follows will influence how patrol officers act toward the public. The eight orientations include 1) Rational, 2) System, 3) Crime Control versus Due Process, 4) Politics, 5) Growth Complex, 6) Social Constructionist, 7) Oppression, and 8) Late Modernity. Having a reference point in which to evaluate good behavior will influence the actions of police officers in the field. However, each orientation is based on assumptions, which must be understood. The eight orientations are described below.

Rational Orientation

The rational orientation simply views law enforcement as a business. Peace and security can be achieved by controlling crime, and crime can be controlled by punishing offenders (Kraska, 2004). In other words, everyone is expected to follow the rules in order to achieve the agreed upon end result, which is peace. When a man, for example, decides not to follow the rules, he creates a tear in the fabric of peace, and this fabric must be repaired, which requires a cost. By not following the rules, this man has encroached upon the rights of other individuals and is forcing them to pay a cost for which he is responsible. Because this is not fair, laws are required to balance things out. The offender must pay a cost high enough, not only to repair the damage, but to deter him from disrupting social order in the future. If the penalty is not high enough to discourage future acts of deviance, then the public's confidence in public safety will be undermined. The greater the cost is to the public, the greater the cost that must be paid by the offender.

The main assumptions of the rational orientation are that everyone in society has equal value, everyone is in alignment, and everyone concedes to follow the agreed upon rules. It assumes that everyone has given up a little bit of personal freedom so that the government can enforce the agreed upon rules in order to promote public safety in a fair and impartial manner (Kraska, 2004). It assumes that crime has a cost and can be managed through payment.

System Orientation

The system orientation views criminal justice as an entity that consists of interacting, yet independent, agencies (Kraska, 2004). The various agencies function by drawing inputs from the external environment, transforming these inputs, and then sending the final product back into the environment as socially approved output. An example would be to collect convicts (input), to rehabilitate them through behavior modification programs (transform), and then to release them back into society (output). The system's independent units strive to maintain balance and internal stability as they sustain each other. It is believed that crime is a rational choice and that the size and power of the system must be increased in order accommodate increases in the crime rate.

The primary purpose of the criminal justice system, according to the system orientation, is to control crime via interagency cooperation (Kraska, 2004). It is believed that public safety can be achieved through efficient operations of each unit of the criminal justice system, including the legislative, executive, judicial, and correctional agencies. In this way, accused persons can be processed, rehabilitated, and returned to society in an effective and efficient manner that promotes social peace.

The main assumption of the system orientation is that those who have legal authority are capable of making rational decisions, which will reduce crime in an efficient manner (Kraska, 2004). It is believed that the system can adapt itself to accommodate changes in the external environment, usually by increasing its resources. By effectively and efficiently using resources and technology, by improving laws and policies, by improving judicial processes, and by improving rehabilitation and re-entry programs, it is expected that crime can be better controlled and public safety will be enhanced.

Crime Control Orientation versus Due Process Orientation

The main purpose of the crime control orientation is to secure peace by arresting as many law violators as possible, as fast as possible, and by using as few resources per arrest as possible (Kraska, 2004). Furthermore, because the defendants are presumed guilty (otherwise they would not have been arrested), releasing suspects due to procedural mistakes is wrong. In other words, suspects are guilty of their alleged crimes, otherwise law enforcement authorities would not spend the resources trying to prosecute the person (i.e., effective crime control does not focus on innocent people). It is believed that this quantitatively based tough-on-crime policy can be achieved by efficiently processing offenders informally and consistently through the legal system. This requires having few constitutional restraints placed upon law enforcers. However, the crime control orientation assumes that law enforcers a) are trustworthy and will enforce laws in a fair and legal manner, and b) can competently reconstruct crime scenes and develop the most accurate account of the actual events in a descriptive and factual manner. In short, mistakes are tolerated up to the point where they start to interfere with the suppression of crime.

The main purpose of the due process orientation is to protect people's rights by placing constraints upon the government and by making government officials defend their investigative procedures in an adversarial courtroom (Kraska, 2004). Due process advocates believe that mistakes are unacceptable, individual freedom is more valuable than absolute security, and that factual guilt does not equate to legal guilt. However, unless a person is provided the opportunity to present evidence, it is assumed that this distinction will not be made. This qualitative based policy assumes that the defendant will be provided adequate legal representation in the courtroom and that the legal system will lead to the discovery of the truth (e.g., whether the police honored procedural safeguards, as guaranteed by law). Indeed, the due process orientation requires that an unbiased third party make an objective evaluation of legal guilt.

Due process advocates view criminal justice as a necessary means to protect social freedom by protecting all citizens from unjust acts committed by government officials (Kraska, 2004). Because the cost of being incarcerated is extremely high, the due process orientation requires that the state eliminate all doubt as to whether constitutional procedural safeguards were violated. In order to control law enforcers, there must be a cost for violating the rules. Thus, in order to ensure that police officers will comply with the law, it is argued that the cost of releasing all suspects whose rights have been violated will be a high enough cost to motivate law enforcers to obey the law when they perform their duties. According to the due process orientation, corrupt police officers will cause the crime control orientation to fail.

Politics Orientation (Right Wing versus Left Wing)

According to the politics orientation, the criminal justice system is interest-based and its primary purpose is contingent upon the political climate at the time, which constantly changes according to who are in power (Kraska, 2004). Many interests groups fight for power and want to protect their own self-interests. Through negotiations, the different groups can protect their interests through checks and balances. This promotes an orderly offender processing system via rational policies. Politics, however, has two sides, a right wing and a left wing.

The right wing is conservative and the left wing is liberal (Kraska, 2004). On the one hand, the right wing believes that a) the system is too lenient with offenders, b) the system favors the rights of offenders over the rights of victims, c) youths no longer respect authorities, d) hard working law-abiding Americans are paying the high cost for crime, and e) society is too permissive involving morality issues. The left wing, on the other hand, believes that a) the system inappropriately includes certain vices as crimes, which indicates a more serious crime problem than really exists, b) authorities label people as criminals, which may stigmatize them and create a self-fulfilling prophecy, c) correctional facilities are warehouses for criminals and they fail to rehabilitate inmates, which lead to recidivism, d) centralized power discourages the involvement of community members in solving local problems, and e) the criminal justice system discriminates against and segregates minorities in order to control them.

The right wing and the left wing each have their own set of assumptions (Kraska, 2004). The right wing's assumptions state that a) people are responsible for their own actions, b) strong morals, based on a religious foundation, are essential for a healthy and well-functioning society, c) people have the right to be safe and secure in the areas where they spend most of their time, d) a healthy society requires that people obey the laws, which will be administered fairly and firmly, and e) social order requires that major categories of persons be segregated so that they can be controlled. The left wing's assumptions state that a) the primary cause of crime lies in dysfunctional social conditions, b) obsolete morality regulations are deficient in meeting the current needs of a majority of the population, c) there is an unequal distribution of power and resources in the country, d) a healthy society cannot discriminate against major categories of persons, e) official authorities stigmatize offenders by labeling them as criminals, which will lead to hardship and future crime, and f) the crime problem is exaggerated (thus, legal codes should be changed so that victimless crimes are not counted toward the crime problem).

Growth Complex Orientation

According to the growth complex orientation, the purpose of the criminal justice system is to build an ever growing bureaucracy; administering justice and controlling crime are tools that are used to increase the agency's size and power (Kraska, 2004). In an effort to meet the organizational ends in the most efficient way, scientific methods are established in order to create rules and regulations, which will get everyone to perform their duties in the same technically efficient and predictable manner. Instead of focusing on the outcome (doing the right thing), the rules and regulations become the standard for performance. Using statistics allows police departments to defend their enforcement practices. When someone challenges their apparently unfair enforcement tactics, the police can claim that individuals are arrested based on objective numeric analysis. They may also argue that without using statistics to classify and sentence people, each person's fate would be inconsistent and uncertain.

Operating under the growth complex orientation, there is an incentive to lock people up. Part of the criminal justice system has become privatized and many investors hope to profit (Kraska, 2004). On the one hand, the investors create many jobs. For example, workers are needed to build prisons, supply prison food, supply prison clothes, and provide medical care. On the other hand, the investors need customers (i.e., inmates); hence, there is an incentive to confine people in prison. By locking people up in prison, the state effectively manages the surplus labor force, which is naturally generated in a capitalistic society (Kraska, 2004). Thus, politicians appear to be effectively serving the public. After all, jobs are created and there are fewer unemployed people in the marketplace.

The main assumptions of the growth complex orientation are that a) a bureaucracy needs to survive and grow, b) people desire to build dynasties that extend their power and create a type of immortality, c) the use of rational and efficient methods are the best way to measure performance, d) capitalism and efficiency take precedence over human dignity (consequently, people lose sight of their morals), e) a matrix of organizations, interests, and resources is needed for growth, f) punishing people is good financial business and creates many jobs, and g) profiteers are not held accountable for their faulty products and their low quality services.

Social Constructionist Orientation

The social constructionist orientation is based upon interpretivism, which has both subjective and objective qualities (Kraska, 2004). On the one hand, interpretivism is subjective and claims that reality and meanings are shaped via individual experiences, which are unique to each individual. On the other hand, interpretivism is objective and claims that individuals constantly negotiate their perceptions with other people with whom they associate, reflecting an intersubjective reality (Weber, 2004). Indeed, there is no one single truth; reality for each person is constructed relative to personal experiences based upon language, symbols, and the interactions with other individuals (Kraska).

According to the social constructionist orientation, the purpose of the criminal justice system is socially constructed and depends on the political climate, social sentiment, cultural values, intellectual perspective, and interests of those in power (Kraska, 2004). Using the media to manage the appearance of the system's legitimacy, the public is continually bombarded with myths until the myths become accepted as facts. The criminal justice system can provide the public with select information, which creates the perception that the status quo must be maintained. Police can effectively create their own jobs by persuading the public to support their current efforts.

The assumptions of the social constructionist orientation are a) police use myths to develop problems that do not really exist, which divert public attention away from the real problems in society (e.g., unemployment and discrimination), and b) the interests of people in power must be protected (Kraska, 2004). Using descriptive statistics and the media, who need exciting crime stories to sell their product, the police can provide the information needed to create moral panic. For example, the police chief can increase the crime rate by ordering the officers to file multiple charges for each case report or the police chief can reduce the crime rate by ordering the officers to file a single charge for each case report. By appearing to effectively react to a problem, which never really existed, the police can gain the public's support.

Late Modernity Orientation

According to the late modernity orientation, the purpose of the criminal justice system is to promote safety and security by effectively identifying and managing classes of people who are assessed to be a threat (Kraska, 2004). The "goal is not to eliminate crime but to make it tolerable through systematic coordination" (Kraska, p. 305-307). Late modernity is not concerned with the underlying causes of crime; rather, it uses statistics to assess risk levels of particular classes of people and then tries to control populations that are identified as high risk. By incarcerating the high risk groups of people, significant aggregate effects in crime can be realized. In other words, crime can be reduced by rearranging the type of people who are still out in the general population (i.e., it reduces the percentage of high risk people who are roaming around in free society).

The main assumptions of the late modernity orientation are that the state cannot provide effective overall security, that private persons need to invest in their own situational crime prevention programs, and that people rationally choose to commit crime (Kraska, 2004). Because situational crime prevention programs require financial resources to implement, this excludes many of the poor people (who end up being labeled as outsiders). Late modernity orientation supporters claim that these misfortunate people are responsible for their own fates. By classifying these misfortunate individuals as outsiders, the dominant classes can effectively control them without the dominant classes giving up their own freedoms. Indeed, authorities can effectively control these misfortunate people because incarceration is easy to implement, it results in immediate consequence, it has few political opponents, it relies on the existing system of regulations, and it leaves the fundamental social and economic systems intact.

Oppression Orientation

Oppression orientation claims that the state protects the interests of the elite and powerful while oppressing the disadvantaged and less powerful (Kraska, 2004). In other words, the state uses the law as a tool for the political repression of those groups that threaten state power. There is a struggle for power and the groups that attain the most power are the ones who dictate the law. According to the oppression orientation, the purpose of the criminal justice system is to control people who threaten the status quo. Groups who are less powerful politically, which include minorities, women, and the poor, are used as scapegoats for America's problems. By using scapegoats, society is able to overlook the underlying factors that actually cause significant social harm (e.g., unemployment and poverty).

The assumption of oppression orientation is that the criminal justice system has built in bias against minorities, women, and the poor (Kraska, 2004). Indeed, because laws in the U.S. are based on men's perspective, the laws are inherently biased. In short, the criminal justice system abuses its power through the practice of institutional racism, sexism, and classism.

<table>
<tr><th colspan="3">Police Department Orientations</th></tr>
<tr>
<td>Crime Control

The overall goal is to control crime by arresting as many people as possible, as fast as possible, using as few resources as possible. Mistakes are acceptable; police are trustworthy and they only arrest the guilty.

</td>
<td>Police Department Orientations

• Rational
• Crime Control
• Due Process
• System
• Politics and Criminal Justice
• Growth Complex
• Social Constructionist
• Late Modernity
• Oppression</td>
<td rowspan="2">Police Department Orientations

What is good police officer behavior?

Police managers have different ideas of right and wrong in which to judge good police officer behavior. Consequently, different police department orientations answer the question, "What is good police officer behavior?" in different manners.</td>
</tr>
<tr>
<td>Due Process

Personal freedom is more valuable than absolute security. People have a right to legal representation; police need to prove case in court. Mistakes by the police are unacceptable.

</td>
<td>Rational

Law enforcement is a business. Everyone agrees to give up some freedom for peace and security. If the cost for crime is high enough, individuals will rationally choose to obey the law.

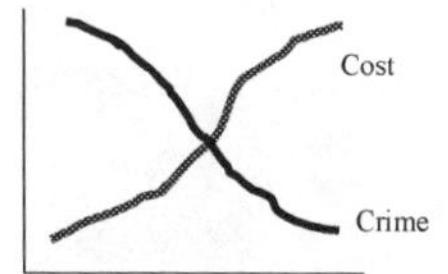</td>
</tr>
</table>

Figure 6. Police Department Orientations.

Police Department Orientations		
System	***Growth Complex***	***Late Modernity***
Independent agencies work together to collect deviants, to transform them, and to return them to society. Public safety can be achieved through inter-agency cooperation and efficient operation of each agency.	Purpose of police is to build an ever growing bureaucracy. Police rules become the standard to measure performance (quotas). Police create problems to ensure jobs. Human dignity is unimportant; punishing individuals is profitable.	Purpose of police is to use statistics to assess risk levels and to promote safety by controlling the classes of people who have been identified as the problem. Individuals need to take responsibility to protect themselves.
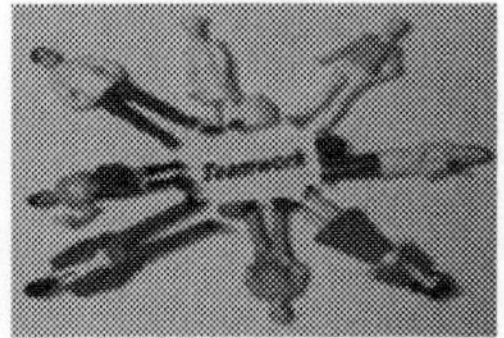		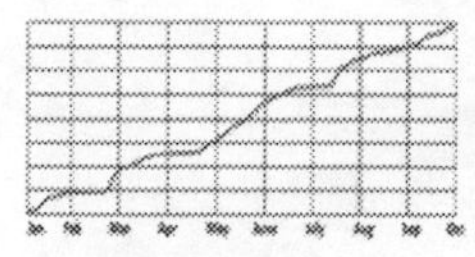
Politics	***Social Constructionist***	***Oppression***
Purpose of police depends on who has political power. Right wing: system is too lenient; left wing: system is too controlling.	Purpose of police is based on interpretivism. Good behavior is determined by culture, by social sentiment, and by people in power. Because there is no single truth, police use media to create myths.	Purpose of police is to protect the elite and powerful while controlling the disadvantaged and less powerful. The police should maintain the status quo by controlling minorities.

Figure 6 (continued). Police Department Orientations.

References

Akers, R.L., & Sellers, C. (2009). *Criminological theories: Introduction, evaluation, and application* (5th ed.). New York, NY: Oxford University Press.

Barkan, S. (2006). *Criminology: A sociological understanding* (3rd ed.). Upper Saddle River, NJ: Pearson Prentice Hall.

Brinkerhoff, J.R. (2009). *Domestic Operational Law: The Posse Comitatus Act and Homeland Security.* Retrieved from http://usacac.army.mil/cac2/call/docs/10-16/ch_12.asp

Cain, W. (2003). Declaring independence. *Society, 41* (1).

Carter, D. (2002). *Issues in police-community relations: Taken from The Police and the community* (7th ed.). Boston, MA: Pearson Custom.

Coleman, S. (2004). When police should say "no!" to gratuities. *Criminal Justice Ethics, 23* (1), 33-44.

Corley, M. (2005). Gratuities. *FBI Law Enforcement Bulletin, 74* (10), 10-13.

Dreisbach, C. (2008). *Ethics in criminal justice*. Boston, MA: McGraw-Hill Irwin.

Christian Police & Prison Association (n.d.). Retrieved from http://cpa-usa.org/law-officers/canons-of-police-ethics/

Hames, J., and Ekern, Y. (2005). *Constitutional law: Principles and practice*. Clifton Park, NY: Thomson Delmar Learning.

Harberfeld, M.R. (2006). *Police leadership.* Upper Saddle River, NJ: Pearson Prentice.

Hensley, W. (1996). A theory of the valenced other: The intersection of the looking-glass-self and social penetration. *Social Behavior and Personality, 24* (3), 293-308.

Hess, K.M., & Bennett, W.W. (2007). *Management and supervision in law enforcement* (5th ed.). Belmont, CA: Wadsworth Thomson.

Hess, K. and Wrobleski, H. (1997). *Police Operations* (2nd ed.). St. Paul, MN: West Publishing.

Kraska, P. (2004). *Theorizing criminal justice: Eight essential orientations*. Long Grove, IL: Waveland Press, Inc.

Liska, A. and Messner, S. (1999). *Perspectives on crime and deviance* (3rd ed.). Upper Saddle River, NJ: Prentice Hall.

Perez, D.W., & Moore, J.A. (2002). *Police ethics: A matter of character.* Incline Village, NV: Copperhouse.

Pollock, J.M. (2004). *Ethics in crime and justice: Dilemmas & decisions*. Belmont, CA: Thomas-Wadsworth.

Pozo, B. (2005). One dogma of police ethics: Gratuities and the "democratic ethos" of policing. *Criminal Justice Ethics, 24*(2), 25-46.

Prenzler, T., and Mackay, P. (1995). Police gratuities: What the public think. *Criminal Justice Ethics, 14* (1).

Reaves, B.A. (2007). Census of state and local law enforcement agencies, 2004. *Bureau of Justice Statistics Bulletin.* Retrieved from http://bjs.ojp.usdoj.gov/index.cfm?ty=dcdetail&iid=249

Ruiz, J., and Bono, C. (2004). At what price a "freebie'? The real cost of police gratuities. *Criminal Justice Ethics, 23* (1), 44-54.

Ryan, K., and Cooper, J. (2007). *Those who can, teach* (11th ed.). Boston, MA: Houghton Mifflin.

Sewell, C. (2007). Gratuities pay now or later. *FBI Law Enforcement Bulletin, 76* (4), 8-12.

Tucker, J., Donovan, D., and Marlatt, G. (Eds.). (1999). *Changing additive behavior: Bridging clinical and public health strategies*. New York: Guilford Press.

U.S. Department of Labor, Bureau of Labor Statistics (2009). *Occupational outlook handbook, 2010-11 edition.* Retrieved from http://www.bls.gov//oco/ocos/60.htm

Weber, R. (2004). The rhetoric of positivism versus interpretivism: A personal view. *MIS Quarterly 28*(1), iii-xii.

White, M. (2002). The problem with gratuities. *FBI Law Enforcement Bulletin, 71* (7), 20-23.

Chapter 4

LENSES OF TRUTH & CRITICAL INQUIRY

What is Truth?

Before police officers can effectively serve the public, they must first understand the public. However, groups of individuals may experience life's events differently from other groups, and one community member may perceive reality differently from another community member. Although not all-inclusive, the following discussion describes several different perspectives of truth. A police officer who understands that there are different interpretations of reality will be able to better serve a greater population. Indeed, a single event may be considered acceptable in one culture yet taboo in another. In short, there are different perceptions of truth based on different references in which to interpret data. If an officer believes that his or her truth is the only truth, then that officer will be at a disadvantage in dealing with other people.

Logical positivists argue that an objective reality exists and is independent of human mind and human behavior (Crossan, 2003). Logical positivists believe that the human experience of the world reflects an objective, independent reality (Weber, 2004). It is this reality that is used as the foundation for human knowledge in the building of a reality beyond the human mind. Logic positivism argues that people are objects whose behaviors can be reliable predicted (Crossan).

Post positivists argue that reality exists but cannot be fully understood or realized due to limited human intelligence (Hatch, 2002). Post positivists believe that knowledge is produced through generalizations and approximations via rigorously defined qualitative studies and low level statistics. To post positivists, the researcher is the data collection instrument.

Post modernists argue that knowledge is partial, fragmented, and contingent (McLaughlin & Muncie, 2006). Indeed, reality and science are socially constructed (Holliday, 2007). In other words, everything in life that is perceived is conditioned by culture, interactions, and institutions. Life's events occur by chance and, although humans are role-makers, their roles are unstable constructions (McLaughlin & Muncie). To post modernists, discourses are a linguistic coordinate system, and language is very influential.

Constructivists reject scientific realism and argue that there are multiple subjective realities and that absolute realities are unknowable (Glesne, 2006; Hatch, 2002). Constructivists believe that knowledge is symbolically constructed and that various realities are constructed via individual perspectives. Constructivists believe that reality is developed when individuals use their own personal beliefs, attitudes, and experiences to fit new information into what they already know. Reality is affected by the context in which an idea is taught and requires the individual to take an active role in constructing her own reality via reflection and interaction. To constructivists, investigators and participants determine truth through mutual agreement. The rules for various games are examples of individuals using social constructionism to understand unique situations.

Post structuralists argue that there is no truth and that order is created within an individual's mind in order to give meaning to the universe (Hatch, 2002). Post structuralists believe that events happen for no particular reason and that there are multiple realities, each being equally valued. Truth is subjective, local, and constantly changes.

Pragmatists believe that truth is defined by what is effective, useful, and brings about positive consequences (Mertens, 2005). Pragmatists avoid the metaphysical concepts of truth and reality because they involve useless debates and discussions. To pragmatists, truth is measured in terms of accomplishment and resolution.

Critical theorists and **feminists** argue that the world consists of historically situated structures that have a real impact on the lives of individuals based on race, social class, and gender and that knowledge is subjective and political (Hatch, 2002). Critical theorists focus on race and social class while feminists focus on gender. Critical theorists and feminists believe that there is a differential treatment of individuals based on race, social class, and gender and that these factors limit opportunities for certain groups of people. Specifically, the poor, minorities, and females are discriminated against in society and are generally at a disadvantage.

Feminist criminology is "a developing intellectual approach that emphasizes gender in criminology" (Schmalleger, 2007, p. G-11). According to feminists, men have dominated the field of criminal justice and have developed theories and written laws for the explanation and control of crime based on their own perspectives (Akers & Sellers, 2009). Indeed, traditional criminal justice theories make no distinction between men and women (Schmalleger). Although some theories may be applied to both men and women, such as the social bonding theory and the biological theory, the traditional criminology theory inadequately accounts for crimes committed by females (Akers & Sellers). Currently there is no single well-developed theory that explains female crime.

In order to better understand female criminality and to address the root causes of female crime, females need to be incorporated into the development of criminal theories (Schmalleger, 2007). After all, women make up about half of the U.S. population and having first-hand data is optimal (i.e., their perspective is essential). Because women obtain unique understandings of reality based upon their social and personal positions within society, their perceptions of crime may be different from men's perceptions of crime (Hammers & Brown, 2004). Thus, because the criminal justice system is predominately run by men, who use their own realities to make social policies, these policies may be ineffective for half of the U.S. population (i.e., women) because they may be based on flawed assumptions (i.e., they assume that there is no behavioral difference between men and women). Indeed, women's perception of truth, which is created by their personal experiences involving social class, culture, and race, may not be adequately represented in the current criminal justice system (Weber, 2004).

For females to more effectively influence public policies, they must be equally represented within the state and federal governments. Although this may be opposed by the men in power, laws could be passed that demand 50% of all positions in the state and federal governments to be held by females. By controlling 50% of the power, females may better influence laws and public policies.

Afrocentrism involves the process of using African principles and standards as the foundation for viewing African customs and conduct (Asante, 2009). Proponents of Afrocentrism state that African cultures and contributions have been downplayed and deliberately kept hidden under the so called *historic records*, which are controlled by Caucasians. The Afrocentrist asks what Africans would do if no Caucasians existed. Afrocentrists claim that African people are underdeveloped as a result of a) the lack of power and b) the lack of control of the global economy.

According to Hall (2000), the U.S. Supreme Court's current equal protection doctrine exploits minority groups in America's increasingly multiracial society. The Supreme Court uses the image of a mosaic America to recast Caucasians as just another group competing against other groups. By transforming Caucasians into a victim group with the same moral and legal claims as minority groups, the Court's actions fail to effectively support programs that will help minorities, such as affirmative action, while providing stronger protections for white entitlements.

According to Dotzler (2000), solutions to racial problems can be solved but only if Caucasians face the fact that many of the current racial problems are due to the massive crime of slavery from long ago. By providing the truly disadvantaged people (i.e., African Americans) with major monetary reparations, African Americans may be able to overcome their hardships. Indeed, African Americans face social environments on a daily basis that are not experienced by Caucasians. Thus, even if a Caucasian has never owned slaves, the U.S. social environment seems to favor and reward Caucasians over African Americans. In other words, Caucasians and African Americans do not experience America in the same manner. Hence, all Caucasians in the U.S. have benefited from slavery and from the discrimination against African Americans.

It is difficult to solve past injustices when the injustices continue even today. Benton Harbor, Michigan is a good example of the struggle for resources and power between Caucasians and African Americans. According to Jesse Jackson, Benton Harbor's high unemployment rate, the lack of job opportunities, and African American residents' sense of hopelessness are all believed to have been created by Caucasians. Furthermore, many individuals feel that the judicial system, the police, and the financial system, which are all under white control, continue to abuse African Americans (Stevens, 2003).

Interpretivists argue that a person's perceptions and knowledge are shaped through lived experiences (Weber, 2004). Perceptions are shaped by individual experiences and are unique to each individual. Individuals constantly negotiate their perceptions with other people with whom they associate, reflecting an intersubjective reality.

Technical rationality supporters argue that scientific theory is more important than other theories because it applies theory to practice (Papell & Skolnik, 1992). Indeed, solving a complex problem depends on the general principles derived from the basic and applied sciences. However, because professional practitioners often use art and intuition to solve complex and unpredictable problems, knowledge and action are causally connected but are inadequate in describing the competencies demonstrated by professionals. Through reflection, people obtain information that allows them to continually adapt their behaviors to overcome obstacles.

Empiricists believe that knowledge comes primarily from sensory experiences (Hamlyn, n.d.). However, knowledge is tentative and subject to continued revision. Indeed, senses change over time, which provide ambiguous knowledge. In addition, different individuals may perceive the same event in different manners, which may result in different learned truths.

Phenomenology focuses on lived experiences and the commonalities and shared meanings in those experiences. Phenomenology explores the essence of experience and gains a deeper understanding of an experience by uncovering hidden phenomena (Hatch, 2002). Phenomenology involves the fundamental nature of reality and it questions what can really be known about it (Ponterotto, 2005). In other words, phenomenology is concerned with human experience and it attempts to reveal phenomena that have been given meaning (Wimpenny & Gass, 2000). Because people are an integral part of the environment and each person has his or her own perspectives, reality is co-created with other individuals.

Hermeneutics study the interpretation of both verbal and nonverbal forms of communication. Hermeneutics interpret life's events through lived experiences and language (Dowling, 2004). Supporters of hermeneutics believe that investigators have biases that are an essential part in the evidence collection, analysis, and interpretation processes because the biases may serve as reference (Ponterotto, 2005). These will allow the investigator to effectively probe individuals for further information during an interview process, perhaps in the form of examples. Indeed, it is believed that these biases will improve an investigator's understanding of the information received from individuals (Dowling, 2004). However, because everyone has different lived experiences, they develop different truths (Chessick, 1990). Indeed, two investigators may evaluate the same information and may arrive at two different conclusions.

Ethnography seeks to describe a culture from the local or indigenous people's point of view (Berg, 2007). Data collection includes participant observation, participant interviewing, and artifact examination in order "to understand the cultural knowledge that group members use to make sense of the everyday experiences" (Hatch, 2002, p. 21). Examining the writings and the types of markers used in gravesites are examples of artifact data.

Table 13

Lenses of Truth

Lens	Beliefs	Critique
Logical positivists	All knowledge comes from logical reasoning and empirical evidence; if a proposition cannot be tested and verified, it is meaningless	Admit using past personal experiences as references for the pre-understanding of the phenomenon being studied; there are assumptions about the world and the nature of knowing; hypotheses cannot be proved true (must show falsification)
Post positivists	Reality exists but cannot be fully understood or realized due to limited human intelligence; world is not predicable due to its ambiguity, complexity, and subjectivity	Does not offer any clear criteria for choosing among the multiple and competing explanations that it produces; may lead to intellectual incoherence
Post modernists	There is no single truth; truth is community-based, does not correspond to reality, and everything in life that is perceived is conditioned by culture, interactions, and institutions; life's events occur by chance and, although humans are role-makers, their roles are unstable constructions	Postmodernism is meaningless, it deliberately restricts knowledge, and it prevents the full facts of a topic from becoming known. The truth that there is no truth is self-refuting.

Constructivists	Reject scientific realism and argue that there are multiple subjective realities; absolute realities are unknowable	May produce negative results when individuals encounter incomplete data or misconceptions; not all people understand the same information in the same way
Post structuralists	There is no absolute truth; order is created within an individual's mind in order to give meaning to the universe; cultural contexts and various languages create equally valid, multiple narratives of truths; objective truth is illusionary	Post structuralists claim that meaning is meaningless, which is a self-refuting; incorrectly attempts to apply narratives to the physical sciences
Pragmatists	Truth is defined by what is effective, useful, and brings about positive consequences	One must constantly evaluate if the standards are in tune with the current times and situation; standards may be influenced by those individuals in power
Critical theorists and feminists	World consists of historically situated structures that have a real impact on the lives of individuals based on race, social class, and gender; knowledge is subjective and political	Critical theorists may be biased to misinterpret information from others as discriminatory; implies a priori assumptions of human nature; radical feminists assume that men and women are indistinguishable beings

Afrocentrists	African principles and standards are used as the foundation of viewing African customs and conduct; asks what Africans would do if no Caucasians existed	In the name of ethnic pride, exaggerated stories are taught to African American children (they are told lies, which impede their future success); most African American students are not exposed to an Afrocentric curriculum
Interpretivists	A person's perceptions and knowledge are shaped through lived experiences; truth is unique to each individual	Subjective; clear patterns may not emerge in data; lack of causal relationships; emotions may bias the views of an interpretivist
Technical rationalist	Scientific theory is more important than other theories because it applies theory to practice to solve complex problems	Does not fully consider the value of social relationships in solving problems; people resist change
Empiricists	Knowledge comes primarily from sensory experiences; knowledge is tentative and subject to continued revision	Senses change over time, which provide ambiguous knowledge; different individuals may perceive the same event in different manners, which may result in different learned truths

Phenomenologist	Explores the essence of experience and gains a deeper understanding of an experience by uncovering hidden phenomena; reality is co-created with other individuals	Small sample size prevents the data from being generalized to other populations; the knowledge is subjective; it is difficult to detect and prevent researcher-induced bias
Hermeneutist	Interprets life's events through lived experiences and language	Because everyone has different lived experiences, each person develops a different truth
Ethnographer	Describes a culture from the local or indigenous people's point of view	Validity of truth is questionable because ethnography studies are difficult to replicate; truth is limited to the subjects in the study; interpretation of truth is heavily dependent on the ethnographer; to collect good data, the ethnographer must take the time to build trust with the community

Personal Bias:
Post positivists, Phenomenology, and Hermeneutics

Should a researcher be totally objective and interpret the data with no personal bias or should the researcher use personal experience to interpret the data? While positivists believe that the investigator is an objective and neutral data analyst, supporters of hermeneutics believe that investigators have biases that play an essential part in the evidence collection, analysis, and interpretation processes because the biases may serve as reference (Ponterotto, 2005). Is a police officer a positivist or does a police officer use personal experience and training to interpret situations?

Post positivists

Ontology

Ontology concerns the fundamental nature of reality and it questions what can really be known about it (Ponterotto, 2005). Post positivists believe that there is a true reality but that it is imperfect. This is because people rely upon their senses to measure and interpret information. Senses are shaped by cultural, gender, political, and other external factors.

Axiology

Axiology involves the role of the researchers' values during a research study (Ponterotto, 2005). Post positivists believe in an objective study, free from personal values and feelings. The goal is for the researcher to identify and separate personal biases from the study. By using standardized and systematic methods, personal biases are minimized. However, the actual decision to study a particular topic may itself be biased.

Epistemology

Epistemology involves the relationship between the researcher and the participants and the study of knowledge (Ponterotto, 2005).

This involves its nature, origin, methods, limits, and justifications (Hofer & Pintrich, 2002. Post positivists believe that the objectivity of researchers should be independent of the participants, although it probably is not. Post positivists acknowledge that the researcher may have some influence upon the participants; however, they do not want to get too emotionally involved with the participants.

Methodology

The process and procedures of a study make up its methodology (Ponterotto, 2005). Post positivists use strict scientific methods to control and manipulate variables in order to be able to objectively explain relationships and to make predictions. Post positivists prefer to use mechanisms that allow for the collection of measurable quantifiable data. Post positivism relies upon the falsification theory.

In performing research, post positivists attempt to identify the closest possible singular truth by using multiple measures and observations, combining both quantitative and qualitative techniques (Crossan, 2003; Ponterotto, 2005). For example, by using multiple raters and performing brief interviews with the participants, the raters can come to a consensus in identifying the themes and arriving at the single proximal reality. Because post positivists use quantitative analysis, they have the advantage of being able to identify patterns and relationships for predicting future events. Furthermore, the data can be validated and generalized to a larger population. The disadvantage of post positivism is that it assumes that the researcher is unbiased. However, because the researcher lives life like everyone else, whose personality, attitude, and perceptions have been shaped by environmental factors, such as social, political, economic, and religious factors, there is no such thing as a biased free researcher. For example, something as simple as language can affect the results of the test. To one person, the word "bad" may be interpreted as a terrible thing. To another person, the word "bad" may be interpreted as a good thing. Thus, the perception and interpretation of the word "bad" could have two different meanings and may affect the interpretation of the test results. Another example may be how physical actions are interpreted. For example, pointing a thumb upward may be perceived as a positive response or a derogatory response. The interpretation depends on culturally developed perceptions.

Phenomenology

Ontology

Phenomenology is concerned with human experience, and it attempts to reveal phenomena which have been given meaning (Wimpenny & Gass, 2000). Because people are an integral part of the environment and each person has his or her own perspectives, reality is co-created by both the researcher and the participant (Hatch, 2002).

Axiology

Phenomenology recognizes that the researcher, who has predetermined concepts, is an active part of the research process. Indeed, the researcher's personal biases are useful and an important part of a research study; this gives the researcher valuable reference in which to interpret the data (Wimpenny & Gass, 2000). However, the researcher must bracket personal preconceptions and presuppositions in order to arrive at the participant's true reality. Phenomenology, in essence, means from the participant's point of view (Camic, Rhodes, & Yardley, 2003).

Epistemology

Phenomenology argues that the researchers do have prejudices because they are a part of the environment, and that they need to distance themselves from the participants by bracketing their biases so that they do not interfere with the objectivity of the study (Dowling, 2004). However, because the researcher may perform in-depth interviews, relationships are developed and the researcher and the participants may develop strong bonds (Wimpenny & Gass, 2000).

Methodology

The methodological objective is to describe what experiences mean to the people who lived them (Sadala & Adorno, 2002). Using phenomenology, the main method of data collection is through an in-depth, three-step interview process (Wimpenny & Gass, 2000). The goal is to establish the context of each participant's experience, to construct that experience, and then to find the meaning of that experience. This can be achieved by the researchers developing the skills in which to probe the participants for further information, perhaps through clarification or by referencing examples. In this manner, a more detailed and actual representation of the lived experiences will be recorded. Other ways of collecting data include examining the participants' writings, observing the participants, and studying experiential descriptions in art and literature (Hatch, 2002).

Hermeneutics

Ontology

Hermeneutics believe that the minds of people along with their values are individually developed by their unique experiences in the worldly environment. In short, each person has a unique perspective in interpreting data (Chesssick, 1990). Hence, there are multiple interpretations of reality.

Axiology

Hermeneutics argues that people are an integrated part of society in which they live and interact (Chessick, 1990). Therefore, researchers will have certain prejudices because their perceptions have already been influenced by their environments prior to the study. This is important because the understanding of information depends on the researcher using linguistic experiences for reference, and because the researcher and participant are connected by a common human consciousness (Dowling, 2004). Indeed, the researcher needs to be aware of personal biases and needs to be opened minded to the participant's meanings so that their uniqueness can be understood. Furthermore, when analyzing historic information, because meanings change over time, the data need to be evaluated in reference to its own time frame. In this way, the data will have relevance for today's applications (Chessick; Fuchs, 1993).

Epistemology

Hermeneutics argue that a researcher's prejudices are an important part of a research study. Experience and education should be used during the data collection, analysis, and interpretation processes. It is believed that experience and education are valuable tools to be used to enhance the understanding of data (Dowling, 2004).

Methodology

For hermeneutics, there are no universal principles, only many equally contingent approaches (Dowling, 2004; Fuchs, 1993). One way of collecting data is through semi-structured in-depth interviews. However, the focus is not on the collection and analysis of data, but on the process of understanding.

References

Akers, R.L., & Sellers, C. (2009). *Criminological theories: Introduction, evaluation, and application* (5th ed.). New York, NY: Oxford University Press.

Asante, M.K. (2009). *What is Afrocentricity?* Retrieved from http://www.asante.net

Berg, B. (2007). *Qualitative research methods for the social sciences* (6th ed.). Boston, MA: Pearson Education, Inc.

Camic, P., Rhodes, J., and Yardley, L. (Editors) (2003). *Qualitative research in psychology: Expanding perspectives in methodology and design.* Washington, DC: American Psychology Association.

Chessick, R. (1990). Hermeneutics for psychotherapists. *American Journal of Psychotherapy, 44*(2), 256-273.

Crossan, F. (2003). Research philosophy: Towards an understanding. *Nurse Researcher, 11*(1), 46-55.

Dotzler, R.J. (2000). Getting to reparations: A response to Fein. *Sociological Practice: A Journal of Clinical and Applied Sociology, 2*(3), 177-182.

Dowling, M. (2004). Hermeneutics: An exploration. *Nurse Researcher, 11*(4), 30-39.

Fuchs, S. (1993). Three social epistemologies. *Social Perspectives, 36*(1), 23-44.

Glesne, C. (2006). *Becoming qualitative researchers: An introduction* (3rd ed.). Boston, MA: Pearson.

Hall, A.A. (2000). There is a lot to be repaired before we get reparations: A critique of the underlying issues of race that impact the fate of African American reparations. *St. Mary's Law Review, 1*, 22-32.

Hamlyn, D.W. (n.d.). *Empiricism*. Retrieved from http://mind.ucsd.edu/syllabi/99_00/Empiricism/Readings/Encyc_Phil/Empiricism.html

Hammers, C., and Brown, A. (2004). Towards a feminist-queer alliance: A paradigmatic shift in the research process. *Social Epistemology, 18*(1).

Hatch, J. (2002). *Doing qualitative research in education settings*. Albany, NY: State University of New York Press.

Hofer, B., and Pintrich, P. (2002). *Personal epistemology: The psychology of beliefs about knowledge and knowing*. Mahwah, NJ: Lawrence Erlbaum Associates, Inc.

Holliday, A. (2007). *Doing and writing qualitative research* (2nd ed.). Thousand Oaks, CA: Sage.

McLaughlin, E., & Muncie, J. (2006). *The Sage dictionary of criminology* (2nd ed.). Thousand Oaks, CA: Sage.

Mertens, D.M. (2005). *Research and evaluation in education and psychology: integrating diversity with quantitative, qualitative, and mixed methods* (2nd ed.). Thousand Oaks, CA: Sage Publications.

Papell, C., and Skolnik, L. (1992). The reflective practitioner: A contemporary paradigm's relevance for social work education. *Journal of Social Work Education, 28*(1), 18-26.

Ponterotto, J. (2005). Qualitative research in counseling psychology: A primer on research paradigms and philosophy of science. *Journal of Counseling, 52*(2), 126-136.

Sadala, M., and Adorno, R. (2002). Phenomenology as a method to investigate the experience lived: A perspective from Husserl and Merleau Ponty's thought. *Journal of Advanced Nursing, 37*(3), 282-293.

Schmalleger, F. (2007). *Criminal justice today: An introductory text for the 21st century* (9th ed.). Upper Saddle River, NJ: Pearson Prentice Hall.

Stevens, L. (2003, June 20). Jackson: All must help the city in wake of violence. *The Herald Palladium* (Benton Harbor, Michigan).

Weber, R. (2004). The rhetoric of positivism versus interpretivism: A personal view. *MIS Quarterly, 28*(1), iii-xii.

Wimpenny, P. & Gass, J. (2000). Interviewing in phenomenology and grounded theory: is there a difference? *Journal of Advanced Nursing, 31*(6), 1485-1492.

Chapter 5

INFORMATION & COMMUNICATION

Quantitative v. Qualitative Studies

Quantitative investigations are scientific, objective, and effective in describing phenomena in terms of magnitude (Balian, 1988). Quantitative investigations use numeric values and statistics to identify patterns, to objectively quantify relationships between variables, and to make predictions. In addition, because large sample sizes are used, data can be generalized to larger populations. However, numeric values are ineffective in describing the subjective interpretations of human emotions (Wakefield, 1995). Because individuals have unique lived experiences and their realities are based on their own perceptions, a single objective truth is unattainable; indeed, there are multiple realities when dealing with perceptions. Thus, quantitative investigations are ineffective for the reconstruction of meanings. In short, quantitative studies ask **how** variables are related but not **why** they are related. For example, a quantitative research question may ask, *Is there a relationship between ice cream sales and the murder rate?* By the way, there is a positive relationship.

When investigating a topic that cannot be quantitatively predicted, such as human nature, qualitative investigations are most effective. Indeed, qualitative investigations are preferred for describing and interpreting experiences in context specific settings because each person's reality is construed in his or her own mind (Adams, 1999; Ponterotto, 2005). Qualitative research attempts to reveal the meanings that participants have given to various phenomena. This kind of information cannot be attained through quantitative analysis and requires probing the participants for greater detail through in-depth interviews using open-ended questions. In short, qualitative studies ask **why** variables are related but not **how** they are related. For example, a qualitative research question may ask, *Why do you feel that ice cream sales are related to the murder rate?*

Falsification

Theories are an organized body of principles and concepts intended to explain specific phenomena (Leedy & Ormrod, 2005). A police officer can test a theory to determine if it is a viable explanation of a phenomenon by developing and statistically verifying a conjecture concerning the relationship between the variables. However, because human knowledge is limited, hypotheses cannot actually be proved true (Shields, 2007). For example, we will never know for sure if any of the many extraneous variables have impacted a particular relationship between known variables (a person may appear to have committed a crime, but appearances can be deceiving). However, we can demonstrate that relationships do not exist between variables (the person was already dead at the time of the crime and could not have committed the crime). Thus, because relationships cannot be proved true, an attempt is made to prove them false. This is called falsification. For example, instead of proving that a defendant is truly guilty of a crime, a prosecutor attempts to prove with a certain confidence level that the defendant is not innocent of the crime. For example, if there is a 95% confidence level that a defendant is not innocent, then jurors may find the defendant guilty. In other words, if hypotheses are not proved false, then they are accepted as true at a certain confidence level. This implies that there is an acceptable level of being wrong. Thus, innocent people may sometimes be wrongly convicted.

For a trial verdict, there are two possible ways to make a mistake. One way is to convict an innocent person. The other way is to set a guilty person free. A juror can ensure that one type of error is never made, but this will require either a) always setting defendants free or b) always convicting defendants. For either case, there is no need for a trial. On the one hand, if one juror wants to ensure that he never makes a mistake by letting a guilty person go free, then that juror must always vote guilty. His reasoning may be that the police do not arrest innocent persons. With this reasoning, there is no need for a trial because everyone arrested will be convicted by this type of juror. On the other hand, if another juror wants to ensure that she never makes a mistake by sending an innocent person to jail, then that juror must always vote not guilty. With this reasoning, there is no need for a trial because everyone arrested will be set free by this type of juror. Thus, in both cases, there is no need for a trial. However, because there are trials in the U.S., compromises are required and there will be chances of making mistakes.

Negotiations are required among jury members. If a mistake is made, then the question is whether U.S. jurors want to error on the side of convicting innocent individuals or to error on the side of setting guilty individuals free. By design, the U.S. legal system is set up to error on the side of letting guilty persons go free. A conviction is based on guilt beyond a reasonable doubt; an acquittal is not based on innocence beyond a reasonable doubt. As indicated in Figure 7, because decisions are based on confidence levels and negotiations, innocent individuals will sometimes be convicted. This is an inherent part of the U.S. legal system. Notice that this argument is not influenced by the penalty of the conviction, such as the death penalty. In other words, it is expected that innocent persons will sometimes be convicted and will be put to death.

Levels of Proof

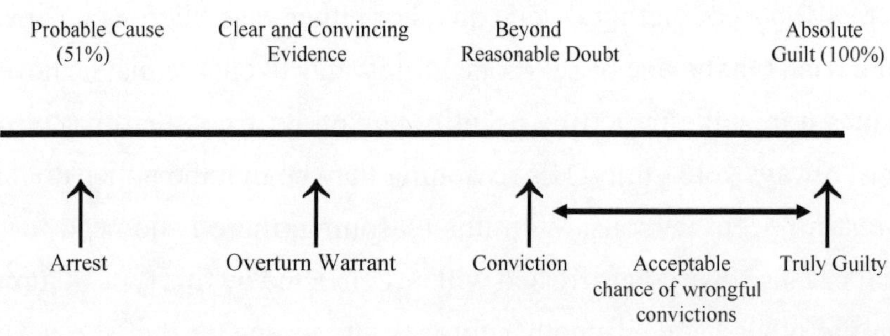

Figure 7. Acceptable chance of wrongful conviction. (not to scale)

Assumptions

Most decisions depend on assumptions, and we will never know if all of the assumptions are 100% accurate. Although we may be confident about a decision, we cannot know with absolute certainty that the decision is correct. However, understanding the assumptions that were relied upon in making a decision is important because the assumptions may change, which may impact an objective decision. In law enforcement, if the assumptions change, then police officers must be willing to modify their position.

Correlation does not mean causation (Leedy & Ormrod, 2005). Just because two events are highly correlated does not mean that one event causes the other. For example, it does not get dark at night because the sun is on the other side of the earth (Verma, 2005). The sun is an additional light source, but it is not the only light source in the sky. Thus, in this case, a wrong assumption may lead one to believe that the lack of sunlight causes it to get dark at night.

Being not false is not the same thing as being true. In order words, if something is not negative does not mean that it is positive (i.e., it may be neutral). For example, if a hockey team has played 10 games and is undefeated, what is the team's record? It is unknown because the team may have tied any number of the 10 games. If by some chance the team had tied all 10 games, a defense attorney may claim that the team has never lost, while the prosecutor may claim that the team has never won. Both statements are true, yet they seem to be contradictory. However, the two statements do not necessarily conflict with one another. This is how statistics can be misleading. Should consumers buy the same shoes used by the team? Either decision may be argued and supported with statistical data.

Police officers need to detect diversionary flares (i.e., deception) that are intended to lead the officer off track. The way to do this is to get the sought-after answers to their questions via active voice questions and answers. For example, if an individual answers questions via double negatives or through misplaced modifiers, the officer must clarify the answers by asking direct questions that elicit active voice responses. See Table 14.

Table 14

Interpretation of Sport Statement

	Interpretation of Results		
	Won (+)	Tied (neutral)	Lost (-)
Suspect statement			
I have not lost =	x	x	
I have not won =		x	x
I have won =	x		
I have lost =			x

It should be pointed out in Table 14 that *I have won* ≠ *I have not lost.* For a second example, suppose you state that the sky was not cloudy all day. All day means 100% of the time. Therefore, you are stating that it was not cloudy 100% of the time; it could have been cloudy 0% of the time up to 99% of the time. In other words, it could have been sunny 1% of the time up to 100% of the time. If you are writing a police report and it is important that the sky was sunny during the crime, stating that the sky was not cloudy all day may be detrimental to your case. See Table 15.

Table 15

Interpretation of Weather Statement

	Interpretation of Statement		
	Sunny all day	**Cloudy up to 99% of time**	**Cloudy all day (100% of time)**
Not cloudy all day =	x	x	

Now suppose that a police officer arrives at a crash scene. A car that was parked near a curb pulled out into traffic and was struck by another car headed in the same direction. If the police officer asks a witness to the crash what she saw, and if she states that she did not see the driver in the parked car look before he pulled out into traffic, the statement is basically valueless. See Table 16.

Table 16

Interpretation of Witness Statement

	Interpretation of Witness Statement		
	I saw driver look	**I was not looking**	**I saw driver not look**
Witness statement provided =		x	x
Answer sought (two good responses) =	x		x

Notice the first four words: *"I did not see."* This is problematic because the police officer wants to know what the witness did see. Indeed, the witness statement never claimed that the driver of the parked car did not look before he pulled out into traffic. The witness statement would be true even if the witness was not looking in the right direction at the time of the crash. It would be wrong to assume that the witness was looking in the right direction. To argue in court that the witness saw the driver of the parked car not look would be changing the truth value of the witness statement. In short, a police officer needs to be careful about relying on assumptions. Get responses that provide direct and positive answers.

In addition, police officers must not assume that all individuals define words in the same way. For example, consider the following statements.

Unclear: Where were you during dinner?
Clear: Where were you during supper?

The above sentence that mentions dinner is problematic because dinner is not time dependent. Although supper is the last meal of the day, dinner is the largest meal of the day. Thus, for some people, dinner may not be the same as supper. In other words, if you were to question a suspect about his or her alibi during dinner time, you may be thinking about 5:00 pm and the individual may be speaking about noon. Therefore, seek precise times of day that do not have different meanings to different individuals.

Misplaced and dangling modifiers

Grammar is important in police writing because an officer's credibility is linked to his or her written reports. If police officers make mistakes in their reports, the officers should expect defense attorneys to ask them if they have performed their jobs to the best of their ability. On the one hand, if the officers claim that they have done their best work, then mistakes in their reports will make them appear incompetent or dishonest. On the other hand, if the officers claim that they have not done their best work, then mistakes in their reports will make them appear lazy and uncaring. Thus, police officers need to use proper grammar when writing police reports.

Although some mistakes in grammar may make police officers look incompetent, lazy, or dishonest in court, other mistakes in grammar may significantly change the meaning of a police report. For example, because a misplaced modifier incorrectly modifies the wrong word, and because a dangling modifier has no referent in a sentence, misplaced and dangling modifiers may alter the meaning of a sentence. Thus, adjectives and adverbs should be placed as closely as possible to the words that they are supposed to modify and active voice should be employed (American Psychological Association, 2010). This may help eliminate any unintended meanings. In this case, the police officers should expect defense attorneys to ask them if they write true and accurate reports. If the officers state that their reports are true and accurate, then the defense attorney may argue that the reports should be accepted at face value, especially if misplaced modifiers change the meanings of sentences in the police reports to mean what the defense attorneys want them to mean. However, if the officers state that their reports are not true and accurate, then the reports will have little value, the officers' credibility will be ruined, and the officers could be criminally charged with filing false police reports.

Consider the following example. Suppose a man and his wife are at school and he tells her that he loves her.

Incorrect statement: He told his wife that he loves her at the school.

Correct statement: While at the school, he told his wife that he loves her.

The incorrect statement does not indicate that he loves his wife, but it does indicate that he loves his wife's presence at the school. This would be appropriate, for example, if his wife worked at a school and he did not want her to quit her job and to leave the school.

Incorrect statement: Running out of gas, she walked to the gas station.

Correct statement: She walked to the gas station because her car ran out of gas.

The incorrect sentence indicates that she ran out of gas (not her car). This may imply that she was jogging, became tired, and started to walk.

Logic: Conditional Statements

Although an if-then statement may be true, the converse of an if-then statement may not necessarily be true (Smith, Eggen, & St. Andre, 2006). In other words, the converse of a conditional statement is not necessarily true. For example, research shows that aggressive behaviors in children are good predictors of adult criminality (Huesmann & Eron, 1992; Huesmann et al., 2002; Miller-Johnson et al., 2005). Thus, if aggression is present then there is crime. However, if crime is present does not necessarily mean that there is aggression (e.g., there may be other reasons why people are arrested).

Suppose a father states to his daughter that if she behaves, then he will give her candy. Then suppose his daughter misbehaves. Will the father be truthful if he gives his daughter candy after she misbehaves? The answer is yes. The only guarantee that the father made was that he will act in a certain way if his daughter behaves. However, the father never addressed what he will do if his daughter misbehaves. Thus, if his daughter misbehaves, the father's actions will be truthful whether or not his gives his daughter candy. The father will only be untruthful if his daughter behaves and he does not give her candy. See Table 17.

Table 17

Interpretation of Conditional Statement

Guarantee		If my daughter behaves . . .	If my daughter misbehaves . . .
If my daughter behaviors, then I will give her candy		Then a truthful statement dictates that I give her candy	Then a truthful statement allows me to either give her candy or to not give her candy

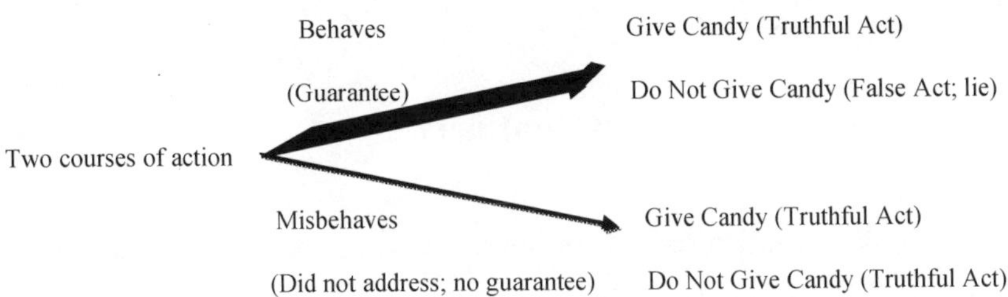

Figure 8. Interpretation of conditional statement.

Let us apply this argument to a law. A U.S. visa is an entry document issued by the U.S. government that allows a non-citizen to seek entry into the U.S. (LexisNexis, 2005). A non-American passport is issued by the person's native country and is a travel document that is used for identification and proof of citizenship. **Suppose federal law states that a particular person cannot enter the U.S. without a passport.** Thus, if the person has entered the U.S., then the person must have had a passport (this is a true statement). However, it is not necessarily true that if the person has a passport, then the person will be allowed to enter the U.S. The law states that not having a passport will prevent the person's entry into the U.S., but the law does not address what will happen if the person does have a passport. See Table 18. Thus, understanding the converse of conditional statements is important in law enforcement.

Table 18
Interpretation of Law

	Passport Law	
	If have, then may enter	**If do not have, then may not enter**
Foreign Passport		x

Quantifiers

Because conditional statements can be objectively assessed by turning them into mathematic equations, police officers need to understand the difference between existential and universal quantifiers. It is important for a police officer not to change the meaning of a statement by changing an existential-quantifier statement into a universal-quantifier statement and vice versa. For an open sentence that uses an existential quantifier, the sentence is true if the truth set is nonempty (Smith et al., 2006). This means that a statement is true if the statement is true at least one time. However, for an open sentence that uses a universal quantifier, the sentence is true only if the truth set is the entire universe. This means that a statement is true only if the statement is true all of the time. For example, if a suspect stated that he likes beer, this statement is true if the suspect likes at least one type of beer. Thus, for the suspect to be lying, an officer will have to prove that the suspect dislikes all types of beer. However, if the suspect stated that he likes all beer, then the officer only needs to show that the suspect dislikes one type of beer for the suspect to be considered untruthful.

Suppose that the signs on a roadway indicate that speed is controlled via RADAR. Then suppose you receive a speeding ticket but the officer used VASCAR to clock your speed. Your argument is that the ticket is invalid because the officer used VASCAR and the signs indicate that RADAR will be used. **What will you have to do in court to show that the signs are not truthful and what does the officer have to do to show that the signs are truthful?** The signs are truthful if at least one officer in the area uses RADAR. Thus, the officer only has to show that one officer in the area uses RADAR. You, on the other hand, will have to show that every officer in the area does not use RADAR.

Subsets

A set is a group of objects that follow a rule or that have something in common (Large, 2007). A subset is a set that belongs to a larger set. Suppose a friend states to you on January 1 that you may borrow his car any day of the year, whenever you want. Then suppose you borrow the car on July 7 and get pulled over by the police. The police charge you with driving another person's car without permission. The police officer asks you, "Did you have permission to drive the car specifically on July 7?" The police officer wants a *yes* or *no* answer. The correct answer is yes, because July 7 is a part of the year. In other words, the year includes July 7 and you had permission to drive the car on every day of the year.

Suppose John has $20. True or false, John has $10. The answer is true because $10 is a subset of $20. If John has $20, then John has $10.

Public Relations vs. Community Relations

Public relations programs are agency oriented and are structured to maximize department image (Hunter & Barker, 2011). Public relations activities are routinized and structured whenever possible, having regular distribution channels. As demonstrated in agency-initiated press releases, information only flows one-way, which is outward from the department to the public. Public relations programs are not an essential component of a police department's operating philosophy; instead, they are tools to be used by police management.

Community relations programs, on the other hand, are difficult to routinize and standardize (Hunter & Barker, 2011). Although some of the elements may be routine, serving the many public interests usually requires flexibility. Community relations programs are an essential component of the police department's operating philosophy and two-way information flow is essential for program success. If the police department is community relations oriented, community relations programs will serve both the community and the police.

Mass Media & Police

Bureaucratic police departments have a vested interest in justifying their existence via statistics (Kappeler & Potter, 2005). Advertising a high crime rate will give the public the perception that the police are needed. In other words, it is good police business when the media create the myth that crime is high, especially when crime is not actually high. If the media continue to repeat the information, it soon becomes a truism.

In addition, the media are for-profit businesses and they like readily available and exciting information (Kraska, 2004). Indeed, their job is to sell information. Thus, the media supply the public with what it demands (the public will only pay for what it wants to hear). Over time, the media's distorted coverage of crime helps to shape crime as a social problem (Kappeler & Potter, 2005). Instead of focusing on the root causes of crime, such as poverty and unemployment, the media limit their discourse on crime control policies to more laws, more police, more prisons, and longer sentences. People who continue to hear the same message over and over again begin to believe that it is true (Kraska). In short, the media are responsible for creating many false conceptions about criminal justice practices, but it is their customers who demand such information.

The police and the media have a common goal, which is to serve the public. The relationship between the police and the media is symbiotic (Miller, Hess, & Orthmann, 2011). For example, the police and the media may work together to put out a crime alert or to advertise unsafe neighborhood practices. However, because the media are guided by the 1st Amendment (public's right to know) and the police by the 4th Amendment (right to privacy), there may be conflict between the agencies (del Carmen, 2010).

The police need to have good relations with the media (Whisenand, 2011). For example, the police may lose their professional reputation and public support if they have poor media relations. The police are accountable to the public and the media are the community watchdogs. Thus, when a crisis event occurs, the police must have a trained officer readily available to communicate with the media. Subsequently, the police need to monitor the messages that the media deliver to the public because police departments are hypersensitive to criticism and will take defensive countermeasures. For example, the department may take away a valuable tool used by officers because one officer was portrayed by the media as using the tool improperly. Finally, police should use the media as a conduit to obtain third-party support. The public often wants to help the police in crisis situations and the media can assist.

Developing a partnership with the media is essential for effective police-community relations (Miller et al., 2011). The media are powerful and they can influence local residents, which may lead to their support. On the other hand, the media can also influence residents to not support the local police.

If the police are required to lie to the media, then the police should offer an explanation or apology at the appropriate time (Miller et al., 2011). For example, public safety may require the police to be less than truthful. However, once the threat has passed, then the police should clear things up.

Mass Media and the Public

Mass communication is a formal system of conveying much information to large groups of people in a short amount of time (Kappeler & Potter, 2005). Consequently, the media can spread fear over great distances very quickly. By advertising particular crimes, the media can create an epidemic where none really exists (Kappeler & Potter, 2005). Media frenzies spread quickly, which give false impressions and magnitudes of criminal events. Once a theme has been established, similar stories are accepted as newsworthy. In addition, stories that do not match the theme may be modified so that they do match the theme. Thus, the misperception of a crime wave may grow out of control.

A small number of people control most of the information (Kappeler & Potter, 2005). Although about 80% of all crime does not attract an audience, the media select the crime problems that they want to publicize, which are often the most gruesome criminal acts that are uncovered. The choice of crime coverage is driven by the competitive market and by the demand of the consumer.

The media have been known to report inaccurate information (Kappeler & Potter, 2005). For example, distorted coverage has exaggerated the degree that African Americans have been portrayed as criminals and Caucasians as victims. Furthermore, media stories have ignored the real social causes of crime and have created the perception that particular crimes are social problems. In short, media coverage gives the perception that the only way to control crime is by hiring more police officers, by passing more laws, by building more prisons, and by handing down longer sentences.

In addition, television media use graphics to get attention (Kappeler & Potter, 2005). Because television media are under time constraints, they are unable to provide the context that gives the information true meaning. Thus, the viewers only hear part of the story and they generate truth based on limited intelligence. Because some repugnant crimes do occur, partial truths that exaggerate such crimes only make the problem seem worse.

Mass Media: The Elite Controlling Minorities

The media have been used by individuals in power to control minorities. For example, hemp, which is collected from the cannabis plant, makes a higher quality paper at a lower cost than does wood pulp (Gahlinger, 2004). However, because William Hearst, a huge newspaper publisher, owned millions of acres of woodland, he lobbied to outlaw marijuana. During the 1920s, Hearst linked the marijuana use in New Orleans to murder, rape, poverty, and disease (Yaroschuk, 2000). This served two purposes: to make money by selling newspapers and to persuade lawmakers in congress to pass laws outlawing the growing of hemp. Although this did not result in the passage of federal laws outlawing the cultivation of hemp, Louisiana jumped on the opportunity to restrict the use of marijuana, hoping that it would be a means to control the black population.

Prior to the Great Depression of 1929, Mexicans in the southwest were considered a welcomed labor force (Gahlinger, 2004; Yaroschuk,

2000). However, once the Great Depression began, that Mexican labor force was no longer needed. In order to reduce the number of Mexican citizens working within the United States, the San Antonio Gazette published newspaper articles that stigmatized the Mexicans, stating that they commonly used marijuana, which turned them into frenzied and dangerous criminals. The media's goal was to force the Mexicans back to Mexico.

Many people distrust the government and formal news media. For example, in 1936, the film *Reefer Madness* was used as a scare tactic to describe the dangers of smoking marijuana (Roleff, 2005; Spurling, 1993). However, because the film overly exaggerated the effects of marijuana use, the formal media lost their credibility; their credibility is still questioned today. Consequently, marijuana advocates now transmit their own information using other types of media, such as bumper stickers, tee shirts, music, magazines, and the Internet.

Media of the Less Powerful

Various forms of the media can be used by individuals not in power to spread their messages. For example, minorities and the poor, who have been labeled as social deviants by the elite and powerful, may use music and magazines to communicate with society. Rappers may speak about police corruption; others may challenge questionable laws. *High Times*, *Cannabis Culture*, *Cloud Magazine*, and *SKUNK* are the voice of the marijuana community. If the police are effectively going to serve the public, then the police need to listen to what the public is saying. Some of the words may be harsh, but they may be truth as perceived by those who speak them.

Small Town Media

Sometimes in small towns, the media may heavily depend on the police to get their stories. If the media upset the police, then there is the chance that the police may no longer cooperate with the media and provide them with needed information. Because the media may need the information to survive, especially in small towns where there is not much activity taking place, the media may hesitate to publish negative information about the police department. The media may publish negative information about an officer that the department wants to discipline, but the media will only target that particular officer and not the department.

Freedom of Information Act

The Freedom of Information Act makes the records of government agencies accessible to the public (Miller et al., 2011). The act supports the idea that the people have a right to know. However, police departments may withhold certain information that involves national security, an active case, or the privacy rights of an individual.

Terrorism

Terrorists use the media to arouse passion for their ideals and to generate anger toward a common enemy, namely America (Friedman, 2005). Anti-Western propaganda is televised around the world where information is carefully manipulated. Persistent broadcasts of biased information may create the desired response of community hatred. In short, terrorists need the media as a way to advertise their violence and to generate support for their cause.

Reference

Adams, W. (1999). The interpermeation of self and world: Empirical research, existential phenomenology, and transpersonal psychology. *Journal of Phenomenological Psychology, 30*(2), 39-65.

American Psychological Association. (2010). *Publication manual of the American Psychological Association* (6th ed.). Washington, DC: Author.

Balian, E.S. (1988). *How to design, analyze, and write doctoral or master's research* (2nd ed.). New York, NY: University Press of America.

Del Carmen, RV. (2010). *Criminal procedures: Laws & practice* (8th ed.). Belmont, CA: Wadsworth.

Friedman, L. (Ed.). (2005). *What motivates suicide bombers?* Detroit, MI: Thomson Gale.

Gahlinger, P. (2004). *Illegal Drugs: A complete guide to their history, chemistry, use, and abuse*. New York: Plume.

Huesmann, L.R., & Eron, L.D. (1992). Childhood aggression and adult criminality. In J. McCord (Ed.), *Facts, frameworks, and forecasts: Advances in criminology theory* (p. 137-156). New Brunswick, NJ: Transaction.

Huesmann, L.R., Eron, L.D., & Dubow, E.F. (2002). Childhood predictors of adult criminality: Are all risk factors reflected in childhood aggressiveness? *Criminal Behaviour and Mental Health, 12*(3), 185-208.

Hunter, R.D., & Barker, T. (2011). *Police-community relations and the administration of justice* (8th ed.). Upper Saddle River, NJ: Prentice Hall.

Kappeler, V.E., & Potter, G.W. (2005). *The mythology of crime and criminal justice* (4th ed.). Long grove, IL: Waveland.

Kraska, P. (2004). *Theorizing criminal justice: Eight essential orientations.* Long Grove, IL: Waveland Press, Inc.

Large, T (2007). The Usborne Illustrated Dictionary of Math. London, England: Usborne.

Leedy, P., & Ormrod, J. (2005). *Practical research: Planning and design* (8th ed.). Upper Saddle River, NJ: Pearson Merrill Prentice Hall.

LexisNexis (2005). *Immigration law handbook.* Longwood, FL: Gould.

Miller, L.S., Hess, K.M. & Orthmann, C.H. (2011). *Community policing: Partnerships for problem solving* (6th ed.). Clifton Park, NY: Delmar.

Miller-Johnson, S., Moore, B.L., Underwood, M.K., & Cole, J.D. (2005). African-American girls and physical aggression: Does stability of childhood aggression predict later negative outcomes? In D. Pepler, K. Madsen, C. Webster, & K. Levene (Eds.), *The development and treatment of girlhood aggression* (p. 75-101). Mahwah, NJ: Lawrence Erlbaum.

Ponterotto, J. (2005). Qualitative research in counseling psychology: A primer on research paradigms and philosophy of science. *Journal of Counseling, 52*(2), 126-136.

Roleff, T. (2005). Drug Abuse: Opposing viewpoints. Detroit: Thomson Gale.

Shields, L. (2007). Falsification. *Pediatric Nursing*, 19(7), 37.

Smith, S., Eggen, M., St. Andre, R. (2006). *A transition to advanced mathematics* (6th ed.). Belmont, CA: Thomson Brooks/Cole.

Spurling, A. (Producer), & Leonard, M. (Director). (1993). *Altered states: A history of drug use in America.* [Motion Picture]. United States: Films Media Group.

Verma, S. (2005). *The little book of scientific principles, theories, & things*. New York, NY: Sterling.

Wakefield, J. (1995). When an irresistible epistemology meets an immovable ontology. *Social Work Research, 19* (1).

Whisenand, P.M. (2011). *Supervising police personnel: The fifteen responsibilities* (7th ed.). Upper Saddle River, NJ: Prentice Hall.

Yaroschuk, T. (Producer & Writer). (2000). Hooked: Illegal drugs and how they got that way (Vol. 1) [Motion Picture]. The History Channel: A&E.

Chapter 6

DEVIANCE & COMMUNITY

Deviance can be described as the source of innovation that results when a person takes one measurable step away from the normally accepted policies and infects the status quo. Deviance is an innovation virus that attacks traditional thinking at the core level. Furthermore, the community's culture may influence what is classified as deviant.

In order to evaluate what is normal behavior and what is deviant behavior, some reference point is needed (Liska & Messner, 1999). Consequently, different interest groups struggle for power and the group that comes out on top, the dominate group, establishes what is considered normal behavior. Some actions are guided by what is defined as proper (acceptable) social etiquette and cultural customs and some are defined by laws. Although many people may violate accepted cultural customs of etiquette at one point or another, this is considered normal if the behaviors are not continued for prolonged periods of time. If the behaviors are practiced over prolonged periods, then those people are labeled deviant.

Some rules are considered serious enough to write down and to enforce, punishing those who do not conform to these specific guidelines. The problem with laws is that they are not universally and evenly applied to all persons (Liska & Messner, 1999). Even though law enforcement knows that certain persons commit crimes, charges are not always filed. Even if charges are files, there is a good chance that prosecutors will dismiss some of the cases for one reason or another (case load, personal acquaintance, etc.). Finally, even if a person is arrested and convicted of a crime, there is no consistency in sentencing. Outside factors, such as jail space availability, the status of the convicted person within the community, and the community's reaction to the conviction may all affect a judge's decision on a case-by-case basis.

Concept of Community

A community is a collection of people within a geographic area who share a mutual identification, loyalty, interdependence, and a common social organization of programs (Fritz, 2002). In addition to the geographic community, where the people develop strong ties as a territorial unit, there may be a) **spiritual community**, where social bonds are developed through friendships, religious beliefs, and language, b) **purposive community**, where social bonds are developed because people have a common objective, such as work, and c) **intentional community**, where social bonds are created through the intentional development of a social collective. A community is comprised of individuals who share a culture, interest, and perspective and that may be recognized as a legal entity, which allows for social and political action (Trojanowicz, Kappeler, & Gaines, 2002). Furthermore, a community is a mechanism that transmits social values and that allows social interactions to collectively shape its character. The socialization process is an ongoing event that is never complete (Robinette & Straus, 2002). Individuals constantly learn new information, skills, and assume ever changing social roles as they proceed through life. The local community is not independent of the larger social scene.

The difference between a) the **functionalism and the systems paradigm** and b) the **critical theory and the conflict paradigm** is that the former states that society is a cohesive system where society works together and changes for the good of the whole, but the latter stresses that social relations are based on conflict due to power differentials and resource allocation (Straus, 2002). Three communities will be discussed: **POLICE, GANGS,** and **INMATES.**

POLICE AGENCY AS COMMUNITY

A police agency may be classified as a community. The police officers may live in the same area, they may be friends, they share the same police jargon, they have a common objective (i.e., to uphold the law), and the group is intentionally formed (perhaps by law). In order to maintain control over police operations, the organization has structure functionalism, where members are "coordinated into a functional system through the operation of specialized 'subsystems' creating 'regularities' in their conduct" (Straus, 2002, p. 26). Indeed, the police department probably has a standard operating procedures manual that will describe how to respond to various situations. Furthermore, the rank of each officer will be defined in the standard operating procedures manual along with each officer's responsibilities. This is important from the police officers' point of view because it will improve the agency's efficiency; everyone will know who will do what. This is important from the general community members' point of view because their peace of mind may rely upon the knowledge that there is a community of protectors near them that will provide help to them when needed.

Police Department Corruption

Law enforcement has a history of being corrupt (Carter, 2002). Indeed, during the *Mapp v. Ohio* case, the U.S. Supreme Court noticed that police officers engage in official misconduct and that their behaviors must be controlled (del Carmen, 2010). The Indiana State Police department is no exception. The media, current and past department employees, and the public have all questioned the integrity of the department.

Media

The Indiana State Police places a lot of emphasis on self-image. However, the department's reputation has been tarnished. For example, the media have reported that the Indiana State Police regularly engage in unethical activities. First, an Indiana State trooper broke into the home of a Michigan couple and robbed them (AR15.com, 2009). The trooper was charged with armed robbery, first-degree home invasion, and using a gun to commit a felony. Second, a 27-year Indiana State Police veteran was arrested and charged with fraud and forgery (South Bend Tribune, November 01, 2006). The officer was charged with forging a signature on a home equity loan and improperly taking $25,000 out of an account. Third, a 31-year Indiana State Police veteran was arrested for stealing more than $90,000 in state money (Lewis, 2010, December 01). In this case, the officer had control over the funds. Fourth, another

Indiana State police officer was charged with having sex with a 14-year-old child (WTHR.com, 2013, Oct 11). Fifth, two Indiana State police troopers assaulted a gay bar patron when he refused to move his vehicle from a parking spot that they wanted (Towle, 2008, July 31). Sixth, an Indiana State trooper was less than truthful and was charged with obstruction of justice when he obtained probable cause that a female was over the legal limit for driving a vehicle while intoxicated but told the police dispatcher that the female tested under the legal limit (Maiorano, 2011, May 25). Seventh, a trooper was charged with groping a 19-year-old female that he pulled over for speeding ("State Police", 2014, October 04). Eighth, an Indiana State Police officer has been charged with criminal recklessness and disorderly conduct for waving his gun inside a restaurant (Associated Press, 2013). Ninth, an Indiana trooper stole fuel when he filled his personal vehicle with gasoline that was owned by the state police department (WISHTV.com, 2010, August 12). Finally, in the David Camm murder investigation, the Indiana State Police conducted a shoddy investigation to ensure a conviction. However, after 13 years in prison, David Camm's conviction was overturned in 2013 (Lama, 2014). This case involved witness tampering, evidence tampering, and perjury.

Quarterly Discipline

The Indiana State Police formally disciplined 24 employees in the fourth quarter of 2010 (Indiana State Police, 2011). Some of the charges in which state troopers were found guilty include criminal offenses, such as a) providing false information, b) seizing property without legal authority (theft), and c) illegally stopping vehicles. Other offenses include a) failing to meet quotas, b) neglect of duty,

c) conduct unbecoming an employee, and d) failing to show official courtesy to a superior officer. It is easy to see how quotas can be used to manipulate the officers' behavior. If the officers challenge the quota system, then they may be suspended for questioning authority. If the officers manipulate the data or act in questionable ways to meet the quota, then the officers may be suspended for conduct unbecoming an officer.

Quotas

Police departments do have quota systems (Miller, Schultz, & Hunt, 2011). Indeed, the Indiana State Police admitted that it has a quota system (Getts, 2011). Quota systems are used by police management to justify their own existence by providing information that uneducated individuals can easily understand (Kraska, 2004). Uneducated individuals may include police employees and local residents. In other words, it is very easy for a police department to show that the officers are doing work by advertising the number of tickets that the officers write. It requires more creativity to show police work if crime is prevented. Indeed, a study by Long & Yerington (2006) indicates that Indiana police administrators do not have a fundamental understanding of information that involves police work. This is supported by the fact that an Indiana trooper has referred to his administrators as the "Indiana Imbecile Club" (Allen, 2011, p. 7). Furthermore, because the Indiana State Police administrators did not dispute this claim during an internal investigation, this is, by definition, an adoptive admission (Klein, 1997).

If quotas are used to assess officer performance, then the objective of serving the public becomes unimportant (Kraska, 2004). For example, suppose there is no quota system in place and a trooper normally stops 5 cars per day and writes 5 citations. If a quota system is then implemented and now requires the trooper to write 20 citations per day, the trooper may simply issue 20 citations to the occupants of the five cars. Instead of stopping more vehicles, the officers may simply provide vehicle occupants with multiple citations.

Quotas may have a negative effect on public perception and the overall morale of the officers. For example, a 10-year Indiana State police veteran recently quit the police department because he stated that the department has lost its focus on serving the public (Getts, 2011, July 10). The ex-trooper stated that the Indiana State Police micro-manages troopers and that the department uses quotas to judge police performance. The ex-trooper stated that the Indiana State Police overemphasizes traffic stops and fails to serve the public by undermining troopers' efforts to fight crime.

If Indiana State Police officers fail to write a certain number of tickets and warnings, then they are placed on probation (Allen, 2011, July 11). Consequently, troopers may be motivated to falsify their numbers in order to stay out of trouble. Moreover, there are many aspects of police work that are not measured by a quota system, such as teamwork, attending public service meetings, and eliminating public bias (Whisenand, 2011). If the public demands that police administration show productivity through quotas, then the officers will give the public what it demands, which are more tickets.

Race Discrimination

Most Indiana police officers are male Caucasians (Long & Yerington, 2006). Allen, a black male trooper, stated that he had been targeted in the past because of his race (Allen, 2011, July 11). For example, Allen stated that he was fired during the Indiana State Police academy because of a medical condition, which was correctable, even though Caucasian officers who had medical conditions were not fired (Allen, personal communication on September 25, 2011). Allen was later rehired during a law suit.

While Allen was at the Indiana State Police academy, Allen was diagnosed with a benign brain tumor (Allen, 2011, July 11). After conferring with his doctor, Allen received a written letter that the condition, once corrected, would not affect his abilities to complete the academy. Allen stated that he informed the Indiana State Police of the situation but the Indiana State Police ordered him to resign. When Allen did not resign, he was fired.

Three Caucasian classmates, who had medical conditions, were also ordered to resign (Allen, 2011, July 11). However, when they failed to resign, they were not fired. Allen stated that race was a factor. The fact that the Indiana State Police did not deny these claims during Allen's internal investigation is an adoptive admission that they do practice race discrimination (Klein, 1997; Whitesell, 2011, August 30).

Addressing Racism

According to Fein (2000), there are four strategies to help resolve racism, which are a) the **moral model**, b) the **social engineering model**, c) the **clinical/educational model**, and d) the **cultural/structural model**. The **moral model** is based on the idea that people are basically good and if they just do the right thing, then racism would disappear. However, change based on the moral model requires a prolonged state of arousal; this is problematic because moral crusades usually fade away before the transformations are completed. The **social engineering model** suggests that variables can be manipulated so that desirable outcomes can be achieved. However, in a capitalistic society, power is decentralized and social engineering may be performed in a piecemeal fashion, leading to dangerous unforeseeable consequences. The **clinical/educational model** indicates that racial problems are psychological based and that the defective behaviors of individuals can be treated and rectified. However, people will only learn new behaviors if they want to learn new behaviors; unfortunately, many people resist change. Finally, the **cultural/structural model**, the most comprehensive model of the four, emphasizes the larger historic context. However, because minority cultures evolve within the dynamic network of social roles and structures, no one has enough power to command a specific endpoint. Indeed, at any point in time, a particular person can only make marginal changes.

There are several steps that police departments may implement in order to help minimize racism. First, fair and honest officers must be hired and this can be accomplished by administering psychological screening tests prior to hiring. Racist candidates, for example, should be eliminated from the hiring process. Second, by allowing civilian oversight groups to investigate police complaints, such as racism complaints, the department will improve police-community relations (Walker, Spohn, & DeLone, 2007). Indeed, by involving community members in law enforcement, police management will get a true community perspective for what local residents perceive as important issues (Carter, 2002). After collecting data that are obtained by the civilian oversight group, the police department can then analyzed the information. In this way, patterns of police officer misconduct can be identified and can provide evidence to support further investigations. Third, police departments need to collect demographics on all individuals stopped for traffic violations (American Civil Liberties Union, 2008). This is important because without the demographics data, police management will have no way of knowing if profiling is taking place. If an officer stands out from the rest of the officers in terms of a) complaints, b) traffic stops of minorities, or c) excessive force, then this will alert management that a problem may exist. Fourth, cameras should be put into police cars and each stop should be recorded. If a complaint is made, then the video footage can be reviewed. Fifth, all officers should receive ethics and multi-cultural training (Shusta, Levine, Harris, & Wong, 2002). In this way, the officers may come to understand the behaviors, attitudes, and perspectives of the various people that they encounter. Sixth, officers need to be trained in verbal judo. Residents often feel that they have been abused, not by what the officers do, but by how the officers do it (Walker et al.). Thus, if officers can be trained to communicate better, then perhaps misunderstandings can be eliminated and problems may be reduced.

Officer Safety

There may be conflict inside the police culture. By placing citizen complaints under the category of unbecoming an officer, which covers many things (e.g., appearance, tone of voice, gestures, comments), police administration needs no further evidence to find a trooper guilty of a violation. The end result is that troopers may second guess their actions during critical situations in fear of receiving a complaint. The results may be fatal.

Education

The Indiana State Police does not encourage advanced education (Allen, 2011, July 11). Although the Indiana State Police did require a college education at one time for new employees, the department has since "dummied down" the department (Allen, p. 7). According to Allen, the Superintendent has stated that lowering the standards will not impact the quality of recruits and will allow minorities to better meet the minimum requirements. Allen stated that this is offensive and suggests that women and blacks lack the ability to achieve. The fact that the Indiana State Police did not deny these claims during Allen's internal investigation is an adoptive admission that the department is intentionally offensive to minorities (del Carmen, 2010; Klein, 1997; Whitesell, 2011, August 30).

Free Speech

Police officers have the Constitutional right of free speech (Peak, Gaines, & Glensor, 2010). Over the years, the courts and legislatures have bestowed or recognized a number of rights that police officers possess. Many of these rights are constitutionally guaranteed, but others have been adopted by legislative bodies or through union negotiations.

Although the right of freedom of speech is one of the most fundamental of all rights of Americans, the Supreme Court indicated in the *Pickering v. Board of Education* case that the State does have an interest in controlling the speech of its employees that differ significantly from the speech of the citizenry in general (Peak et al., 2010). Hence, the state may impose restrictions on its employees that it would not be able to impose on the citizenry at large. These restrictions must be reasonable, however.

A police regulation that is overly broad may be found to be an unreasonable infringement on a police officer's freedom of speech. (Peak et al., 2010). For example, there was a Chicago Police Department rule that prohibited any activity, conversation, or discussion that was derogatory toward the department. That policy was found unreasonable by the court. The policy was unreasonable because such a rule prohibited all criticism of the agency by its officers, even in private conversation. Essentially, a department cannot arbitrarily regulate officers' speech. However, if officers make statements that adversely affect the department's operation, such as leaking information about an ongoing investigation or by making false statements, then the courts will generally rule in the State's favor to prohibit that kind of speech.

One way to discourage police officer untruthfulness is for the state to implement the *Giglio* policy (U.S. Department of Homeland Security, 2004). The federal government employs the *Giglio* policy, which requires officers to tell the truth when they are required to be truthful. The *Giglio* policy states that any findings of misconduct that reflect upon the truthfulness or possible bias of an employee, which could impact of credibility of the officer as a witness, may be used to impeach the officer in court. Thus, if federal officers get caught lying during their official duties, then they will be fired because they are no longer credible witnesses. Thus, if the *Giglio* policy is adopted at the state level, then officers who engage in misconduct that reflects negatively upon their truthfulness would be fired. The *Giglio* policy would force police officers to tell the truth when they are required to tell the truth. A police department would only oppose such a policy if being truthful was problematic.

Indiana State Police Alliance

In a recent letter issued by the Indiana State Police Alliance (ISPA), a club that supposedly represents the interests of troopers, the club condemned the actions of troopers who lodged complaints against the Indiana State Police (Rader, 2011). The ISPA condemned the complaints because a) they reflected personal opinions, b) they tarnished the department's image, c) the complaints have already been investigated by the state, and d) only the ISPA has the right to file complaints on behalf of state employees. Furthermore, the ISPA stated that feeding off opinions that reflect negatively upon the department is a destructive process, that only members of the ISPA can attend ISPA meetings, and that the Indiana State Police administration sends a representative to monitor the ISPA meetings.

The preceding argument appears to be biased against troopers. First, administrators are responsible for leading a team of diverse employees, who have a variety of skills (Whisenand, 2011). Good leadership requires listening to employees and it has been estimated that about 85% of a leader's abilities involve the ability to understand and use the power of emotions. Human nature involves emotions and opinions, and they provide information that cannot be obtained elsewhere. Thus, when the ISPA stated that they condemned the opinions troopers, they are basically stating that qualitative information is unimportant (Rader, 2011). However, qualitative information is the only way to investigate why problems exist, and, therefore, opinions should be sought. Indeed, quantitative studies are ineffective for this type of study (Creswell, 2009). In other words, the ISPA does not understand the value of qualitative information and this limits their effectiveness at being trooper representatives. In addition, profound dissatisfaction is the catalyst for change (Whisenand). Only a person who is deeply dissatisfied, has much energy, is willing is break old bonds, and who has the insight to address sensitive issues can motivate change. In short, instead of dismissing the complaints of disgruntled employees, the ISPA should seek them in order to understand truth from the troopers' perspective (Berg, 2007).

Second, the courts and legislatures have recognized that police officers have a constitutional right to free speech (Peak et al., 2010). The Court ruled that an officer's derogatory remarks toward the police department are not necessarily unreasonable. According to the Indiana State Police policy, troopers cannot exercise their right to free speech (Whitesell, 2011, August 30). This rule is not supported by the *Muller v. Conlisk* ruling and should be challenged by troopers in court.

Third, the ISPA stated that complaints made against the state were investigated by the state, but this is inherently biased (Rader, 2011). The methodology of the investigation and the actual data should be made available to the public for review (Creswell, 2009). If the data are not made available for others to scrutinize, then the study has little credibility and would not be seriously considered by the experts. The ISPA failed to provide the study and, consequently, the argument is valueless.

Fourth, the ISPA implied that it engages in unethical behavior. For example, only ISPA members are allowed to attend meetings, only the ISPA can file complaints on behalf of troopers, and the Indiana State Police administration sends a representative to monitor the meetings (Rader, 2011). This is problematic because the ISPA discriminates against troopers who are not members. In addition, troopers may not want to file a complaint against the department in front of Indiana State Police management. This is an unethical practice because anonymity is lost (Creswell, 2009). In fact, the practice actually implies that Indiana State Police management has corralled troopers into ISPA meetings in order to control complaints.

Finally, the ISPA stressed that the Indiana State Police's integrity was important (Rader, 2011). However, the ISPA did not explain why the Indiana State Police destroyed personnel records, destroyed electronic records, and failed to honor a subpoena during a 2011 court case (*Davis v. Whitesell, 2011*). In addition, the ISPA did not explain why the department destroyed Allen's records during his law suit against the department (Allen, personal communication on 11/1/2010).

Gaining the Public's Trust?

In 2007, Orland, Indiana had a civilian who may have been patrolling as a police officer. The Indiana State police would not investigate. A civilian handcuffing individuals and transporting them to other places may be a violation of law. Below is part of a letter that was massed-mailed to local residents.

> On Oct 3, 2007, an Orland town board member was threatened with violence because she is investigating town corruption and conspiracy. It has recently been discovered that the local town deputy marshal may have never been certified as a law enforcer, or at least lost her certification long ago. It appears that she has never been to the Indiana Law Enforcement Academy for certification.
>
> In an attempt to cover up the deputy marshal's lack of credentials, it appears that two of the three town board members stated that she would be sent to the law enforcement academy in mid-October, 2007 so that she may be certified as a deputy marshal (stated at town meeting on Sept 10, 2007). The third board member challenged and investigated the deputy marshal's credentials. Having been caught in their possible act of conspiracy, on Sept 24, 2007 the two other board members acknowledged that they knew that the female deputy marshal was uncertified. On that day, they then pulled the deputy marshal off of the job. (These same two board members have been "out voting" the third board member for some time in hiring a certified marshal). It appears that these two board

> members knowingly allowed a civilian to enforce the laws of the state of Indiana by providing her, a civilian, the tools of the trade. Consequently, several laws may have been violated. (Albright, 2007).

A small town in Indiana may have its own town marshal. According to the conflict theory, town board members, who hire the town marshal, do not want outside police officers in their town (Schmalleger, 2011). In order to get rid of a trooper in their town, different residents may file complaint-after-complaint against the trooper. Residents know that the trooper will get disciplined, even if the officer did nothing wrong. Consequently, small towns know how to force troopers out of their towns.

Investigating Problems via Academic Research

Quantitative & Qualitative Studies

Quantitative investigations are scientific, objective, and effective in describing phenomena in terms of magnitude (Balian, 1988). Quantitative investigations use numeric values and statistics to identify patterns, to objectively quantify relationships between variables, and to make predictions. In addition, because large sample sizes may be used, data can be generalized to larger populations. For a quantitative study, a hypothesis must be written so that it includes the variables being tested (i.e., the hypothesis must include the independent and depend variables within the statement) (Balian, 1988). Furthermore, although directional hypotheses may be used in a study, all statistical tests are measured against the null hypothesis.

However, numeric values are ineffective in describing the subjective interpretations of human emotions (Glesne, 2006; Hatch, 2002).

When investigating a topic that cannot be quantitatively predicted, such as human nature, qualitative investigations are most effective. Indeed, qualitative investigations are preferred for describing and interpreting experiences in context specific settings because each person's reality is construed in his or her own mind; qualitative research attempts to reveal the meanings that participants have given to various phenomena (Adams, 1999; Ponterotto, 2005). Feelings, opinions, and emotions cannot be accurately assessed via quantitative analysis; probing the participants for more detail through in-depth interviews using open-ended questions is required. The investigator needs to obtain the proper software for content (data) analysis in order to identify themes in the data (Berg, 2007). Themes in the data provide meaning. However, there are some limitations to qualitative studies: a) the small sample size associated with qualitative studies may prevent the findings from being generalized to a larger population; and b) due to forgetfulness and intentional deception, experiences from the past may be reported less than accurate.

Types of Research Questions

There is a difference between a quantitative research question and a qualitative research question. The appropriate type of question will depend on what the researcher is trying to answer. Quantitative research questions ask **how** variables are related. Qualitative research questions ask **why** variables are related.

Quantitative Research Question

R_1. What is the relationship between the number of years that African American girls have participated in school-sponsored contact sports prior to graduating from high school and their amount of aggression as young adults?

Null Hypotheses (HO)

HO There is no relationship between the number of years that African American girls have participated in school-sponsored contact sports prior to graduating from high school and their amount of aggression as young adults.

Qualitative Research Question

R_1. How do African American female adults describe their perceptions that participating in school-sponsored contact sports prior to graduating from high school has impacted their amount of aggression as young adults?

Research is a systematic process of collecting, analyzing, and interpreting information in order to better understand the subject of study (Leedy & Ormrod, 2005). Research attempts to solve a problem by answering a question. Below are several different types of qualitative research studies. The appropriate research design will depend on the purpose and focus of the study.

Table 19

Qualitative Research (Berg, 2007; Hatch, 2002; Leedy & Ormrod, 2005).

Qualitative Study Research Design	Purpose	Focus	Data Collection	Data Analysis
Phenomenological	To understand truth and reality from the participants' point of view	A specific event as perceived by an individual	Purposive sampling consisting of 5-25 individuals for in-depth and unstructured interviews	Identify common themes and synthesize them into an overall concept
Ethnography	To understand how the participants' behaviors reflect the culture of a group in a natural setting	A specific location where a group of people share a common culture	Artifact collection, participation observation, and structured and unstructured interviews	Identify underlying beliefs and phenomena and synthesize into a general behavior
Focus Group Study	To understand truth and reality from the participants' point of view	Specific events as perceived by a small group of individuals	Interviews and any other relevant data sources	Identify common themes and synthesize into an overall concept
Case Study	To understand one person or event in great detail because of the situation is poorly understood	One case in its natural environment or a few cases in their natural environment	Interviews, observation, written documents, and audiovisual information	Identify common themes and synthesize into an overall concept

Grounded Theory	To derive a theory by collecting and interpreting data in a natural setting in multiple stages	The process of human actions and interactions and how they impact each other	Interviews and any other relevant data sources	Prescribed and systematic way of coding the data to identify interrelationships in the data in order to construct a theory
Content Analysis	To identify themes and patterns in a body of material through a systematic examination of the data	Any communication displayed in verbal, visual, or behavioral fashion.	Sampling the specific material to be analyzed and coding the material in a precisely defined manner.	Tabulation of the frequency of each coded theme for descriptive and inferential statistical analysis.

Implementation of a Focus Group Study

Focus group interviews, where individuals who share common traits and experiences interact and provide data beyond what any single participant could provide, are most appropriate for studies that are explanatory in nature (Hatch, 2002). However, a weakness in this technique is that the group consensus may overshadow a particular individual's perspective (Berg, 2007; Hatch). Following is a focus group study on police profiling.

Focus Group Instrument

The topic of discussion is community members' perceptions of police profiling.

Following is a statement of the basic rules (Berg, 2007). The discussion will be conducted in a polite and professional manner. Indeed, different points of view and experiences will provide an overall understanding of the issue. Therefore, all opinions are valued. A question will be asked, each participant will be asked to provide a short response, and then the question will be open for group discussion. Everyone is encouraged to respond.

Five open-ended questions will be asked during the interviews. The five questions are listed below.

- What is your perception of the relationship between the police and community?
- What is your perception of the relationship between the police and minorities?
- What is your perception of the relationship between minorities and whites?
- What is your experience with police profiling or racial discrimination?
- Do you think that the police have earned your respect?

Probe questions

Does the community support the police or is there a lot of conflict?
Do community members file a lot of complaints against officers?
Are there gangs in the area?

Do the police effectively serve minorities?
Are minorities adequately represented in local police?

Do minorities and whites struggle over political power?
Are minorities adequately represented in the local judicial government?

Can you provide an example of a profiling experience?

Why do you trust the police?
Why do you not trust the police?
Have you ever had an encounter with a rude (or polite) police officer?

In order to gather a general feeling of civilians' perceptions of the local police, a focus group interview was conducted involving 7 participants. The interview was conducted in a room at a local university. The ground rules were described to the participants as 1) a question will be asked, 2) each participant will be asked to provide a short response, and 3) the question will then be open for group discussion (Berg, 2007). The seven participants are as follows: 1) O. Zing, a 32 year old Asian American female who was born in China; 2) L. Cloud, a 50 year old Native American female; 3) P. Cheddar, a 50 year white male, retired from the U.S. Army; 4) O. Twinkles, a 50 year old white female with 9 years of business experience; 5) T. Witne, a 50 year old white female with 5 years of manufacturing experience; 6) P. Proud, a 50 year old white female and homemaker; and 7) L. Rodriguez, a 41 year old Hispanic female who was born in Panama. It should be noted that all of the participants who have stated that they are 50 years of age are probably not actually 50. Three of the females did not want to provide their actual ages. They simply stated "50 plus or minus." In short, the focus group participants are from different backgrounds and are able to provide different perspectives about the topic. Below is the essence of what the focus group participants stated.

Research Question: *What is your perception of the relationship between the police and community?*

"In general, the community does not respect the local and state police because the police are idiots. In fact, one state police officer was forced to resign because he is a thief" (P. Cheddar, personal communications of September 22, 2011). Because this event was advertised in the local media, the case being described is common knowledge for the group. Thus, all participants agreed with this statement.

Research Question: *What is your perception of the relationship between the police and minorities?*

"The police do profile. Anyone who is dark they profile. My son was walking with two blond hair boys. A cop pulled up to them and questioned them about smoking. The cop let the two blond hair boys go but made my son empty out his pockets to prove that he did not have any cigarettes" (L. Cloud, personal communications of September 22, 2011). Although all of the Caucasians in this group stated that they have had no personal experiences with the police, the Native American, the Chinese American, and the Hispanic American stated that they are aware of police discrimination against minorities. Only one female Caucasian stated that she believes discrimination occurs against minorities, but only because of what she has seen in the movies.

Research Question: *What is your perception of the relationship between minorities and whites?*

"Some minorities exaggerate ethnic problems. Some Chinese do not like to talk to whites because they do not think that whites like them. I say, how would they know until they talk with them? People feel comfortable talking to those who look similar" (O. Zing, personal communications of September 22, 2011). Zing also stated that several years ago at Indiana University, a Chinese American mom had a sick 12 year old son. She let her son sleep with her so that she could take care of him. Zing stated that this is common practice in China. However, social workers came, they charged the mom with sexual abuse, and they took her son away; consequently, her son, shortly thereafter, died. Zing stated that whites need to learn different cultural practices. The general consensus of the group is that whites do not communicate well with other cultures. The rest of the group backed this up with another example. They stated that, just a little while ago, there was an accident nearby and a Hispanic was killed. No one in the area knew how to speak Spanish and no one could communicate with the victim's family. Thus, the entire group claimed that there is definitely a communication problem between cultures.

Research Question: *What is your experience with police profiling or racial discrimination?*

"I only know what I have seen on T.V. and in the movies. White police officers pick on minorities" (P. Proud, personal communications of September 22, 2011). The overall consensus is that the participants have had no personal experience with police profiling or racial discrimination and that they have learned their perceptions through second-hand information. Only the Hispanic female may have actually experienced a profiling incident. In her case, she stated that she had pulled into a grocery store and that a white male city police officer was staring her down (L. Rodriguez, personal communications of September 22, 2011). She stated that after she left the store, about 20 minutes later, the officer followed her for about 4 miles out of the city. He then pulled her over and gave her a bogus excuse.

Research Question: *Do you think that the police have earned your respect?*

"I respect the police out of fear" (O. Zing, personal communications of September 22, 2011). The overall consensus is that those who respect the police do it because of the officers' position, not because of the officers' behaviors. Overall, it appears that all of the participants believe there are police-community concerns. Only the minority females, however, specifically believe that there are police-minority concerns. Finally, the group consensus is that the police are respected only because of their position of authority and not because of their behaviors.

Implementation of a Case Study

Case studies can be performed in many types of social environments and can provide rich, in-depth information on simple or complex phenomenon (Berg, 2007). Indeed, case studies are effective in performing qualitative research on a person, a process, an institution, an event, a program, or a social group involving a contextualized contemporary (as opposed to historic) phenomenon within specified parameters (Hatch, 2002).

Case studies are among of the most popular research designs in law enforcement today (Champion, 2006). Case studies allow for thorough investigations of individuals in specific social settings and include detailed behavioral and psychological descriptions of persons in those settings. Because there are philosophical, political, and ethical issues involving police officer behaviors, a qualitative case study would be effective in understanding how police officers develop their attitudes. Indeed, a case study, which focuses on very few participants (perhaps only one participant), can provide the in-depth, detailed information that is necessary to understand police behavior (Berg, 2007). Furthermore, case studies allow formal interviews to supplement observations (Hatch, 2002).

There are five advantages to case studies (Champion, 2006). First, case studies are flexible and they allow the researcher to collect data via multiple techniques, such as observation, interviewing, and examination of records. Second, this flexibility can be extended to virtually any dimension. Third, case studies can be performed in many types of social environments. Fourth, case studies can be inexpensive if the researcher collects the data firsthand. Finally, a longitudinal case study will allow behavioral changes to be measured at specific points in time. This may be important if the incremental changes are small.

There are two disadvantages in performing case studies (Champion, 2006). First, case studies may not be generalized to larger populations. Because the research design is qualitative in nature, it is subjective and depends on how each person perceives truth and reality (Weber, 2004). Second, findings from case studies may not always support theories. In other words, the findings are not conclusive proof of anything. Therefore, an accumulation of case studies is important in investigating similar phenomena so that confident statements can be made about the social world.

Personal Interview with State Police Officer (name changed for anonymity)

Y. Bell - State Police (personal communication on October 1, 2011)
B/m 45 years old, born in U.S.
6 years corrections, 14 years police
About half of life lived in the city, half in the country

Research Question: What is your perception of the relationship between the police and the community?

Response: The community generally does not like the police. Many people are involved with some sort of crime, whether it be smoking marijuana or underage drinking, therefore they do not want the police to know their business. They only want the police when they need help. The community members in general, both blacks and whites, do not generally like the police department. If there is a shooting for example, whites will support the police and blacks will claim racism and oppose whites.

Research Question: What is your perception of the relationship between minorities and the police in your community?

Response: The police department absolutely profiles. White officers will pull black drivers over simply because of race. Many blacks get tired of this.

Research Question: What is your perception of the relationship between minorities and whites in your community?

Response: Anytime a shooting happens, white and blacks will divide. This is due to economic reasons and because of the racism the blacks perceive that whites practice against them.

Research Question: What is your experience with profiling or racial discrimination?

Response: I do not profile based on race or gender but I do profile behaviors. For example, when I pull up next to a driver and he will not look at me but looks straight forward with both hands on the steering wheel, this is suspicious behavior and I will look for valid reasons to pull the driver over. Also, one night several years ago, I was driving home from the gym and a county police officer was in the crossover with his headlights shining across the roadway. I was in an unmarked police car and wearing a rag on my head. As soon as I passed him, I knew that he was going to pull out and stop me, even though traffic was heavy. Sure enough, he pulled out and stopped me. I immediately showed him my police badge and asked him why he stopped me. He stated that I was weaving a little bit. That was untrue but I did not argue with him.

Research Question: Do you respect the police?

Response: Because I work with police officers, I trust them. We share a common experience. However, I do not trust the administration. The police department does not like complaints and will give too much credence to civilians and totally distrust the officers.

Recommendations for State Police Problem

There are several ways for a police department to improve its police-community relations. First, the department must hire educated officers. Proper police decisions require critical thinking. Second, officers must be persuaded to change their own behaviors. However, change must come from the top. Third, the *Giglio* policy should be implemented at all levels of law enforcement. If the officers cannot be truthful when they are required to be truthful, then they should not have authority over other people's freedom. Fourth, the police department should send their Quarterly Disciplinary reports to the media. If police management expects to get the respect and trust of the community, then management needs to be less secretive. Fifth, all police officers need to join Zoomerang, which is a web-based company that allows members to participate in surveys (Zoomerang, 2010). By joining Zoomerang, academic research can be performed on a variety of topics by many experts in the field and the department will have no way of controlling the information or its publication. Finally, to better understand local problems, the police department must represent the community that it serves.

Table 20

Improving Police Performance

5 Ways to Improve Police-Community Relations
Hire educated officers
Officers must change their own behaviors
Giglio policy should be made into state law
Department should send their Quarterly Disciplinary reports to the media
All officers should join Zoomerang
Department must represent the community that it serves

It is quite important that the government represents the community that it serves (Carter, 2002). For example, women make up 51% of the American population but only hold about 25% of the country's elected official positions (Iowa National Education for Women's Leadership, n.d.). Of the 535 members of the 113th U.S. Congress, only about 18% are females and only about 5% are black females. To enhance public trust, justice, and job effectiveness, the police department must reflect the local community. This will ensure that the police department is striving toward the right goal. Indeed, it is important that everyone understands what is happening so that everyone can work in harmony toward the same goal.

STREET GANG AS COMMUNITY

Social deviants are a part of the community and, if crime is to be reduced and the general health of society is to be improved, their perspectives must be considered. A street gang may be defined as a community. The members may live in the same area, they may be friends, they may share the same language and religious beliefs, they may have a common objective, and the group may be intentionally formed. Indeed, a gang may improve the quality of life for some, while diminishing the quality of life for others. It all depends on whose perspective is being used as reference. For example, during the 1980s, there was a civil war in El Salvador and over one million Salvadoran refugees entered the U.S. (Werner, 2007). Many of these Salvadoran refugees entered the ghettos of Los Angeles and were attacked by Mexican gangs. In order to survive, they intentionally formed the La Mara Salvatrucha (MS-13) gang to protect themselves. Thus, the members formed a gang as a matter of survival. As the MS-13 gang grew, however, the gang's objectives changed. Today, MS-13's primary business involves illegal drugs, which supports its primary mission of killing people (Castaneda, 2006; Poe, 2006).

Gang Definition

The definition of criminal street gang differs from state to state. The Virginia State Code basically defines a gang as three or more persons who associate in an ongoing organization whose primary purpose is the commission of crime (Harrisonburg, 2008). The Virginia State Code also states that gang members are physically identifiable in some manner and have a criminal history of violence.

MS-13

The MS-13 gang is a serious social problem (Cosby, 2006; McLemore, 2006; Poe, 2006). The MS-13 gang is becoming more structured and organized than ever before, proving to be effective business opportunists (Cosby, 2006; McLemore, 2006). They are quite diverse in their crimes, preying on law abiding citizens and law breakers alike. For example, some of their crimes involve prostitution rings, dealing drugs, extortion, robbery, contract killings, alien smuggling, and protecting drug lords. In short, the MS-13 does meet the definition of a gang.

The MS-13 gang members are so violent that they attack police officers, other gang members, and brutally murder innocent women and children with machetes (Cosby, 2006; McLemore, 2006; Poe, 2006). Because the MS-13 members engage in violence so casually, even hardened police offers are intimidated; MS-13 gang members have placed bullets on the doorsteps of police officers' with the officers' names on them. In addition, the U.S. Department of Homeland Security has recently warned its officers that they could be targeted by MS-13 assassins. In short, the federal government has declared the MS-13 a national security risk.

Because gang affiliation eventually leads to one of three paths, the hospital, jail, or the grave, something must be motivating people to join gangs (Poe, 2006). There are several factors that lead young children to join gangs. Some of these factors include broken families, poverty, peer pressure, language barriers, comradeships, protection from other youths, and boredom (Harrisonburg, 2008). Some families, especially in single parent households, may live in poor areas, the parents may be required to commute long distances to work, and the parents may be required to work long hours. These parents may sometimes leave their children at home for extended periods of time. Instead of building strong bonds with the parents, these children may build bonds with gang members. They end up joining gangs for structure and a sense of belonging (Harrisonburg; "Keys", 1999). In addition, the media promote gang affiliation through glorified gang life in the movies, in the news, on the Internet, and in music. Even police-sponsored gang prevention programs may unintentionally promote gang affiliation when children equate attention to respect and prestige.

Criminal Theories

Several theories may explain the gang problem. According to Sampson's theory of collective efficacy, juveniles commit crimes because they need resources, because the neighborhood is disorganized, because there is a lack of social control, and because there is anonymity (Vold et al., 2002). Cooley has indicated that individuals are heavily influenced by other people with whom they associate (Hensley, 1996). By caring about other people's expectations, bonds are created. Thus, when youths hang around gang members and develop bonds, they may end up replacing the family unit with the gang unit. According to Akers' social learning theory, behaviors are reinforced over time according to the intensity, duration, and frequency of social learning experiences (Akers &Sellers, 2009). According to the rational choice theory, rewards encourage certain behaviors while punishments discourage other behaviors. According to the looking glass self, each person's identity is determined by how that person believes he or she appears to others, how he or she perceives others judge that appearance, and then by how he or she reacts to the judgments of other people (Hensley, 1996). This means that each gang member is very concerned about what the other gang members think of him or her. Because youths have a strong passion to belong to a gang, this gives the gang leverage over those who want to belong, which influences their behaviors.

If MS-13 gang members do not consider the rewards of following society's rules very valuable, and if gang members are not afraid of possible punishments from society, then they will not care how society perceives them. Not caring about how society perceives them means that they will not react to society's judgments. Not reacting to society's judgments means that they will not obtain their identities from society. In the MS-13's case, however, they do care about what society thinks of them. The problem is that they want to be seen as mean and tough, and, in order to get that recognition, they must do the opposite of what society demands of them. For example, the MS-13 gang requires that a new member kill someone and to bring money into the gang, usually through extortion. This will meet society's expectations of what an MS-13 gang member is supposed to be (Poe, 2006).

Over the years, individuals who identify themselves as being deviant learn to associate with other deviants, developing personal relationships with them (Ulmer, 2000). This eventually develops into a moral commitment with one another. Over time, they perfect their skills of executing criminal activities and live for excitement. If they continue their activities without getting caught, they learn that the costs associated with their acts are quite low, which encourages additional deviant acts (Liska & Messner, 1999).

The rational choice theory involves a simple business decision: the act is performed if it is profitable (Schmalleger, 2011). Some individuals commit crimes when the extrinsic rewards are high. By performing deviant acts supported by the gang, gang members can be rewarded handsomely, such as when they rob people, as long as they do not get caught by the police. In addition, because there is a huge amount of money involved in the drug business, it is the backbone of gang activity (Poe, 2006). As long as the U.S. demand for illegal substances is high, there will be gang activity.

Some individuals commit crimes when the intrinsic rewards are high (Schmalleger, 2011). When MS-13 gang members are arrested and prosecuted, it only makes the gang problem worse (Poe, 2006). First of all, prison is not considered punishment. MS-13 gang members equate prison with universities, and those that are released back into society are considered to be graduates. Second, if MS-13 gang members are released from prison and then deported back to their home countries, they end up recruiting other refugees in their home countries who are experienced in guerilla warfare. They then reenter the U.S. in greater numbers, with military style expertise. Therefore, whether they serve time in prison or are deported back to their home countries, U.S. punishments are considered rewards by MS-13 gang members, which only enhance the MS-13 gang problem.

Some individuals commit crimes because the severity of punishment is low (Schmalleger, 2011). MS-13 gang members know that U.S. law enforcement agencies talk tough but lack substance. Of the 55 thousand illegal aliens in U.S. prisons, each has been arrested an average of 8 times after committing an average of 13 crimes (Farah, 2006; Farah, 2007). Thus, illegal alien gang members serve short sentences and then are deported. Once deported, it takes them about one month to get back into the U.S. Although an average of 12 Americans are killed every day by illegal aliens, the task of deporting all of the illegal aliens is overwhelming. Furthermore, illegal aliens know how to manipulate and tie up the U.S. legal system (Werner, 2007). Therefore, American citizens must evaluate how much they are willing to pay to deal with this problem.

Some individuals commit crimes because the certainty of punishment is low (Schmalleger, 2011). MS-13 gang members know that there is a shortage in police manpower and that police officers cannot effectively perform their duties. In fact, there would need to be a tenfold increase in the number of police officers to bring back the peace of 40 years ago (Walinsky, 1995). Indeed, the U.S. Department of Homeland Security is ineffective in handling the illegal immigration problem, as evidenced by the 12 million foreigners currently living within the U.S. (Levin, 2007). In fact, the work environment of U.S. Customs at the U.S. border is not conducive to catching illegal aliens. Catching illegal aliens is not the number one priority for Customs Officers; the number one goal is to catch terrorists.

Some individuals commit crimes because the celerity of punishment is slow (Schmalleger, 2011). It takes a very long time to resolve illegal immigration cases. At the border, if illegal aliens are caught, they are told that they will be required to appear in immigration court at a later date. The illegal aliens are then released and allowed to proceed on their way. However, only about 30 percent show up for the immigration proceedings (Bellantoni, 2005). Of those that do appear, about 85 percent of those who are ordered deported become fugitives. Consequently, there are about 465,000 illegal alien fugitives within the U.S. Because illegal immigration is a huge political issue, the federal government has passed the responsibility of dealing with the problem to the states (Boulard, 2006). However, a federal judge has ruled that it is unconstitutional for state and local law enforcement agencies to enforce federal immigration laws (Kivlan, 2007). Hence, the immigration problem may take many years to resolve.

Once people are arrested and labeled deviant, there is a stigma that is attached to them (Liska & Messner, 1999). Indeed, being labeled a deviant by society may create stigma for gang members, thereby, limiting their legitimate economic activities. On the other hand, labeling gang members as criminals may promote respect from within the gang. For example, Mara Salvatrucha is street slang for Salvadoran guard posse, or street tough Salvadorans; Mara is taken from the word marabunta, which is a fierce ant that defends its colony. Hence, MS-13 means army ant (Florida, 2007; McLemore, 2006; Nesarajah, 2006; Poe, 2006). Members have a reputation of labeling themselves as MS-13 gang members by tattooing their upper bodies, including their arms and faces. These tattoos represent gang commitment, gang beliefs, specific gang clique (area) associations, deeds of violence, and respect for the dead. Tattoos also earn respect from other gang members. In short, tattoos are status symbols, worn with pride.

Intervention and Prevention

Because gangs target youths for recruitment, youths must be the source for finding resolution. Evidence indicates that participating in valuable activities unrelated to substance abuse, such as the Midnight Basketball Project, has a positive impact in the reduction of deviant behaviors (Tucker et al., 1999). However, due to a lack of research that establishes this point without question, executives, administrators, and politicians who fund intervention treatment programs, do not share a common set of concepts about the nature of substance abuse. They are treating substance abuse as an addiction and disease without considering the social environment. Thus, they have eliminated the Midnight Basketball Program because they do not understand the big picture. In their minds, there is no credible research that correlates valued activities to reduced substance abuse.

Instead of attacking the supply side of drugs, a more effective strategy may be to address the demand side. If there is no demand, then supply is inconsequential. To attack the gang problem, the government needs to manage the demand for drugs in the general community. This can be achieved through various treatment programs. There is much money available from the federal government in the forms of grants to help state and local governments manage the substance abuse problem.

The U.S. Office of National Drug Control Policy provides funding for addiction related programs (U.S. Office of National Drug Control Policy, 2007). States and local governmental agencies may apply online for financial benefits, such as grants, along with other assistance (e.g., from the U.S. Drug Enforcement Agency) to combat drug related problems in their areas. Many states and local governments just do not have the resources to combat drug related problems and the U.S. Office of National Drug Control Policy funding site is a vital tool that provides the necessary resources.

Because gangs actively recruits school children, it is here where gang preventative measures need to be taken. Because young children are very impressionable and are targeted for gang recruitment, they need to be educated about the costs associated with gang affiliation, such as going to prison and not being able to find good jobs later in life. The U.S. government, however, has responded by implementing a nationwide campaign called Operation Community Shield, seeking out and arresting known gang members (Werner, 2007). However, as stated earlier, when gang members are locked up and then released back into society, the gang violence becomes worse. Therefore, the best solution is to develop and implement a preventative strategy.

There are a couple of other ways to make positive change (Carter, 2002; Tucker et al., 1999). First, neighborhood-watch programs can be developed. This will allow neighbors to get to know one another. Second, parents can create a caring family unit. Indeed, good role models will help children to develop pro-social values.

INMATES AS COMMUNITY

Inmates may be classified as a community. Inmates live in the same area, they may be friends, they share the same jargon, they have a common objective (i.e., to be free), and the group is intentionally formed (by court order). In order to maintain control over inmate behaviors, the department of corrections will have an inmate handbook, which describes the rules and regulations that control inmate behavior. It is important not to forget about inmates because they may be released one day. Once they are released, they may live in the neighborhood.

Individuals convicted of crimes are confined in prisons where violence is not uncommon. Because there are many more prisoners than correctional officers, and because 25% of the prison population has antisocial personality disorder, it is easy to understand why violence occurs (DeLisi & Vaughn, 2008; State of Indiana, 2008). However, there are several ways to help manage prison violence.

Causal Factors

There are several causal factors related to inmate perpetrated violence within correctional facilities. These factors include prison overcrowding, lack of effective supervision, inexperienced staff members, ineffective classification and placement of inmates (e.g., violent offenders are mixed with nonviolent offenders), boredom and sexual frustration among prisoners, inadequate programming within the correctional facility, tensions between rival gang members, abundance of weapons, and prison-specific offender profiles, which include race and childhood aggression (Byrne, n.d.; Human Rights Watch, 1998; Knowles, 1999). Furthermore, because many inmates lack the ability to peacefully resolve conflict, many factors can set them off. Some of these factors include confrontational demeanors, privacy issues, disrespect, and turf-based challenges.

Basically, there are three categories of inmates who resort to violence: 1) the antisocial offenders, who have learned that force produces successful result; 2) the special needs offenders, who act violent due to mental impairments; and 3) the psychopathic offenders, who are predatory, lack empathy, and are violent for no good reason (Seiter, 2008). Furthermore, there are two strains of criminal predatory behavior, which are proactive and reactive aggression

(Walters, 2008). Proactive aggression is cold-blooded, calculated, goal oriented, and is used to achieve a tangible reward. Reactive aggression, on the other hand, is hot-blooded, unplanned, and is used in retaliation to a provocation or perceived injustice.

Understanding the difference between proactive and reactive aggression is important because the proper intervention strategies must be matched to the appropriate aggression type (Walters, 2008). For example, proactive aggression may be best managed by offering programs that alter outcome expectancies involving crime. Reactive aggression, on the other hand, may be best managed by teaching skill development techniques via anger and stress management classes. However, because there is a direct relationship between these two types of aggression, the most effective programs will address both types of aggression.

Inmate-on-Inmate Violence

About half of all male inmates incarcerated in state correctional facilities have been convicted of violent offenses, and a large percentage of them have long criminal histories (Seiter, 2008). This sets the stage for a hostile environment. Because of boredom, sexual tensions, and feelings of powerlessness, many inmates engage in violence as a way to mentally escape the reality of prison. Thus, by engaging in proactive aggression, they can focus their attention on fighting other inmates. Consequently, the more they fight, and the more hostile the environment, they more they see themselves as victims and less as offenders. Hence, they look for reasons to fights. On the other hand, the inmates who are challenged must engage in reactive aggression in order to defend their reputations and to prevent being perceived as vulnerable and weak.

Inmate-on-Staff Violence

Inmates may attack staff members if the inmates perceive that injustices are committed by staff members (Walters, 2008). For example, the Indiana prison system has several inadequacies in protecting the health and rights of inmates. First, according to the inmate's *Adult Offender Handbook*, only medical services that are considered necessary shall be provided to prisoners (Indiana Department of Correction, n.d.). Indeed, all medical services for elective or non-emergency concerns will be denied. Second, if a prisoner has been prescribed a particular diet but fails to follow that diet, such as by eating a snack, then the diet will be terminated; terminating such assistance seems to be vindictive, and thus, cruel and unusual punishment. Third, routine dental cleaning is only provided to inmates as long as they practice good oral hygiene. In other words, if the prisoners do not brush their teeth, then they will not be allowed to see the dentist. Finally, dentures are only provided to prisoners if they are determined to be medically necessary. In other words, chewing food is not considered necessary. Again, this may seem like cruel and unusual punishment. Consequently, inmates may engage in proactive aggression against staff members in order to earn prestige among other prisoners (simply for assaulting a common enemy), or they may engage in reactive aggression in order to bring attention to the injustices.

Inmates Who are Likely to Commit Violence

Research indicates that most incarcerated murderers do not continue violence in prison (Cunningham, 2008). For those convicted of homicide, it is unclear as to whether the severity of the homicide impacts prison violence. However, the evidence does indicate that inmates who serve life sentences without parole are not more likely to engage in prison violence than those who are eligible for parole.

Those who are likely to engage in prison violence are the criminal predators who are psychopaths. Criminal predators lack remorse, they have a sense of entitlement, their desire for objects justifies the means to obtain them, and they rarely accept blame for their actions (Timmins, 2008). Indeed, "psychopaths constitute the most violent population of human aggressors known" (DeLisi & Vaughn, 2008, p. 159). Furthermore, about 25% of the prison population has a psychiatric disorder similar to psychopathy. Thus, this confines a violent group of individuals who are likely to commit violence in a single place.

Techniques to Limit Inmate Violence

One way to help protect inmates is to redirect some of the money that is being used to fight the war on drugs to the penal system. The $75 billion that is used to fight the war on drugs annually could be funneled into the prison system (Buckley, Nadelmann, Schmoke, McNamara, Sweet, Szasz, T., et al., 1996). With this extra money, specific failures in the prison system can be addressed. Because placing prisoners together in confined areas may lead to violence, and because isolating them may lead to frustration and aggression, this money could be used to hire more officers, to purchase more recreational equipment, to provide more complete medical treatment, and to provide more counseling sessions (Seiter, 2008). Thus, by more providing more resources, health will be promoted, security will be improved, and anxieties will be reduced.

Another way to help reduce prison violence is to employ alternate sentencing options (Seiter, 2008). First, by reducing the prison population, the standard of living inside the prisons will improve. This means that inmates will have access to better healthcare services (i.e., more resources will be available). In addition, reducing the number of inmates in prison will reduce the number of inmates available to be assaulted.

Structural Aspects and Violent Behavior

Prisons are structures that are design to confine individuals convicted of crimes (Seiter, 2008). Concrete walls and metal bars take away personal freedoms and privacy. Inmates are thrown into an environment where they are under the control of the government and are in the presence of violent predators. Having no way to physically escape, inmates may be physically and emotionally challenged. In Indiana, for example, there are over 20,000 adult male prisoners in medium and high level security prisons (State of Indiana, 2008). With a correctional staff of about 6,300 employees, this is a little more than 3 inmates for every employee. However, there are only about 4,600 custody officers. Dividing the officers into three shifts, this makes it about 13 inmates for every correctional officer.

The Indiana Department of Correction provides an *Adult Offender Handbook* to all inmates (Indiana Department of Correction, n.d.). The handbook describes the depression and suicide prevention program, sexual assault prevention procedures, and the grievance process. Although Indiana seems to be proactive in protecting the Eighth Amendment rights of inmates, inmates who report depression or suicide thoughts may appear weak, and those who report sexual assaults may appear to be untrustworthy. Indeed, inmates may be intimidated or threatened by other inmates if they seek outside help (Seiter, 2008).

Human Behaviors

Humans, like other animals, need food, water, shelter, and they have the desire to reproduce (Bartol & Bartol, 2008). In order to secure these needs and desires, people stake out territories. This has been true in America for centuries, as Native American tribes secured good hunting grounds as they fought with other tribes over these territories.

Because there is the risk of death when one human fights another human, compliance can be achieved via ritualized aggression, where aggression takes place solely through a show of force (Bartol & Bartol, 2008). For example, it is not uncommon for the U.S. navy to send ships to foreign shores as a show of U.S. might. It is hoped that this show of force will discourage foreign countries from attacking the U.S.

Although there are exceptions, human beings are about equal in strength and size. Thus, there is a natural inhibition to fight one another because there is no guarantee of superiority. In other words, when two people fight, there is an equal chance that either party may die in combat. Even if one person is bigger and more muscular than another person, there are many weapons that are capable of neutralizing the difference.

Males in the U.S. tend to be more physically aggressive than females (Bartol & Bartol, 2008). Many boys are expected to act like men and to deal with their problems via physical force. Crying and backing down from bullies may make the person appear weak, which may promote additional violence.

Females in the U.S. tend to engage in interpersonal forms of aggression (Bartol & Bartol, 2008). Females tend to employ relational aggression to hurt other people. They may gossip, ridicule, and ostracize others who have threatened their territory.

Female Prisons

There are several problems associated with female prisons. First, because there may be only one or two female prisons within a state, this creates a problem for families and children who may want to visit the female inmates (Peak, 2007). Second, because there are so few female prisons, there is less separation of inmates by security classification; this could be dangerous. This means that violent female offenders will be housed with non-violent female inmates. Third, because most female prisons are located in town with less than 25,000 residents, this makes it hard to locate and recruit qualified and experienced staff to work in these remote areas (Peak; Schmalleger, 2007). Staff employees include counselors.

Female inmates cannot be treated the same as male inmates. First, female inmates have different communication styles from that of male inmates (Peak, 2007). Second, there are about 101,000 females prisoners in state prisons and about 53% of them have minor children. Because females are generally the caregivers, the separation from their children creates a special concern (the separation affects their children too). Indeed, female inmates suffer from this separation differently than do male inmates (Seiter, 2008). In response to this problem, some prisons are providing parenting programs and Girl Scouts Behind Bars programs, which allow female inmates to spend time with their children.

Administrators of female correctional facilities state that there are several ways to help limit violent behaviors (Seiter, 2008). These include a) hiring dedicated and qualified staff members, b) using inmates help run the programs, c) using role model inmates to help provide positive peer influence, d) providing parenting and educational classes, e) creating an open communication system, f) providing administrative and staff interactions, g) meeting specific needs of the inmates, and h) developing an outside private-public partnership and interagency coordination. By treating female inmates like human beings and by meeting their needs, when feasible, their tensions and frustrations will be reduced. Consequently, this will help manage their tendencies toward violence.

Many female inmates are in prison due to drug related offenses, which continue even after incarceration (Schmalleger, 2007). The state of Pennsylvania has developed the *Pennsylvania Plan*, which is a zero-tolerance drug policy (Peak, 2007). Inmates who are caught with drugs are criminally prosecuted; those who test positive for drug use, via hair testing, are required to serve disciplinary custody time. Furthermore, by utilizing highly sensitive drug detection equipment, packages, visitors, and correctional officers can all be examined for illegal drugs. As a result of the *Pennsylvania Plan*, inmate-on-inmate assaults have decreased by 70%, and inmate-on-staff assaults have decreased by 57%. Thus, there is evidence that crime in prison can be reduced.

Finally, because inmates are confined in tightly clustered areas, situational crime prevention (SCP) measures, which are designed to prevent specific crimes in specific locations, may be implemented to reduce crime inside prisons (LaVigne, 1994). By removing the rewards for crime, there will be fewer incentives to commit crime. For example, instead of using cash to make purchases inside prison, debit cards can be used. All purchases can be tracked and the purchaser must show proof of purchase to possess an item. An advantage of using SCP measures is that SCP measures do not have to understand the underlying causes of crime. Instead, they focus on the settings for crime.

Indiana's Rehabilitation Programs

The Indiana Department of Correction (IDOC) offers many programs to help rehabilitate offenders (Donahue, 2008). First, IDOC has a division called Prison Enterprises Network (PEN) that employs 1,744 offenders in meaningful jobs. The work provides inmates with job skills and work ethics so that they can function in a self-sustaining manner. Some of the items that PEN offenders make include yo-yos, sweaters, furniture, children's costumes, toilet paper, and pallets.

Second, in 2007, thousands of Indiana offenders provided 919,371 hours of community service (Donahue, 2008). The value was estimated at $5.3 million. This included roadside trash pickup, clean-up of state parks, clean-up of state and county fair locations, tree planting in city parks, and landscaping in military bases.

Third, IDOC offers many vocational classes (Donahue, 2008). These classes include automotive mechanics, automotive body repair, agricultural mechanics, computer aided design, barbering/ cosmetology, business finance, graphic arts, culinary arts, marketing, welding, equine, and engine repair.

Fourth, IDOC offers addiction treatment classes, which 12,148 offenders utilized in 2007 (Donahue, 2008). These classes include 1) Clean Lifestyle is Freedom Forever, which is a specialized therapeutic community to help treat methamphetamine addiction, 2) Integrity and Purpose Units, which help with addictions other than methamphetamine, and 3) outpatient substance abuse programs, which help offenders whose substance abuse is less severe.

Fifth, IDOC offers education programs (Donahue, 2008). These include Literacy Education, which aims to ensure that offenders can at least read their certificates when they complete the class (there were 1,949 students in 2006-2007), general education development, which is equivalent to a high school diploma (there were 2,002 students in 2006-2007), college degrees (there were 2,070 students in 2006-2007), and technical certificate classes for specific occupations.

Sixth, IDOC offers classes to help build an offender's sense of responsibility (Donahue, 2008). These classes include a purposeful living program, which is a faith based program (enrollment in 2007 was 1,200), a fatherhood program, which provides the tools for an offender to become a more responsible parent (enrollment in 2007 was 453), and animal rehabilitation programs, which allow for the training of dogs and horses so that they can be adopted as pets (there were more than 293 participants in 2006-2007).

Seventh, IDOC offers programs that give back to the community (Donahue, 2008). For example, in 2006-2007, inmates fixed 1,356 bicycles for persons who needed this kind of transportation. In addition, they fixed wheelchairs for the disabled (there were 7 inmates employed in this program).

Eighth, IDOC offers sex offender treatment programs (Donahue, 2008). The offenders are taught that they are accountable for their own actions. The program also assists sex offenders in obtaining residence, employment, and support services. In 2006-2007, there were 1,932 Indiana inmates who participated in sex offender treatment.

Ninth, IDOC offers mental health programs to a large number of inmates (Donahue, 2008). A chronic care unit is available for severely mentally ill inmates and a suicide watch program is implemented system-wide. In fact, "the Indiana Department of Correction is the largest provider of mental health services in the state of Indiana" (Donahue, p. 83).

Finally, parole may be offered to inmates (Office of Code Revision Indiana Legislative Services Agency, n.d.). According to IC 35-50-6-1, when a person who has been sentenced for a felony is released early, due to credit time earned, the person shall be placed on parole until the fixed term expires, not to exceed 24 months. Parole is an incentive to rehabilitate.

In sum, these programs are offered to help rehabilitate offenders so that they can assume their responsibilities when they are released back into the community. When inmates are believed to have reformed, and when they are ready to be released back into society, they may be released on parole (Seiter, 2008). With this hope of early release, inmates may try to self-improve in order to meet parole standards.

References

Adams, W. (1999). The interpermeation of self and world: Empirical research, existential phenomenology, and transpersonal psychology. *Journal of Phenomenological Psychology, 30*(2), 39-65.

Akers, R.L., & Sellers, C. (2009). *Criminological theories: Introduction, evaluation, and application* (5th ed.). New York, NY: Oxford University Press.

Albright, (2007, October 5). *Law suit involving town board members and deputy marshal.* Letter mass mailed to residents of Orland, Indiana.

Allen, C. (2011, July 11). *The Indiana State Police facade*. Electronic letter mailed to Indiana state employees on July 11, 2011.

American Civil Liberties Union (2008, August 6). *ACLU releases report on racial profiling in Louisiana.* Retrieved from http://www.aclu.org/racialjustice/racialprofiling/36358prs20080806.html

AR15.com (2009, Oct 21). *Indiana state trooper involved in home invasion . . . faces life in prison.* Retrieved from http://www.ar15.com/forums/t_1_5/944698_.html&page=1

Associated Press (2013, Aug. 29). *Indiana trooper formally charged in gun-waving case*. Retrieved from http://www.dailyherald.com/article/20130828/news/708289883/

Balian, E.S. (1988). *How to design, analyze, and write doctoral or master's research* (2nd ed.). New York, NY: University Press of America.

Bartol, C., and Bartol, A. (2008). Criminal behavior: A psychosocial approach (8th ed.). Upper Saddle River, NJ: Prentice Hall.

Bellantoni, C. (2005). Officials failed to deport alien. *Washington Times,* A01.

Berg, B.L. (2007). *Qualitative research methods for the social sciences* (6th ed.). Boston, MA: Pearson.

Boulard, G. (2006). Immigration-left to the states. *State Legislatures, 32*(9), 14-17.

Buckley, W., Nadelmann, E., Schmoke, K., McNamara, J., Sweet, R., Szasz, T., et al. (1996). The war on drugs is lost. *National Review, 48*(2), 34-48.

Byrne, J. (n.d.). *Commission on safety and abuse in America's prisons: Summary of testimony.* Retrieved from http://www.prisoncommission.org/

Carter, D. (2002). *Issues in police-community relations: Taken from The Police and the community* (7th ed.). Boston, MA: Pearson Custom Publishing.

Castaneda, R. (2006, Sept. 27). MS-13's primary goal is killing, prosecutor says at start of trial. *Washington Post.*

Champion, D. (2006). *Research methods for criminal justice and criminology* (3rd ed.). Upper Saddle River, NJ: Pearson Merrill Prentice Hall.

Cosby, R. (2006, Feb 13). 'MS-13' is one of nation's most dangerous gangs. *MSNBC*. Retrieved from *http://www.msnbc.msn.com/id/11240718/*

Creswell, J.W. (2009). *Research design: Qualitative, quantitative, and mixed methods approaches* (3rd ed.). Los Angeles, CA: Sage.

Cunningham, M. (2008). Institutional misconduct among capital murderers. In M. Delisi, and P. Conis (Eds.), *Violent offenders: Theory, research, public policy, and practice* (p. 237-253). Boston, MA: Jones and Barlett Publishers.

Davis v. Whitesell, No. 10-2617 (7th Cir. July 5, 2011).

Del Carmen, R.V. (2010). *Criminal procedures: Laws & practice* (8th ed.). Belmont, CA: Wadsworth.

DeLisi, M., and Vaughn, M. (2008). Still psychopathic after all these years. In M. Delisi, and P. Conis (Eds.), *Violent offenders: Theory, research, public policy, and practice* (p. 155-168). Boston, MA: Jones and Barlett Publishers.

Donahue, D. (2008). *Indiana department of correction 07 annual report*. Retrieved from http://www.in.gov/idoc/

Farah, J. (2007). Declare war on MS-13. *WorldNetDaily.* Retrieved from *http://www.worldnetdaily.com/news/article.asp?ARTICLE_ID=54768*

Farah, J. (2006). Illegal aliens murder 12 Americans daily. *WorldNetDaily.* Retrieved from *http://wnd.com/*

Fein, M.L. (2000). Race relations: A survey of potential intervention strategies. *Sociological Practice: A Journal of Clinical and Applied Sociology, 2*(3), 147-162.

Florida Gang Investigators Association (2007). Gang-related information. *The Official Florida Gang Investigators Association.* Retrieved from *http://www.fgia.com/*

Fritz, J.M. (2002). Community matters. In R. Straus (Ed.), *Using sociology: An introduction from the applied and clinical perspectives* (3rd ed.) (p. 235-264). New York, NY: Rowman & Litterfield Publishers, Inc.

Getts, M. (2011, July 10). *Trooper resigned because of traffic policies.* KPCnews.com

Glesne, C. (2006). *Becoming qualitative researchers: An introduction* (3rd ed.). Boston, MA: Pearson.

Harrisonburg Police Department (2008). Charge gang task force. *Harrisonburg Police Department* web site. Retrieved from *http://www.harrisonburgva.gov/*

Hatch, J. (2002). *Doing qualitative research in education settings.* Albany, NY: State University of New York.

Hensley, W. (1996). A theory of the valenced other: The intersection of the looking-glass-self and social penetration. *Social Behavior and Personality, 24*(3), 293-308.

Human Rights Watch (1998). *Behind bars in Brazil.* Retrieved from http://www.hrw.org/sites/default/files/related_material/BRAZL98D.pdf

Indiana Department of Correction. (n.d.). *Adult offender handbook.* State of Indiana: Author

Indiana State Police (2011). *Discipline actions: Quarterly report October-December, 2010.* Report generated and distributed by Indiana State Police management.

Iowa National Education for Women's Leadership (n.d.). Changing the face of leadership [Brochure]. University of Iowa: Author.

Keys to Safer Schools.com (1999). Worst of the Worst. *Safer Schools News, 96*. Retrieved from *http://www.keystosaferschools.com/ms-13.htm*

Kivlan, T. (2007). Federal failure on immigration opens doors for localities. *CongressDaily.*

Klein, I. (1997). *Law of evidence for criminal justice professionals* (4th ed.). Belmont, CA: Wadsworth.

Knowles, G. (1999). Male rape: A search for causation and prevention. *The Howard Journal, 38*(3), 267-282.

Kraska, P. (2004). *Theorizing criminal justice: Eight essential orientations*. Long Grove, IL: Waveland Press, Inc.

Lama, D. (2014, Oct 24). *David Camm files lawsuit against Floyd County alleging he was framed for murder.* WDRB. Retrieved from http://www.wdrb.com/

LaVigne, N. (1994). Rational choice and inmate disputes over phone use on Rikers Island. *Crime Prevention Studies*, 3.

Leedy, P., & Ormrod, J. (2005). *Practical research: Planning and design* (8th ed.). Upper Saddle River, NJ: Pearson Merrill Prentice Hall.

Levin, Y. (2007). Fixing immigration. *Commentary, 123*(5), 49-54.

Lewis, B. (2010, Dec 01). *Former commander of ISP toll road post arrested.* Retrieved from http://www.wndu.com/home/headlines/Former_commander_of_ISP_toll_road_post_arrested_111044914.html

Liska, A. and Messner, S. (1999). *Perspectives on Crime and Deviance* (3rd ed.). Upper Saddle River, NJ: Prentice Hall.

Long, B., & Yerington, C. (2006). Police administrators in Indiana: A descriptive study of attitudes, perceptions, and stressors. *Internet Journal of Criminology*, 1-23.

Maiorano, K. (2011, May 25). *Former trooper charged with felony.* Retrieved from http://www.wlfi.com/

McLemore, D. (2006, Oct 29). MS-13 gang seen as growing threat. *The Dallas Morning Star.*

Miller, M.R., Schultz, D.O., & Hunt, D.D. (2011). *Police patrol.* Mason, OH: Cengage.

Nesarajah, V. (2006). Minority issues in charlotte: gang related issues – ms-13. *University of Wisconsin.* Retrieved from *http://www.uwec.edu*

Office of Code Revision Indiana Legislative Services Agency (n.d.). *Indiana code 35-50-6. Chapter 6. Release from imprisonment and credit time.* Retrieved from https://iga.in.gov/legislative/laws/2014/ic/

Peak, K. (2007). *Justice administration: Police, courts, and corrections management* (5th ed.). Upper Saddle River, NJ: Pearson Prentice Hall.

Peak, K.J., Gaines, L.K., & Glensor, R.W. (2010). *Police supervision and management in an era of community policing* (3rd ed.). Upper Saddle River, NJ: Prentice Hall.

Poe, C. (Executive Producer) & Poe, C. & Parker, G. (Writers). (2006). *World's most dangerous gang* [Motion Picture]. United States: National Geographic.

Ponterotto, J. (2005). Qualitative research in counseling psychology: A primer on research paradigms and philosophy of science. *Journal of Counseling, 52*(2), 126-136.

Rader, J. (2011, July 14). *Department morale.* Letter distributed by Indiana State Police Alliance.

Robinette, P.D, and Straus, R.A. (2002). Sociology of the individual and the group: Social psychology. In R. Straus (Ed.), *Using sociology: An introduction from the applied and clinical perspectives* (3rd ed.) (p. 89-121). New York, NY: Rowman & Litterfield Publishers, Inc.

Schmalleger, F. (2007). *Criminal justice today: An introductory text for the 21st century* (9th ed.). Upper Saddle River, NJ: Pearson Prentice Hall.

Schmalleger, F. (2011). *Criminology: A brief introduction.* Upper Saddle River, NJ: Prentice Hall.

Seiter, R. (2008). *Corrections: An introduction* (2nd ed.). Upper Saddle River, NJ: Pearson Prentice Hall.

Shusta, R., Levine, D., Harris, P., and Wong, H. (2002). *Multicultural law enforcement: Strategies for a peacekeeping in a diverse society* (2nd ed.). Upper Saddle River, NJ: Prentice Hall.

South Bend Tribune (2006, November 1). *Indiana State Police officer charged with fraud and forgery.*

State of Indiana (2008). *Offender population statistical report May 2008*. Retrieved from http://www.in.gov/idoc/

State police trooper charged with groping woman during traffic stop. The Elkhart Truth. 2014, Oct. 4). Retrieved from http://www.elkharttruth.com/news/2010/09/02/State-Police-trooper-charged-with-groping-woman-during-traffic-stop.html

Straus, R. (2002). Using sociological theory to make practical sense out of social life. In R. Straus (Ed.), *Using sociology: An introduction from the applied and clinical perspectives* (3rd ed.) (p. 21-43). New York, NY: Rowman & Litterfield Publishers, Inc.

Timmins, D. (2008). Prosecuting criminal predators. In M. Delisi, and P. Conis (Eds.), *Violent offenders: Theory, research, public policy, and practice* (p. 221-235). Boston, MA: Jones and Barlett Publishers.

Towle, A. (2008, July 31). *Indiana troopers fired for assault on gay bar patron*. Retrieved from http://www.towleroad.com/2008/07/indiana-trooper.html

Trojanowicz, Kappeler, & Gaines (2002). *Community policing: A contemporary perspective* (3rd ed.). Cincinnati, OH: Anderson Publishing.

Tucker, J., Donovan, D., and Marlatt, G. (Eds.). (1999). *Changing additive behavior: Bridging clinical and public health strategies*. New York: Guilford Press.

Ulmer, J. (2000). Commitment, deviance, and social control. *The Sociological Quarterly, 41*(3).

U.S. Department of Homeland Security (2004). *Law course for customs and border protection officers.* Longwood, FL: Gould.

U.S. Office of National Drug Control Policy (2007). *Funding.* Retrieved from http://www.whitehousedrugpolicy.gov/

Vold, G., Bernard, T., and Snipes, J. (2002). *Theoretical criminology* (5th ed.). New York, NY: Oxford University Press.

Walinsky, A. (1995). The crisis of public order. *The Atlantic Monthly, 276*(1), 39-54.

Walker, S., Spohn, C., and DeLone, M. (2007). *The color of justice: Race, ethnicity, and crime in America* (4th ed.). Belmont, CA: Thomson Wadsworth.

Walters, G. (2008). Criminal predatory behavior in the Federal Bureau of Prisons. In M. Delisi, and P. Conis (Eds.), *Violent offenders: Theory, research, public policy, and practice* (p. 191-203). Boston, MA: Jones and Barlett Publishers.

Weber, R. (2004). The rhetoric of positivism versus interpretivism: A personal view. *MIS Quarterly, 28*(1), iii-xii.

Werner, Z. (2007). FBI targets ms-13 street gang. *The Online NewsHour*. Retrieved from http://www.pbs.org/

Whisenand, P.M. (2011). *Supervising police personnel: The fifteen responsibilities* (7th ed.). Upper Saddle River, NJ: Prentice Hall.

Whitesell, P. (2011, August 30). *Disciplinary actions – finding and order.* Indiana State Police, Indianapolis, IN.

WISHTV.com (2010, August 12). *ISP trooper quits after internal review.* Retrieved from http://www.wishtv.com/

WTHR.com (2013, Oct. 11). *State police officer arrested, charged with sex offenses.* Retrieved from http://www.wthr.com/story/23673428/2013/10/11/state-police-officer-arrested-charged-with-sex-offenses

Zoomerang (2010). Retrieved from http://zoomerang.com/

Chapter 7

INDIVIDUALS WITH DISABILITIES

General Practices for Interviewing People with Disabilities

When a police officer interviews a person with has a disability, it is important to talk directly to the individual without appearing to be uncomfortable (Indiana Protection, 2008). If the person appears to be confused and agitated, it might be wise to discontinue the use of sirens and emergency lights, if possible. An officer should identify herself and explain the reason why she is there. Use a steady, calm voice. Ask simple, direct questions. Be prepared to repeat any of the questions, if necessary.

If the person has a caregiver, seek to gain the caretaker's assistance to help ensure that the person with the disability understands the requests (Indiana Protection, 2008). It is important not to jump to conclusions when working with someone with a disability. For example, a person who has a physical disability may be mistaken for someone who is under the influence of alcohol. Agitation due to the inability to understand, or from being understood, could be misinterpreted for aggressive, challenging behavior. It is important to look and ask for any identification and medical alert bracelets, which could provide emergency contact information. Do not assume a person with a physical disability has an intellectual disability.

Before assisting a person with a disability, the officer should first found out, in a direct manner, the way in which the person can be assisted (Indiana Protection, 2008). This is important because each disability can be different. Do not assume that a person needs help solely on the fact that the person has a disability.

Interviewing People with Intellectual Disabilities

Individuals with intellectual disabilities may not be able to understand the importance of the police officer's role in a particular situation (Indiana Protection, 2008). They may not understand the seriousness of their actions and they may appear to be nonsensical in how they discuss the situation. They may not understand what they have agreed to in the interview, and they may say anything in order to gain the approval of the officer involved in the interview.

Individuals who have intellectual disabilities may be unsure of what they remember and they may give confusing answers (Indiana Protection, 2008). It is important to allow enough time for them to think about what they are being asked. The officer may have to use illustrations or to point to objects to ensure that the individuals are able to follow the questions. In order to maintain rapport and cooperation, it is crucial to avoid using "baby talk" when talking with a person who has an intellectual disability. Use simple, direct sentences, speak at a moderate pace, and ask one question at a time.

Interviewing Individuals with Autism Disorders

Autism is a disorder in which social and communication skills are impaired (Indiana Protection, 2008). The ability of the person to communicate is often limited; the person may demonstrate no verbal ability. Instead, the person may rely on gestures or repeated phrases. The person may make limited eye contact and could interpret any colloquial phrases in a literal manner. Individuals with autism may show signs of distress or erratic behavior for no observable reason and they can be very sensitive to touch and excessive lighting. Individuals with autism may not comprehend the consequences of their actions or understand their legal rights. They may have trouble remembering details of situations and may not understand the questions being asked of them.

In order to best assist individuals with autism, the officer should speak clearly and slowly and should ask direct and simple questions (Indiana Protection, 2008). In some cases, it may be best to remove them from situations in which there is a high level of visual and auditory stimulation. In addition, unless it is dangerous behavior, the officer should not stop them from performing repetitive motions. If the officer does, this may escalate their erratic behaviors.

Interviewing Individuals with Mental Illness

If an individual begins to act strange and show odd behaviors, it is best to ask the person if he or she has any mental health issues (Indiana Protection, 2008). Ask the question in the most respectful manner possible, but be prepared for the person to avoid giving an answer or denying any problem. The stigma of mental illness is quite severe in U.S. culture and most people will want to avoid that particular label.

If the person acknowledges having a mental illness, it is important to not overwhelm the person with questions (Indiana Protection, 2008). Keeping questions clear and short may produce optimal results. Give the person ample physical space in order to keep him or her from feeling cornered or trapped.

Interviewing Individuals with Visual Impairment

When dealing with individuals who are experiencing visual impairment, it is best for officers to announce their presence before entering the area (Indiana Protection, 2008). If another person enters the room, the officers should tell the person with the visual impairment who has entered the room and the reason for the arrival. Avoid speaking louder to the person (they are not hearing impaired). Any written information will need to be orally communicated to the visually impaired person.

If assistance is offered to a visually impaired person, the officer should avoid grabbing the person's arm to guide him or her (Indiana Protection, 2008). The officer should ask the person to describe the assistance needed. The officer should offer her arm to the visually impaired person to hold for guidance and should let the person know if he or she is approaching areas such as stairs, narrow hallways, or other challenging areas. When guiding the person to a place to sit, the officer should place the person's hand on the back of the chair.

Interviewing Individuals with Hearing Impairments

Interviewing individuals with hearing impairments can create a series of challenges, particularly when a sign language interpreter is not available (Indiana Protection, 2008). Some people with hearing impairments are not deaf; they may simply be hard of hearing. A hearing aid is not a sign that the person can fully hear and understand what is being said. Some individuals can read lips.

If someone is deaf, written communications can be very useful, as long as the officer and person with the hearing problem understand the same language (Indiana Protection, 2008). When an officer interviews a person with a hearing problem, the officer should face the person directly and should speak in a clear voice with a normal tone. Do not shout at the person. Attempt to reduce any noise in the background that could inhibit communications. Utilize writing, if possible. Write clearly and give the person enough time to read and process the questions.

A person with hearing problems may appear to be extremely confused or disoriented; this should not automatically be taken as aggressive and oppositional behavior (Indiana Protection, 2008). If a person with a severe hearing impairment is the focus of an investigation, it is important to remember that only a certified sign language interpreter should be utilized when the Miranda warning is given.

Following is a summary of how police officers should respond to individuals with disabilities (Indiana Protection and Advocacy Services, 2008). Individuals with disabilities may be suspects, victims, or witnesses. Some disabilities are easily recognizable while other disabilities are not easily recognizable. Most people with disabilities react the same way to law enforcement situations as does the general public. Some will need special accommodations specific to their disabilities.

Police Officers Encountering Individuals With Disabilities

- General tips for all people with disabilities
- Intellectual Disabilities
- Autism/Autism Spectrum Disorder
- Epilepsy
- Cerebral palsy
- Mobile Impairments
- Mental Illness
- Visual Impairment/Blind
- Hearing Impairment/Deaf
- People with Service Animals
- Other Disabilities/conditions
- Helpful Resources

General Tips

- Refer to the individual before the disability.
- For example:
- Correct: I am speaking to a person who is blind.
- Incorrect: I am speaking to a blind person.
- Check for hearing aid; see if it is working.
- Ask simply questions; wait for a response.
- Give one direction at a time; too many directions may confuse the person.
- Provide simple choices; some individuals may only respond to the last choice.
- Explain written documents in easy to understand terms (this includes the Miranda warning).
- Before seeking assistance from a caregiver, the officer should find out from the person the help that is needed.
- Every person and every disability is unique.
- Respect the individuals' independence as much as possible; allow them to move on their own, if possible.
- Ask the individuals if they need help before help is provided.
- If possible, gather all of the person's medications before the person is moved from a location.
- Collect needed communication devices (speech synthesizers, alphabet board, head pointer, etc.).
- Department should provide contact information for support personnel who can assist with a variety of disabilities.

Interpreting Behavior

- Be cautious about interpreting behaviors because different conditions may exhibit similar characteristics. For example, a person with cerebral palsy may appear to be intoxicated.
- Non-compliant behavior may be due to a lack of understanding or due to fear.
- Some individuals may require extra time to process what is happening and to respond.
- Person may have an ID bracelet, emergency medical card, or a medical alert bracelet.
- Officer should seek assistance from the person's caregiver, who may understand the person's needs and method of communicating.

Police Response	
If the individual	***Police officer should...***
Does not seem to understand	Reword questions using different and easier words; use direct and concrete phrases; if no improvement, check for hearing loss.
Seems preoccupied	Get the attention of the person before asking questions.
Cannot seem to concentrate	Be brief and repeat directions.
Agitated or over-stimulated	Be calm, remove distractions, and give firm and clear directions.
Is displaying poor judgment	Not expect to engage in rational conversation.
Is having trouble with reality	Be simple, direct, and truthful.
Is delusional	Ignore delusions and do not argue. Redirect thoughts to current situation.

Is disoriented/confused	Check for hearing loss. If no hearing loss, redirect thoughts to current situation. Give one direction at a time and use direct and clear phrases.
Is fearful	Reassure the person that he or she is safe.
Seems to be changing emotions	Remain calm and ignore change in emotions.

Intellectual Disabilities

- Individuals with intellectual disabilities strongly object to the term "mental retardation"
- Officers should call it "intellectual disability"
- Individuals may not understand the seriousness of their actions
- Individuals may not understand their Constitutional rights
- They may easily be persuaded by others
- They may eagerly confess in order to please officer
- Allow extra time for person to process information and to respond.
- Treat the person with dignity and respect (do not use baby talk).
- Use short sentences and simple words.
- Point at pictures and objects to illustrate words.
- Make eye contact with the person; use the person's name often.
- Look for an identification card, which may provide contact information.
- Give one direction or ask one question at a time.
- Ask the person to repeat the direction/question in his or her own words to assess the person's understanding.
- Tell the person how long the encounter is expected to last and when things will return to normal (if known).
- Using a watch to indicate time may be meaningless to the person. Tie time to common everyday events, such as breakfast or lunch.
- Clearly indicate when the person may contact other people (family members, case managers, etc.).

Autism/Autism Spectrum Disorder

- Communication and social skills impaired
- May not be initially obvious
- Individual may be non-verbal or have limited verbal skills
- Individual may have difficulty expressing needs
- Individual may gesture or point instead of speaking
- Individual may repeat phrases instead of communicating conventionally
- Individual may appear deaf; may not respond to verbal cues
- Individual may make little, if any, eye contact
- Individual may interpret language in a literal manner

  For example: if asked if they want to waive their Miranda warning, they may wave their hand

- Officers should avoid using words that have multiple meanings
- In a criminal justice scenario, person may not understand consequence of his or her actions
- Individual may have hard time remembering facts and details
- Individual may not understand what he is agreeing to
- Individual may not provide credible responses
- Individual with autism do feel pain
- Individual may display extreme distress for no apparent reason
- Individual may show no fear of danger
- Individual may exhibit inappropriate giggling
- Individual may engage in self-stimulating behavior (body rocking, repeating phrases, etc.)
- Individual may be extremely sensitive to sound, light, or touch

Interacting with a Person who has Autism/Autism Spectrum Disorder

- Speak slowly and clearly
- Use simple language; rephrase as necessary
- Explain what is going to happen before it happens, at every step
- People with autism have difficulty with change; they prefer the routine
- Person may have trouble concentrating in highly-stimulating area
- Officer may have to lead the person to a quiet area
- Approach individuals from front because they startle easily
- Do not shout or touch the person; talk in calm voice
- Do not encroach upon the individual's personal space
- Allow repetitive movements (biting self, body rocking, flickering an object) unless it is a safety concern; intervention can escalate behaviors

Individuals with Epilepsy

- Episodic medical condition in which individuals have no control; seizure activity in brain
- Seizure may cause person to act strangely; may cause disturbance
- May affect speech, consciousness, and movement
- Person may not be able to respond or interact normally during seizure or for quite a while afterward
- Person may be confused and disoriented and may not be able to understand officer

Seizure Symptoms

- Spitting
- Running
- Biting
- Shouting/Screaming
- Flailing movements
- Abusive language

Partial Seizure Symptoms

- Eyes flutter
- Blank stare
- Acts dazed

Interacting with Person who has Epilepsy

- Check for medical identification bracelet
- Note length of seizure; seizure more than 5 minutes could be a medical emergency
- If seizure > 5 minutes, have person transported to hospital
- If it is known that the person has epilepsy, assume observed behaviors are seizure-related
- Some individuals have a Vagus Nerve Stimulator (VNS) to help control seizures; it is an implant just under the skin in the upper chest
- Person may have Patient Emergency Medical Card and Cyberonics Magnet; follow instructions on card
- Do not forcibly restrain person during seizure or just after seizure
- Restraints may injure the person
- Person may perceive such actions as an attack
- Person may try to protect self by forcibly resisting
- If person has seizure while in custody, provide medical attention
- If person has convulsive seizure, place person on side to prevent choking
- Do not place anything in person's mouth (to hold tongue down)
- Hog-tying, placing a person face down, or using a choke hold on a person who is having a seizure or who has just had a seizure can obstruct breathing and cause death
- Failure to provide medication in a timely manner to a person with epilepsy could produce fatal rebound seizures

Person with Cerebral Palsy

- Disorder caused by damage to the brain
- Affects ability to control movements and posture
- May vary from mild to extreme
- Mild cerebral palsy impacts balance and may make the person appear to be intoxicated or under the influence of drugs
- Severe cerebral palsy will alter major motor activities

Cerebral Palsy

- Sometimes associated with other problems, such as epilepsy, hearing problems, vision problems, or intellectual problems
- Do not assume person with cerebral palsy has intellectual disability
- Do not assume the person is intoxicated
- If have difficulty understanding the person's speech, slow down and ask one question at a time
- Give person time to respond; ask person to repeat, if necessary
- If person is using communication board or other communication device, allow the person time to communicate
- If person has a mobility or intellectual problem, deal with those issues too

Interacting with Individuals with Mobility Impairment

- Do not make assumptions about the mobility limitations
- Communicate with person about ability to move about
- Two individuals may be using mobility devices for different reasons (one may use them to alleviate pain while moving about and one may need them to move about)
- If conversation will take several minutes, sit down and speak with the individual at eye level
- If the officer needs to move the individual out of the wheelchair, the officer should ask the individual about the most effective way to accomplish this task
- Placing individual in police car may not be safe
- Consider using a van suitable for transporting an individual in a wheelchair
- Individuals who use wheelchairs are trained to move about
- Officer should offer assistance but should provide only what the individuals request
- If individual is placed into a paddy wagon, officer should ensure individual knows how to hold onto the railing when handcuffed
- Officer should not assume that an individual who has a mobility impairment has an intellectual impairment
- Officer should speak normally to the individual
- Only move the individual when required; inform the individual what needs to be done
- Use care when removing individuals from their mobility devices because it may cause harm

Interacting with Individuals with Mental Illness

- Individual with a mental illness may become confused
- Individual may exhibit bizarre behavior
- Officer should ask person about mental health issues
- Individual may refuse to discuss personal health concerns
- Officer should use simple, clear, and brief language
- Officer should address one item at a time
- If individual becomes agitated, move to a quiet area
- Officer should speak calmly and should give individual plenty of space
- Officer should keep focused on the purpose of the assignment
- If remove individuals from site, let them bring along their prescription medications

Interacting with Individuals with Visual Impairments/Blind

- Some individuals are legally blind but still have some sight; others are totally sightless
- Officer should speak out and announce presence before entering area
- Officer should announce when people enter and leave the area
- Officer should announce if bystanders are around
- Visual impairment does not equate to hearing impairment; thus, speak normally and do not avoid words like "see" and "look"
- Do not touch the person unless assistance is needed
- Officer may need to let individual grasp arm for guidance
- Individual may walk slightly behind the officer to gauge the officer's reactions to obstacles
- Officer should announce doors, steps, etc.
- When about to sit down, officer should place the individual's hand on back of the chair
- Officer will have to read out loud any written information

Interacting with Individuals with Hearing Impairments/Deaf

- There are varying degrees of hearing impairment; some are totally deaf
- Hearing aids may increase volume, which includes background noise, and may not necessarily enhance clarity
- Individuals may not understand what is being said
- Officer may have to communicate by written means; some may not understand English
- Some individuals may read lips, others may require a sign language interpreter
- When entering a room, officer should toggle lights to get the individual's attention
- Officer should get the individual's attention before speaking
- Officer should face the individual when speaking and should not obstruct mouth
- Officer should reduce background noise and speak slowly and normally
- If interpreter is present, officer should make eye contact with the individual and not with the interpreter
- Officer may be able to write down information
- One officer should communicate at a time
- Officer may use hand gestures as visual cues
- Individual may appear confused as a result of miscommunication
- Miranda warning should be provided by a certified sign language interpreter

Individuals with Service Animals

- There are many different kinds of animals that are used to assist individuals with disabilities
- Service animal = dog or other common domestic animal specifically trained to assist person with a disability
- Animals may help with psychiatric, cognitive, and mental disabilities
- Service animals ≠ wild animals, farm animals, rabbits, reptiles, ferrets, rodents, amphibians
- Service animals provide services that include guiding individuals who are visually impaired, alerting individuals who are hearing impaired, pulling wheel chairs, fetching items, warning individuals when they are about to have a seizure, retrieving the phone or medications, assisting individuals with navigation
- Animals that provide comfort, emotional support, therapeutic benefits, and emotional support are companion animals and not service animals
- Service animals should be moved with the owner
- The owner must have control over the service animal
- The service animal can be removed if it is a threat
- Seek the owner's permission before touching the animal or speaking to the animal
- Use the leash, if required to move the animal
- An individual who employs a service animal is not required to show an officer proof that a service animal is required
- Officer may ask about the service that the animal provides to the individual
- If have doubt about the legitimacy of the service animal, investigate with a supervisor later

Individuals with Communication Impairments

- Individuals may stutter or may have had a stroke
- Officer should slow down and ask one question at a time
- Individuals may use an electronic communication board
- Officer should provide the individual enough time to use the board and to answer the questions

Individuals with Traumatic Brain Injury

- Individuals with traumatic brain injury may perceive information differently than the officer
- Individual may be argumentative or belligerent
- Officer needs to keep the individual focused on the issue at hand
- Officer should slow down, ask one question at a time, and allow enough time for response

Individuals with Tourette's Syndrome

- Individual may display frequent and repetitive movements of face, arms, and limbs
- Individual may have vocal tics
- Individual may involuntarily swear

Behavioral Disturbance

- Individual who displays a medical or psychiatric problem and is a safety concern should be evaluated by medical personnel

Reference

Indiana Protection and Advocacy Services (2008). *TIPS for law enforcement and corrections personnel: Encounters involving people with disabilities*. Indianapolis, IN.

Chapter 8

DISADVANTAGED PEOPLE

Immigrants

Years ago, America was considered a melting pot of many different kinds of people (Ryan & Cooper, 2007). Immigrants were expected to give up their language and customs so that they could be assimilated into the dominant American culture. However, many cultural groups have maintained their own identities after moving to America; various cultures have maintained their unique customs and beliefs. Thus, instead of a melting pot where all cultures blend into one identity, America can better be described as a mosaic of cultures. Police officers need to appreciate cultural differences in order to better serve the public.

Police officers may encounter several problems while trying to help immigrants. The first problem may be the language barrier. Because the number of immigrants entering the U.S. is increasing, police officers have a greater possibility of encountering persons who do not speak English (Shah, Rahman, & Khashu, 2007). If officers cannot effectively communicate with the people that they serve, then they cannot effectively perform their duties. However, there are several ways to help resolve the language barrier. First, the department can train officers in the language of interest by providing them with a working knowledge of the language (e.g., having the officers learn the words that they will most likely encounter). Second, summary sheets of commonly used words and hand held language translators can be provided to the officers to help them in the field. Finally, police departments may pool their resources together so that a live translator can always be available for an entire area.

Another problem is that undocumented aliens may be afraid to cooperate with the local police because they fear that they will be deported (Shattell, Hamilton, Starr, Jenkins, & Hinderliter, 2008). Therefore, it is important for police officers to ease the fears of immigrants by focusing only on the state-related crimes and not on federal immigration issues. The officers can make it clear to the immigrants that it is not their responsibility to enforce immigration laws. Furthermore, the police need to inform immigrants that there are a variety of services available to them, including shelters, hospitals, police services, and legal aid.

Shattell et al. (2008) conducted a qualitative community-based participatory research study that identified the factors that affect a Latino population's perception, access, and use of mental health services. The researchers collected data by employing focus group interviews. The focus group was comprised of 12 members, including seven Latino community members, three nursing students, one public health employee, and a researcher. The findings indicated that, although many Latinos may have mental health problems, the Latinos perceived language barriers and their immigration statuses to be barriers in obtaining needed mental health services. Consequently, the general health of the community may be less than optimal. In short, effective communication is required to help immigrants ease their fears and to help them utilize the social services that are available to them.

Scapegoating Minorities for Profit

If you assume that marijuana became illegal in the U.S. to promote the good health of residents and/or for spiritual/religious reasons, then you have made a wrong assumption. The motives for making marijuana illegal in America were greed and power. African Americans and Hispanics were used as scapegoats for financial gain.

The only reason that marijuana became illegal in the U.S. in the first place was because a small group of people in power arbitrarily defined it that way so that they could protect their own financial interests (Gahlinger, 2004). Being in a capitalistic society, those individuals with power may be encouraged to pass laws that discriminate against different cultures, if the laws prove profitable. The reason why marijuana became illegal in the U.S. was because it was profitable to those in power. Cultural discrimination and the control of information were the mechanisms used to pass the law.

Marijuana is classified by the federal government as an illegal drug. However, marijuana has been in this country for centuries and it is part of the American culture (Gahlinger, 2004). In fact, some people claim that marijuana is no worse than cigarettes or alcohol (Roleff, 2005). Although the federal government has declared a War on Drugs, which includes marijuana, the results are proving similar to the results of the 1920-1933 Prohibition Act against alcohol (Buckley, 1996).

Worldwide there are about 300 million people who smoke marijuana (cannabis), and it is the number one illegally consumed drug within the United States (Earleywine, 2002). In America, an estimated 4,477,000 pounds of marijuana are consumed each year by all age groups. In fact, about 40% of all Americans have smoked it at least once in their lifetime. To give an idea about who is smoking marijuana, in 1999 about one third of all U.S. adults have smoked it, about half of the adults between 18 and 25 years of age have smoked it, and about 19% of those from 12 to 17 years of age have smoked it. Thus, marijuana consumption is a national pastime event.

Records indicate that marijuana has been used for about 4,000 years (Gahlinger, 2004). People would sit in tents, burn marijuana, and inhale the smoke. Several thousand years later in Europe, the Romans served marijuana to guests. However, marijuana was only tolerated when used for medical or religious purposes. When people started to use it for recreational purposes, the public became concerned. In 1484, the Pope condemned marijuana, stating that it was the devil's plant. Consequently, the public put pressure on the government to outlaw marijuana. However, during the 16th century, the demand for hemp, part of the cannabis plant, had significantly increased because of the need for rope, fabric, and paper. Consequently, in 1533, King Henry VIII commanded that farmers use part of their lands to grow cannabis. Because the demand for cannabis continued to grow, Parliament, about one hundred years later, passed laws that granted citizenship to anyone who would grow cannabis. However, this was not enough. In 1611, Britain encouraged the Virginia colonies to grown cannabis. In fact, King James I and King George III both ordered cannabis to be grown in the American colonies. By 1850, there were 8,327 American plantations that grew cannabis.

In 1876, America was celebrating 100 years of independence from Britain in the form of a world exposition in Philadelphia (Yaroschuk, 2000). During this celebration, the Sultan of Turkey introduced the water pipe into America. This pipe was used to smoke marijuana for recreational purposes. Capitalistic American entrepreneurs saw this as a business opportunity and immediately opened Turkish smoking parlors in the north. This attracted people of all types, but attending such parlors was done in secrecy. Although this continued for several decades, alcohol was still the preferred drug. Then, in 1920, Prohibition outlawed the use of alcohol. Consequently, people turned to the use of marijuana as a replacement drug.

During the 1920s, New Orleans was the largest party city in America (Yaroschuk, 2000). New Orleans consisted of many different cultures, which included American, European, French Cajun, Spanish, African American, and Chinese. Jazz music was quite popular in that environment and was directly related to the pleasures of marijuana consumption. Furthermore, marijuana was the only legal drug available in New Orleans, since alcohol was banned. Marijuana cigarettes were commonplace, were relatively cheap, and were socially acceptable. However, the media were about to get involved.

Hemp, collected from the cannabis plant, makes a higher quality paper at a lower cost than does wood pulp (Gahlinger, 2004). Hence, up until the 1880s, hemp was commonly grown. However, because

William Hearst, a huge newspaper publisher at the time, owned millions of acres of woodland, he lobbied to outlaw marijuana. During the 1920s, Hearst linked the marijuana consumption in New Orleans to murder, rape, poverty, and disease (Yaroschuk, 2000). This served two purposes: a) to make money by selling newspapers, and b) to persuade lawmakers in Congress to pass laws outlawing the growing of hemp. Although this did not result in the passage of federal laws outlawing the cultivation of hemp, Louisiana jumped on the opportunity to restrict the use of marijuana, hoping that it would be a means to control the black population.

Then the Great Depression of 1929 hit. Prior to that time, Mexicans in the southwest were considered a welcomed labor force (Gahlinger, 2004; Yaroschuk, 2000). However, once the Great Depression hit, the Mexican labor force was no longer needed. In order to reduce the number of Mexican residents working within the United States, the *San Antonio Gazette* published newspaper articles that stigmatized Mexicans, stating that they commonly used marijuana, which turned them into frenzied and dangerous criminals. The goal of the media was to force Mexicans back to Mexico.

In the early 1930s, there was no federal law that prohibited marijuana use (Gahlinger, 2004; Yaroschuk, 2000). After the Prohibition Act was repealed, Harry Anslinger, who was a lead enforcer of Prohibition laws, became head of the newly formed Federal Bureau of Narcotics. Although Anslinger saw no dangers in the use of marijuana, Texas, California, Arizona, and Colorado pressured Congress to pass marijuana laws in order to reduce the number of Mexicans in their states. Anslinger then visited Hearst and they became allies in the campaign against marijuana. Together, they used the media, in terms of newspapers articles, radio announcements, and films to stigmatize the use of marijuana. By exaggerating the effects of marijuana, by labeling marijuana as Mexico's devil's weed (a foreign product), and by linking marijuana with violent predatory crimes committed by Mexicans toward Americans, this helped feed the fear that already existed due to the Great Depression (Yaroschuk). This pressured Congress to pass the Marihuana Tax Act of 1937. Although this Act did not directly outlaw marijuana possession, it did indirectly outlaw its possession. It accomplished this because in order to legally possess marijuana, a person had to purchase a marijuana stamp. However, the federal government refused to issue any marijuana stamps. Furthermore, the law stated that in order to get a marijuana stamp, one must have the marijuana in hand; however, to have it in hand without the stamp was illegal.

Although the enforcement of marijuana laws had relaxed during World War II, immediately afterwards Anslinger began an aggressive enforcement campaign (Yaroschuk, 2000). In order to get the public's attention, he utilized the media and targeted celebrities, such as movie stars and musicians. However, marijuana consumption continued.

In 1970, America was involved in the Vietnam War. Because President Nixon became concerned that the war may be lost due to drug use by soldiers, he became aggressive toward illegal drug consumption (Gahlinger, 2004; Yaroschuk, 2000). As a result, Congress passed the Comprehensive Drug Abuse Prevention and Control Act of 1970, which is the legal foundation for drug regulation today. In 1972, President Nixon declared the War on Drugs, and, in 1973, he created the Drug Enforcement Administration (DEA). Consequently, the Commissioner of the DEA was immediately sent to

Saigon where he implemented Operation Golden Flow. This required each U.S. soldier to provide a urine sample to be tested for marijuana. If a soldier failed the drug test, then that soldier was not allowed to leave Vietnam. However, in the states, there were 76 million adolescents who were experiencing unprecedented prosperity, who practiced free love, who were rebellious toward the government, and who preferred marijuana as their recreational drug of choice.

Conflicting Points of View

There are two opposing sides to how marijuana is perceived. When evaluating a problem, effective investigation requires that both sides of an argument be objectively examined. In this way, the benefits and the costs of using marijuana can be evaluated.

One side believes that the government must not control the use of marijuana (Roleff, 2005). This side claims that no one has ever died from a marijuana overdose, that marijuana is no different than alcohol or cigarettes, that marijuana could be a safer prescription than other medicines, that marijuana is not addictive, and that laws that ban marijuana have created a black market, which has led to street and gang violence. In addition, marijuana is associated with the peace movement of the 1960s (i.e., the civil rights struggle), the free speech movement, the rise of feminism, and the people's disapproval of the Vietnam War (Spurling & Leonard, 1993). In other words, marijuana consumption is a statement of protest against the establishment. Proof that marijuana is no more dangerous than cigarettes was demonstrated during the 1969 Woodstock concert, where there were about 500,000 people standing in the rain on a 35 acre lot with no food or restrooms. Much marijuana was consumed at Woodstock, yet there was absolutely no violence. Furthermore, if law enforcement agencies do strictly enforce marijuana laws, it is by nature discriminatory. This is true because marijuana consumption in urban areas is overt as compared to the covert use of marijuana in suburb areas. Because police officers have a tendency to arrest the easy targets, they focus on urban residents, who are mostly black minorities. Thus, by default, marijuana enforcement targets minorities. Because about 60% of the people incarcerated in the U.S. are imprisoned due to drugs and alcohol related convictions, marijuana enforcement is inherently unfair (Spurling & Leonard).

On the other hand, some believe that marijuana is dangerous (Roleff, 2005). It is claimed that marijuana, due to improved growing techniques, is about 20 times more potent that it was a generation ago. Furthermore, it is claimed that the use of marijuana impairs cognitive abilities, that it contains hundreds of carcinogens, that it causes respiratory infections and lung disease, that it impairs infants' motor development skills (when breast fed), and that it is both psychologically and physically addictive (Indiana, 1997; Roleff). Furthermore, using marijuana during pregnancy can cause neurological damage to the fetus. Delta-9-tetrahydrocannabinol (THC) is the main chemical in marijuana and it is stored in fatty tissues of the body, which include the brain, liver, lungs, spleen, and reproductive organs. Within the brain, THC can cause permanent damage by widening the synapses gaps, thus decreasing the transmission of communication impulses. This can result in memory and speech problems. In short, THC can damage all of these fatty tissue organs.

Furthermore, marijuana cigarettes purchased on the streets may be impure and contain elements of other substances, such as herbicides or more dangerous drugs (Indiana, 1997). Thus, there are no benefits whatsoever in using marijuana. If this drug were introduced into the market today, a healthy society would not welcome it (Spurling & Leonard, 1993). Moreover, not strictly enforcing marijuana laws can be harmful to society. For instance, if law enforcement agencies do not enforce marijuana laws in the cities, those neighborhoods would be overrun with drug dealers and drug users. Basically, the law-abiding residents who live in these areas and who are unable to escape would effectively be abandoned. Indeed, it is law enforcement's responsibility to protect all people, even the poor.

Another problem is that marijuana users become intoxicated and drive motor vehicles. When driving a car, being intoxicated with marijuana is equivalent to being intoxicated with alcohol. To be charged with operating a vehicle while intoxicated by marijuana, a person's urine only needs to test positive for THC. The urine can test positive for up to 30 days after its use (Erowid, 2011). Driving while intoxicated may lead to the death of innocent people.

Finally, marijuana consumption can impair decision-making abilities, which may lead to casual, unplanned, and unprotected sex (Marr, 1998; Yancey, 2002). This could lead to unwanted pregnancies or to the contraction of sexually transmitted diseases. Thus, smoking marijuana may lead to a lifetime of other concerns.

The media are divided. This is essential because the media have a major impact on the public's and government's perception involving the use of marijuana. The more formal media tend to support the government's point of view, while the informal media tend to oppose the government's point of view.

On the one hand, the news media have stigmatized marijuana and have linked it to predatory and violent crimes (Yaroschuk, 2000). In this case, the media advertise that marijuana is harmful via posters, brochures, radio announcements, and television commercials. With the 1986 drug overdose death of the Boston Celtics' number one draft choice, Len Bias, the media took advantage of this opportunity as a means to generate support for the Partnership for a Drug Free America (Spurling & Leonard, 1993).

On the other hand, there are some media that promote marijuana consumption. There are many songs, websites, and several magazines, such as *High Times*, *Weed World*, *The Cannabis Grow Bible*, and *Cannabis Culture*, which all endorse marijuana use. They distrust the government and the formal news media. For example, in 1936, *Reefer Madness* was used by the formal media as a scare tactic to describe the dangers of smoking marijuana (Roleff, 2005; Spurling & Leonard, 1993). However, because the film overly exaggerated the effects of marijuana use, the formal media lost their credibility; their credibility is still in question today. Consequently, marijuana advocates now transmit their own information using other types of media, such as bumper stickers, tee shirts, music, and magazines.

The War on Drugs cannot be won (Tucker et al., 1999). Because Americans demand illegal substances and are willing to pay a lot of money for them, there will always be someone there to meet that demand. Just as learned during Prohibition, the government can only govern with the consent of those being governed. Thus, to manage the marijuana problem, other strategies are necessary.

Addressing the Problem

There are two approaches that may be implemented to reduce the criminal use of marijuana: a) educate the young on the dangers of marijuana, or b) legalize and restrict marijuana, like cigarettes (Roleff, 2005).

The Indiana State Excise Police department is the law enforcement division within Indiana whose primary goal is to educate school-aged children about the dangers of drug use (Huskey, 2007). As a solution to the marijuana problem, Indiana State Excise Police officers travel from school to school and they present students with information in the form of coloring books, videos, and brochures; they also engage the students in practical exercises. For example, the officers may have the children wear goggles that emulate different levels of intoxication. By having the children wear the goggles and attempt simple tasks, the children will get a better understanding of what it means to be intoxicated. Because childhood is a time of great learning, this is the time to teach them. Indeed, the Indiana State Excise Police believe that preventative medicine is the right medicine. However, marijuana is more than a law enforcement issue; it also involves parents and teachers. As mentioned earlier, positive role models need to encourage children to engage in worthwhile activities. By developing positive relationships, children will come to realize that they are a valuable part of society.

Legalize Marijuana

Since marijuana is already rooted in American culture, it is almost impossible to eliminate it (Spurling & Leonard, 1993). This being the case, the government could legalize and regulate it, like cigarettes. In this way, the government can control and tax it, leading to a healthier society (Roleff, 2005). Currently, the War on Drugs consumes about $75 billion per year in public funds, about $70 billion per year in consumer expenses, about half of all court time, about half of all jail expenses, and the valuable time of about 400,000 police officers (Buckley et al., 1996). This is a lot of resources spent on a war that cannot be won (Tucker et al., 1999). Thus, by legalizing marijuana, much of this money could be saved and applied to other areas. Moreover, by legalizing marijuana, taxes can be collected on it. This will boost the U.S. budget and will create jobs.

Incarcerated Minorities

Although the U.S. has less than 5% of the world's population, it has nearly 25% of the world's total prison population (Liptak, 2008). Having such a large incarceration rate is due, in part, to get tough policies and longer prison sentences (Kelley, Mueller, & Hemmens, 2004). Indeed, at the end of 2007 in the U.S., there were about 2.3 million people incarcerated, 4.2 million people on probation, and 800,000 people on parole (Fears, 2008; McCarthy, 2009). The large number of convicts in the U.S. legal system has resulted in an annual cost of about $45 billion to U.S. taxpayers.

In 2009, for example, the state of Indiana's general population was about 6,423,113 (Stats Indiana, 2010). According to the Indiana Department of Correction (2010a; 2010b) and the Indiana Supreme Court Division (2010), at that same time there were about a) 28,389 adult inmates, b) 810 juvenile inmates, c) 10,955 residents released on parole, and d) about 147,333 residents released on probation. Hence, in 2009 there were about 2,919 per 100,000 Indiana residents on some sort of criminal supervision and the cost was assumed by Indiana taxpayers. The current trend in America is to be tough on crime, but evidence indicates that the public and law makers support crime preventative techniques (Kelley et al., 2004). In fact, most states employ treatment programs as important crime preventative measures.

African Americans and Crime Rate

African Americans are being charged with crimes at an extraordinarily high rate all across the country (McCarthy, 2009). For example, African American males are 660% more likely to be arrested than Caucasian males, and African American females are 350% more likely to be arrested than Caucasian females. In Indiana, for example, African Americans comprise about 9% of the state's total population (Stats Indiana, 2010). However, African American men account for about 39% of the state's adult male prison population, African American women account for about 27% of the state's adult female prison population, and African American juveniles account for about 34% and 24% of the state's juvenile prison population for boys and girls, respectively (Indiana Department of Correction, 2010a). Indeed, there is a high arrest rate and conviction rate for African Americans and it is important to understand the causes.

Racism and the Courts

There are several court rulings that have paved the way for racial conflict. These court rulings have set the stage and have allowed the police to continually stop, investigate, and harass African Americans.

In addition, African Americans have been denied due process in court. For example, in the Calvin Burdine case, the fact that his lawyer was asleep during parts of the trial, and Burdine was still convicted in court, demonstrates the power of the government and how the application of the law may be unfair at times. In this case, the lower courts appeared to be following the letter of the law and not the intent of the law. When this happens, decisions are made that seem irrational.

In 1985, the U.S. Supreme Court ruled in *Tennessee v. Garner* that, under the 4th Amendment, the police may only use deadly force to stop a fleeing suspect if the officer has probable cause to believe that the suspect poses a significant threat of death or serious bodily injury to the officer or to other persons (Oyez Project, 1985). The police can consider a person driving a vehicle at high speeds as dangerous to bystanders. Thus, the police may be able to selectively use deadly force against African Americans by ramming their vehicles. The police just need to articulate why the situation was dangerous.

In 1996, the U.S. Supreme Court ruled in *Whren v. United States* that the police can stop vehicles for violations of the traffic code and any criminal activities discovered as a result of the traffic stops are not unreasonable under the 4th Amendment (Hames & Ekern, 2005). However, because many traffic violations are subjective in nature, this gives the police a free pass to stop African Americans. In other words, pretexual stops are legal (del Carmen, 2010).

In 1999, Michigan passed a law that forbids state trial judges from appointing counsel to criminal defendants after a plea of guilty is made (Oyez Project, 2005). This is significant if the defendant wants to redraw the plea or if there are errors made during the sentencing phase. Although this ruling was overturned in 2005, it is clear that the poor (i.e., minorities) were legally discriminated against.

Racial Profiling Study

According to the American Civil Liberties Union (2008), a year-long racial profiling research study has been performed in Louisiana. The findings indicate that people of color are disproportionately targeted by law enforcement officers. Indeed, people of color are arrested at a higher percentage rate than their representation in the general population, which gives the perception that profiling is taking place.

Use of Force

Because the actual number of incidents related to the use of force depends upon police reports, the actual number may never be known. There may be several reasons why police officers do not report all use of force incidents. These reasons may include a) not wanting to be required to complete additional paperwork, b) not wanting to appear too aggressive to the department and perhaps disciplined, and c) not wanting to advertise possible liability concerns.

Although it may be easy to say that racism and the use of excessive force have no place in law enforcement, it is difficult for a single police officer to do anything about it. For example, if a good police officer makes a complaint against another police officer for racial discrimination, the good officer's career may be in jeopardy. Due to police culture, corrupt officers may band together and start filing bogus complaints against the good officer. Furthermore, the corrupt police officers are smart enough to spread out their complaints so that they do not look suspicious. The complaints are usually subjective in nature (e.g., being rude to the public) so that little defense can be provided. From police management's point of view, corroboration may equate to guilt. Thus, the complaint system may need to be improved.

The use of force is a factor that may impact police-community relations (Hess & Wrobleski, 1997). The police obtain the authority to use force from the same people that they may be required to use that force against. This may have a negative impact on the police-community working relationship. In order to help minimize conflict, the police must educate the public about the legitimate use of force (when it will be used and to what extent). Furthermore, by the police allowing the public to have input on use of force policies, the public will at least understand that the police are acting within appropriate guidelines. Another way to make positive change is to ensure that police management reflects the same racial proportion as the community (Carter, 2002). This will help ensure that the rights of minorities are protected.

Riot: Benton Harbor, Michigan

Introduction

On June 16, 2003, a 28 year old Benton Harbor, Michigan resident, Terrance Shurn, a black male, died as the result of a police chase (Downer, 2003). As he was fleeing police, Shurn crashed his motorcycle into an abandoned house. Because the pursuing officer,

Wes Koza, was perceived to be white, this developed into a racial riot (Race riots, n.d.). This resulted in Berrien County officials declaring a state of emergency (BH riots, 2003). However, although Officer Koza was perceived to be Caucasian, he is actually half Caucasian and half African American, and, according to the U.S. Census Bureau, Koza may be classified as African American (Race riots; U.S. Census Bureau, n.d.). Thus, residents' perception played a key factor in the Benton Harbor riot.

Purpose

Because local residents, who were mostly African Americans, considered that the police had used excessive force during this traffic incident, a riot broke out (CityData, 2008; Race riots). However, upon further examination, it is clear that the racial tension in Benton Harbor had been brewing for years. Indeed, the riot is only a symptom of the local problem. Hence, further investigation is necessary.

Theoretical Framework

There are three theories of crime causation that describe the racial turmoil in Benton Harbor, Michigan. These theories are 1) the social learning theory, 2) the conflict theory, and 3) the strain theory (Siegel, 2003; Vold et al., 2002). African American residents in Benton Harbor claim that the problems in Benton Harbor are the result of Caucasians taking most of the money, jobs, and political power out of Benton Harbor (NEFAC, n.d.). Furthermore, the local police officers, who are mostly white, seem to target black drivers. Hence, crime is due to class conflict, limited resources, and limited job opportunities.

Social Learning Theory

In 1973, Albert Bandura developed his social learning of aggression (Vold et al., 2002). Combining operant conditioning and cognitive psychology, behaviors can be learned and reinforced through personal rewards and punishments; behaviors can also be learned by observing the rewards and punishment of other people. According to Edwin Sutherland, behavior is a social learning process where crime is learned and is a by-product of interaction (Siegel, 2003). Indeed, criminal behaviors are learned in proportion to the duration, frequency, and intensity of the social learning experiences. Furthermore, if the laws are perceived to be unfairly enforced, then individuals will learn "different views on the utility of obeying the legal code" (Siegel, p. 221). Thus, this theory seems relevant in the Benton Harbor incident because the residents feel that they have been discriminated against as a group for a long time. They have learned that if they do nothing, then they will continue to be persecuted.

Conflict Theory

According to the conflict theory, the public disagrees on many social issues, which are usually due to differentials in wealth and power (Barkan, 2006). The most powerful groups gain control of the government and they adopt their values as the legal standards of behavior. Instead of serving the public, those individuals in power pass laws to protect their own self-interests (Vold et al., 2002). Consequently, those people with power are able to pursue their self-interests while those people with less power, usually minorities, are unable to pursue their self-interests because their actions are defined as criminal. This theory seems relevant in the Benton Harbor incident because one of the major complaints of community residents is that Caucasians control the local wealth and legal power.

Strain Theory

In the 1930s, Robert Merton argued that personal goals originate in the culture (Vold et al., 2002). Basically, humans are conforming beings who are strongly influenced by the values and attitudes of the culture in which they live (Bartol & Bartol, 2008). In the U.S., which is a capitalistic society, the cultural goal is to achieve financial success. However, when the legitimate means to achieve this success are blocked, strain and frustration are generated (Siegel, 2003). Consequently, other methods, which may be defined as illegal by the dominant class, must be employed in order to achieve personal goals. This theory seems relevant in the Benton Harbor incident because residents have complained that there are few job opportunities in town and they have little hope of legitimately achieving success.

Statement of the Facts

Police Facts

On June 16, 2003 at about 2:00 am, a Berrien County (Michigan) police officer clocked two high performance motorcycles over 100 mph on U.S. 31 in Royalton Township (Downer, 2003). The county deputy pursued the motorcycles but disengaged because of the high speeds involved. Shortly thereafter, a Benton Township officer, Wes Koza, observed one of the motorcycles as the driver continually disregarded stop signs. Subsequently, Officer Koza began to pursue the motorcycle. Eventually, the pursuit entered the city of Benton

Harbor. According to police, Koza was several blocks behind Shurn when Shurn crashed his motorcycle into an abandoned house. Shurn died at the scene.

Perceived facts (by community residents).

According to local witnesses, Koza rammed his police vehicle into the back of the motorcycle, causing Shurn to lose control of his motorcycle before he crashed into the house (NEFAC, n.d.). After Shurn died, witnesses claim that two officers (one of them being Koza) slapped each other's hand in praise.

Furthermore, according to Jesse Jackson, Benton Harbor's high unemployment rate, the lack of opportunities, and residents' sense of hopelessness are all perceived to have been created by whites (Stevens, 2003). Then, to top it off, the police, the judicial system, and the financial system, which are all under white control, continue to abuse them. The death of a local black youth at the hands of a white police officer is considered by the black community as going too far (NEFAC, n.d.). Indeed, local residents have engaged in rebellion against the government in order to make a statement (Weiner & Kelly, 2003).

Reactions to Incident

On June 17, 2008 at about 8:00 pm, local residents arrived at the Benton Harbor City Hall meeting (Hartzell, 2003; Strode, 2003). They were angry and protested high-speed police pursuit policies. During their complaints, they made threats against the Benton Harbor Police Department. In addition, according to local residents, on that same evening local residents gathered together at the crash site and began praying and singing church songs (Maass & Taylor, 2003). Local residents claim that the police arrived at the scene and told them to break it up and to vacate the premises. Residents claim that this angered them, that they were fed up with the police, and that they were not going to be pushed around anymore. Consequently, at 11:00 pm, street violence broke out (Hartzell, 2003). Residents began throwing bricks and bottles at the police (Ast & Eliasohn, 2003). Soon afterwards, three to four hundred rioters took to the streets. They began to set homes on fire, they shot at police, they dragged people from their cars and set fire to the cars, and they continued to throw rocks and bottles at police officers and firefighters, preventing them from helping victims (Aiken, 2003; Ast & Eliasohn; Hartzell, 2003). The police responded by using tear gas. However, the violence only grew. By the end of the first night, two homes were burned and residents continued to throw rocks and heavy objects at police officers and firefighters (BH riots, 2003).

The next night, residents escalated their acts of violence (BH riots, 2003). They engaged in arson, they overturned cars, they continued to fire guns, and they continued to assault police officers and firefighters. Local law enforcement responded by declaring a state of emergency so that other police agencies would be able to assist. The 17 police officers in Benton Harbor immediately received help from other law enforcement agencies (Aiken, 2003). The Michigan State Police immediately sent 150 troopers. In addition, Berrien County, Van Buren County, Kalamazoo County, and Macomb County sent deputies to the scene. At the same time, local church leaders urged residents to stop the violence. Due to the overwhelming police presence, a third night of violence was prevented.

Overall, the estimated property damage was about $500,000 (Aiken, 2003). Twenty-eight homes were destroyed or damaged and several fire trucks and police cars were damaged. Although some individuals were beaten and stabbed, there were only 15 injuries. Some of the injuries were serious, but there were no fatalities. As a result, there were at least seven arrests.

Analysis of the Incident

Incident Background

During the 1930s till 1966, Benton Harbor, Michigan was a major tourist area and industrial center and was the most prosperous city in the county (NEFAC, n.d.). Although many African Americans flocked to Benton Harbor during this time in order to work, they did not gain political power. Instead, they congregated together and developed their own cultural community. Then, in 1966, after years of being abused by local authorities, a Caucasian male shot and killed an African American youth. Consequently, a riot broke out.

Following the riot of 1966, many of the whites, along with their businesses, moved out of Benton Harbor and into the neighboring city of St. Joseph (NEFAC, n.d.). This financially hurt Benton Harbor. Furthermore, the Caucasians took the political, legal, judicial, and financial power with them to St. Joseph. By seizing control of county power, St. Joseph authorities were able to divert federal and state funds to St. Joseph and away from Benton Harbor. Moreover, by controlling the banks, financial authorities in St. Joseph declined to grant loans to Benton Harbor businesses. Consequently, over the years, Benton Harbor has become concentrated with poor African Americans, many of who are jobless.

Even though the chief of police, the mayor, and the entire city council in Benton Harbor are African Americans, the police force is still mainly white (NEFAC, n.d.). Because Benton Harbor consists of 95% Blacks, there is racial tension between the police and community members. Indeed, it appears that white police officers (i.e., those who are in authority), are arresting more black residents than white residents.

Evaluation

Following the Benton Harbor riot of 1966, the current residents of Benton Harbor claimed that many of the whites, along with their businesses, moved out of Benton Harbor and into the neighboring city of St. Joseph (NEFAC, n.d.). As a result, there are few opportunities in which to advance in Benton Harbor and residents feel hopeless (Stevens, 2003). Benton Harbor residents may have valid arguments, which may explain the reasons behind the 2003 riot. For example, Benton Harbor consists of over 90% African Americans while St. Joseph consists of 90% Caucasians (CityData, 2008; Fedstats, n.d.). Thus, Caucasians appeared to have moved from Benton Harbor to St. Joseph, as claimed. Furthermore, the income in Benton Harbor is well below the U.S. average, the state of Michigan average, and the average in St. Joseph. Indeed, there does appear to be few good job opportunities in Benton Harbor.

Recommendations

There are several ways to help reduce racial tensions and to prevent this incident from happening again. The goal is to improve police-community relations and to improve police officer performance (Carter, 2002). This can be achieved by a) improving police officer hiring practices, b) increasing community involvement, c) developing an early warning system, d) enhancing police officer training, e) enhancing police officer equipment, and f) employing use of force alternatives.

Improving Police Officer Hiring Practices

In order to minimize police officer misconduct, the department should only hire good police officer candidates. This can be accomplished through a screening process prior to hiring. By administering psychological screening tests prior to hiring, bad officer candidates, who appear racist, for example, can be eliminated from the hiring process.

Increasing Community Involvement

In order to get the community involved in law enforcement efforts, citizen complaints can be investigated by civilian oversight groups (Walker et al., 2007). In this way, police management will get a feel for what the public perceives as important. Following complaint investigations, the data can be analyzed by police management to identify high-risk police employees.

Developing an Early Warning System

Early warning systems need to be developed to identify high-risk officers who are engaging in misconduct (Human Rights Watch, 1998). These officers need to be accountable for their actions and appropriately disciplined. Statistics can easily be collected on each officer and this data can then be compared with the data from other officers who work in the same area under the same conditions (Walker et al., 2007). This information will indicate if disparities exist between similar officers.

Enhancing Police Officer Training

Officers need to be better trained as communicators. Officers need to be trained in the use of verbal skills to control potentially volatile situations ("Appendix A", n.d.). Training should include cultural awareness and verbal judo (Verbal Judo Institute, Inc., 2004).

Officers need to be better trained in properly using their weapons. Officers can be trained by using shoot-no shoot video simulations ("Expertise", 2007). These scenarios are interactive; the individuals in the videos actually respond to police actions. Indeed, research has shown that training and experience reduce the number of police officer decisions that are based on stereotyped views. This is essential in reducing racial bias in law enforcement.

Enhancing Police Officer Equipment

Police departments should use available technology. Cameras could be installed in police vehicles to document events (Walker et al., 2007). Cameras will help expose police officer misconduct along with false complaints. Furthermore, a police officer who receives a complaint could be required to take a polygraph exam. This could be required as part of the job. This will help keep the police officers honest.

Use of Force Alternatives

There are workable alternatives to the use of deadly force when the police confront violent situations. Basically, the amount of force that police officers are allowed to employ is the least amount necessary in order to resolve the situation (Walker et al., 2007). Generally, a police officer may use one level of force above that employed by the violator in order to gain compliance. However, because there is no universal agreement on a standard continuum of force, different departments may be able to use different weapons to control different levels of resistance (Federal Law Enforcement Training Center, n.d.). The various levels of resistance are 1) psychological intimidation, 2) verbal noncompliance, 3) passive resistance (e.g., going limp), 4) active resistance (e.g., pulling away), 5) aggressive resistance (e.g., striking the officer), and 6) attempted murder. The various levels of force used by police officers are 1) officer presence, 2) verbal commands, 3) soft empty hand control (e.g., pressure points), 4) hard empty hand control (e.g., striking), 5) hard weapons (e.g., baton and chemical weapons), and 6) deadly force. The actual level of force employed by a police officer, however, depends on the tools that are available to the officer along with situational variables, such as the number and size of the suspects. A police officer may be more justified in using a gun when weapon availability is limited. This is why alternative less-than-lethal weapons need to be available to police officers.

There are a variety of non-lethal weapons that police officers can use to contain violent individuals. These weapons can be broken down into the following categories: electric shock, chemical, impact projectiles, physical restraints, and light (U.S. Department of Justice, 2002). First, the electric shock weapon of choice is the Taser gun, which delivers a 50,000 volt shock through barbed wires (Hambling, 2005). Although the weapon produces immediate effects, the officers must be in close proximity to the violators because physical contact must be maintained. Second, chemical weapons include pepper spray, tear gas, anesthetics, and calmatives (U.S. Department of Justice). However, problems with chemical weapons are the some people may be vulnerable to health problems and other people may be able to work through the effects of the chemicals. Third, impact projectiles include rubber bullets and bean bags (Pilant, 2000). Being hit with these is immediately painful and promotes compliance. However, at close range, these impact projectiles can be deadly. Fourth, physical restraints include net guns, electrified nets, chemical substances applied to surfaces that impede movement, and flexible cuffs (U.S. Department of Justice). Concerns involving the nets and cuffs are that officers must be in close proximity to the suspects; for the chemicals applied to the surface, this may also affect the officers' movement. Finally, weapons of light include lasers, plasma flash bangs, and LED flashlights. All three light weapons gain compliance by using light pulses that cause disorientation and nausea in humans (Hambling; Shachtman, 2007). The laser, however, can cause eye injury, resulting in blindness.

Future non-lethal weapons under development include using radio frequencies. One radio frequency weapon uses a 95-gigahertz microwave beam that heats the body to 130 degrees Fahrenheit, creating great, but temporary, pain (Hambling, 2005). Also under development is a weapon that uses acoustic energy, both audible and inaudible. Whether it is ear splitting sounds or low frequency signals, the goal is to create nausea and sudden diarrhea. However, because these weapons affect the human central nervous system, they can be potentially lethal.

In short, the police must make every effort to do their jobs safely. Technology is always improving and police must use this technology to promote peace and safety. After all, the goal of the police is to serve and protect.

References

Aiken, S. (2003, June 19). Huge police presence, rain keep rioters off the streets. *The Herald Palladium* (Benton Harbor, Michigan).

American Civil Liberties Union (2008, August 6). *ACLU releases report on racial profiling in Louisiana.* Retrieved from http://www.aclu.org/racialjustice/racialprofiling/36358prs20080806.html

Appendix A: Christopher Commission recommendations (n.d.). Retrieved from http://www.usc.edu/libraries/archives/cityinstress/options/appena.html

Ast, W. III, and Eliasohn, M. (2003, June 18). Second night of violence leaves at least 15 injured in Benton Harbor. *The Herald Palladium* (Benton Harbor, Michigan).

Barkan, S. (2006). *Criminology: A sociological understanding* (3rd ed.). Upper Saddle River, NJ: Pearson Prentice Hall.

Bartol, C., and Bartol, A. (2008). *Criminal behavior: A psychosocial approach* (8th ed.). Upper Saddle River, NJ: Prentice Hall.

BH riots: Rumor, mistrust help fuel senseless street violence (2003). *The Herald Palladium* (Benton Harbor, Michigan).

Buckley, W., Nadelmann, E., Schmoke, K., McNamara, J., Sweet, R., Szasz, T., et al. (1996). The war on drugs is lost. *National Review, 48*(2), 34-48.

Carter, D. (2002). *Issues in police-community relations: Taken from The Police and the community* (7th ed.). Boston, MA: Pearson Custom Publishing.

CityData (2008). *Michigan profile*. Retrieved from http://www.idcide.com/citydata/mi/

Del Carmen, R.V. (2010). *Criminal procedures: Laws & practice* (8th ed.). Belmont, CA: Wadsworth.

Downer, K. (2003, June 17). Police: Chase exceeded 100 mph. *The Herald Palladium* (Benton Harbor, Michigan).

Earleywine, M. (2002). *Understanding marijuana: A new look at the scientific evidence*. New York: Oxford University Press.

Erowid (2011). *Cannabis drug testing.* Retrieved from http://www.erowid.org/plants/cannabis/cannabis_testing.shtml

Expertise improves shoot-no shoot decisions in police officers and lessens potential for racial bias (2007, June 4). *ScienceDaily.* Retrieved from http://www.sciencedaily.com/releases/2007/06/070603215445.htm

Fears, D. (2008, June 12). New criminal record: 7.2 million. *The Washington Post.*

Federal Law Enforcement Training Center (n.d.). *Use of force continuum (podcast transcript).* Retrieved from https://www.fletc.gov/training-catalog

Fedstats (n.d.). *Mapstats: Michigan.* Retrieved from http://fedstats.sites.usa.gov/

Gahlinger, P. (2004). *Illegal Drugs: A complete guide to their history, chemistry, use, and abuse*. New York: Plume.

Hames, J., and Ekern, Y. (2005). *Constitutional law: Principles and practice*. Clifton Park, NY: Thomson Delmar.

Hambling, D. (2005). Police toy with 'less lethal' weapons. *New Scientist*. Retrieved from http://www.newscientist.com/

Hartzell, T. (2003, June 17). House burned, police vehicles vandalized during Benton Harbor riot. *The Herald Palladium* (Benton Harbor, Michigan).

Hess, K. and Wrobleski, H. (1997). *Police Operations* (2nd ed.). St. Paul, MN: West Publishing.

Human Rights Watch (1998). *Shielded from justice: Police brutality and accountability in the United States. Los Angeles.* Retrieved from http://www.hrw.org/

Huskey, A. (2007). *Message from the superintendent*. Indiana State Excise Police. Retrieved from http://www.in.gov/atc/isep/

Indiana Department of Correction (2010a). *2009 annual report*. Retrieved from http://www.in.gov/idoc/

Indiana Department of Correction (2010b). *Indiana Department of Correction fact card.* Retrieved from http://www.in.gov/idoc/files/FACT_CARD_JULY_2009.pdf

Indiana State Police (1997). [Brochure]. *Marijuana: get straight on the facts.* New Orleans, LA: Syndistar, Inc.

Indiana Supreme Court Division, State Court Administration (2010). *2009 Indiana probation report: Statewide summary.*

Kelley, L., Mueller, D., & Hemmens, C. (2004). To punish or rehabilitate revisited: An analysis of the purpose/goals of state correctional statutes, 1991-2002. *Criminal Justice Studies, 17*(4), 333-351.

Liptak, A. (2008, April 23). U.S. prison population dwarfs that of other nations. *International Herald Tribune.*

Marr, L. (1998). *Sexually transmitted diseases: A physician tells you what you need to know.* Baltimore, MD: John Hopkins University Press.

Maass, A., and Taylor, K. (2003). Police abuse & chronic poverty fueled Benton Harbor riots. *Counterpunch.* Retrieved from http://www.counterpunch.org/maass07082003.html

McCarthy, K. (2009). *Growth in prison and jail populations slowing: 16 states report declines in the number of prisoners.* Retrieved from Bureau of Justice Statistics Web site: http://www.bjs.gov/

NEFAC (n.d.). Tale of two cities: Benton Harbor and St. Joseph, Michigan: A study of poverty and racism in Berrien County, Michigan. *North Eastern Federation of Anarchist Communists.*

Oyez Project, Halbert v. Michigan, 545 U.S. ___ (2005). *OYEZ: U.S. Supreme Court Media.*

Oyez Project, Tennessee v. Garner, 471 U.S. 1 (1985). *OYEZ: U.S. Supreme Court Media.*

Pilant, L. (2000). Less-than-lethal weapons: New solutions for law enforcement. *Science and Technology.* Retrieved from http://www.ncjrs.gov/pdffiles1/nij/grants/181653.pdf

Race riots in Benton harbor: Blacks burn their town (n.d.). *Adversity.net.* Retrieved from http://www.adversity.net/BentonHarbor/BentonHarborRaceRiots.htm

Roleff, T. (2005). Drug Abuse: Opposing viewpoints. Detroit: Thomson Gale.

Ryan, K., and Cooper, J. (2007). *Those who can, teach* (11th ed.). Boston, MA: Houghton Mifflin.

Shah S., Rahman, I, & Khashu, A. (2007). Overcoming language barriers: Solutions for law enforcement. *Community Oriented Policing Services.* Retrieved from http://www.cops.usdoj.gov/

Shachtman, N. (2007, August 6). Homeland security's new weapon makes people sick. *Aftermath News.*

Shattell, M.M., Hamilton, D., Starr, S.S., Jenkins, C.J., & Hinderliter, N.A. (2008). Mental health service needs of a Latino population: A community-based participatory research project. *Issues in Mental Health Nursing*, 29, 351-370.

Siegel, L. (2003). *Criminology* (8th ed.). Belmont, CA: Wadsworth – Thomson.

Spurling, A. (Producer), & Leonard, M. (Director). (1993). *Altered states: A history of drug use in America.* [Motion Picture]. United States: Films Media Group.

Stats Indiana (2010). *States IN profile.* Retrieved from http://www.stats.indiana.edu/sip/

Stevens, L. (2003, June 20). Jackson: All must help the city in wake of violence. *The Herald Palladium* (Benton Harbor, Michigan).

Strode, K. (2003, June 19). Reporter caught in riot looks rage in the eye. *The Herald Palladium* (Benton Harbor, Michigan).

Tucker, J., Donovan, D., and Marlatt, G. (Eds.). (1999). *Changing additive behavior: Bridging clinical and public health strategies.* New York: Guilford Press.

U.S. Census Bureau (n.d.). *State and county quick facts: Race.* Retrieved from http://quickfacts.census.gov/

U.S. Department of Justice, Office of Justice Programs, National Institute of Justice (2002). *Less-than-lethal weapons.* Retrieved from http://ojp.gov/

Verbal Judo Institute, Inc. (2004). *"Excellence in tactical communication."* Retrieved from http://www.verbaljudo.org/verbaljudolawenforcement.html

Vold, G., Bernard, T., and Snipes, J. (2002). *Theoretical criminology* (5th ed.). New York, NY: Oxford University Press.

Walker, S., Spohn, C., and DeLone, M. (2007). *The color of justice: Race, ethnicity, and crime in America* (4th ed.). Belmont, CA: Thomson Wadsworth.

Weiner, S., and Kelly, M. (2003). Rebellion against police brutality. *Fight Back! News*, *6*(3).

Yancey, D. (2002). *STDs: What you don't know can hurt you.* Brookfield, CT: Twenty-first Century Books.

Yaroschuk, T. (Producer & Writer). (2000). Hooked: Illegal drugs and how they got that way (Vol. 1) [Motion Picture]. The History Channel: A&E.

Chapter 9

COMMUNITY POLICING

Normative Sponsorship Theory

Community policing relies on the normative sponsorship theory, which indicates that people who have a convergence of interest may cooperate with one another in order to satisfy their needs (Sower, Holland, Tiedke, & Freeman, 1957). However, the community members will only work together as long as the goals are within the normal limits of established standards (Sower & Gist, 1994). Hence, the more congruent the beliefs and values of the stakeholders, the more likely they will sponsor change and work together to solve their problems. Therefore, it is imperative that the police and community members work together to define common goals, to effectively mobilize community resources, and to sponsor change in order to reduce crime and to promote community health.

Critical Social Theory

Community policing also relies on the critical social theory, which is the practical social science that encourages individuals to become socially and politically active in order to change and improve their current social conditions (Agger, 2006). Indeed, critical social theory endorses the enlightenment, empowerment, and emancipation of the people (Fay, 1987). First, people are enlightened when they obtain empirical knowledge about their states of oppression and their potential capacity to improve their situations. Second, people are empowered when they are galvanized to engage in a socially transformation action. Finally, people are emancipated when they know who they are, what they genuinely want, and when they have collective autonomy and power to freely and rationally determine the nature and course of their collective existence. In short, the critical social theory raises the people's awareness of their current oppression, it demonstrates the possibility of a qualitatively different future, and it holds community members responsible for actively getting involved and creating their own liberation.

Staffing

Because law enforcement is a police-community endeavor, good relations require that the police are representative of the population. In order to achieve this, while at the same time recruiting qualified employees, police departments must set standards. One of those standards may be education. There are many benefits for officers to have an education: it equips officers to make complex decisions with little supervision; it helps officers understand problems experienced by minorities; and it enables officers to readily adapt to change (Carter, 2002). However, educational requirements may be discriminatory if minorities are presented with fewer educational opportunities.

If the population is not adequately represented, the police may not understand the needs of the community. For instance, even though the police and the community both strive toward public safety, they may have different interpretations of what that means (Thacher, 2001). The police officer may focus only on serious and violent crimes, while the public may focus on the everyday quality-of-life problems.

Rapid Response

Some police departments react to crime and use rapid response times as the measure of community satisfaction (Vito, Walsh, & Kunselman, 2005). For example, computerized statistics (COMPSTAT) was introduced in 1994 by the New York City Police Department as a strategy that uses information technology to control neighborhood crime. By using accurate and timely information, COMPSTAT allows for the rapid, focused deployment of police resources to address identified problems (Willis, Mastrofski, & Weisburd, 2007). However, COMPSTAT places most of the responsibility for reducing neighborhood crime on police management (Magers, 2004). Consequently, by overlooking line officers and community members, local problems are not well understood and police-community relations are less than optimal (Eterno & Silverman, 2005).

There are several problems associated with relying solely on rapid response time strategies. First, if police departments rely on crime statistics to solve their problems, and because many crimes are not reported to the police, the police may be ineffectively allocating resources (Magers, 2004). Second, crime statistics do not indicate quality of life issues or the reasons for crime. For example, a high unemployment rate, a down turn in the economy, a changing social class, and the lack of public services may be the reasons for crime and public dissatisfaction (Barkan, 2006). Thus, data driven decisions based on incomplete information may be faulty. Third, if the police are to better serve the public, then the police must understand what is important to the public. The police must get community members involved (Carter, 2002). Indeed, the health of the community requires a team effort. By police officers and community members working together via community policing, resources can be better utilized in taking proactive measures to improve the quality of life (Lombardo & Lough, 2007).

COMPSTAT has been implemented by several cities as a mechanism for collecting accurate intelligence in a timely manner so that the police can rapidly respond to high crime areas (Bratton, 1997). By effectively allocating adequate resources in a timely manner to high crime areas, evidence indicates that crime can be prevented (Shepherd, 2002). Although COMPSTAT does not indicate the reasons for crime, COMPSTAT does stress accountability (Teal, 2007). If crime statistics indicate that problems exist, and if nothing is being done about them, such as assigning more officers to patrol a particular area, then police managers will be perceived as not doing their job. This will negatively affect police-community relations. In this regard, COMPSTAT can be used as a publicity tool to calm the public. Residents will be able to enjoy their lives if they believe that they are safe.

In short, COMPSTAT is a tool that can provide valuable information in a timely manner, which could help improve police performance. However, police actions must not be controlled by a single tool. Another tool, which incorporates police officer experience, must be created and utilized in conjunction with COMPSTAT.

Technology and Public Service

Law and order depend largely on local residents. Thus, police departments must utilize the public as a resource. This means the police must engage community members in crime preventative strategies. This can only happen if the police work with community members.

Police officers need to combine technology with project-based activities that encourage public participation. Cooperation will require residents to internalize new concepts. Residents are eager to work with computers and they are more receptive to information when it is presented via technology. Furthermore, technology-based activities will allow the residents to have some control over projects and this will allow them to learn through trial and error. Thus, using technology to perform project-based activities will create a more active and engaging environment, it will foster the local residents' ability to think critically and to solve problems, and it will help local residents to better communicate with the larger community.

Computers & Intellectual Capacities

Technology allows for different learning styles. According to Howard Gardner, a leading psychologist, people learn through seven different intellectual capacities (Ryan & Cooper, 2007). These distinct intelligences are a) linguistic, b) logical-mathematical, c) bodily-kinesthetic, d) musical, e) spatial, f) intrapersonal, and g) interpersonal. Officers can use technology in a way that matches the way that different individuals learn. Thus, technology can help local residents learn according to their own unique abilities.

Linguistic

Linguistic learners learn best through language (Ryan & Cooper, 2007). Thus, officers can utilize computers to teach concepts through writing and editing. For example, officers can teach local residents to express abstract concepts by using poems and word processing documents.

Logical-mathematical

Logical-mathematical learners learn best through tangible and inquiry-based projects (Ryan & Cooper, 2007). Officers can use computer games to teach critical thinking skills and drill-and-practice programs to teach essential knowledge. In addition, database programs can be used to illustrate quantitative information.

Bodily-kinesthetic

Bodily-kinesthetic learners learn best through movement (Ryan & Cooper, 2007). Computers are effective tools for bodily-kinesthetic learners because when using a computer, local residents must actively use the keyboard, joystick, mouse, disk burner, and other devices. In addition, officers can use presentation software to simulate real-life scenarios. In these cases, the local residents will interact with the computer, make important decisions, and act out their choices.

Musical

Musical learners learn best by listening and by creating rhythms and patterns (Ryan & Cooper, 2007). Computers are effective tools for musical learners because many computer programs are readily available that play music. Furthermore, local residents can develop critical thinking skills by breaking down and rebuilding melodies.

Spatial

Spatial learners learn best through visual experiences (Ryan & Cooper, 2007). Computers are effective tools for spatial learners because residents can learn through graphic programs, such as computer-aided designs and paint programs. These programs allow local residents to visualize concepts. Furthermore, local residents can express themselves with the use of presentation software.

Intrapersonal

Intrapersonal learners are self-motivated and learn best through meta-cognitive processes (Ryan & Cooper, 2007). Because local residents have different learning abilities, computers allow residents to learn at their own pace. Furthermore, computers can provide residents with additional instruction and training in areas where they need help. Because intrapersonal learners are not sure how to share their ideas beyond their own community, they can be encouraged to use blogs, which will allow them to express themselves in an ordered manner and to a larger community.

Interpersonal

Interpersonal learners learn best through interactions with other people (Ryan & Cooper, 2007). For these residents, computers encourage cooperative learning by allowing individuals to work together. For example, interpersonal learners can use online survey tools to generate data for one another. This will enhance the creative and communication skills of the residents.

Barriers to Technology

There are several barriers to implementing technology. Some of the major barriers may include a lack of adequate training, a lack of hardware, a lack of software, and a lack of input concerning choice of software. Although there is a lot of technological information available, overwhelming officers with this information is an ineffective way to promote the use of technology. Instead, administrators need to focus on sound educational principles and to create the conditions, as well as the motivation and competencies, so that officers are able to implement the technology. In short, learning is a team effort and administrators must provide officers with the necessary support so that they can achieve their goals. As in football, without proper training, equipment, and direction, it is unreasonable to expect success.

Overcoming Barriers

There are several ways to overcome the barriers that impede the use of technology. First, because officers will respond to technology that is directed at helping them achieve their goals, training should be curriculum rich and should focus on properly applying technology. Second, administrators need to provide professional development plans and mentors to ensure that adequate support is provided. Finally, before officers will be able to effectively use available technology, they must know that the tools exist. Hence, management must provide that knowledge via training and mentoring.

Factors for Success

There are several factors that will enhance the effectiveness of technology. First, a detailed plan that provides a clear vision of the goals and steps necessary for the effective management and implementation of the technology will need to be developed. This will include funding, which may be obtained from the government, and the installation of the technology. Second, officers will need to know how to integrate the technology, which will require on-going training. Third, administrators will need to support the process by providing funding and other support, such as by restructuring the officers' schedules. Finally, administrators will need to reflect on the process so that any corrective adjustments can be made. Indeed, a system without feedback is unstable.

Community Policing in America

Police departments are formed to serve the public. Thus, police departments are responsible for effectively using all available resources (e.g., community members) when performing their duties because they are accountable to the public. In addressing a community's needs, a police department must decentralize its power so that each officer has the flexibility to be creative in resolving the issues at hand (Wilson, 2006). Indeed, police officers and community leaders must work together to determine how to best meet the community's needs. Instead of reacting to social problems, police departments and community members must work together to implement a proactive community-policing strategy.

Community policing is a philosophy that proactively addresses immediate public concerns in the community via police-community partnerships and problem solving efforts (Hess & Wrobleski, 2003). Indeed, there is a collaborative partnership between law enforcement agencies and community members as they work together to solve social problems. In short, the police encourage and empower community members to take an active role in promoting public safety and in reducing social problems, both by working with law enforcement agencies and by resolving their own problems (Wilson, 2006).

Community members are the ones who set the standards for social order. Indeed, residents are accountable for maintaining their own neighborhoods. However, any particular neighborhood may be served by city, county, and state law enforcement agencies. Thus, because each type of law enforcement agency may have a different geographical jurisdiction, communities may overlap.

Community-policing will not only reduce crime, but it will make for a healthier society. For example, if community-policing reduces the use of drugs, then this may reduce other community problems. For example, marijuana contains hundreds of carcinogens and these chemicals can damage the brain, liver, lungs, spleen, and reproductive organs (Indiana, 1997; Roleff, 2005). Thus, marijuana use can lead to increased medical expenses. Furthermore, marijuana is an intoxicant that can impair decision-making abilities. This may lead juveniles to engage in casual, unplanned, and unprotected sex, which, in turn, may lead to unwanted pregnancies and to the contraction of sexually transmitted diseases (Marr, 1998; Yancey, 2002). In short, community-policing may promote public health and reduce community costs.

Social Constructs of Policing

A social system involves every interrelated component of a unified whole and every external factor that influences every element of that organized structure (Carter, 2002). In law enforcement, the components include the police department, the police programs, the police officers, other cooperative police departments, the prison guards, the jails, the judges and judicial officers, federal, state, and local legislatures, firearm manufacturers, automotive manufacturers, and bullet proof vest manufactures. External factors are those elements that affect the system but are not directly part of the system. For example, external factors that may affect the successful execution of various police programs, such as the marijuana eradication program, the Drug Awareness Resistance Education (DARE) program, the Selective Traffic Enforcement Program (STEP), the seat belt enforcement program, and the driving while intoxicated enforcement program, will include school principals, teachers, and the media. For individual officers, external factors will include the family, economic institutions, educational institutions, religious affiliations, and friends. All of these external factors help shape the components of the system.

Community Involvement Programs

There are many different techniques and programs that the police may employ to enhance social order. Some of these techniques and programs include Community Oriented Policing Services (COPS), Citizen Oriented Police Enforcement (COPE), Problem Oriented Policing (POP), Youth-Focused Community Policing (YFCP), Teaching, Education and Mentoring (TEAM), Citizen Patrol (e.g., Guardian Angels), Citywide Crime Prevention Program (CCPP), Special Crime Watch Programs, National Night Out (NNO), Crime Stoppers, Mothers Against Drunk Drivers (MADD), Reserve Police Officers, Police Explorers, Youth Safety Corps (YSC), McGruff, Police Athletic League (PAL), Drug Awareness Resistance Education (DARE), Police Assisted Community Enforcement (PACE), Gang Resistance, Education and Training (GREAT), Gang Resistance Is Paramount (GRIP), Foot Patrol, Community Profile, Fear-Reduction, Burglary Prevention Program, Citizen Advisory Boards, Citizen Police Academies (CPA), community prosecutors, community courts, Crime Resistance in a Municipal Environment (CRIME), San Antonio Fear Free Environment (SAFFE), and Domestic Violence/ Sexual Assault (DVSA) (Lurigio & Skogan, 2000; Miller, Hess, & Orthmann, 2001; Sadd & Grinc, 2000; Trojanowicz, Kappeler, & Gaines, 2002; Weisel, & Eck, 2000). Table 21 is a comparison of how different types of police officers feel about community policing, citizens, and their roles as police officers. How police officers perform their duties will impact how well a program works (Miller et al., 2011; Sadd & Grinc, 2000; Trojanowicz et al., 2002).

Table 21

Police Officers' Attitudes

		Tough cops believe	**Clean-Beat Crime Fighting cops believe**	**Problem Solving cops believe**	**Professional cops believe**
Community Policing	=	Not real police work	May impede efforts to fight street crime	Encourage citizen involvement	Encourage citizen involvement
Citizens	=	Hostile and uncooperative	Unappreciative	Help identify root causes of problems	Needed to maintain positive relations with community
Supervisors	=	Unsupportive	Unsupportive	Support is valued	Approval is valued
Procedural Guidelines	=	Do more harm than good	Valued to protect due process	Too restrictive and impede efforts to solve problems	Acceptable restrictions
Law Enforcement	=	Narrow and focuses on enforcing laws	Very rigid in enforcing laws	Not most important function of officer	Accept role as defined by department
Aggressiveness	=	Police should be aggressive, part of image	Police should aggressively enforce law	Results in negative police-community relations	Police should only be aggressive when necessary
Order Maintenance	=	Not real police work	Part of role if can enforce order formally by law	Part of police job	Seeks additional police roles and responsibilities
Selectivity of Enforcement Actions	=	Focus on serious violations	Focus on all illegal activities	Discretionary and informal law enforcement	Handle full range of offenses, both formal and informal

Following is a discussion on several community policing programs. The programs include a) citizens on patrol, b) neighborhood speed watch, c) crime-free multi-housing, d) lock out auto theft, and e) community patrol officer program. First, for the citizens on patrol program, community members help provide public services that the police officers may not have the time to provide (National Association Citizens on Patrol, n.d.). The services may include checking the welfare of elderly and disabled individuals, checking the homes of vacationers, and providing extra patrol in areas where there are non-violent crimes, such as loitering and the playing of loud music. Second, for the neighborhood speed watch program, the department of transportation may loan out radars to community members so that they can record information about speeding vehicles (Seattle Department of Transportation, n.d.). The information is then used by the department of transportation to create a traffic calming strategy to promote street safety. Third, for the crime free multi-housing program, law enforcement agencies and property managers work together in an effort to eliminate illegal activities on rental properties (Phoenix Police Department, n.d.). Crime prevention tactics may include redesigning the properties to discourage crime, performing criminal background checks on applicants, displaying signage that advertises anti-crime facilities, and strengthening the rental agreements. Fourth, for the lock out auto theft program, law enforcement agencies provide information to residents so that the residents can take proactive steps in reducing auto theft (Missouri State Highway Patrol, n.d.). Some of the steps that residents may take to prevent auto theft include locking their cars, parking their cars in well-lighted areas, installing audible alarms, installing vehicle immobilizers, and installing tracking systems. Finally, for the community patrol officer program, law enforcement agencies provide civilians with vans in an attempt to reduce illegal drug activity in schoolyards (Sadd & Grinc, 2000). Volunteers park the vans outside of elementary and middle schools and they provide children with youth counseling and drug prevention information. All illegal drug activities are reported to the police departments at a later time. In short, each community policing program needs to be tailored to the particular problems being addressed.

Community Policing Applied in Several Large Cities

Chicago

In 1993, Chicago's Mayor introduced the Chicago Alternative Policing Strategy (CAPS) as a community policing program (Lurigio & Skogan, 2000). The CAPS program consisted of six basic features to reduce crime. The first feature required police officers to develop partnerships with community members and to know crime hot spots, community organizations, and community resources in their beats. The second feature involved making police officers responsible for crime control in specific locations. The third feature involved creating a system that differentiated between emergency and non-emergency calls for assistance, and, thus, allowed the department to prioritize its responses. The fourth feature involved focusing on the root causes of neighborhood problems, such as building decay. The fifth feature involved making the police officers responsible for effectively using community organizations and other city agencies to resolve crime. Finally, the sixth feature involved efficiently collecting crime data, analyzing the data at the district level, and then sharing the information among the street officers. Indeed, the CAPS program was designed to increase police officer presence, to improve police officer response to crime, and to reduce crime by addressing the root causes of crime.

Houston

In an effort to reduce local drug problems, the Houston Police Department employed a type of community policing called Innovative Neighborhood Oriented Policing (Sadd & Grinc, 2000). The program was based on the idea that drug problems can only be resolved if the police and the community work together. First, local residents formed patrol groups and they monitored local cantinas. Second, the police provided residents with citizens' band radios so that the groups could report suspicious activities. Third, the police also helped elderly homeowners employ situational crime prevention measures by providing them with improved locks and doors, free of charge. Indeed, in order to aggressively address the community's fear of drug related crimes, the police attacked the problem in multiple ways. However, the police department did not develop formal partnerships with other city agencies. Instead, line officers formed informal relationships with certain individuals within other agencies.

Cincinnati

In an effort to reduce crime and to improve police-community relations, Cincinnati employed a Community Sector (COMSEC) Team Policing program in high crime problem areas with diverse residents (Lurigio & Rosenbaum, 1994). A police district was divided into six sectors, which included a business sector, two low-income high-crime sectors, a middle class sector, a mixed residential and business sector, and a racially mixed low-income sector. To offer a full range of police services, teams of officers were permanently assigned to small demographically and geographically defined neighborhoods. Each team was autonomous under a decentralized operational system. Officers performed both investigative and patrol functions.

To assess the program, self-administered surveys were issued to police officers at 6 months, 12 months, 18 months, and 30 months after the program began (Lurigio & Rosenbaum, 1994). The department wanted to assess the officers' job satisfaction and their attitudes toward their work and the community. In addition, the police interviewed residents inside their respective sectors to assess their experiences with police along with their attitudes toward the police. The findings indicated that the police officers were initially very satisfied with their jobs and that residents received good police service. However, during the study police management moved away from a decentralized government and gained greater control over the daily operations of the police officers in the district. Consequently, the positive changes were undermined.

San Diego and Oakland

In an effort to reduce crime, to improve the cleanliness of their neighborhoods, and to provide safe environments for children, the San Diego and Oakland police departments employed a type of community policing called Neighborhood Watch (City of Oakland, n.d.; City of San Diego, n.d.; Oakland Police Department, n.d.). Employing Neighborhood Watch, the San Diego and Oakland police departments developed a partnership with local community members and enlisted their active participation in community policing. Some of the activities that local residents actively engaged in included a) walking around the neighborhood and identifying suspicious activities and potential problems, b) cleaning the streets and parks, c) painting over graffiti, d) painting home address numbers on curbs, and e) developing an activity profile of local residents to help fellow members recognize suspicious or unusual activities. Thus, by using local residents to gather information, by listening to what the residents perceived to be community issues, and by involving the public in the decision-making process, the San Diego and Oakland police departments have improved their relations with community members and have effectively addressed community issues.

Evaluation of Community Policing

Because the police are supposed to serve community stakeholders, community policing must be judged from the perspectives of stakeholders. Community stakeholders include all community members, such as police officers, homeowners, children, and inmates. Indeed, community policing involves all community members in solving social problems.

Police Officers

To enhance police-community relations, police departments must train their officers to improve their performance. Saus et al. (2006) conducted a study of 40 police officer cadets in order to investigate whether attending a brief training session in situational awareness will improve the cadets' performance. Half of the participants received scenario-based training on a simulator that used realistic field situations, and the other half received marksmanship training on a simulator that focused on shooting skills. Data were collected on the participants by a) scoring their responses on shoot-no shoot police scenarios via an interactive firearms training simulator, b) having them complete self-administered questionnaires, and c) measuring their cardiovascular responses. The findings indicated that the cadets who had received the brief training session in situational awareness had a greater number of shots on target, they scored higher on critical decision making, and they showed less mental stress as demonstrated by their cardiovascular output. Thus, it is imperative that police departments provide proper training to their officers because training can reduce officer stress, improve police performance, and improve police-community relations.

Homeowners

Homeowners can take preventative measures to reduce crime. Weisburd, Bushway, Lum, and Yang (2004) conducted a 14 year study in Seattle to determine if crime is prevalent and stable in micro places, or hot spots, over time. Using official crime data, crime appeared to be clustered in specific street segments. Thus, by recognizing crime hot spots, local authorities and community members can focus their efforts in these locations in order to prevent crime. For example, barriers that increase the risk of being caught can be installed around a residential home to discourage burglary (Taylor & Harrell, 2000). Some of these barriers may include fences, cameras, alarms, and lights (Clarke, 2000). Thus, by hardening the targets of crime, local residents may prevent crime themselves through environmental design.

Children

Several studies indicate that anti-social behaviors committed by children can be reduced. For example, Vieno, Nation, Perkins, and Santinello (2007) assessed the relationship between civic participation and adolescent deviant behaviors, such as alcohol consumption and bullying. Civic participation included the involvement in structured organizations, which promoted the common good (e.g., church, athletic clubs, dance clubs, choir, etc.). The participants consisted of 7,097 students from 11 to 15 years of age and data were collected through self-report questionnaires. The findings indicated that youths who had engaged in moderate civic participation had fewer behavioral problems than the other participants.

In addition, Xue, Zimmerman, and Caldwell (2007) conducted a longitudinal study of 824 ninth graders in four public schools in Michigan in order to assess whether the participation in pro-social activities will reduce the anti-social behavior of cigarette smoking. Pro-social activities included extracurricular school activities, community activities, and church activities. Data on adolescent cigarette use were collected through face-to-face interviews and through self-administered surveys. The findings indicated that the participation in pro-social activities had helped children who resided in disadvantaged neighborhoods to overcome risk exposures. In other words, civic participation has demonstrated to promote healthy behaviors in children.

Finally, Smith (2003) conducted a study and evaluated crime from the offenders' points of view. Smith collected data from 461 students who were 11 to 16 years of age and who resided in an area where there was a high amount of graffiti and fence damage. By providing the students with situational scenarios, Smith evaluated whether existing vandalism encouraged children to commit additional vandalism. Through multivariate analysis, the findings indicated that youths were more likely to target fences that appeared to be easy targets to vandalize. Thus, the rapid repair of fences and paint out campaigns may be effective in reducing youth vandalism.

Inmates and Faith-Based Programs

Messemer (2007) conducted a study involving the influence of faith-based programs on the academic achievement of low-literate inmates in a southeastern U.S. prison. The sample consisted of 124 male inmates who were 14 to 50 years of age and who participated in a faith-based Adult Basic Education program. The inmates were grouped into two categories: Christians (n=55) and non-Christians (n=69). Furthermore, the participants were administered pretests and posttests in math, reading, and language skills. The researcher then performed *t*-tests in order to determine if there were differences between the pretest and posttest scores. The findings indicated that there were significant learning gains in math, reading, and language skills for both the Christian and non-Christian groups. Thus, the faith-based programs have demonstrated to be beneficial to Christian and non-Christian inmates alike.

In a second study, Armour et al. (2008) conducted a pilot study of a faith-based program for 102 male inmates in a Texas prison. The sample included 66 Christian and 33 non-Christian participants who attended a 14-week faith-based program, called Restoring Peace, which was based on restorative justice principles. The researchers administered surveys to the participants in a pretest and protest format to measure characteristics like empathy, the propensity to forgive, and the quality of relationships with others. Using paired sample *t*-tests, the findings indicated that the participants in both groups had increased their ability to adopt the perspectives of other individuals, they were more likely to forgive, and they had improved the quality of their relationships with other people. Again, a faith based program has demonstrated to be beneficial to Christian and non-Christian inmates alike.

Ten Principles of Community Policing

Below are 10 principles of community policing (Trojanowicz et al., 2002).

1) Community policing is an organizational strategy that allows police and the community to work closely together to explore new and creative ways to address quality of life concerns. Community members provide input into the police process in exchange for their participation and support.
2) Community policing grants greater autonomy to patrol officers, recognizing their judgment as police professionals. In addition, community policing demands that everyone in the police department, both sworn personnel and civilians, practice solving problems in new and challenging ways.
3) Police departments need to create and develop Community Policing Officers, who are outreach specialists and who act as the direct link between the police department and the community. The Community Policing Officers must be given

the time and resources to meet face-to-face with community members and to effectively perform their specialized duties.

4) The Community Policing Officers must be in contact with community members on an on-going basis so that they can work together in new and creative ways to reduce the fear of crime and to enhance quality of life. Community Policing Officers focus on long-term solutions to community problems and they link the community to public and private agencies.
5) Police serve as the catalyst in challenging residents to accept their share of the responsibility for solving their own problems and for handling minor issues. This will allow police to focus efforts on major problems and to work on long-term solutions. As a result, trust will be enhanced between the police and the community members, vigilantism will be restrained, and apathy among community members will be reduced.
6) Community policing allows for a full-spectrum of police services. Because police departments are the only social control agencies that are open 24 hours a day, every day, community policing provides a vital proactive element to the role of police officers in making communities safer.
7) Community policing requires that the entire police department work with the public to develop mutual trust and accountability. Community policing stresses new ways to protect those individuals who are most vulnerable: elderly, juveniles, poor, disabled, homeless, and minorities.
8) Although community policing employs new technologies, community policing mostly relies on the input from patrol officers and community members. The judgment and wisdom of people are trusted above all else.

9) Community policing is a team effort and requires the commitment of the entire department. Support must come from upper management. Community Policing Officers are the specialists in **bridging the gap** between the department and the community.
10) Public order cannot be imposed by police force alone. Community members are a resource that must be utilized in order to solve social community problems. Community policing allows officers to provide personalized police services to the community by decentralizing police authority. Community policing is not a tactic that is to be applied and abandoned, but it is an on-going tactic that is modified to suit specific needs.

Police Culture

Effective law enforcement requires the collaboration of police, citizens, and community-based organizations (Gardner, 2000). There have been many community policing programs that have failed over the years because communities change over time. The traditional communities were homogeneous, demanded conformity, and experienced little change from year to year. Contemporary communities, however, are pluralistic, adaptive, and require change to survive. Therefore, traditional police practices are outdated and ineffective.

Organizational change requires much effort and time and is often met with resistance (Zhao, Thurman, & Lovrich, 2000). First, police officers' education and training are important factors in effectively implementing community policing strategies. Second, the values that police officers hold may impact the officers' receptiveness to change. Moving a police department from incident-driven to outcome-driven is no easy task (Glensor & Peak, 2000). Areas that must be recast are a) leadership and management, b) organizational culture, c) field operations, and d) external relationships. Community policing requires a strong foundation and its growth must be nurtured.

Planners of community-policing strategies need to examine the attitudes of police staff in order to identify pockets of resistance (Lurigio & Skogan, 2000). This is because community policing breeds a new type of police officer who is knowledgeable about the local community, who is a stakeholder in the community, and who is allowed to exercise independent thought and action. The police officer is an expert in problem solving and community engagement activities, which lead to greater job satisfaction and productivity. This is a win-win scenario for the police and the public. If police officers like what they do, they will become good at it. If they are good at what they do, then they will get promoted. If the traditional officers resist change, then the police culture will not be compatible with successful community policing programs. Thus, organizational change is necessary for community policing to be successful (Weisel & Eck, 2000). However, because the cost of forcing change may be extremely high, it may be best to let the opponents die off before moving forward.

For an effective community policing program, the proper kind of leadership is required (Carter, 2002). An authoritarian leadership style represents traditional law enforcement practices. A participatory leadership style represents community involvement. Police management must support a participatory leadership style for effective community involvement (Miller et al., 2011; Trojanowicz et al., 2002). See Table 22.

Table 22

Police Leadership Styles

Authoritarian Leadership Style	Participatory Leadership Style
Responds to problems	Problem solving and prevention
Individual Competitiveness	Teamwork
Professional expertise	Seeks input from community (customers)
By the book; emotional decision making	Data-based decision making
Tell/Order subordinates	Asks and listens to employees
Boss as patriarch	Boss as coach and teacher
Maintains status quo	Create, innovate, experiment
Monitors and controls employees	Trusts employees
Relies upon technology	Relies on people
Failure is the result of employees	Failure is the result of system/process
Organization is closed to outsiders	Organization is open to outsiders

Table 23 is a comparison between traditional policing, community policing, and problem-oriented policing (Miller et al., 2011; Trojanowicz et al., 2002).

Table 23

Interpretation of Police Work

Principle	Traditional policing	Community Policing	Problem-Oriented Policing
Focus of policing	Law enforcement	Community building via crime prevention	Law, order, and major problems

Focus of intervention	Reactive, based on criminal law	Proactive, based on criminal, civil, and administrative law; prevent crime via community building	Mixed, based on criminal, civil, and administrative law; focus on major problems
Focus of police culture	Inward, rejecting community	Outward, building partnerships	Mixed, depending on problem
Amount of community involvement	Low and passive	Always	Determined on a problem-by-problem case
Range of community involvement	Low and passive	High and active	Mixed, depending on particular problem
Communication flow	Downward from police to community	Horizontal	Horizontal
Police authority and command	Centralized	Decentralized with community linkage	Decentralized with local command accountability
Community's input in decision-making	Nominal	Shared, joint responsibility	Varied; final decision to be made by police
Range of police activity and measure of success	Narrow and crime focused activities based on statistics and quotas; arrests for serious violations	Broad activities, including quality of life issues; implementation of intellectual and analytical skills to provide public service, to reduce fear, and to make safer neighborhoods	Narrow to broad activities, depending on identified problems; implementation of interpersonal skills to resolve identified problems

Level of discretion by patrol officer	High and unaccountable	High and accountable to the community and local commanders	High and primarily accountable to the police administration
Implications for organizational change	Few, status quo maintained	Many and dynamic	Varied, minimized
Linkage to other agencies	Poor and intermittent	Participative and integrative	Participative and integrative, depending on problem

Table 24 indicates of how a police department dealt with local problems (Trojanowicz et al., 2002).

Table 24

Examples of Police-Community in Action

Problem	**Solution/Partnership**
Gang activities; intimidation of residents; burglaries	Neighborhood watch; increased patrols; youth programs
Shoplifting	Post pictures of shoplifters; monitor items taken into dressing rooms
Trashing parking lot of night club; underage drinking	Cite owner for trash in parking lot; cite owner for underage drinking on property; focused police patrol; violators required to clean parking lot as part of community service
Traffic; drug dealing; failure to leave park after hours	Additional patrol; horse patrol; use gates to seal park after hours

Fighting; public intoxication; drug sales; underage drinking; robberies; burglaries	Road blocks; bike patrol; field interviews; neighborhood watch; enforce loitering laws
Poor lighting and speeding near liquor store resulting in vehicle accidents with intoxicated pedestrians who cross street	Enforce jaywalking and public intoxication laws
Breaking into cars near theater; women leaving purses in plain view	Suggested camera use; increased lighting; increased signage
Public urination; panhandling; burglaries; homeless congregate; trash	Place toilets in area; work with churches to establish homeless shelters
Gangs; drug sales; loitering; graffiti; vandalism; burglaries in low-income area	Improved lighting; undercover sting operations; increased patrols; work with churches to develop outreach programs
Prostitution; loitering; public drinking; vandalism	Have fire marshal inspect premises; enforce traffic, parking, and open container laws
Tractor-trailers run traffic lights, causing crashes	Intensify enforcement and public education
Residential burglaries by juveniles	Field interviews; requested that items be marked with ID; increased patrol
Thefts from autos; auto theft; truancy	Neighborhood watch; increased guardians
Domestic violence; fights; disorderly conduct; drug sales; public intoxication; theft	Increased police patrols and number of arrests
False alarms/bank alarms	Pass false alarm ordinance
Vacant homes used for drug sales	Rolling roadblocks and stakeouts; request FEMA to destroy buildings

Many young females in public housing draw males who drink, fight, and sell drugs	Implement trespass program; work with public housing to reduce number of females in facility; enforce evictions; get social workers involved
Gas station drive-offs	Encourage employees to collect money in advance
Speeding in school zone	Educate students; place radar trailer in area; increase citations

Citizen Involvement – Volunteer Police

Police officers are public officials who fulfill a vital role of a) protecting life and property, b) detecting, preventing, and investigating crime, c) identifying and apprehending criminals, d) regulating public conduct, e) detecting conditions that affect public welfare, and f) performing miscellaneous public services (Indiana State Police, n.d.). In order to keep up with modern crime levels, police departments must utilize all available resources at their disposal, like private security companies do. The number of private security companies has grown in recent years and security officers now outnumber the police by at least 300% (Joh, 2004). This indicates that community members perceive the police as either unable or unwilling to adequately protect them. Indeed, police departments often receive criticisms of citizens, prosecutors, defense attorneys, judges, politicians, and the media for their inadequacies (Wootson, 2011). One resource that police departments can utilize to help maintain public order is volunteer officers.

It may be unwise not to utilize civilians in law enforcement (Greenberg, 1984). Unless law enforcement agencies effectively use their available resources to combat crime, they may lose the public's confidence. If they lose the public's confidence, they may also lose the public's support. Without the public's support, the police cannot adequately function. Hence, in order to change the perception of police inadequacy, police departments need to make use of auxiliary police officers.

Auxiliary Police Officers

Originating in Europe, organized extralegal efforts for social control advanced across America with the Western frontier over one hundred years ago (Hoffman, 2011). In the earliest days of the frontier, businesses financially sponsored law enforcement (Prassel, 1972). With the development and growth of mercantile activity, businessmen banded together to form special-forces called Merchants' Police. Because businesses financially supported these officers, state governments permitted the local sheriffs and chiefs of police to grant special commissions. In short, the needs of the population in the expanding West quickly outgrew the services that the local law enforcement agencies could provide, and the public was willing to pay for increased security. As a result, local governments were legally authorized to appoint private policemen to help combat crime. At that time, the public was directly responsible for helping the police maintain law and order.

Although these low-cost, special policemen (today called auxiliary officers, volunteer officers, reserve officers, or constables) were commissioned by local governments as an operating police force for social control, the absence of effective law enforcement agencies often times allowed them to act outside the realm of the law

(Prassel, 1972). Although their actions at the time may have fitted into the developing pattern of social control, they often times failed to provide the accused with their constitutional rights. Consequently, friction developed between the full-time police officers and these special police officers to the point where police departments no longer welcomed the public's help. However, due to increasing crime rates, an increasing demand for police services, and tightened budgets, many law enforcement agencies realized the need to again recruit civilian volunteers (Joh, 2004). Indeed, the Commission on Accreditation of Law Enforcement Agencies (CALEA) encourages police departments to utilize auxiliary police officers (Orange County Sheriff, n.d.).

Auxiliary versus Reserve

There may be some confusion about the difference between a "reserve" police officer and an "auxiliary" police officer. Reserve police officers are considered an extension of the police department. Auxiliary officers, on the other hand, originally came under the Police Emergency Division for civil defense (Greenberg, 1984). This is an important point because, although it is clear that reserve police officers fell under local police department control, auxiliary officers fell under civil defense control, which may affect their work assignments.

CALEA is a nationally recognized accreditation board that sets standards for reserve and auxiliary police officers (Orange County Sheriff, n.d.). Generally, a "reserve" police officer refers to a non-regular, sworn member of a police agency who has regular police powers while on duty and who is required to participate in department activities on a regular basis (Greenberg, 1984). An "auxiliary" officer, on the other hand, refers to a non-regular peace officer whose functions are usually limited to emergency situations related to civil defense activities, which include drills. Drills can take the form of assisting a police department in maintaining law and order on a regular basis. Hence, because reserve officers and auxiliary officers often perform the same duties, the terms are used interchangeably across the nation. Today, states and local jurisdictions will have exact titles and corresponding duties codified for their specific agencies.

Increased professionalism and authority are associated with advanced knowledge, training, skills, and abilities (Greenberg 1984). Reserve officers should have the same training as their corresponding full-time officers, wear the same styled uniforms, have the same authority, and may perform the same duties. Auxiliary officers, on the other hand, may have less training than their corresponding full-time officers, may wear different styled uniforms, must not be armed, and will only have citizen's arrest authority. Hence, reserve officers generally have more training than auxiliary officers, granting them more authority.

Uniforms for Volunteer Officers

When volunteer officers are seen in uniform, the public does not necessarily distinguish them from full-time officers. The public expects them to be competent enough to handle the various situations that they encounter; after all, they represent the police department and its authority. Accordingly, volunteer officers need to feel good about their appearance as they project a command presence.

There is much controversy about whether volunteer officers should wear uniforms identical to those of the full-time officers (Greenberg, 1984). One argument against volunteer officers wearing uniforms indistinguishable from that of the full-time officers is that tax paying citizens want to know whether they are being serviced by full-time officers or by persons less qualified. A second argument is that citizens who cannot distinguish between full-time officers and volunteer officers may bypass the full-time officers and may approach the volunteer officers. This type of situation creates several immediate problems. First, volunteer officers may be forced into command situations that they cannot effectively handle. Second, full-time officers may feel as though their authority is being undermined. Finally, full-time officer may come to resent the volunteer officers.

On the other hand, there are some who feel that volunteer officers should wear uniforms and equipment identical to that of the full-time officers (Greenberg, 1984). If the volunteer officers are dressed differently, the public may distrust, disrespect, and become overly aggressive toward the volunteer officers, questioning their authority. By outfitting the volunteer officers with identical uniforms to that of the full-time officers, the volunteer officers will be more accepted as police members.

The obvious solution for this dilemma is to dress volunteer officers according to their training. If the volunteer officers are trained as well as the full-time officers and are state certified, then there is no reason to distinguish between full-time and volunteer officers (Greenberg, 1984). However, if the volunteer officers have less than adequate training, then they should be distinguished.

Need for Reserve/Auxiliary Officers

American citizens increasingly oppose tax increases, yet they continue to demand increased police services. This means that law enforcement agencies must now consider themselves as private enterprises and seek means to achieve their goals as efficiently as possible. Therefore, as fiscal constraints get tighter, department heads must look toward auxiliary police officers as a way to meet public demand for increased services.

There are about 250,000 auxiliary police officers who assist about 700,000 sworn officers in the U.S. (Weinblatt, 2011). Since 9/11/2001, there has been much interest in using reserve police officers (Hoffman, 2011). These reserve officers, who include lawyers, bankers, school teachers, engineers, doctors, and many other professions, have a variety of skills that can be quite useful to law enforcement agencies (Minnesota Police Reserve Officers Association, 2005; Weinblatt, 2011). Because law enforcement agencies perform so many different kinds of work, it is generally not difficult to utilize these volunteers in at least some capacity.

Public

Champions who support the use of civilians in law enforcement argue that auxiliary officers provide great benefits (Minnesota Police Reserve Officers Association, 2005). They argue that when civilians join police departments, they help co-produce public safety, which benefits both the police and public. One benefit realized by the public is reduced fear of being victimized by criminals. As a result of having more uniformed officers on the streets, people will be influenced to act lawfully simply by the use of conspicuous patrol tactics (Siddle, 2005). The auxiliary program places officers on the street who otherwise would not be there. Thus, law and order can be better maintained simply by having more officers out on the streets who are visible to the public.

A second benefit gained by using auxiliary police officers is improved relations between the community and the police (Joh, 2004). By having civilians witness police officers actually work, police officers will become more accountable to the public. Furthermore, civilians will come to better appreciate law enforcement techniques and may be more willing to engage in behaviors that will help police.

A third benefit gained by using auxiliary police officers is improved law enforcement effectiveness (Minnesota Police Reserve Officers Association, 2005). Because auxiliary officers get relatively smaller doses of the more depressing side of law enforcement, their jobs often seem very exciting. As a result, auxiliary officers' on-duty awareness is acute, their dedication is sincere, and they are much less vulnerable to stress-induced burnout. Furthermore, civilians in police work do not have to be promoted out of their areas of expertise, as often happens with full-time officers, allowing them to do what they do best.

Police

Police departments benefit in several ways by utilizing volunteers (Minnesota Police Reserve Officers Association, 2005). One way auxiliary programs benefit police departments is through crime prevention and control. The public's support is much needed because there are about 400 U.S. residents for every full-time sworn police officer (Reaves, 2007; U.S. Department of Labor, 2009). If a police department builds grassroots political support and if the police department makes the community at large a special interest group, the police department is more likely to gain the public's support (Joh, 2004).

A second way that police departments benefit from auxiliary programs is in cost savings. For example, about 90% of a police department's budget may be allocated for personnel costs (Reading Police Department, 2011). As budgets grow tighter, as grant monies become scarcer, and as demands for police services continue to grow, police administrators must seek improved ways to utilize available resources. Many auxiliary officers work for free, meaning that, in addition to no salaries, there are no union contract hearings and cost-of-living increments to be concerned about (Texas Municipal League, 2011). Thus, using auxiliary police officers can be quite cost efficient.

A third benefit gained from using auxiliary officers is that, because the workload of full-time police officers is reduced, the full-time officers may be allowed to perform more sophisticated police functions. By allowing auxiliary officers to perform the more routine functions and services within the police department, the regular officers will be allowed to focus on the tasks that require their specialized skills and training. Furthermore, this will enhance the professionalism of the full-time police officers because they will work within more clearly defined areas of expertise.

A fourth benefit gained by police departments from using civilians in law enforcement is related to the wide variety of experiences and expertise that civilians bring into the department (Minnesota Police Reserve Officers Association, 2005). Because law enforcement activities cover so many different areas, having officers educated only in law enforcement procedures may not be sufficient. Indeed, as crimes become more sophisticated, using civilians to combat crime becomes increasingly important.

Finally, a fifth way that police departments can benefit from auxiliary programs is from the opportunity to evaluate those who want to become full-time officers. Some departments may use their auxiliary programs as recruitment tools, evaluating potential applicants through their volunteer work. Knowing whether candidates will be successful police officers before the department incurs salary and police academy expenses is good business.

Residents' Perspective

Not all citizens may approve of letting civilians execute law enforcement functions. Although involving the community in police work generally enhances relations between the police agency and community, some individuals may resent such involvement. One reason why they may not want civilians to get involved with the police department is that they may perceive that their tax dollars are inefficiently being spent on training and outfitting people other than real police officers. They feel that they have a right to be served by regular police officers and that this right is undermined when regular police officers are substituted with less qualified civilians. Because auxiliary officers engage in law enforcement activities sporadically, their skills may be less than optimal.

Volunteers' Perspective

There are several reasons why civilians may volunteer to work for police departments as auxiliary officers. Some volunteers use auxiliary police work as a way to gain experience in the process of pursuing careers in law enforcement (Weinblatt, 2011). Others, however, may join in an effort to serve the community, for recreational activities, and/or for educational purposes. Lastly, there are some who may join auxiliary units because they may not have been able to qualify as full-time police officers and they seek a means to satisfy their personal needs.

Regular Officers' Perspective

There may be resistance from within the police community regarding the use of auxiliary police officers. Full-time police officers may feel that auxiliary officer participation negatively impacts their income, may threaten job security, may reduce the number of promotional positions available, and may undermine police solidarity and their professional image. Furthermore, some full-time police officers may feel that auxiliary officers who ride double invade their personal space and demand constant supervision.

Some full-time police officers feel that auxiliary police officers negatively affect their income. Full-time officers may feel that auxiliary officers will reduce the amount of overtime available for them to work; the department could simply call in volunteer police officers who will work for free (Gill & Mawby, 1990). However, this problem can be addressed by limiting the number of auxiliary officers who are employed by the department, by limiting the maximum number of hours that they may work, and by limiting the maximum number of auxiliaries that can be called in at any single time. The role of the auxiliary unit is to augment the police department, not to displace the officers (Minnesota Police Reserve Officers Association, 2005). Furthermore, full-time police officers may resent civilians performing hazardous police work because police officers rely on the hazards of their jobs to earn sympathy from the public for increased salaries. Thus, regular police officers are concerned that auxiliary officers may directly affect their income. For example, although many full-time officers may welcome the extra set of eyes and help that auxiliary officers provide, the regular police officers may perceive volunteer police officers as scab labor. In other words, full-time officers may feel that auxiliary officers encourage management not to hire more full-time police officers. In addition, if fewer full-time police officers are hired, then fewer supervisors will be needed.

Full-time police officers may be concerned that civilians performing police work may undermine their professional image. If auxiliary officers dress poorly, perform poorly, display a lack of commitment, and jump the chain-of-command, then conflict may develop. A possible solution for this concern is to develop a rank structure within the auxiliary unit, where the unit is charged with maintaining its own order and discipline. However, with a rank system, the auxiliary officers must understand that even the highest ranking auxiliary officer is still subordinate to the lowest ranking full-time officer.

Some full-time police officers may feel that auxiliary officers who ride double with them invade their personal space. Full-time police officers who ride one-man cars may resent the intrusion of company into their vehicles. Some full-time officers get used to riding alone and may feel pressured when someone else is inside their vehicles because they know that someone else is watching them, which may lead them to modify their performance. In addition, some full-time police officers may be suspicious of auxiliary police officers, at least until they get to know them.

Auxiliary police officers may need too much supervision (Miller et al., 2011). One shortcoming of auxiliary officers is that they rarely gain the experience of those who have totally committed themselves to law enforcement. As a result, auxiliary officers may not have had the time to adequately develop their critical thinking skills. In addition, because auxiliary police officers may not have full police powers (i.e., the authority to arrest), their effectiveness may be diminished.

Departments' Perspective

There is a possibility that a police department may spend a lot of time and money on training auxiliary officers only to have them leave. If civilians join auxiliary units in order to become full-time police officers, then the police departments should expect them to apply for full-time police positions when given the chance, even if the positions are with other departments. This concern may be minimized by evaluating the reasons why civilians want to become auxiliary officers in the first place.

Collecting Data to Assess a Community-Policing Program

Once a community policing strategy has been implemented, it will be necessary to evaluate the strategy (Carter & Sapp, 2000). Indeed, any system without feedback is unstable. A police department's vision, the availability of resources, the demands of the community, and the characteristics of the community may all impact how community policing is implemented. Community policing is not a program but a philosophy of management and service delivery. This makes it difficult to assess.

Traditional law enforcement has focused on improving staffing, management, equipment, and the organization instead of focusing on the outcome of police work (Goldstein, 2000). Indeed, how fast officers arrive at the scene and how many arrests they make are objective ways to assess performance. On the other hand, assessing the crimes that have been prevented is a more difficult task. Effective program evaluation will depend on having a developed initiative (Carter & Sapp, 2000). Therefore, it is essential to have an established framework with clear criteria at the outset that will be used as the basis for meaningful evaluation.

Community policing is a partnership between the police and public, which focuses on preventative strategies through early interventions (Rosenbaum, 2000). Community policing does not discontinue traditional policing functions, it just reprioritizes the services that the police provide. Community policing stresses nonemergency services and alternate means for achieving the goal of peace. For example, it is the fear of crime that plays a crucial role in determining the stability of a neighborhood, which may lead to serious crime and a destabilized housing market. Thus, if the police can reduce social and physical signs of disorder, then perhaps neighborhoods can be stabilized before social problems get out of control. In short, serious organizational change is necessary to sustain a community policing strategy. This will require support from the public, police management, and patrol officers. In addition, public education is needed to build a more functional relationship between the police and public.

There are several ways to assess a police-community program. Once way to assess the program is to survey the community to see how satisfied residents feel. Another way is to assess how the officers feel about the program. See below for examples of surveys for collecting data in order to assess a police-community program.

Table 25

A survey to assess the community members' point of view

On a scale of 1 to 3, rate the following conditions. Three is a more positive response than one. 1 < 2 < 3				
1	I feel secure in my neighborhood.	1	2	3
2	What is the quality of police services?	1	2	3
3	What is the chance of becoming a victim of a serious crime in my neighborhood?	1	2	3
4	What is your overall satisfaction with police services?	1	2	3
5	The officers respond quickly to calls for service.	1	2	3
6	The officers are courteous.	1	2	3
7	Do officers identify themselves?	1	2	3
8	Are officers knowledgeable about solving problems?	1	2	3
9	Officers speak clearly and are easily understood.	1	2	3

Table 26

A survey to assess the police officers' point of view.

On a scale of 1 to 3, rate the following conditions. Three is a more positive response than one. 1 < 2 < 3				
1	The department is a decentralized operational system.	1	2	3
2	I am satisfied with my job.	1	2	3
3	Leaders willingly accept ideas for improvement.	1	2	3
4	I am allowed to make decisions in the face of ambiguity.	1	2	3
5	I work as part of a team to solve problems.	1	2	3
6	I serve as a role model to peers.	1	2	3
7	I serve as a role model to local residents.	1	2	3
8	I meet with local community groups on a regular basis.	1	2	3
9	My purpose as a community policing officer is well defined.	1	2	3

References

Agger, B. (2006). *Critical social theories: An introduction* (2nd ed.). Boulder, CO: Paradigm.

Armour, M.P., Windsor, L.C., Aguilar, J., & Taub, C. (2008). A pilot study of a faith-based restorative justice intervention for Christian and non-Christian offenders. *Journal of Psychology and Christianity, 27*(2), 159-167.

Barkan, S. (2006). *Criminology: A sociological understanding* (3rd ed.). Upper Saddle River, NJ: Pearson Prentice Hall.

Bratton, W. (1997). Blood, sweat, and databases. *Forbes, 160.*

Carter, D. (2002). *Issues in police-community relations: Taken from The Police and the community* (7th ed.). Boston, MA: Pearson Custom Publishing.

Carter, D. & Sapp, A.D. (2000). Community policing evaluation. In R. Glensor, M. Correia, & K. Peak (Eds.), *Policing communities: Understanding crime and solving problems, an anthology* (p. 284-302). Los Angeles, CA: Roxbury Publishing.

City of Oakland. (n.d.). *The Oakland community policing philosophy.*

City of San Diego. (n.d.). *Police department: Neighborhood watch.*

Clarke, R. (2000). Situational crime prevention: Successful studies. In R. Glensor, M. Correia, & K. Peak (Eds.), *Policing communities: Understanding crime and solving problems, an anthology* (p. 182-225). Los Angeles, CA: Roxbury Publishing Company.

Eterno, J.A., & Silverman, E.B. (2005). The New York City Police Department's compstat: dream or nightmare? *International Journal of Police Science & Management*, *8*(3), 218-231.

Fay, B. (1987). *Critical social science*. Ithaca, NY: Cornell University Press.

Gardner, J. (2000). Building a responsive community. In R. Glensor, M. Correia, & K. Peak (Eds.), *Policing communities: Understanding crime and solving problems, an anthology* (p. 67-74). Los Angeles, CA: Roxbury Publishing.

Gill, M.L. & Mawby, R.I. (1990). *A special constable: A study of the police reserve*. Brookfield, VT: Gower.

Glensor, R.W., & Peak, K.J. (2000). Lasting impact: maintaining neighborhood order. In R. Glensor, M. Correia, & K. Peak (Eds.), *Policing communities: Understanding crime and solving problems, an anthology* (p. 117-122). Los Angeles, CA: Roxbury Publishing.

Goldstein, H. (2000). Improving policing: A problem-oriented approach. In R. Glensor, M. Correia, & K. Peak (Eds.), *Policing communities: Understanding crime and solving problems, an anthology* (p. 5-21). Los Angeles, CA: Roxbury Publishing.

Greenberg, M.A. (1984). *Auxiliary police: The citizen's approach to public safety.* Westport, CT: Greenwood.

Hess, K.M., & Wrobleski, H.M. (2003). *Police operations: Theory and practice* (3rd ed.). Belmont, CA: Thomson Wadsworth.

Hoffman, E. (2011). *A history of reserve law enforcement.* Reserve Police Officer Association. Retrieved from http://www.reservepolice.org/

Indiana State Police (n.d.). *Career overview.* Retrieved from http://www.in.gov/isp/

Indiana State Police (1997). [Brochure]. *Marijuana: Get straight on the facts.* New Orleans, LA: Syndistar, Inc.

Joh, E. (2004). The paradox of private policing. *Journal of Criminal Law & Criminology, 95*(1), 49-131.

Lombardo, R., & Lough, T. (2007). Community policing: Broken windows, community building, and satisfaction with the police. *The Police Journal, 80*(2), 117-140.

Lurigio, A.J., & Rosenbaum, D.P. (1994). The impact of community policing on police personnel. In D. Rosenbaum (Ed.), *The challenge of community policing: testing the promises* (p. 147-163). Thousand Oaks, CA: Sage.

Lurigio, A.J., & Skogan, W.G. (2000). Winning the hearts and minds of police officers. In R. Glensor, M. Correia, & K. Peak (Eds.), *Policing communities: Understanding crime and solving problems, an anthology* (p. 246-256). Los Angeles, CA: Roxbury Publishing Company.

Magers, J.S. (2004). Compstat: A new paradigm for policing or a repudiation of community policing? *Journal of Contemporary Criminal Justice*, *20*(1), 70-79.

Marr, L. (1998). *Sexually transmitted diseases: A physician tells you what you need to know.* Baltimore, MD: The John Hopkins University Press.

Messemer, J.E. (2007). The influence of Christian programs on the academic achievements of low-literate male inmates. *The Journal of Correctional Education*, 58(3), 222-248.

Miller, L.S., Hess, K.M. & Orthmann, C.H. (2011). *Community policing: Partnership for problem solving* (6th ed.). Clifton Park, NY: Delmar Cengage.

Minnesota Police Reserve Officers Association (2005). Retrieved from www.mnproa.org/

Missouri State Highway Patrol. (n.d.). *You hold the key: Lock out auto theft.*

National Association Citizens on Patrol (n.d.). *Frequently asked questions.*

Oakland Police Department. (n.d.). *Crime prevention: Neighborhood watch.*

Orange County Sheriff (n.d.). Retrieved from www.ocso.com/

Phoenix Police Department. (n.d.). *Crime free multi-housing.* Retrieved from http://phoenix.gov/

Prassel, F.R. (1972). *The western peace officer: A legacy of law and order.* Norman, OK: University of Oklahoma.

Reading Police Department (2011). Retrieved from www.readingma.gov/

Reaves, B.A. (2007). Census of state and local law enforcement agencies, 2004. *Bureau of Justice Statistics Bulletin.* Retrieved from http://www.bjs.gov/

Roleff, T. (2005). *Drug abuse: Opposing viewpoints.* Detroit, MI: Thomson Gale.

Rosenbaum, D.P. (2000). The changing role of the police: Assessing the current transition to community policing. In R. Glensor, M. Correia, & K. Peak (Eds.), *Policing communities: Understanding crime and solving problems, an anthology* (p. 46-64). Los Angeles, CA: Roxbury Publishing.

Ryan, K., and Cooper, J. (2007). *Those who can, teach* (11th ed.). Boston, MA: Houghton Mifflin Company.

Sadd, S., & Grinc, R.M. (2000). Implementation challenges in community policing: Innovative neighborhood-oriented policing in eight cities. In R. Glensor, M. Correia, & K. Peak (Eds.), *Policing communities: Understanding crime and solving problems, an anthology* (p. 97-116). Los Angeles, CA: Roxbury Publishing.

Saus, E., Johnsen, B.H., Eid, J., Riisem, P.K., Andersen, R., & Thayer, J.F. (2006). The effect of brief situational awareness training in a police shooting simulator: An experimental study. *Military Psychology, 18*, S3-S21.

Seattle Department of Transportation. (n.d.). *Neighborhood speed watch program.* Retrieved from http://www.seattle.gov/

Shepherd, J. (2002, June 4). Police patrols crime hotspots. *The Times* (United Kingdom).

Siddle, B.K. (2005). *Defensive tactics instructor manual.* Millstadt, IL: PPCT Management Systems, Inc.

Smith, M. (2003). Exploring target attractiveness in vandalism: An experimental approach. *Crime Prevention Studies, 16*, 197-236.

Sower, C., & Gist, G.T. (1994). *Formula for change: Using the urban experiment station methods and the normative sponsorship theory.* East Lansing, MI: Michigan State University Press.

Sower, C., Holland, J., Tiedke, K., & Freeman, W. (1957). *Community Involvement: The webs of formal and informal ties that make for action.* Glencoe, IL: The Free Press.

Taylor, R.B., & Harrell, A.V. (2000). Physical environment and crime. In R. Glensor, M. Correia, & K. Peak (Eds.), *Policing communities: Understanding crime and solving problems, an anthology* (p. 167-181). Los Angeles, CA: Roxbury Publishing Company.

Teal, K. (2007, May 26). New philosophy unites cops: Compstat program isolates numbers, sites of crimes. *Florida Keys Keynoter.*

Texas Municipal League (2011). Retrieved from http://tml.associationcareernetwork.com/

Thacher, D. (2001). Conflicting values in community policing. *Law & Society Review*, 35 (4), 765-798.

Trojanowicz, R., Kappeler, V., and Gaines, L. (2002). *Community policing: A contemporary perspective* (3rd ed.). Cincinnati, OH: Anderson Publishing.

U.S. Department of Labor, Bureau of Labor Statistics (2009). *Occupational outlook handbook, 2010-11 edition.* Retrieved from http://www.bls.gov/ooh/

Vieno, A., Nation, M., Perkins, D.D., & Santinello, M. (2007). Civic participation and the development of adolescent behavior problems. *Journal of Community Psychology, 35*(6), 761-777.

Vito, G.F., Walsh, W.F., & Kunselman, J. (2005). Compstat: The manager's perspective. *International Journal of Police Science & Management*, *7*(3), 187-196.

Weinblatt, R. (2011). Retrieved from http://www.policereserveofficer.com/

Weisburd, D., Bushway, S., Lum, C., & Yang, S. (2004). Trajectories of crime at places: A longitudinal study of street segments in the city of Seattle. *Criminology*, *42*(2), 283-321.

Weisel, D.L. & Eck, J.E. (2000). Toward a practical approach to organizational change: Community policing initiatives in six cities. In R. Glensor, M. Correia, & K. Peak (Eds.), *Policing communities: Understanding crime and solving problems, an anthology* (p. 257-271). Los Angeles, CA: Roxbury Publishing.

Willis, J.J., Mastrofski, S.D., & Weisburd, D. (2007). Making sense of COMPSTAT: A theory-based analysis of organizational change in three police departments. *Law & Society Review*, *41*(1), 147-188.

Wilson, J.M. (2006). *Community policing in America.* New York, NY: Routledge.

Wootson, C.R. (April 20, 2011). Study by CMPD calls Charlotte airport police inadequate. *Herald-online.* Retrieved from www.heraldonline.com/

Xue, Y., Zimmerman, M.A., & Caldwell, C.H. (2007). Neighborhood residence and cigarette smoking among urban youths: The protective role of prosocial activities. *American Journal of Public Health*, *97*(10), 1865-1872.

Yancey, D. (2002). *STDs: What you don't know can hurt you.* Brookfield, CT: Twenty-first Century Books.

Zhao, J., Thurman, Q., & Lovrich, N. (2000). Community-oriented policing across the U.S.: Facilitators and impediments to implementation. In R. Glensor, M. Correia, & K. Peak (Eds.), *Policing communities: Understanding crime and solving problems, an anthology* (p. 229-238). Los Angeles, CA: Roxbury Publishing.

Chapter 10

SOCIOLOGY & COMMUNITY INTERVENTION

Sociology

During the 19th century, the industrial revolution and urbanization created disruption in maintaining social order (Turner, 1974). French sociologists no longer felt that social order was ensured by open and competitive economic conditions. Consequently, social thinkers began to ask why and how society is possible. During this time, advances in the biological sciences significantly influenced the social and intellectual disciplines. Hence, sociology was created as a self-discipline with a biological basis.

Although natural sciences rely on biological explanations for behavioral variations, sociology relies on learning and environmental explanations for the same behaviors (Goldenberg, 1997). Auguste Comte gave sociology a place among the sciences during the 19th century (Park & Burgess, 1969). Comte believed that sociology, which he had initially called social physics, could be treated as a technical science and could be used as a foundation to establish governments. Comte believed that progress demanded order, and he had hoped that the character of natural law could be extended to legislation where the scientific study of human nature could be realized. Although the elementary sciences, such as physics and chemistry, give people control over external nature, sociology gives people control over themselves.

Sociology deals with the reactions that result from voluntary and involuntary contact that human beings have with one another (Park & Burgess, 1969). Sociology has two main competing perspectives (Goldenberg, 1997). On the one hand, the macro-structural perspective claims that the human behavior lies in the structure of the social system. Thus, people's actions can be explained by evaluating the forces that impinge on their positions within the system. On the other hand, the micro-structural perspective claims that human behavior is motivated and can be explained by individualistic and social-psychological factors. Indeed, Max Weber, a founder of the micro-structural perspective, believed that sociology is based on intentional behavior.

During the early 20th century in the U.S., Chicago School sociologists viewed society as a process involving the complex and multifaceted interplay of associations and disassociations (Buckley, 1967). Social structure was considered a temporary, accommodative representation of the interactive process. In other words, society continually shifts its structure in order to adapt to internal and external conditions. Indeed, the process "focuses on the actions and interactions of the components of an ongoing system" (Buckley, p. 18). Furthermore, in an effort to intervene in social problems, Chicago School sociologists employed clinical sociology, which pairs science and action, to improve the quality of life (Fritz, 2002; Straus, 2002).

Paradigms of American Society

The four major paradigms, or theoretical perspectives, dominating American sociological thinking are a) **functionalism and the systems paradigm**, b) **interactionism and the conduct paradigm**, c) **critical theory and the conflict paradigm**, and d) **exchange theory and ecological perspective** (Straus, 2002). The **functionalism and the systems paradigm** states that the properties of a society are based on the interrelatedness of its members and not on the individual characteristics of the members themselves. The **interactionism and the conduct paradigm** states that people interact with one another in determining their realities. The **critical theory and the conflict paradigm** states that social conditions are influenced through group conflicts. The **exchange theory and ecological perspective** states that social conditions are influenced through interpersonal and intergroup transactions. Thus, all four paradigms dominate contemporary American sociology, they all involve the interaction between society's members, and they all help make practical sense of everyday life.

The Functionalism and the Systems Paradigm

The functionalism and the systems paradigm states that society has functional needs and that the form of society will change to meet those needs (Straus, 2002). According to this paradigm, society is a cohesive system and members are naturally integrated into systems so that they can work for the common good of the whole. In other words, social behaviors contribute toward the well-being of society and a healthy society is one of harmonious equilibrium.

The Interactionism and the Conduct Paradigm

The interactionism and the conduct paradigm states that human conduct is self-conscious and self-directed (Straus, 2002). According to this paradigm, human behaviors are influenced by social rules and this is what distinguishes human behavior from other biological creatures. Furthermore, human beings interact through symbolic communication and, consequently, they socially construct reality. In addition, this paradigm assumes that social members start life about equal, it downplays the impact of larger social factors, it assumes that social order is based on mutual conspiracy, and it assumes that society as a whole buys into it. This paradigm directly challenges the functionalism and the systems paradigm.

The Critical Theory and the Conflict Paradigm

The critical theory and the conflict paradigm states that conflict is the result of power differentials and resource allocation, it is universal, and it strongly influences a person's relationship to society (Straus, 2002). On the one hand, conflict can be destructive and can escalate into social disputes. On the other hand, conflict can promote social cohesiveness through problem resolution. According to this paradigm, conflict is a fact of social life and the manner in which it is handled will influence social relationships. Furthermore, this perspective challenges the functionalism and the systems paradigm by claiming that there is nothing natural or necessary about economic inequality.

The Exchange Theory and Ecological Perspective

Unlike the functionalism and the systems paradigm that focuses on the needs of society, the exchange theory and ecological perspective states that technology, population characteristics, and the physical environment are the primary factors of social organization (Straus, 2002). According to this paradigm, social life is based on interpersonal and intergroup transactions involving social, physical, and biological factors in which each person attempts to maximize personal gain. By having accepted norms that govern fair trade, competition can be realized without conflict.

Children with Special Needs

Various paradigms may apply to the same sociological situation. For example, involving special education children, although the **interactionism and the conduct paradigm** stresses that individuals start about equal, which may not be the case for children with special needs, the paradigm does stress that society will act in harmony toward a common end in an effort to promote social good (Straus, 2002). This does seem to be the case as evidenced by the U.S. government's passage of laws, such as No Child Left Behind, to help such kids (Guillaume, 2004). Although the law may have problems, it does show signs of effort. The **exchange theory and ecological perspective** may also apply in special needs situations. This is because technology, population characteristics, and the physical environment may affect how social changes are implemented in particular communities (Straus). For example, children with special needs in urban communities may experience interpersonal and intergroup transactions differently than special needs children in rural areas. Thus, the potential to maximize personal gains may not be the same in all communities.

Applied & Clinical Sociology

Level and Function of Theory

There are four levels of theory within the sociological field. The first and most basic level of theory is through simple observation (Straus, 2002). The theory's function is simply to allow individuals to think more clearly about the world by fitting the observed facts to the proposed explanation. However, in order to improve a theory's credibility, science (i.e., the systematic examination of the world through observation), measurement, analysis, and reflection must be applied to the theory. The second level and function of theory is based on the pure social science, which "is concerned with the development of scientific theory about society and social life" (Straus, p. 12). By applying science to theory, this academic level helps individuals think more clearly and accurately about the social world and generates an enhanced understanding of how individuals actually affect society. In the end, the value of this level of theory is measured by the extent to which its generalizations are supported by hypothesis-testing situations. The third level and function of theory is based on applied sociology. Applied sociology uses evaluation research to solve subjective problems which will better society in the future, such as using opinion polls to assess social values (Straus). This level is more advanced than pure sociology because it attempts to solve practical problems that will change society for the better. Finally, the highest level and function of theory is based on clinical sociology. Clinical sociology pairs science and action to solve current problems through immediate intervention. Thus, although applied sociology plans to solve problems in the future, clinical sociology plans to solve problems today.

There is a difference between **applied** and **clinical** sociology. As practiced in the U.S., applied sociology stresses research for practical purposes while clinical sociology stresses hands-on intervention (Fritz, 2002). Applied sociology is anthropocentric and focuses on the objective, end, or purpose in solving subjective problems that will better society in the future, using evaluation research to measure how successful human wants are satisfied (Straus, 2002; Ward, 1906). An example of applied sociology includes using large scale surveys for advertising, market research, and opinion polling (Straus). Clinical sociology, on the other hand, pairs science and action in a humanistic manner to improve the quality of life through analysis and action (Fritz). Examples of clinical sociology include marriage counseling, community consulting, and developing national policies.

For **applied sociologists**, the **interactionism and the conduct paradigm** and the **exchange theory and the ecological perspective** are most valuable (Straus, 2002). Using the interactionism and the conduct paradigm, sociologists can help solve future problems by using the media to construct reality through symbolic communication. Furthermore, using the exchange theory and ecological perspective, programs that use fair trade to maximize profits through competition can be promoted. Hence, for applied sociologists, there is ample time to shape social attitudes through effective communication.

For **clinical sociologists,** the **critical theory and the conflict paradigm** is most valuable because Americans practice capitalism

(Straus, 2002). If clinical sociologists are to solve current problems in the U.S., they must recognize that the practice of capitalism, which creates groups of rich people and groups of poor people, is a variable with which they must contend (Kraska, 2004). Capitalism by nature creates a surplus of poor people, and these poor people threaten the status quo. Thus, as long as there is capitalism and a struggle for limited resources, there will be conflict.

The social structure is the "relatively stable patterns of personal and interpersonal action, relationships, and processes that serve as the organizing framework of social life" (Straus, 2002, p. 380). The clinical sociologist will attempt to promote peace and to make life better for all social groups (Shostak, 2002). This includes making life better for family members and improving personal relationships. When clinical sociologists observe oppression and injustice, they have a responsibility to get involved.

Clinical Sociologists Responding to Family Problems

Clinical sociologists can facilitate problem-solving meetings between couples while helping them to learn the proper ways to manage conflict. There are eleven steps that clinical sociologists follow, and attempt to get couples to follow, for problem resolution (Cohen, 2002). As a result, couples may be able to resolve personal conflict and improve relationships.

Step 1: When stating a problem, individuals should always begin with positive statements (Cohen, 2002). This will switch the participants' perception from a negative track to a positive track. Indeed, emotions are associated with conflict and negative statements may only agitate the situation and block effective communications.

Step 2: When stating a problem, individuals should be specific and state the problem in behavioral terms (Cohen, 2002). By stating what behaviors need to be changed, this will clearly indicate how changes can be made. Otherwise, general criticisms do not provide for clear actions.

Step 3: When discussing a problem, individuals should state personal feelings (Cohen, 2002). Sometimes one person may not know how the other person feels. Instead of making assumptions about how each other feels, each person needs to clearly state his or her feelings so that there are no misunderstandings.

Step 4: When discussing a problem, individuals need to admit their personal roles in the problem (Cohen, 2002). There are always two sides to a problem. Therefore, each person must evaluate his or her own contribution to the problem.

Step 5: When defining the problem, individuals need to define it briefly (Cohen, 2002). When the problem becomes too complicated, people become overloaded and forgetful. Thus, the problem needs to be easily defined so that it can be effectively addressed.

Step 6: When discussing a problem, individuals need to limit the problem to only one problem at a time (Cohen, 2002). Otherwise, if one person diverts attention to other problems, the current problem will not be resolved. Thus, individuals need to stay focused on the current problem.

Step 7: When discussing a problem, individuals need to paraphrase it (Cohen, 2002). By doing this, each person will receive confirmation that he or she is interpreting the problem correctly. Indeed, before a problem is effectively resolved, it must first be properly understood.

Step 8: When discussing a problem, individuals should not make inferences (Cohen, 2002). Indeed, each person has developed his or her own reality based upon unique personal experiences. Thus, if a person uses personal realities to judge other people, this may lead to wrong assumptions. Therefore, individuals should focus on behaviors and they should avoid attributing causes and meanings to other people's behaviors.

Step 9: When discussing a problem, individuals need to be neutral rather than negative (Cohen, 2002). The goal is to find a win-win resolution. Thus, instead of using threats, demands, and derogatory statements, which may lead to withdrawal or counterattacks, each person should address the problem in a constructive manner.

Step 10: When discussing a problem, individuals need to focus on solutions (Cohen, 2002). Individuals need to avoid restating old problems, which may only promote negative feelings. Indeed, individuals need to brainstorm and to work toward constructive resolutions.

Step 11: When discussing a problem, individuals need to promote mutuality and compromise (Cohen, 2002). Healthy relationships need to be balanced. Thus, each person needs to work for resolutions that are satisfactory to both parties.

In short, these 11 steps are used to manage conflict. By following these 11 steps, individuals will be able to focus their efforts on the problem at hand. Once learned, these steps may be performed inside the home by family members.

Police Officer as Sociologist

A police officer may wear many hats, one of them being the role of a sociologist. There are eight roles that sociologists may assume (Shostak, 2002). The sociologist may assume the role of 1) cultural translator, 2) peace publicist, 3) assessor of novel ideas, 4) defender of the language, 5) thoughtful advocate, 6) peace scholar, 7) peace historian, and 8) futurist. The police officer needs to select the most appropriate method that best resonates with the community.

There are many different ways for a police officer to get involved to better society, and each sociologist role addresses problems from a different perspective (Shostak, 2002). The first role that a police officer may assume is that of a cultural translator. In this case, the police officer attempts to lessen misperceptions between parties and to build trust between them. The second role that a police officer may assume is that of a peace publicist. In this case, the police officer attempts to redirect resources to improve social life in a more efficient manner. The third role that a police officer may assume is that of an assessor of novel ideas. By pointing out the pleasures gained by misconduct, a better understanding of why people engage in conflict may be realized. The fourth role that a police officer may assume is that of a defender of the language. In this case, the police officer describes hurtful actions as they really are, without trying to sugarcoat them. The fifth role a police officer may assume is that of a thoughtful advocate. In this case, the police officer lets the facts of the data speak for themselves (objective analysis). The sixth role a police officer may assume is that of a peace scholar. In this case, the police officer performs a literature review and uses information already available to help resolve conflict. The seventh role a police officer may assume is that of a peace historian. In this case, the police officer attempts to introduce honesty, reconciliation, and privacy by reminding individuals of the complexity and futility of conflict. The eighth role a police officer may assume is that of a futurist. In this case, the police officer attempts to use modern technology to simulate future conditions based on proposed solutions.

Table 27
Police Officer as Sociologist

#	Title	Role of Police Officer
1	Cultural translator	Police officer attempts to lessen misperceptions between parties and to build trust between them.
2	Peace publicist	Police officer attempts to redirect resources to improve social life in a more efficient manner.
3	Assessor of novel ideas	Police officer points out the pleasures gained by misconduct so that a better understanding of why people engage in conflict may be realized.

4	Defender of the language	Police officer describes hurtful actions as they really are, without trying to sugarcoat them.
5	Thoughtful advocate	Police officer lets the facts of the data speak for themselves (objective analysis).
6	Peace scholar	Police officer performs a literature review and uses information already available to help resolve conflict.
7	Peace historian	Police officer attempts to introduce honesty, reconciliation, and privacy by reminding individuals of the complexity and futility of conflict.
8	Futurist	Police officer attempts to use modern technology to simulate future conditions based on proposed solutions.

Self-Regulated Communities

Local problems are best understood at the local level. To gain control over their local issues, communities need to become self-regulated (Garland & Sparks, 2000). A self-regulated community provides two advantages. First, local residents will be able to handle their local issues more effectively because they understand the nature of local problems and the capabilities of available resources. Second, any individuals who feel that they cannot live in a particular area where certain activities are illegal may simply move to a region where the activities are not illegal. In other words, individuals may align themselves with others who feel the same way. In this way, everyone is satisfied.

Social Engineering, Duluth, & Back of Yards

There are several different strategies to help resolve social problems (Alinsky, 1984; Duluth Model, n.d.; Fein, 2000). Three models to address social problems are a) the social engineering model, b) the Duluth Model, and c) the Back of Yards. The social engineering model systematically eliminates barriers until all the barriers are removed, the Duluth model employs a systemic form of community intervention, and the Back of Yards uses a local community council and interagency collaboration to handle local problems (Alinsky, 1984; Rivett, & Rees, 2004). By implementing these intervention strategies, problems can be identified, solutions can be presented, and, by working together, community members can provide a coordinated effort to overcome their problems.

Social Engineering Model

The social engineering model suggests that variables can be manipulated so that desirable outcomes can be achieved (Fein, 2000). In other words, the root causes of social problems are objectively identified and resolved so that change is possible. Once the problems are resolved, there will be no barriers left to impeded change. Subsequently, change may occur, which will enhance the health of the community. However, in a capitalistic society, because power is decentralized, social engineering may be performed in a piecemeal fashion, leading to dangerous and unforeseeable consequences. Hence, to strengthen the community's efforts in managing social problems, interagency cooperative efforts are needed.

Duluth Model

The Duluth model employs a systemic form of community intervention to handle local problems (Duluth Model, n.d.; Rivett, & Rees, 2004). Because each individual on the community team has unique skills and performs special functions, each person's contribution is essential for social success via interagency collaboration. In other words, organizations do not need to become one big melting pot. Instead, the team needs to resemble a mosaic. In the mosaic model, each organization retains and adds its own unique strengths to the team for overall success. This same argument applies to various team sports (e.g., football, baseball, soccer, hockey, basketball, etc.).

The Duluth model exploits the natural synergy between companies. In other words, the team is greater than any single player. In addition, the Duluth model promotes equal gender relationships and creates a means to end violence toward women and children (Rivett, & Rees, 2004).

The aim of the Duluth model is to generate a coordinated community response to change the legal system to better promote the health of society (Duluth Model, n.d.). The goal is to change the practice of local professionals so that they will work effectively together to promote the safety of individuals-in-need. In other words, the health of victims is the highest priority and offenders are required to receive treatment.

However, getting agencies to work together can be difficult. First, there may be communication problems. Agencies need to keep each other informed about the process so that the entire problem involving both victims and offenders can be addressed. Indeed, there must be a case manager to ensure that each agency is performing its function. Second, workers may put their personal agendas over that of the victims. Finally, the way each worker is rated on his or her performance review may affect how each person performs his or her duties. Thus, the agencies need to develop an overall plan that meets the model's goal.

Back of Yards

According to Alinsky (1984), the Back of Yards, which is a local community council, was formed in a Chicago neighborhood as a way to handle local problems. Because local residents believed that one social problem may influence many other social problems, and that the community is part of the larger social scene, "the organizational procedures must direct their attention toward those larger socioeconomic issues which converge upon" (p. 26) the local scene and are readily identified as problems. In other words, problems are not independent of one another, extraneous variables must be considered, and the root causes of the problems must be resolved.

Local communities must face and solve their own area problems. Thus, by uniting the various organizations within a community to promote the welfare of all local residents, it is hoped that all individuals have an opportunity to find health, happiness, and security. Above all, it is important that the united organization is not controlled by outside groups, whose interests may not be in alignment with the local community's interests. Indeed, health and safety are the focus of problem management, not punishment and labeling.

Applying Sociological Models to Prostitution

Several sociological models can be applied to prostitution. By implementing a combination of these intervention strategies, social problems can be resolved and social health can be enhanced. Community groups need to provide a coordinated effort to overcome their local problems via totality of circumstances.

Self-Regulated Communities

When power is centralized, the government is less flexible in handling complex social issues. Because individuals of different cultures in different geographical regions under a single government may have different attitudes of what is best in their local areas, a single law not be equally effective everywhere (Garland & Sparks, 2000). This may be particularly true for prostitution, which involves laws based on the elite's subjective interpretations of morality. Thus, an effective solution to the problem is to let the communities be self-regulated, where the decision to legalize prostitution can be decided at the local level.

By splitting society into communities of choice, different groups will be able to pass laws that best meet their needs (Garland & Sparks, 2000). If individuals did not like the local laws in one area, they can simply move to another area that is in alignment with their values. Thus, through this type of social governance, prostitutes will cease to be exceptions to the mainstream. In addition, residents will feel less threatened that moral minorities will gain control of a centralized government through a political majority and threaten the lifestyle of their community.

Back of Yards

Applying Back of Yards to prostitution, the violence, sexually transmitted diseases, and the mental health of the prostitutes can be addressed. Because a national solution is not forthcoming, local communities must face and solve the problems themselves. By developing a unity of purpose, the Back of Yards Neighborhood Council may use indigenous organizations to mobilize the sentiment of the community (Alinsky, 1984). Furthermore, by developing a community congress, with elected officials, appropriate policies can be approved. In short, the Back of Yards Neighborhood Council is flexible, local residents socially identify with the community congress, and policies represent the residents' interests.

Duluth Model

Applying the Duluth model to prostitution, women's health and safety take precedence over punishing their sexual activities. Because each agency in the community has limited resources, the output of the various organizations will be greater if they combine their efforts. In short, the local community organizations will work as a team to meet the needs of prostitutes.

The Duluth program uses four primary strategic principles for inter-organization intervention (Duluth Model, n.d.). First, change must occur within the basic infrastructures of the various agencies. For example, participating organizations must develop a plan to work cooperatively to protect female prostitutes by providing them with the appropriate resources. Second, the overall strategy must focus on the victim's health and safety. This can be achieved by providing the prostitutes with essential public services and by providing anyone who abuses them with mandatory treatment programs. Third, the various organizations must be collaborating partners. Indeed, each agency's workers must focus on the overall goal and not on personal agendas. Finally, individuals who threaten the health and safety of prostitutes must consistently be held accountable by the police and courts for their acts of recklessness and violence. When these four strategic principles are followed, the Duluth model will be quite successful.

Social Engineering Model

The social engineering model suggests that variables can be manipulated so that the root causes of society's concerns about prostitution can be resolved in an orderly and rational manner (Fein, 2000). Society's concerns about prostitution include violence, sexually transmitted diseases, and the mental health of the prostitutes. Using the social engineering model, each problem is addressed below.

Reducing Violence

Research conducted by Brents and Hausebeck (2005) indicates that the legalization of brothels in Nevada has resulted in fewer acts of violence toward prostitutes. This is because government approved brothels bring a level of public scrutiny, official regulation, and bureaucratization. Furthermore, by employing situational crime prevention measures, violence inside brothels can be effectively prevented (Clarke, 2000). Situational crime prevention measures do not focus on offenders or the many reasons why they may commit crime. Instead, they focus on the opportunities to commit crime, the settings for crime, and on the prevention of crime. Thus, strong defense mechanisms can be placed inside the brothels. These measures will increase the effort, increase the perceived risks, and reduce the anticipated rewards associated with committing crimes of violence against prostitutes.

Preventing Sexually Transmitted Diseases

Research conducted by Velu (2002) indicates that knowledge and awareness of HIV/AIDS and a positive social support system promote condom use. Indeed, sexually transmitted diseases may be effectively managed through mandated education. Therefore, the local community may develop an educational program that will require all parties of commercial sex to attend before they engage in sexual business. In other words, prostitutes and clients must pass a government approved test about effective condom use before they will be allowed to engage in commercial sex. The test may be provided at the local brothels and the records maintained at the source. The law will requirc that condoms be used during commercial sex. Furthermore, the local government can require the prostitutes to undergo periodic medical exams. These services may be funded by tax revenue collected from the brothels or by union dues paid by the prostitutes.

Promoting Prostitutes' Mental Health

Research conducted by Vanwesenbeeck (2005) indicates that female prostitutes suffer mental distress because they are stigmatized, because they work in harsh working environments, and because they lack social support. Thus, if the local community provides prostitutes with safe work environments (i.e., brothels), if the prostitutes are treated as human being and not as deviants (e.g., by legalizing prostitution), and if prostitutes are provided the necessary social services that they need (e.g., professional counseling), then the mental health of the prostitutes may be enhanced. In addition, an appropriate exit program needs to be developed so that women can leave the field of prostitution, if desired.

Alcoholism: A Social Problem

There are about 100,000 Americans killed each year due to alcoholism, costing about $116 billion annually (Firshein, 1997). Although alcohol is harmful and additive, it is a socially accepted and desirable drug. Americans demand alcohol and, in a capitalistic society, that demand will be supplied. Indeed, history has shown that attacking the supply side of alcohol is futile (Tucker et al., 1999). Therefore, to manage the problem, other tactics must be used.

There are more than 700,000 Americans who receive treatment for alcoholism on any given day (U.S. Department of Health and Human Services, 2000). Addiction is a medical condition involving chemicals inside the brain (Lemonick, 2007). The human body has a way to compensate for the presence of foreign substances (e.g., alcohol), which may include the need for certain chemicals.

Medical Model

According to the medical model, addiction is a progressive disease that needs to be treated at the individual level (Morse, 2004; Nunes-Dinis & Barth, 1993). The medical model states there is a large biological difference between a normal person's brain and an addict's brain. In fact, the brains of addicts have been shown to possess common elements of addiction, independent of the kind of substance abused. Consequently, the addicts are not responsible for their cravings of harmful substances. The behaviors exhibited by addicts are only the symptoms of the disease and not the disease itself. Therefore, instead of punishing the addict, nonjudgmental and therapeutic responses are appropriate. Addiction requires intervention treatment, not incarceration (Grose, 2007). The addict is, however, responsible for seeking treatment.

Intervention treatment is intensive, costly, and involves a trained professional in a clinical environment (Morse, 2004; Nunes-Dinis & Barth, 1993). The proper treatment program will often produce a high rate of change for an addict. In the medical model, change is an inch wide and a mile deep.

Public Health Perspective

According to the public health perspective, an addiction problem is a community and environmental problem (Tucker et al., 1999). The public health perspective seeks to address substance abuse problems at the community level and tries to help as many people as possible at one time in natural environments. Thus, a specific individual's motivation to change is irrelevant. Because the entire population of high-risk groups is targeted, the intervention is brief and cost effective. However, the rate of change is low. Thus, in the public health perspective, change is a mile wide and an inch deep.

According to the public health perspective, an addict's inappropriate behaviors are influenced by the environment. Addicts need to identify and prevent inappropriate behaviors before they happen (Blanchard & Tabachnick, 2002). Addicts need to be educated so that their attitudes and beliefs about harmful substances can be changed. In addition, addicts need to remove themselves from harmful environments. Addicts need to move to friendlier environments with family members, peer groups, and others who will have a positive influence.

MATCH

Project MATCH, which stands for Matching Alcoholism Treatments to Client Heterogeneity, was the largest and most expensive treatment study related to alcoholism (Tucker et al., 1999). The research study investigated whether patients responded better to particular treatment programs if they were matched to a particular program based upon personal characteristics that they possessed. The three treatment programs investigated were 1) the twelve-step facilitation (TSF) program, 2) the cognitive-behavior therapy (CBT) program, and 3) the motivational enhancement therapy (MET) program. The findings indicate that there is no significant difference between patient characteristics and treatment therapies. Generally, all three programs are equally effective in terms of reducing the amount of alcohol consumed. Therefore, alcoholics have three equally viable alternatives, allowing them to select the treatment program that best satisfies their personal interests.

However, the MATCH research study has several limitations (Tucker et al., 1999). First, there was no control group. Thus, there is no fixed reference in which to compare the test results. Second, researchers dropped subjects from the study who did not have a permanent home address or who had legal problems. Dropping these high risk clients from the study meant the loss of valuable data. Finally, because MATCH researchers had strict screening and recruitment processes, because they performed one-on-one treatment sessions instead of group therapy, and because they performed personalized follow-up sessions, the study's external validity was compromised.

Dealing with Alcoholics

Police Tactics

There are three police tactics for dealing with those individuals who abuse alcohol. The first tactic is the pay officers to work overtime and to specifically look for alcohol-related violations. These officers are not given any other details during these special projects because their sole focus is to make alcohol-related arrests. These special patrols are advertised to the public, via the media, as a warning not to drink and drive. The second tactic is to set up sobriety check points during normal patrol hours. Normal patrol hours include Friday and Saturday nights. The fear of arrest may scare people straight. A third tactic is for police officers to travel from school to school and to present information to students as part of a prevention program. As a way of educating the students, police officers may let the students wear intoxication goggles, which emulate the effects of various levels of intoxication. The goal is to educate the young about the negative consequences associated with consuming alcoholic beverages.

Excise Police

The Excise Police are the law enforcement officers whose primary goal is to restrict the availability of alcohol to minors (Huskey, 2007). They use two tactics that they believe are effective. One tactics is to have excise police officers pose as employees or customers at places where alcoholic beverages are sold. Because this tactic is advertised to the general public, it is hoped that minors will be discouraged from purchasing alcoholic beverages due to the inflated risk of being arrested. An added benefit to this tactic is that the officers can teach the store clerks on how to recognize modified and fake identifications. Furthermore, officers have a chance to experience firsthand some of the problems that the clerks face in their stores. This open communication between the police officers and clerks improves overall success. A second tactic used by the Excise Police is to educate the young. Officers travel from school to school and present information to students about the negative consequences associated with alcohol consumption. Similar to the regular police, the goal is to prevent the problem in the first place.

Community Treatment

Local communities may have resources to help alcoholics. For example, Cameron Counseling Center in Indiana offers personalized therapy to persons suffering from compulsive, addictive behavioral problems (Cameron Counseling Center, n.d.a; Cameron Counseling Center, n.d.b). The process that is used to determine which treatment method is made available to each client is based on the addiction counselor's interpretation of an interview with the client. Based on the interview, an individualized treatment program is matched to each client. There are four different groups that a client can be assigned: a) the didactic group, b) the addictions group, c) the relapse prevention group, and d) the non-violence group. The didactic group assists those individuals who exhibit significant drug abuse problems by educating them to take appropriate actions to prevent future problems. The addictions group assists those individuals who exhibit significant alcoholic dependency problems by having them complete exercises, which will help them abstain from future alcohol use. The relapse prevention group assists those individuals who are at high risk of returning to their addictive behaviors by helping them learn to identify and control their relapse warning signs. Finally, the non-violence group assists those individuals who exhibit inappropriate aggressive behaviors by teaching them how to manage their anger through role-playing. Because Cameron Counseling Center is located in a rural area, there is not a big enough market for the Cameron Counseling Center to offer extensive services. Therefore, if a person has needs that cannot be met by the Cameron Counseling Center, then that person is referred to the Fairbanks Alcohol and Drug Treatment Center in Indianapolis, Indiana.

Fairbanks, the oldest nonprofit addiction treatment center in Indiana, offers both impatient and outpatient programs (Fairbanks, n.d.). Fairbanks advertises that its medical director is one of the top addictionologists in the country and that he has specialized training in the disease of addiction. Fairbanks states that a) its highly trained professionals conduct research, which helps determine new substance abuse treatment methods, b) its long-term success proves that its methods are effective, c) its staff members have been involved in several long-term studies on substance abuse, which support the effectiveness of its major treatment programs, and d) it works with the Indiana University Medical School to better understand addiction and the effectiveness of treatment.

At Fairbanks, a medical professional assesses each client through an interview process and develops a personalized step-by-step plan of treatment, which matches each client's needs (Fairbanks, n.d.). For impatient services, Fairbanks has three different programs: the detoxification program, the rehabilitation program, and the residential services program. First, the detoxification program is designed for those individuals who may experience serious withdrawal complications. Patients are continuously supervised. Being under medical management, comprehensive evaluations take place to ensure that the appropriate levels of care are being provided. Second, the rehabilitation program uses a multidisciplinary team, group therapy, and medical observations to assist in the treatment program. The rehabilitation group promotes the 12-step recovery program. Finally, the residential services program is for those individuals who do not need medical intervention but who still need a structured environment to ensure that they abstain from drug use.

For outpatient services, Fairbanks offers three programs: the partial hospitalization program, the intensive outpatient program, and the adolescent discovery program (Fairbanks, n.d.). First, the partial hospitalization program is for medically stable clients who live in stable environments, but who still need support. The support may consist of having the clients participate in the 12-step care program. These clients return home every night. Second, the intensive outpatient program provides education and group therapy several days a week. This program also promotes participation in the 12-step care program. Finally, the adolescence discovery program is designed to educate the young, as a preventative technique. By helping young individuals see the damage that drugs can inflict, it is hoped that they will make wise decisions not to use them.

Two ethical issues involving managed care are cost and confidentiality. For example, the impatient detoxification program at Fairbanks costs $1,278 per day plus physician fees (T. Martin-Nichols, personal communication on November 20, 2007). The rehabilitation program costs $868 per day plus physician fees. Finally, the residential services program costs $524 per day. Concerning the outpatient programs, the partial hospitalization program and the intensive outpatient program costs $451 per day and $5,500 for a ten week program, respectively. Indeed, the programs may be cost prohibitive and may eliminate many people from the treatment process.

Confidentiality is another ethical issue involving treatment programs. Although there are federal laws that require licensed professionals to keep client communications confidential during treatment sessions, these law does not apply to other clients who are present during group sessions (Scott, 2000). The other clients may report information that they hear at the group meetings to other people, including the legal authorities. Furthermore, even if the treatment sessions are private, many state laws only protect privileged information in civil cases and not in criminal cases. Thus, there may be a conflict of interest that may be detrimental to the treatment process.

Alcoholic Anonymous

Alcoholic Anonymous (AA) is a fellowship of men and women in over 105,000 groups worldwide with over 2 million members (Alcoholics Anonymous, 2005). There is strength in numbers. By working together and by supporting each other, people are encouraged and motivated to overcome their addictions. Furthermore, AA has a sponsorship program (Alcoholics Anonymous, 1983b). By receiving continual, one-on-one support from another alcoholic who has shown some progress in the program, hope is gained. Hope promotes success. A study of 7,000 AA members indicated that 29% stayed sober over 5 years, 38% stayed sober between 1 to 5 years, and 33% stayed sober less than 1 year (Alcohol Anonymous, 1987).

Individuals attend AA meetings because they have a problem that they have not been able to resolve by themselves. Alcoholics must humble themselves and admit that alcoholism is a serious problem (Alcohol Anonymous, 1981). Once the problem is accepted, then more effort can be directed at solving the problem. Although individuals who turn to AA may feel that their drinking problems are overwhelming, they are taught that there is a power greater than their addiction. In this manner, members are given hope that change is possible. AA's philosophy claims that to start a new life built upon a solid foundation, the old foundation must totally be discarded.

Because alcohol is a legal drug and is commonplace, alcoholics are going to be continually tempted. AA meetings create a supportive atmosphere, providing fellowships with those who empathize. Indeed, those who have experienced the pain of alcoholism can help other individuals without labeling. As far as anonymity is concerned, AA members are not allowed to disclose their real names when dealing with media (Alcoholics Anonymous, 1983a; Alcoholics Anonymous, 1990). In fact, AA does not even put "AA" on the envelopes that the organization sends out. In short, AA is anonymous to outsiders.

The 12-step care approach utilized by AA is a valuable resource necessary for alcohol addiction treatment (Alcoholics Anonymous, 1981). Because alcohol addiction treatment is outside the mainstream healthcare system, because the U.S. government has a limited budget for government sponsored treatments, and because stigma labeling discourages many alcoholics from attending government sponsored treatment programs, the AA 12-step program provides a needed service to community members (Tucker et al., 1999). See Tables 28 and 29.

However, the 12-step program would not be appropriate for a person who requires inpatient treatment. A personalized step-by-step plan of treatment that matches each client's needs must be developed (Fairbanks, n.d.). For example, detoxification may be required for those who may experience serious withdrawal complications. This could not be accomplished at the 12-step care meetings.

Alcoholics Anonymous 12-Step Program

Table 28

Alcoholics Anonymous 12 Step Care Program

(Alcoholics Anonymous, 1981)

Alcoholics Anonymous 12 Step Care Program The 12 steps are only suggestions.	
1	A person must admit that he or she is powerless over alcohol. A person cannot solve a problem until the person admits that the problem exists.
2	There is a higher power that can help restore sanity. Faith has healing power.
3	A decision has to be made to surrender to that higher authority. Willingness to change requires submission.
4	A person should take a moral inventory of self. Liabilities must be discovered. This is the start of a lifetime of practice.
5	A person must confess the problem. Others are there to help.
6	Persons must submit and ready themselves to have God remove their character defects. Persons needs to grow spiritually.
7	Individuals must humble themselves and ask God to remove their shortcomings.
8	Persons must identify all individuals whom they have harmed and they must be willing to make amends. Isolation must be ended.
9	Persons must make amends to all individuals whom they have harmed without causing any additional injuries.
10	Persons must continually take personal inventories and they must admit flaws right away so that the flaws can be patiently corrected.
11	Persons need to pray and meditate to improve personal relations with God for a better understanding of His will and the power to carry it out.
12	Having a spiritual awaking, alcoholics shall spread the message to other alcoholics and attempt to practice the principles in all aspects of life.

Table 29

Alcoholics Anonymous 12 Traditions

(Alcoholics Anonymous, 1981)

Alcoholics Anonymous 12 Traditions	
1	The common welfare of Alcoholics Anonymous is top priority. Unity of the group is essential for personal survival.
2	AA gets its direction from God. Leaders are simply trusted servants.
3	AA membership only requires a desire to stop consuming alcoholic beverages.
4	As long as it does not negatively impact AA as a whole, each group of AA is autonomous.
5	The primary purpose of AA is to spread the message to suffering alcoholics.
6	AA will not endorse or get involved with outside entities because problems may arise that may divert efforts away from AA's primary purpose.
7	Each AA group needs to be self-sufficient and must decline outside contributions. Exploitation must be prevented.
8	Except for special workers, AA should not employ professionals to run the group. Capitalism should not control the group's purpose.
9	AA should not subject itself to a governing board, but it will have service workers. AA cannot dictate what members must do.
10	AA will not get involved with outside issues, which may draw efforts away from AA's primary mission.
11	Personal anonymity is essential. Public relations are essential. AA seeks publicity for its principles and not for its members.
12	Anonymity is essential because principles come before personalities.

Funding Site for Substance Abuse Assistance

There are several sponsors that provide monies to state and local governments for substance abuse assistance. These sponsors are 1) the Center for Substance Abuse Treatment (CSAT), 2) the Bureau of Justice Assistance (BJA), 3) the Substance Abuse and Mental Health Services Administration (SAMHSA), and 4) the U.S. Office of National Drug Control Policy (Substance Abuse and Mental Health Services Administration, 2014; U.S. Department of Justice, n.d.; U.S. Office of National Drug Control Policy, 2007). First, the CSAT sponsors the Addiction Technology Transfer Center, which provides a national computer bank of knowledge and experience from recognized experts in the field of drug addiction treatment practices. Second, the BJA provides financial and technical assistance to states, local governments, and courts. The BJA supports the Residential Substance Abuse Treatment for State Prisoners Program, which helps states and local governments develop and implement residential substance abuse treatment programs. Third, the SAMHSA sponsors the Recovery Community Services Program, via grants, in order to provide peer-to-peer recovery support services and to offer support to family members. The SAMHSA also helps finance domestic conferences involving knowledge synthesis and dissemination of treatment, recovery, early intervention, and prevention services. Finally, the U.S. Office of National Drug Control Policy provides grants to state and local agencies to combat drug related problems in their local areas. However, federal funding for addiction treatment programs is only granted to state or local agencies who request it. Therefore, it is imperative that state and local governments take the time to ask for the funds.

In conclusion, alcoholism is a significant social and personal problem. Community members must work together to manage the problem. It is important that the community not attach any stigma to those individuals who need help. Otherwise, those individuals who need help may not seek the help that they need. This would be detrimental to society as a whole. There are various factors that contribute to excessive drinking, but there is also help available to those individuals who want it. Furthermore, the federal government has resources that are available to state and local governments to combat addiction problems, if they request them.

References

Alcoholics Anonymous World Service, Inc. (1981). *Twelve Steps and Twelve Traditions* (40th ed.). Grand Central Station, NY: Alcoholics Anonymous Publishing.

Alcoholics Anonymous World Service, Inc. (1983a). *AA tradition: How it developed.* Grand Central Station, NY: Alcoholics Anonymous Publishing.

Alcoholics Anonymous World Service (1983b). *Questions & answers on sponsorship* [Brochure]. The A.A. Grapevine, Inc.: Author.

Alcoholics Anonymous World Service (1987). [Brochure]. *AA membership survey.*

Alcoholics Anonymous World Service, Inc. (1990). *The AA group . . . where it all begins.* Grand Central Station, NY: Alcoholics Anonymous Publishing.

Alcoholics Anonymous World Service (2005). [Brochure]. *A.A. at a glance.*

Alinsky, S.D. (1984). Community analysis and organization. *Clinical Sociology Review*, 2, 25-34.

Blanchard, G. and Tabachnick, J. (2002). The prevention of sexual abuse: Psychology and public health perspectives. *Sexual Addiction & Compulsivity, 9.*

Brents, B.G., & Hausebeck, K. (2005). Violence and legalized brothel prostitution in Nevada: Examining safety, risk, and prostitution policy. *Journal of Interpersonal Violence, 20*(3), 270-295.

Buckley, W. (1967). *Sociology and modern systems theory.* Englewood Cliffs, NJ: Prentice-Hall, Inc.

Cameron Counseling Center (n.d.a). *Cameron Memorial Community Hospital* [Brochure]. Cameron Hospital: Author.

Cameron Counseling Center (n.d.b). *Caring is the key* [Brochure]. Cameron Hospital: Author.

Clarke, R. (2000). Situational crime prevention: Successful studies. In R. Glensor, M. Correia, & K. Peak (Eds.), *Policing communities: Understanding crime and solving problems, an anthology* (p. 182-225). Los Angeles, CA: Roxbury Publishing Company.

Cohen, H. (2002). Sociology and you: Good living. In R. Straus (Ed.), *Using sociology: An introduction from the applied and clinical perspectives* (3rd ed.) (p. 291-324). New York, NY: Rowman & Litterfield Publishers, Inc.

Duluth Model (n.d.). Retrieved from http://www.theduluthmodel.org/

Fairbanks (n.d.). *Experts in addictions. Focused on recovery.* [Brochure]. Fairbanks Alcohol and Drug Treatment Center: Author. Retrieved from http://www.fairbankscd.org/

Fein, M.L. (2000). Race relations: A survey of potential intervention strategies. *Sociological Practice: A Journal of Clinical and Applied Sociology*, *2*(3), 147-162.

Firshein, J. (1997). Alcohol-treatment programmes are comparable. *Lancet, 349*(9044).

Fritz, J.M. (2002). Community matters. In R. Straus (Ed.), *Using sociology: An introduction from the applied and clinical perspectives* (3rd ed.) (p. 235-264). New York, NY: Rowman & Litterfield Publishers, Inc.

Garland, D, and Sparks, R. (Eds.). (2000). *Criminology and social theory*. New York, NY: Oxford University Press.

Goldenberg, S. (1997). *Thinking sociologically* (2nd ed.). New York, NY: Oxford University Press.

Grose, T. (2007). Abuse as a disease, not a crime. *U.S. News & World Report*, *142*(11).

Guillaume, A. (2004). *K-12 classroom teaching: A primer for new professionals* (2nd ed.). Upper Saddle River, NJ: Pearson - Merrill Prentice Hall.

Huskey, A. (2007). Message from the superintendent. *Indiana State Excise Police*. Retrieved from http://www.in.gov/

Kraska, P. (2004). *Theorizing criminal justice: Eight essential orientations*. Long Grove, IL: Waveland Press, Inc.

Lemonick, M., and Park, A. (2007). The science of addiction. *Time, 170*(3).

Morse, S. (2004). Medicine and morals, cravings and compulsion. *Substance Use & Misuse, 39*(3).

Nunes-Dinis, M. and Barth, R. (1993). Cocaine treatment and outcome. *Social Work, 38*(5).

Park, R.E., and Burgess, E.W. (1969). *Introduction to the science of sociology* (3rd ed.). Chicago, IL: The University of Chicago Press.

Rivett, M., and Rees, A. (2004). Dancing on a razor's edge: Systemic group work with batterers. *Journal of Family Therapy*, 26, 142-162.

Scott, C. (2000). Ethical issues in addiction counseling. *Rehabilitation Counseling Bulletin, 43*(4).

Shostak, A.B. (2002). Clinical sociology and the art of peace promotion: Earning a world without war. In R. Straus (Ed.), *Using sociology: An introduction from the applied and clinical perspectives* (3rd ed.) (p. 325-345). New York, NY: Rowman & Litterfield Publishers, Inc.

Straus, R. (2002). Using what? The history and nature of sociology. In R. Straus (Ed.), *Using sociology: An introduction from the applied and clinical perspectives* (3rd ed.) (p. 3-20). New York, NY: Rowman & Litterfield Publishers, Inc.

Substance Abuse and Mental Health Services Administration (2014). *Center for Substance Abuse Treatment*. Retrieved from http://www.samhsa.gov/

Tucker, J., Donovan, D., and Marlatt, G. (Eds.). (1999). *Changing additive behavior: Bridging clinical and public health strategies*. New York: Guilford Press.

Turner, J.H. (1974). *The structure of sociological theory*. Homewood, IL: The Dorsey Press.

U.S. Department of Health and Human Services (2000). New advances in alcoholism treatment, updated Feb 2001. *National Institute on Alcohol Abuse and Alcoholism*.

U.S. Department of Justice, Bureau of Justice Assistance (n.d.). Retrieved from https://www.bja.gov/

U.S. Office of National Drug Control Policy (2007). *Funding*. Retrieved from http://www.whitehouse.gov/ondcp

Vanwesenbeeck, I. (2004). Burnout among female indoor sex workers. *Archives of Sexual Behavior*, 34(6), 627-639.

Velu, S. (2002). Factors associated with condom use among women commercial sex workers in Chennai, India: A study of issues related to HIV/AIDS. *Dissertations & Theses*. (UMI No. 3066561).

Ward, L.F. (1906). *Applied sociology: A treatise on the conscious improvement of society by society.* Boston, MA: Ginn & Company.

Chapter 11

HOT SPOTS, CPTED, & SCP

Routine Activities Theory

Different lifestyles equate to different risks of being victimized (Vold et al., 2002). The spatial and temporal characteristics of each person's normal, legal, and daily activities, known as routine activities, affect the amount and type of illegal activities that the person is exposed to in certain areas (Akers and Sellers, 2009; Cohen and Felson, 2004). For example, if there are a lot of people congregated in a certain spot, such as inside a home, that spot will be less attractive to criminals. On the other hand, if a person is alone in a dark alley, that individual becomes more attractive to criminals.

Cohen and Felson (2004) considered the variables of place, time, objects, and individuals and have developed a routine activities theory of crime. The three minimal elements for crime to successfully occur are motivated offenders, suitable targets, and the lack of capable guardians. When these elements converge in space and time, then the situation is right for crime. Indeed, routine activities theory has elements of both the rational choice and deterrence theories. This is because potential offenders consider the rewards (i.e., obtaining the items of desire) and the risks (i.e., having guardians present) in determining their actions. Thus, situational circumstances can influence the opportunities for crime.

Hot Spots

Crime is not evenly distributed and some people and places are victimized more often than other people and places (Glenson, Peak, & Correia, 2000). Knowing where crime will occur will allow individuals to focus their efforts and limited resources in those areas. A small number of offenders commit a disproportionate amount of crime against a small number of victims in few locations. For example, once burglarized, a home is 400% more likely to be re-burglarized than un-burglarized homes. Indeed, being victimized is a good predictor of being re-victimized.

Situational Crime Prevention & Crime Prevention Through Environmental Design

Since the 1980s, there has been a growing movement to reduce the amount of crime in specific geographical areas by using Situational Crime Prevention (SCP) programs (Clarke, 2000). SCP is a crime prevention strategy that attempts to eliminate or reduce the opportunities to commit specific crimes in specific locations by making crime more risky to attempt and more difficult to accomplish (Siegel, 2003). Instead of relying upon law enforcers, the SCP strategy depends upon public and private organizations (Clarke). Furthermore, SCP does not focus on the persons committing the crimes or the underlying causes of crime, such as unjust social and economic conditions, but focuses instead on the settings for crime (Clarke; Vold et al., 2002). For example, SCP can be implemented in school settings to reduce bullying. By eliminating the need to carry cash in school, by requiring students to use school-issued debit cards, the taking of school money by bullies may be significantly reduced. According to Clarke, SCP does not seek to eliminate crime but seeks only to forestall the occurrence of crime in particular areas by minimizing the opportunities available for crime.

Some crime prevention programs are focused on the individual, some are focused on the community, some are focused on the family, and some are focused on the specific types of locations (U.S. Department of Justice, n.d.). One program that focuses on specific types of locations is called Crime Prevention Through Environmental Design (CPTED). CPTED is a component of SCP (Siegel, 2003). The CPTED is based on the concept that people can take advantage of their available environmental assets, or they can make appropriate changes, if necessary, in order to deter crime. This includes improving structural and environmental designs (such as by building parking garages), hardening targets, increasing surveillance, promoting territoriality, promoting support for legitimate public activities, controlling access to specific areas, and keeping up environmental maintenance (Clarke, 2000). Thus, by denying would-be criminals easy access to suitable targets and by increasing the amount of surveillance in the area, the increased effort to achieve success and the increased risk of getting caught are deterrents for committing crimes.

There are several ways to reduce crime by using SCP and CPTED (Siegel, 2003; U.S. Department of Justice, n.d.). One way to reduce crime is to reduce the anticipated rewards. This can be achieved by a) removing the target, such as by removing the jewelry from under the counter after hours, b) identifying the property, such as by marking products with identification numbers, c) reducing temptation, such as by using gender-neutral telephone lists, and d) denying the benefits, such as by requiring a security code for a car radio to work. A second way to reduce crime using SCP and CPTED is to increase the perceived effort. This can be accomplished by a) hardening the target, such as by using unbreakable glass and slug rejector devices, b) controlling access to the area, such as by using parking lot barriers and fences, c) deflecting offenders, such as by closing off certain streets and by strategically relocating bus stops, and d) controlling the facilitators, such as by using caller ID and credit cards with photographs on them. Finally, a third way to reduce crime using SCP and CPTED is to increase the perceived risks. This can be accomplished by a) screening the entry/exit points, such as by using automatic ticket gates and merchandise tags, b) using formal surveillance, such as by using burglar alarms and security guards, c) using employee surveillance, such as by using closed-circuit televisions and parking attendants, and d) using natural surveillance, such as by using street lights.

For example, to reduce crime in the Washington, D.C. subway system, the subway was designed with an open view of the entire station, winding corridors and corners were eliminated, closed-circuit televisions were constantly used to monitor the area, and multiple-use fare cards were implemented, eliminating the need for passengers to carry cash (LaVigne, 1996). Indeed, the whole idea of SCP and CPTED is to deter crime by reducing benefits and increasing costs. This is directly connected to the rational choice theory. According to the rational choice theory, people commit crimes when the rewards are greater than the efforts, risks, and any other costs associated with the crime (Akers & Sellers, 2009). In short, engaging in crime is a simple business decision.

Effectiveness of Situational Crime Prevention Methods

There are many cases of successful implementation of situational crime prevention methods in a variety of settings (Clarke, 2000; Taylor & Harrell, 2000). Different studies have evaluated the strategy from different perspectives. When employing SCP tactics, the basic question is whether situational crime prevention is an effective strategy for reducing specific crimes in specific locations.

A qualitative study, for example, evaluated SCP involving two shopping centers in England, one that was built in the 1960s, which is called Tricorn, and one that was built in the 1990s, which is called Gunwharf Quays (Poyser, 2005). This study investigated the relationships between the shopping centers' environmental designs, maintenance and criminal opportunities, nuisance behaviors, and customers' fears of being victimized. The researcher conducted semi-structured interviews with the shopping centers' architects, the city council crime prevention planning officer, and the local police department's crime reduction officer. In addition, the researcher administered semi-structured questionnaires to shoppers. The findings indicate that during the 1960s, the goal of the architect was to build the center for functionality. Without giving any thought to environmental crime prevention, and without consulting the public for any input, the architect for Tricorn designed the building as he saw fit and in a manner that did not appeal to the public. Consequently, there were many nooks and crannies, there were many exits that led to numerous streets, and the lighting was poor. In addition, the building was not well maintained. Hence, the ambience attracted the criminal element. Theft, public homosexuality, shoplifting, assaults, and graffiti were commonplace. In sum, the poor design of the building promoted fear among shoppers. As a result, the Tricorn failed to attract customers and the center eventually closed up.

The Gunwharf Quays' architect, on the other hand, consulted the public and took environmental crime prevention considerations into account (Poyser, 2005). The Gunwharf Quays was designed to eliminate the problems experienced by Tricorn. Consequently, the architect eliminated many nooks and crannies and the excessive number of exits, creating highly visible areas with well-defined entrance and exit points. Furthermore, the building is well maintained. As a result, shoppers are attracted to Gunwharf Quays because they feel safe. In sum, community members and local authorities feel that SCP methods are effective in reducing levels of crime, nuisances, and shoppers' fears of being victimized.

Another study was conducted using secondary data and quantitative analysis on crime rate statistics. The Washington, D.C.'s Metro subway system is considered one of the safest subway systems in the world (LaVigne, 1996). There are three reasons why the Metro subway system is believed to be safe, which include a) the system environment is designed to prevent crime, b) the area is well maintained, and c) the rules are stringently enforced. Thus, it is believed by Metro officials that these measures minimize the opportunities for persons to successfully commit crimes. By reviewing the Metro's history and design to determine the extent that the system embodies crime prevention characteristics, and in order to determine if the system's crime rate is actually low statistically, the Metro subway system was compared, via analysis of variance (ANOVA) and F-tests, to Atlanta's, Chicago's, and Boston's subway systems. In addition, Pearson correlation was used to determine the extent that the Metro has insulated itself from crime outside the subway and directly above the subway. The findings indicate that the Metro's mean crime rate is significantly lower than the other three subway systems ($F = 8.45$, $p = 0.001$). Factors that may be helping to reduce crime in the Metro subway system include Metro's high visibility design, closed-circuit televisions usage, well lit and maintained areas, and stringent enforcement of the laws. These efforts reduce the opportunities for crimes to successfully take place. Indeed, the Metro's overall ambience is attractive and comfortable and riders feel safe and secure. However, although some crime rates have demonstrated to be significantly lower in the Metro subway system than above ground, there is no significant difference for assaults above ground and in the Metro subway system.

Another study was conducted from the potential offenders' point of view and explores whether vandalism leads to additional vandalism by examining rapid repair and paint out campaigns (Smith, 2003). The data were collected in 1994 from children 11 to 16 years of age who were attending school in an area where there was a high amount of fence damage and graffiti. The researcher explored the likelihood that juveniles vandalize fences by evaluating several factors, which include a) whether the targets are easy to damage, b) whether the fences are wide or narrow, c) whether graffiti is already present, d) whether the target is already damaged, e) whether the potential offender is male or female, f) whether the juveniles are responsible for damaging a target recently, and g) whether the juveniles are responsible for graffiti recently. Data were collected first by providing 461 participants with self-report questionnaires, which asked questions about whether they have damaged or written on fences, wall, or barriers. Second, the participants were provided situational scenarios in order to assess what they consider attractive potential targets and the likelihood that they would vandalize such targets. Via multivariate analysis of variation (MANOVA), the findings indicate that juveniles who have engaged in graffiti in the last 6 months are more likely to commit acts of vandalism than those who have not engaged in graffiti in the last 6 months. Furthermore, the participants are more likely to target wide fences over narrow ones and targets that are made of easy-to-damage material. In short, there are multiple variables that need to be considered when designing SCP programs.

Another study examined whether situational crime prevention can be applied to the sex abuse of children by priests (Terry & Ackerman, 2008). Because sex offenders come from a heterogeneous population, one generic policy may be ineffective in reducing sexually abusive behaviors. After examining data collected on priests, the data indicate that there is a situational component to sex abuse. The data indicate that the priests are not pedophiles or persistent sex abusers. Instead, priests commit child sex abuse because of increased opportunities to be alone with children, because of the ease of access to the children, and most importantly, because of the availability of adequate locations to commit the acts.

Two other studies investigated whether crime rate is prevalent and stable in micro places over time (Sherman, Gartin, & Buerger, 1989; Weisburd, Bushway, Lum, & Yang, 2004). Examining Seattle and Minneapolis, the data indicate that most of the reported crime is tightly clustered in relatively few hot spots and that there is little crime in most other places. In Minneapolis, for example, 50% of the 323,979 calls to police over a one-year period occurred in 3% of the area. In Seattle, crime was clustered in specific micro areas over a period of 14 years. Thus, because much crime consistently occurs in very specific areas, SCP may be very effective in addressing these crimes.

SCP methods have been applied to a local hot spot by modifying the traffic flow in the area (Atlas & LeBlanc, 1994). SCP was implemented by changing street designs and by closing roads. Over a 7-year period, burglaries, larcenies, and auto theft decreased while robberies and aggravated assaults remained constant. By using physical barriers, such as concrete barriers to close streets, and by using symbolic barriers, such as signs that indicate road closure, vehicular traffic can be controlled. Having reduced traffic, residents feel safer. Feeling safer, residents go outdoors more and increase natural surveillance, thereby reducing crime. However, this study indicates that crime during this time had increased in neighboring areas, perhaps due to displacement.

SCP methods have been applied to a city park (Knutsson, 1997). By examining drug activity in a central city park before and after a redesign of the park, which attempted to make it less attractive to drug dealers, the results indicate that a park redesign can reduce crime. By trimming the hedges in areas where drug dealers are known to congregate, by creating a place for pets to defecate in areas where drug dealers are known to congregate, and by redesigning the layout of the area to increase visibility, the natural surveillance and the number of potential guardians had increased, which discouraged crime. However, displacement of drug dealing to neighboring areas did occur, but they were in areas where the ambience attracted fewer users. Thus, the overall crime rate did decrease.

SCP methods have been applied to a retail store (Farrington et al., 1993). This study used a pretest-posttest design that involved the application of SCP to a retail store in the form of electronic tagging, store redesign, and uniformed security guards. The store redesign included using Perspex shields in front of merchandise, putting up posters that warned visitors of security cameras, and lowering the height of stacked items to increase general visibility. The data indicate that electronic tagging and store redesign are significantly linked to decreased shoplifting but that uniformed security guards are not. However, because the security guards in this study were not experienced and their capabilities were questionable, these factors may have influenced their impact.

SCP methods have been applied to a prison environment (LaVigne, 1994). In 1993, to reduce illicit inmate telephone use, New York City authorities implemented SCP methods and installed a new calling card telephone system within the Rikers Island correctional facility. Student t-tests were used to evaluate the program's effectiveness. First, the new phone system increases the effort to successfully use the system by making it quite difficult to access outside lines. Second, the new system requires more effort for one inmate to intimidate another inmate because a phone card and a personal identification number must be used (the old system only required an inmate to hang up the phone). Third, the risk of getting caught is greater because the use of the new telephone system is recorded electronically, which provides evidence when complaints are investigated. Finally, the rewards are limited and uncertain. If an inmate takes another inmate's calling card, the offending inmate has no idea of how much time is stored on the card. In addition, by limiting the daily amount of time that can be used for telephone calls, the incentive (i.e., reward) for the crime is limited. Thus, this study's findings indicate that the new system is linked to a lower crime rate. In addition, there is no evidence of crime displacement.

Finally, SCP methods have been applied to school environments (O'Neill & McGloin, 2007). This study examined SCP in 3,366 public school settings across the U.S. The results indicate that several SCP methods did significantly reduce the school crime rate. For example, schools that locked their outside access doors, that did not close their campuses for lunch, and that allowed fewer classroom changes during the school day realized lower crime rates. However, other SCP methods had no significance impact on crime reduction in school settings. These results may be due to improperly matching SCP methods to the actual problems or due to the improper implementation of SCP tactics (due to school authorities being unable to find the balance between individual civil rights and community safety). Indeed, properly implementing SCP methods to solve specific crimes in specific locations is essential for proper program evaluation.

In sum, various studies have evaluated situational crime prevention by evaluating data from different perspectives in different environments. For example, one researcher employed qualitative analysis using semi-structured interviews, one researcher employed quantitative statistical analysis on secondary data, and one researcher performed quantitative statistical analysis on data obtained from potential perpetrators of crime (LaVigne, 1996; Poyser, 2005; Smith,

2003). Furthermore, studies were performed in a variety of settings, which include city streets, a park, a retail store, a prison, and public schools (Atlas & LeBlanc, 1994; Farrington et al., 1993; Knutsson, 1997; LaVigne, 1994; O'Neill & McGloin, 2007). Thus, these studies demonstrate that SCP can be applied and analyzed in different ways in different environments. Indeed, by examining as many perspectives as possible, a more complete picture of the effectiveness of the overall program can be obtained.

References

Akers, R., and Sellers, C. (2009). *Criminological theories: Introduction, evaluation, and application* (5th ed.). New York, NY: Oxford University Press.

Atlas, R., and LeBlanc, W. (1994). The impact on crime of street closures and barricades: A Florida case study. *Security Journal*, 140-145.

Clarke, R. (2000). Situational crime prevention: Successful studies. In R. Glensor, M. Correia, & K. Peak (Eds.), *Policing communities: Understanding crime and solving problems, an anthology* (p. 182-225). Los Angeles, CA: Roxbury Publishing Company.

Cohen, L., and Felson, M. (2004). Social change and crime: A routine activity approach. In J. Jacoby (Ed.), *Classics of criminology* (3rd ed.) (p. 52-60). Long Grove, IL: Waveland Press, Inc.

Farrington, D., Bowen, S., Buckle, A., Burns-Howell, T., Burrows, J., and Speed, M. (1993). An experiment on the prevention of shoplifting. *Crime Prevention Studies, 1*, 93-119.

Glenson, R.W., Peak, K.J., & Correia, M.E. (2000). Focusing on prey rather than predators: A problem-oriented response to victimization. In R. Glensor, M. Correia, & K. Peak (Eds.), *Policing communities: Understanding crime and solving problems, an anthology* (p. 160-166). Los Angeles, CA: Roxbury Publishing Company.

Knutsson, J. (1997). Restoring public order in a city park. *Crime Prevention Studies*, 7, 133-151.

LaVigne, N. (1994). Rational choice and inmate disputes over phone use on Rikers Island. *Crime Prevention Studies*, *3*, 109-125.

LaVigne, N. (1996). Safe transport: Security by design on the Washington metro. *Crime Prevention Studies*, *6*, 163-197.

O'Neill, L., and McGloin, J. (2007). Considering the efficacy of situational crime prevention in schools. *Journal of Criminal Justice, 35*(5), 511-523.

Poyser, S. (2005). Shopping centre design, decline and crime. *International Journal of Police Science and Management*, *7*(2), 123-136.

Sherman, L., Gartin, P., and Buerger, M. (1989). Hot spots of predatory crime: Routine activities and the criminology of place. *Criminology, 27*(1), 27-55.

Siegel, L. (2003). *Criminology* (8th ed.). Belmont, CA: Wadsworth – Thomson Publishing Company.

Smith, M. (2003). Exploring target attractiveness in vandalism: An experimental approach. *Crime Prevention Studies*, 16, 197-236.

Taylor, R., and Harrell, A. (2000). Physical environment and crime. In R. Glensor, M. Correia, & K. Peak (Eds.), *Policing communities: Understanding crime and solving problems, an anthology* (p. 167-181). Los Angeles, CA: Roxbury Publishing Company.

Terry, K., and Ackerman, A. (2008). Child sexual abuse in the Catholic church. *Criminal Justice and Behavior, 35*(5).

U.S. Department of Justice, Office of Justice Programs, Bureau of Justice Assistance (n.d.). *Crime prevention through environmental design.* Retrieved from http://ojp.gov/

Vold, G., Bernard, T., and Snipes, J. (2002). *Theoretical criminology* (5th ed.). New York, NY: Oxford University Press.

Weisburd, D., Bushway, S., Lum, C., and Yang, S. (2004). Trajectories of crime at places: A longitudinal study of street segments in the city of Seattle. *Criminology*, *42*(2), 283-321.

Chapter 12

ESTIMATES & ASSESSMENTS

In order to determine how effective a community policing program has been implemented, an implementation estimate can be calculated (Wilson, 2006). The estimates of the scale, which have been developed from surveys of large U.S. municipal police agencies, can range from 0 to 3.178. There are 10 activities that are scored. Each activity is multiplied by a weight factor for a total score in each activity. The total scores in all 10 activities are summed for a total implementation estimate. The closer the total estimate is to 3.178, the more effective is the implementation process.

Calculating the Community-Policing Implementation Estimate

Determine the item value for each factor by determine the number that appropriately answers each question. Transfer the item value for each factor to Table 30.

Factor 1. New Recruit Training **Item Value ______**
In the last 3 years, what percentage of new officer recruits have received at least 8 hours of community policing training?
0 = none, 1 = less than half, 2 = more than half, 3 = all

Factor 2. Sworn Officer Training **Item Value ______**

In the last 3 years, what percentage of sworn officers have received at least 8 hours of community policing training?

0 = none, 1 = less than half, 2 = more than half, 3 = all

Factor 3. Non-sworn Employee Training **Item Value ______**

In the last 3 years, what percentage of non-sworn personnel have received at least 8 hours of community policing training?

0 = none, 1 = less than half, 2 = more than half, 3 = all

Factor 4. Resident Training **Item Value ______**

In the last 12 months, did the police department train local residents in community policing?

0 = no

1 = yes

Factor 5. Problem Solving **Item Value ______**

In the last 12 months, did the department engage in problem solving activities? Consider the following:

A = Department encouraged officers to engage in problem-solving projects on their beat

B = Patrol officers' performance reviews were based on problem-solving projects

C = Patrol officers formed problem-solving partnerships with community groups

Score

0 if (A U B U C) = false

1 if one event of A, B, or C is true

2 if two events of A, B, or C are true

3 if (A ∩ B ∩ C) = true

Factor 6. Written Community-Policing Plan Item Value ______

Does the department have a formal written plan on community policing?

0 = no, 1 = yes

Factor 7. Crime Data Accessibility Item Value ______

Can residents routinely access crime statistics or crime maps? Add 1 point for each source of information used by the department to provide residents with data.

0 = residents cannot routinely access crime data supplied by the department.

Television ___ Radio ___ Newspaper ___
Telephone ___ Internet ___ Newsletter ___
In-person ___ Public kiosk/terminal ___ Other ___

Factor 8. Group Meetings Item Value ______

In the last 12 months, did the department regularly meet with any of the following groups to address crime-related problems? Add 1 point for each group that the department met with to determine the total score.

0 = department did not meet with any groups

School groups ___ Religious groups ___
Youth service groups ___ Tenants' associations ___
Neighborhood Associations ___ Business groups ___
Advocacy groups ___ Other ___

Factor 9. Department Website Item Value ______

Does the department maintain an official Website?

0 = no

1 = yes

Factor 10. Geographical Assignments **Item Value ______**

In the last 12 months, did the department assign community policing details for specific geographic areas?

0 = no

1= Yes, patrol officers were assigned to specific geographic areas OR detectives were assigned cases based on geographical areas

2 = Yes, patrol officers were assigned to specific geographic areas AND detectives were assigned cases based on geographical areas

Table 30

Calculating the Community-Policing Implementation Estimate (Wilson, 2006)

	Factor	Item Value	Weight Factor	Item Score
1	New Recruit Training		0.0519	
2	Sworn Officer Training		0.1427	
3	Nonsworn Employee Training		0.040	
4	Resident Training		0.142	
5	Problem-solving		0.308	
6	Written Police-Community Plan		0.111	
7	Crime Data Accessibility		0.052	
8	Group Meetings		0.075	
9	Department Website		0.057	
10	Geographical Assignment		0.086	
Total Score for Community Policing Implementation Estimate = (Range = 0 – 3.178)				

Table 31

Best Possible Implementation Estimate (Wilson, 2006)

	Factor	Item Value	Weight Factor	Item Score
1	New Recruit Training	3	0.0519	.1557
2	Sworn Officer Training	3	0.1427	.4281
3	Nonsworn Employee Training	3	0.040	.12
4	Resident Training	1	0.142	.142
5	Problem-solving	3	0.308	.924
6	Written Police-Community Plan	1	0.111	.111
7	Crime Data Accessibility	9	0.052	.468
8	Group Meetings	8	0.075	.6
9	Department Website	1	0.057	.057
10	Geographical Assignment	2	0.086	.172
Total Score for Community Policing Implementation Estimate = (Range = 0 – 3.178)				3.178

Evaluability Assessment

During the 1960s the federal government created and funded many programs to address issues of poverty, health care, housing, and education (Trevisan & Huang, 2003). After their implementation, program managers and policymakers wanted feedback on the programs. However, due to the challenges of conducting evaluations in complex environments, there was a lack of clarity between program managers, policymakers, and stakeholders in the programs' objectives, in the proper allocation of resources, and in the kind of feedback needed. Moreover, program resources and activities did not appear to be related to stated outcomes, which were often irrelevant and impossible to measure. As a result, in 1979 Joseph Wholey developed an evaluability assessment (EA) in order to systematically determine the feasibility of a program evaluation. An EA helps to determine if a program evaluation will provide useful information to program managers, policymakers, and stakeholders that can be used to help improve program management and, consequently, program performance (U.S. Department of Justice, n.d.).

The purpose of an EA is to a) explore the objectives, expectations, and information needs of policy makers and program managers, b) explore the reality of programs and the likelihood that progress toward objectives can be measured, and c) assess the extent that the information will be used by program managers, policymakers, and stakeholders for future program and policy decisions (Trevisan and Huang, 2003). By reviewing the coherence and logic of a program and by clarifying the data that are available, an EA can be performed prior to a program's evaluation in order to determine whether an evaluation is worthwhile in terms of the program's likely benefits, costs, and consequences (European Commission, n.d.; Sourcebook, 2003). Additional purposes of an EA include a) determining whether a program needs to be modified, b) determining whether the program should move forward or be terminated, c) determining whether the program's assumptions, intended mechanisms, and expected outcomes and clearly stated, d) determining the appropriateness of the program's design, strategy, and resource allocation, e) determining the extent to which the program is likely to lead to its goals, f) determining the availability of essential information and the costs for obtaining that information, g) improving the program's coherence and logic, h) clarifying to stakeholders how to use an evaluation, and i) determining if program improvements will result in benefits that are greater than any associated costs (European Commission).

An EA is a descriptive and analytic process intended to provide policymakers and stakeholders with a reasoned basis for proceeding with an evaluation (Schmidt, Scanlon, & Bell, 1979). Steps that have been identified to be performed as part of an EA include a) determining the program's purpose, b) identifying work members and securing their commitment, c) defining the boundaries of the program to be studied, d) identifying and analyzing program documents, e) developing and clarifying a program theory, f) identifying and interviewing stakeholders, g) identifying stakeholders' perceptions of the program, h) identifying the stakeholders' needs and concerns, i) determining the plausibility of the program model, j) drawing conclusions and making recommendations, and k) planning specific steps for utilizing the EA data, such as continuing with the program evaluation or doing nothing at all (Trevisan & Huang, 2003).

EA is most appropriate early in a program's design before it has become operational (European Commission, n.d.). This is the best and most cost efficient time to remedy any weaknesses in the program. However, the EA should also be performed in the early stage of a program's life, to ensure that essential data for future program evaluations will be available. Indeed, a successful EA can lead to better defined outcomes, to improved program implementation stability, and to more effective program evaluations (Trevisan & Huang, 2003). Additional benefits in performing an EA include a) being able to distinguish between program failure and evaluation failure, b) improving program development and evaluation skills, c) improving predictions of long term outcomes, d) increasing the visibility of the program, e) improving policy choices, and f) improving the stakeholders' understanding of the program, which may impact continued financial support.

Almost all federal and state agencies demand feedback of their federal and state sponsored programs during the deliberation, legislation, and funding of their respective programs (Trevisan & Huang, 2003). The program evaluation process includes assessing data through scientifically based research, determining a set of performance measures, and determining results. However, this requires that programs are capable of being evaluated. An EA determines the extent to which programs are ready for evaluation.

Policymakers and stakeholders need to assess the effectiveness of a program and to ensure that managers are making optimal use of limited resources (Trevisan & Huang, 2003). An EA will determine which programs can be evaluated so that useful information can be obtained in order to make future decisions. An EA will provide government agencies, policymakers, and stakeholders with the information necessary to decide which programs should be promoted and which programs should be terminated. In short, EA is designed to increase the probability that program evaluations are relevant, responsive, and timely. This is a cost effective way to improve the quality of a program's implementation, to minimize evaluation costs, and to better allocate limited resources.

Police-Community Survey Problem-Analysis Report

Another way to assess a police department's efforts for solving a local problem is via a police-community survey, problem-analysis report. The problem is first identified and analyzed. Responses are then recommended and implemented. Finally, the responses are evaluated. See Table 32 for an example of a police-community survey, problem-analysis report.

Table 32

Example of a Police-Community Survey, Problem-Analysis Report (Whisenand, 2011)

LoGiudice Police Department Police-Community Survey, Problem-Analysis Report	
Identification of Problem	
Description of Problem	Burglary
Location of Problem	111 Alberta St – Zone 4
Date & Time Problem Occurs	10:00 pm – 4:00 am, every several months
Problem Analysis	
Shifts affected	midnight
Information Sources	Police case reports; witnesses
Findings	The home at that location has many bushes and yard items in the front yard that obscure the house.
Responses	
Goals	Remove items that conceal house.
Recommendations	Provide crime prevention through environmental design information to the home owner.
Date of recommendations implementation	2/11/2015
Termination date	2/18/2015
Expected resources	Brochure; time to meet with home owner
Evaluation	
What kind of results were realized?	Home owner was partially receptive
List any additional resources used	Routine patrol
List any additional action required	Continue monitoring area

Police Officer Public Service Performance Review

In order to encourage police officers to serve the public, their performance reviews must reflect activities related to community policing. In other words, using quotas to gauge police performance will only promote egoism, which is self-serving. Thus, qualities such as problem solving, teamwork, initiative, judgment, commitment, and work quality must be assessed. See Table 33.

Table 33

Police Officer Public Service Performance Review (Whisenand, 2011)

CUSTOMER SERVICE (Problem Solving)	1	3	5
Participates in crime preventative programs (e.g., Neighborhood watch meetings)			
Positive community image			
Responsive to community requests			
Uses available community and government resources			
Follows up on services provided to residents			
TEAMWORK			
Displays behaviors that gain respect/trust from fellow officers			
Assists other officers			
Adequately resolves conflict			
Helps eliminate bias within the department			
Shares information that promotes police-community efforts			
COMMUNICATIONS			
Radio			
Reports			
Courtroom			
Listens to citizens			
Ability to adjust to audience			

INITIATIVE			
Identifies and addresses community concerns			
Requires minimal supervision			
Serves as a role model			
Strives to improve performance			
Follows up on work details on own initiative			
Productivity meets the expectations that were agreed upon			
JUDGEMENT			
Aware of consequences of work-related decisions			
Ability to make best-practice decisions with available information			
Sensitive to the needs of the community			
Use of discretion			
Willing to take reasonable risks			
WORK QUALITY			
Knows law			
Applies law			
Effectively uses available equipment			
Completed work product (e.g. reports, collecting evidence)			
PERSONAL APPEARANCE			
Uniform			
Police Car			
Driving			
COMMITMENT			
Pride in department			
Loyalty to department			
Helps eliminate conflict in the community			
OVERALL SCORE			
REMARKS TO IMPROVE PERFORMANCE			
INCREASE IN SALARY BASED ON PERFORMANCE SCORE: IF SCORE > 50% THEN INCREASE IN SALARY = [% SCORE] x [.07] CURRENT SALARY IF SCORE < 50% THEN DECREASE IN SALARY = [% SCORE] x [.07] CURRENT SALARY			

In short, some police departments may use quotas as a way to collect and report numbers that are easy for the general public to understand. Quotas provide a mechanism to inform that public that the police are doing work. Indeed, if a police-community program was most effective and prevented all crime, then there would be no arrests. Therefore, in order to better serve the public by using crime preventative techniques, police administration must be willing to change its paradigm and implement a new method for assessing police officer performance (Whisenand, 2011).

Implementation of a Police-Community Relations Program

There are 11 steps to implement a police-community relations program (Whisenand, 2011). The 11 steps may be broken down into 3 categories, which are problem identification, problem analysis, and options. It is important that the police effectively communicate with the public and to receive quality information. This includes feedback on the program. Indeed, any system without feedback is unstable. Feedback should be used to enhance the program. See Table 34.

Table 34
11 Steps to Implement a Police-Community Relations Program
(Whisenand, 2011).

PROBLEM IDENTIFICATION	
Group Problems	Is it a police problem? How much support will the community provide?
Focus of Most Important Problems	Group related problems Focus on serious problems

Effectiveness	Solving problems in correct order as perceived by police and community
PROBLEM ANALYSIS	
Setting System Up	Contact residents and find facts; analyze data
Redefining Problem	Solve root cause of problem
Stakeholders	Who is being harmed? What are the costs?
Current Successful Practices	If system is working, do not change it
OPTIONS	
Customize or Discard	Resolutions are community specific Equipment from other departments may not work locally
Proactive	Systematic identification of problems Educate the public and give choices Have an advocate in the community provide feedback to the police
Communicating Decisions	Explain police decisions Police may not have authority Police may fail
Evaluation & Feedback	Make adjustments and improvements as needed System is unstable without feedback

References

European Commission (n.d.). *Evaluability assessment.* Retrieved from http://ec.europa.eu/

Schmidt, R., Scanlon, J., and Bell, J. (1979). *Evaluability assessment: Making public programs work better.* Retrieved from http://www.ncjrs.gov/App/publications/abstract.aspx?ID=65018

Sourcebook (2003, December). Evaluability assessment. *Final Materials.*

Trevisan, M., and Huang, Y. (2003). Evaluability assessment: A primer. *Practical Assessment, Research & Evaluation, 8*(20).

U.S. Department of Justice, Office of Justice Programs, Bureau of Justice Assistance (n.d.). *Center for program evaluation.* Retrieved from https://www.bja.gov/

Whisenand, P.M. (2011). *Supervising police personnel: The fifteen responsibilities* (7th ed.). Upper Saddle River, NJ: Prentice Hall.

Wilson, J.M. (2006). *Community policing in America.* New York, NY: Taylor & Francis.

Chapter 13

INSTRUMENTS, RELIABILITY, VALIDITY, & PILOT STUDY

Good decisions require good data. All research collects some type of data (Balian, 1988). Primary data are data collected specifically for the current study; secondary data are not collected specifically for the current study. The validity and reliability of the data must be assessed for both primary and secondary data. If the data are valid, then the data are reliable; however, if the data are reliable does not necessarily mean that the data are valid. In other words, the converse of a conditional statement is not necessarily true.

Reliability	=	consistency
Validity	=	true and accurate information; measures what it is supposed to measure

An alarm clock that is 30 minutes slow every day is reliable. However, it is consistently wrong. Thus, just because data is reliable does not make the data valid. See Table 35 for examples of reliability and validity.

Table 35

Reliability & Validity (Balian, 1988)

Actual Time (True Data)	Valid = Yes Reliable = Yes	Valid = No Reliable = Yes	Valid = No Reliable = No
1:00 pm	1:00 pm	1:30 pm	1:00 pm
2:00 pm	2:00 pm	2:30 pm	2:11 pm
3:00 pm	3:00 pm	3:30 pm	3:24 pm
4:00 pm	4:00 pm	4:30 pm	5:03 pm

Research instruments are used to collect data. Consequently, the validity of the instruments need to be assessed. Because there are many variables in life, it may be hard to determine if an instrument is actually measuring what it is supposed to measure.

Validity

Basically, there are three types validity that need to be assessed: content validity, criterion-related validity, and construct validity (Balian, 1988). Content validity is a subjective approach, criterion validity is an objective approach, and construct validity is a combination of the subjective and objective approach. See Table 36.

Table 36

Types of Validity (Balian, 1988; Salkind, 2007)

Type of Validity	Pros	Cons
Content Validity	Easy to implement; Easy to understand; No statistics required; Fast, cheap	Lack of statistical analysis; Depends on opinions
Criterion-related Validity (Concurrent/Predictive)	Statistically objective; Widely used, accepted; Easy to calculate; Fast, if concurrent; Can be cheap (depends on number of participants)	Power of statistical analysis depends on individuals involved; If predictive, may take long time; Can be costly (depends on number of participants)
Construct Validity	Sophisticated statistics; Fast results (computer analysis); Provides more complete information	Requires many instrument questions and participants; Difficult to learn; Difficult to explain; May be expensive (depends on number of participants and software needed)

Content validity is a subjective way to assess validity (Balian, 1988). The method uses opinions and judgments to determine if the instrument measures what it is supposed to measure. Experts or a formal panel of judges may evaluate an instrument's questions and the researcher may add or drop questions based on that information. Using a panel of judges may be more credible than using the opinion of one person. Although not scientific in its approach, content validity can be valuable in certain research situations. In addition, other validity methods may be used in conjunction with content validity in order to enhance the overall validity of the instrument.

Criterion-related validity is determined by creating correlation coefficients (Balian, 1988). There are two common types of criterion-related validity: concurrent validity and predictive validity. For example, if a researcher develops an instrument, the researcher may determine the validity of the new instrument by comparing it to a published instrument (the criterion), which is supposed to measure the same information. In this case, the researcher may provide both instruments (the new and published instrument) to the sample and the sample's responses to both instruments will be statistically compared via a correlation coefficient. The range of the correlation coefficient is 0.0 to +1.00. The closer the correlation coefficient is to +1.00, the more valid is the instrument.

The researcher may then use the new instrument to collect data over time (Balian, 1988). Subsequently, the researcher may calculate the correlation coefficient between a person's score on the new instrument and another variable, such as future income. Thus, the researcher may be able to predict future income, for example, based on the new instrument's test scores. This is predictive validity. If there is a positive relationship between the new instrument and another variable, such as future income, then the researcher must determine the strength of the relationship. The strength of the relationship is described by the correlation coefficient. The range of the correlation coefficient is 0.0 to +1.00. The closer the correlation coefficient is to +1.00, the stronger is the relationship.

It must be noted that although a strong correlation between two instruments may exist, it does not mean that the instruments are measuring what they are supposed to measure. In other words, two instruments can be equally bad. For example, a verbal aggression instrument may be highly correlated to a physical aggression instrument, but both may be unrelated to the type of ice cream that individuals buy.

Construct Validity is the highest form of validity and utilizes a combination of both content validity and criterion-related validity. Construct validity uses multivariate factor analysis to develop factors (constructs) within each instrument (Balian, 1988). For example, an instrument that is used to measure aggression may be broken down into specific types of aggression, each type being a construct (e.g., physical aggression, verbal aggression, indirect aggression, anger, and hostility). For a group of individuals, aggression may not be uniformly high or low, but certain types of aggression may be high or low. If a specific type of aggression is detected, then corrective actions may focus on that specific type of aggression.

For a new instrument, the researcher can assess the interrelations between the questions (Balian, 1988). Construct validity improves as the number of questions and respondents increase. When the respondents answer questions, relations among the answers are determined. Thus, the respondents determine the constructs and not the researcher.

Correlation Coefficient

Once the correlation coefficient has been determined, what does the number mean? Below are two scales to determine the strength of the relationship based on the correlation coefficient for criterion-related validity measures (Balian, 1988; Salkind, 2007). See Table 37.

Table 37

Strength of Correlation Coefficient

correlation coefficient	relationship	correlation coefficient	relationship
1.0 - .90	excellent	1.0 - .8	very strong
.89 - .80	good	.6 - .8	strong
.79 - .70	fair	.4 - .6	moderate
.69 or less	poor	.2 - .4	weak
		.0 - .2	weak or none
(Balian, 1988)		(Salkind, 2007)	

Reliability

An instrument is reliable if it provides consistent results. Like validity coefficients, the range of the correlation coefficient is 0.0 to +1.00 (Balian, 1988). The closer the correlation coefficient is to +1.00, the more reliable the instrument. Some common types of reliability include a) test-retest reliability, b) split-half reliability, c) equivalent forms reliability, and d) internal consistency reliability. See Table 38 for different types of reliability.

Table 38

Types of Reliability (Balian, 1988)

Type of Reliability	Pros	Cons
Test-Retest	Easy to use; Easy to understand	Takes much time; Costly; Practice effect in respondents
Split-Half	One test administration; Easy to understand	May be difficult to split test
Equivalent Forms	Two separate tests	Takes much time; Hard to write equivalent test items; May be costly
Internal Consistency	Statistically most sophisticated; Well respected; May provide much information	Hard to understand; Hard to explain

Test-Retest

A survey instrument is administered to the same group of participants at two different points in time (Balian, 1988). If the survey is consistent, then the responses should be the same at the two different times. A correlation coefficient is calculated between the participants' first and second scores. The correlation may be determined for the item score or for the total score. However, the test-retest may produce spurious results due to practice effects. This reliability test should only be performed when other methods are not feasible.

Split-Half

The Split-Half reliability test is an enhanced variation of the test-retest reliability procedure (Balian, 1988). All of the survey items are placed in order of difficulty (for cognitive surveys) or by subject matter (for attitudinal surveys). The items are numbered and then split into two groups. One group (test A) will consist of the even numbered items and the other group (test B) will consist of the odd numbered items. If the instrument is reliable, then the scores on the two surveys should be highly correlated. The assumption is that the two tests are relatively equal in content and difficulty. Because the surveys are only administered at one time, this procedure is cost effective.

Equivalent Forms

For the equivalent forms method, two completely separate but equal surveys are created (Balian, 1988). The same participants are surveyed twice, once for each survey. If the instruments are reliable, then the scores on the two surveys will be highly correlated. This method requires many questions, it may be costly, and creating similar surveys can be difficult.

Internal Consistency

Internal consistency techniques utilize more sophisticated statistics to determine reliability coefficients (Balian, 1988). The theory behind this technique is that each item on the survey will be answered in the same direction as the total score direction. Although this method only needs to be administered once, it may require many survey items (the more, the better).

Validity of Study

If a study is not valid, it will not be credible. In other words, a study's validity may limit the usefulness of the study's findings. Below are factors that should be considered and disclosed during a study, which will demonstrate the study's internal and external validity.

Study's Internal Validity

Internal validity indicates that the research design tests the hypothesis that it is supposed to test (Bordens & Abbott, 2008). In other words, the changes in the dependent variable are due to the changes in the independent variables and not due to some unintended variables (Mertens, 2005). There are seven factors that demonstrate internal validity: **1) history, 2) maturation, 3) testing, 4) instrumentation, 5) statistical regression, 6) biased selection of participants, and 7) experimental mortality (**Bordens & Abbott, 2008). These factors are discussed below.

The **history factor** involves specific events, other than the treatment, that occur between multiple observations and that may affect the results (Bordens & Abbott, 2008). If only one observation takes place during a study, and if all of the data are collected within a short amount of time, then there is minimal risk that the history factor will impact a study's internal validity.

The **maturation factor** involves performance change due to age or fatigue (Bordens & Abbott, 2008). For example, participants may discontinue answering the questions on a survey before they finish answering all of the questions. In order to minimize the threat, a study's survey can be short and the questions can be easy to answer. Furthermore, if the surveys are administered on-line, this will allow the participants to take breaks whenever necessary.

The **testing factor** involves the pretest sensitizing of participants (Bordens & Abbott, 2008). In other words, administering a test prior to treatment may change how the participants respond on a posttest. However, if only a posttest is administered, then there is minimal risk that the testing factor will impact a study's internal validity.

The **instrumentation factor** involves the unobserved changes in researcher criteria or the changes in the sensitivity of the instruments to measure what they are supposed to measure (Bordens & Abbott, 2008). In other words, internal validity is threatened a) if the researcher changes definitions during the data collection process or b) if the measures used to collect data become more or less sensitive over time. If data in a study are collected via surveys, if data are collected from each participant only once, and if standard instructions are provided, then there is minimal risk that the instrumentation factor will impact a study's internal validity.

The **statistical regression factor** involves recruiting participants for treatment based upon their extreme scores prior to treatment (Bordens & Abbott, 2008). If measured again, their scores will move closer to the population average, regardless of the actual treatment. However, if participants in a study are not selected based on any type of pretest scores, then there is minimal risk that the statistical regression factor will impact a study's internal validity.

The **biased selection of participants factor** involves administering different treatments to different groups and then comparing the groups after the treatments (Bordens & Abbott, 2008). If the groups are not randomly selected, then there is the potential that a group may have pre-existing biases prior to the treatment. Thus, the pre-existing biases and not the treatments may cause differences among the groups. However, if a study's participants are homogeneous (e.g., African American females), and if there is only one group, then there is little risk that the biased selection of participants factor will impact a study's internal validity.

The **experimental mortality factor** involves the differential loss of participants from groups, resulting in nonequivalent groups (Bordens & Abbott, 2008). If a study only considers one group (e.g., African American females), and if the participants are surveyed only once, then there is little threat that the experimental mortality factor will impact a study's internal validity.

Study's External Validity

External validity refers to the extent to which a study's findings can be applied to a target population beyond the specific individuals and settings (Mertens, 2005). There are four factors that demonstrate external validity: **1) reactive testing, 2) interactions between participant selection biases, 3) reactive effects of experimental arrangements,** and **4) multiple treatment interference** (Bordens and Abbott, 2008**).** These factors are discussed below.

The **reactive testing factor** indicates that a pretest may affect how participants react to the treatment (Bordens & Abbott, 2008). Consequently, the participants' responses may not be representative of the general population. However, if a pretest is not administered in a study, then the reactive testing factor will pose little threat to the study's external validity.

The **interactions between participant selection biases factor** indicates that by selecting a purposive non-random group, the effects of the treatment may only apply to that group (Bordens & Abbott, 2008). For example, if a study only surveys African American females, then the findings may not be applied to individuals of other races. Thus, in order minimize the risk of applying the findings to inappropriate groups, the target population's characteristics to which the study's findings may apply need to be disclosed.

The **reactive effects of experimental arrangements factor** indicates that because the participants know they are involved in an experimental treatment, their responses may be artificial (Bordens & Abbott, 2008). However, if a study is non-experimental (e.g., ex post facto), and if the identities of the participants are anonymous, then there is little motivation to be less than truthful. Thus, in this case, the reactive effects of experimental arrangements factor will pose little threat to the study's external validity.

The **multiple treatment interference factor** indicates that, for multiple experimental treatments, the participants' exposure to prior treatments may affect the participants' responses to later treatments (Bordens & Abbott, 2008). However, if data are only collected at one point in time in a non-experimental study, then the multiple treatment interference factor will pose little threat to the study's external validity.

Validity and Reliability of a Pre-existing, Published Instrument

A pre-existing, published instrument should advertise its psychometric qualities (Balian, 1988). If validity and reliability information is not provided for the published instrument, then the researcher should become suspicious. On the one hand, an advantage of using a pre-existing instrument is that its psychometric qualities should have already been determined. One good source for finding pre-existing measures is the Mental Measurements Yearbook Website. The researcher cannot presume that a pre-existing and published instrument is valid and reliable. On the other hand, if a researcher creates a new instrument, then the researcher may be required to put much work into establishing the instrument's validity and reliability. Indeed, the researcher is responsible for defending the data and the data are only as good as the instrument used to collect them.

Example of How to Describe an Instrument's Psychometric Qualities

Religious Emphasis Scale

The Religious Emphasis Scale is a 10-item self-administered survey that uses a six point Likert-type scale to measure "the extent to which one's parents emphasized the family religion as one was growing up" (Hunsberger, 1999, p. 208). For each item on the measure, a rating of zero indicates, "no emphasis was placed on the behavior" and a rating of five indicates "a very strong emphasis was placed on the behavior" (Hunsberger, p. 210). The total score, which is a continuous variable, is calculated by summing the points for the 10 items. The higher the person's total score, the greater is the person's childhood religiosity.

The Religious Emphasis Scale is a reliable instrument. The Religious Emphasis Scale was standardized using two primary samples (Altemeyer, 1988). The first sample consisted of 513 college students in Altemeyer's introductory psychology class. The second sample consisted of 549 parents of these college students. Average scores on the scale were 17.7 for the college students and 25.0 for their parents. In addition, the mean inter-item correlation for the measure's 10 items was .55, which produced a Cronbach's alpha of .92 for both the students and their parents. Thus, the Religious Emphasis Scale has very strong internal consistency.

The Religious Emphasis Scale is also a valid instrument. Indeed, the Religious Emphasis Scale has been correlated to many other religious measures and the results indicate that the Religious Emphasis Scale has moderate to strong concurrent validity (Altemeyer, 1988, Salkind, 2007). For example, for the student sample and parent sample respectively, the Religious Emphasis Scale has been correlated to the Religious Pressures Scale (.59, .43), the Christian Orthodoxy Scale (.59, .49), the Intrinsic Orientation Scale (.58, .50), the Church Attendance Scale (.62, .44), the Frequency of Prayer Scale (.55, .52), and the Control Impulses Scale (.63, .53). Indeed, these correlation coefficients demonstrate moderate to strong concurrent validity (Salkind).

Aggression Questionnaire

The Buss and Warren (2000) Aggression Questionnaire is an updated version of the Buss-Durkee Hostility Inventory measure, which is one of the most frequently used instruments on aggression. The Aggression Questionnaire is a 34-item self-administered survey that uses a five point Likert-type scale to measure five variables: a) physical aggression, b) verbal aggression, c) indirect aggression, d) anger, and e) hostility. For each item on the measure, a rating of one indicates, "Not at all like me" and a rating of five indicates "Completely like me" (Buss & Warren, p. 30). Using the scores from the subscales, the measure also provides a total score for aggression. For each type of aggression, the individual raw scores are converted into *t* scores, which are continuous values and based on an interval scale of measurement.

The Aggression Questionnaire was standardized using 2,138 individuals from 9 to 88 years of age from four geographical regions in the U.S. (Buss & Warren, 2000). Of the 2,138 individuals, 59% were female, 41% were male, 72% were Caucasian, and 15% were African American. In addition, the Aggression Questionnaire only requires a third grade reading capability.

The Aggression Questionnaire is a reliable instrument, which sufficiently gauges aggression (Buss & Warren, 2000). First, the internal consistency alpha coefficients are .94, .88, and .76 for total aggression, physical aggression, and verbal aggression, respectively. Thus, the internal consistency for aggression is considered adequate to excellent. In addition, the test-retest correlations for a sample of 26 participants over a one week period are .85, .73, and .85 for total aggression, physical aggression, and verbal aggression, respectively. Thus, the test-retest correlations are considered adequate to good (Balian, 1988).

The Aggression Questionnaire is also a valid instrument (Buss & Warren, 2000). According to Buss and Warren, the Aggression Questionnaire was correlated to the Attitudes Toward Guns and Violence Questionnaire and to the Navaco Anger Scale. The correlation coefficients between the Aggression Questionnaire and the Attitudes Toward Guns and Violence Questionnaire are .38, .46, and .30 for total aggression, physical aggression, and verbal aggression, respectively. In addition, the correlation coefficients between the Aggression Questionnaire and Navaco Anger Scale are .59, .48, and .46 for total aggression, physical aggression, and verbal aggression, respectively. Thus, although the Aggression Questionnaire has weak to moderate concurrent validity with the Attitudes Toward Guns and Violence Questionnaire, the Aggression Questionnaire has moderate current validity with the Navaco Anger Scale (Salkind, 2007).

Validity and Reliability of an Original Instrument

The researcher must demonstrate that a new instrument is valid and reliable. If the instrument's questions are not valid, then the data collected are not valid. If the data collected are not valid, then the study's findings have little value. In other words, researchers cannot just go out and ask any questions that they want simply because they want to investigate something. The researcher must show that the survey is valid and reliable.

If an original instrument is used to collect data, then 13 steps will help develop the instrument (Balian, 1988).

1. Review other surveys that are broadly similar (that collect similar information). Look at the question form, survey length, response scales, techniques used for validating the instrument, and other similar factors. Using other published instruments as examples will provide a reference for what professional surveys should look like.
2. Start by listing the research questions; keep the major concepts as autonomous as possible.
3. Using numeric values, weigh the importance of each research question.
4. Decide on the total number of questions that the survey will contain; it is better to use a low conservative number (20-50 total questions). Consider the interest level, attention span, and fatigue factors. The more importance research questions should correspondingly require more survey questions.
5. Write each survey question and code it to match its corresponding research question.
6. Develop a response scale for each survey question; be consistent throughout the test section. In other words, survey questions that relate to a particular research question should all have the same scale.
7. Categorize all survey questions by research questions and read them to a peer. Feedback will help the researcher to make corrections and to better word the survey questions, reducing any ambiguity. Combine similar survey questions into autonomous sections.

8. Refine the number of survey questions; make sure that the final number of survey questions is at an acceptable level.
9. Revise 10% - 20% of the response scaled survey questions and ask them in reverse order. This may help reduce the Halo effect.
10. Do not overestimate or underestimate the respondents' reading aptitude. If a researcher overestimates the participants' reading level, the participants may not understand the survey questions and may provide data that are not valid. If a researcher underestimates the participants' reading level, the participants may become insulted and may provide data that are not valid.
11. At this stage, the survey will possess a certain amount of content validity. This can be objectively assessed during a pilot study.
12. Conduct an informal test with a small group similar to the target participants to assess the clarity of the survey. Use a minimum of 20 participants.
13. Conduct a formal pilot study.

Limitations of Instrument

A researcher must be aware of the instrument's limitations and must attempt to assess their impact on the instrument. Below are four limitations that need to be considered.

1. Participants may try to help the researcher by providing the answers that they believe the researcher wants them to provide.

2. Participants may provide responses that reflect the way that they want to see themselves.
3. If a researcher asks many questions using the same Likert-type scale, participants may simply begin to select the same level response (Halo effect) for all of the responses.
4. Participants may alter their behavior if they know that they are being studied.

Pilot Study

A pilot study allows the researcher to objectively assess a new instrument's validity and reliability. Therefore, if an instrument is original, then a pilot study should be mandatory (Balian, 1988). After a pilot study is completed and data are obtained, the researcher must determine if the instrument is within acceptable standards. The four factors to consider include a) whether the validity and reliability coefficients of the instrument are satisfactory, b) whether item analysis is statistically satisfactory (if performed), c) whether the limitations of the instrument are controlled and at minimal levels, and d) whether the administration of the survey and the time of completion are within acceptable time limits. Below is an example of a pilot study.

Example of the Pilot Study Procedure

In an effort to ensure that the instrument is valid prior to its use in the proposed research study, the researcher will recruit several experts in the field to help evaluate the validity of the instrument. The researcher will informally ask seven faculty members if they are willing to provide their input to enhance the face and content validity of the instrument. If the faculty members are willing to participate, then they will be provided a form in order to rate the instrument. The form will also allow the faculty members to make recommendations for improvement.

The experts will assess both face validity and content validity. The experts will determine the face and content validity of the instrument by determining whether the language and directions on the instrument are clear and easily understood, and whether the instrument provides an accurate range of responses. A valid instrument will measure what it is intended to measure and will collect complete and accurate information. For example, the newly developed Emotional Intelligence Questionnaire should accurately measure the control that individuals exercise over their emotions. The experts' feedback will be used to modify the instrument, if necessary, in order to help ensure that the instrument is accurately collecting the data that it is intended to collect.

After the Emotional Intelligence Questionnaire has been determined to have face and content validity, the reliability of the instrument will be determined. The reliability of the instrument will be determined by performing a test-retest about two weeks apart. The instrument will be offered to 10 to 15 individuals who match the characteristics of the study's population.

In order to gain access to potential participants, the researcher will informally approach faculty members and will ask them if they are willing to offer the instrument to the students in their classrooms. If the faculty members agree, then the questionnaire will be offered in their classrooms to those students who voluntarily agree to participate. This process will continue until 10 to 15 participants have completed the questionnaire.

However, before any data are collected, the researcher will provide the students will a confidential health care information form, a letter of informed consent, and an invitation to participate in the pilot study. The students who want to participate in the pilot study must sign the necessary forms. In addition, as part of the invitation process, several screening questions will be asked so that they students may be able to determine if they qualify to partake in the study. If the students meet the qualifications, then they will be allowed to complete the questionnaire.

The study will be conducted in an ethical manner. In order to protect the anonymity of the participants, certain precautions will be taken. First, each participant will place the first completed questionnaire, the signed confidential health care information form, and the signed letter of informed consent into an envelope. The participants will then seal the envelopes and sign their names over the sealed flaps. The envelopes will then be collected and secured in a locked safe until the retest. The purpose of signing the envelopes over the sealed flaps is to indicate to the participants that their envelopes have not been breached and that the information within the envelopes has remained secured. If the participants fail to return to retake the test, then their sealed envelopes will be destroyed at the end of the pilot study.

On the day of the retest, the participants will a) open their sealed envelopes, b) staple their two completed questionnaires together, c) place both of their questionnaires into a new envelope designated for containing both of their completed questionnaires, and d) place their signed informed consent forms and signed confidential health care information forms into a new envelope designated for them. As a result of employing this strategy, the first test will be appropriately matched to the second test for each participant and the questionnaires will not be directly linked to any of the signed forms. The data will then be recorded and the forms will be locked in a safe for seven years. After seven years, the forms will be destroyed. Below is an example of a pilot study form used to assess a new instrument.

Pilot Test Evaluation

Date: ____________________

Setting: ____

Instrument Name: _________________________

Expected Test Time: ________________________________

Pilot Sample Size: _________________________

Grade each factor from A (excellent) to E (poor)	*Grade*	*Comments*
1. Reading of Instructions	_____	____________
2. Clarity of survey questions	_____	____________
3. Effort completing the survey	_____	____________
4. Validity check: __________________________		____________
5. Reliability check: _______________________		____________
6. Actual time of completion __________________	_____	____________
7. Limitations of survey	_____	____________

Figure 9. Pilot study survey (Balian, 1988).

Below is an example of a completed pilot study form used to assess a new instrument.

Example of Completed Pilot Study Form (from Experts)

Date: 10/17/2014 Setting: Classroom; undergraduate level

Instrument Name: Emotional Intelligence Questionnaire

Expected Test Time: 10 minutes

Pilot Sample Size: 40

Grade each factor from A (excellent) to E (poor)	*Grade*	*Comments*
1. Reading of Instructions	*A*	Instructor did not mention purpose of study. Add new sentence to better describe study's purpose.
2. Clarity of survey questions	*B*	Question 4 is ambiguous. Question 5 should be eliminated.
3. Effort completing the survey	*A*	-----
4. Validity check: *Concurrent* *(r = + .88)*		Clark's Standard Statistical test

5. Reliability check : *(r = +. 74)*		LERTAP analysis; item analysis indicates that question 5 be removed.
6. Actual time of completion *12 minutes*	*B*	Survey took 2 minutes longer than expected; within acceptable limits.
7. Limitations of survey	*B*	Halo effect possible on questions 1, 3, and 8. Possibly reverse wording on question 3.

Figure 10. Completed pilot study survey (Balian, 1988)

References

Altemeyer, B. (1988). *Enemies of freedom: Understanding right-wing authoritarianism.* San Francisco, CA: Jossey-Bass.

Balian, E.S. (1988). *How to design, analyze, and write doctoral or master's research* (2nd ed.). New York, NY: University Press of America.

Bordens, K., & Abbott, B. (2008). *Research design and methods: A process approach* (7th ed.). Boston, MA: McGraw Hill.

Buss, A.H., & Warren, W.L. (2000). *Aggression questionnaire manual.* Los Angeles, CA: Western Psychological Services.

Hunsberger, B. (1999). Religious emphasis scale (Altemeyer, 1988). In P.C. Hill & R.W. Hood (Eds.), *Measures of religiosity* (p. 208-210). Birmingham, AL: Religious Education.

Mertens, D.M. (2005). *Research and evaluation in education and psychology: integrating diversity with quantitative, qualitative, and mixed methods* (2nd ed.). Thousand Oaks, CA: Sage.

Salkind, N.J. (2007). *Statistics for people who (think they) hate statistics* (Excel ed.). Thousand Oaks, CA: Sage.

Chapter 14

RESEARCH PROPOSAL

(First 3 Chapters of a Research Study)

Research Proposal Version 1

CH 1. Introduction

Background/Significance of Problem/Purpose of Study
Research Questions/Null Hypotheses (for quantitative study)

CH 2. Literature Review

Variables/Theoretical Framework (scholarly peer-reviewed academic articles)
Assumptions & Limitations of Theory
Possible Solution to Problem based on Theory

CH 3. Methodology

Research Design
Participants

Sampling Technique/Method of Data Collection

Instrument with Psychometrics or new survey with pilot study design Variables/Scales of Measurement and Planned Data Analysis

Assumptions, Limitations, Reliability & Validity of Study

Tentative Budget

Letter of Invitation

Letter of Informed Consent

HIPAA form, if needed

Philosophical, Political, Ethical Issues, and personal bias (for qualitative research)

References

Research Proposal Version 2

Abstract

Introduction, problem statement, research questions, null hypotheses (quantitative study)

Background section

Literature review

Planned data collection methods

Planned data analysis and expected results

Discussion and conclusions section

Limitations

Future research section

References

All appendices and lists of figures and tables

Research Proposal Version 3

Chapter 1: INTRODUCTION AND STATEMENT OF THE PROBLEM

Introduction to the Problem
Background/Context
The Problem
Problem Statement
Purpose Statement
Research Questions and Null Hypotheses
Study Variables
Rationale, Relevance, and Significance of the Proposed Study
Nature of the Study
Definition of Terms
Assumptions and Limitations

Chapter 2: LITERATURE REVIEW

Introduction to Literature Review
Theoretical Framework
Advancing Theories
Adding to Knowledge
Theoretical Criticisms
Bridging the Gap
Review of the Critical Literature
Evaluation of Viable Research Designs
Chapter 2 Summary

Chapter 3: METHODOLOGY

Introduction to the Methodology
Researcher's Philosophy
Research Design Guide
Research Design Strategy
Sampling Design and Setting
Measures
Data Collection Procedures
Pilot Test
Data Analysis Procedures
Limitations of Research Design/Methodology
Internal Validity
External Validity
Expected Findings
Ethical Issues
Chapter 3 Conclusion

References

The goal of this section is for individuals to learn how to assess a police-community relations program via academic research. Research is the gathering and analyzing of data in order to make best-practice decisions. Understanding research will allow policy-makers to make educated decisions for resource allocation. Every research study has limitations and failure to consider the limitations may result in severe consequences.

It does not matter that a particular research study supports or contradicts other research studies. All research studies are important because each study only provides a small piece of the puzzle. Police officers make decisions based on the totality of the circumstances. Additional research provides more information in which to make better decisions.

Some of the decisions that need to be considered include the following.

- Quantitative or qualitative study
- Variables – parametric vs. nonparametric
- Sample – random vs. non-random
- Data Collection – instrument (psychometrics)
- Data Analysis - statistics vs. themes

Research Variables – Scales of Measurement

How the researcher defines the scales of measurement for the independent and dependent variables will impact the statistical analyses (Leedy & Ormrod, 2005). The scales of measurement for the study's variables should be defined at the outset of the study in a manner that will allow for the desired statistical analyses. Indeed, researchers need to look at what they are trying to accomplish and they should collect data in the format that will allow them to accomplish their goal. The researcher can dictate the scales of measurement by controlling how the survey questions are asked. See Table 39.

Table 39

Scales of Measurement (Field, 2005; Leedy & Ormrod, 2005)

Variable Types			
Categorical	**Nominal**		Categories without quantitative measurement and without rank. Ex: Male or female; number on a sports uniform; Democrat or Republican; property record & receipt #; social security #.
	Ordinal		Categories with rank, but without precise differences between data values. Ex: Much or few; rich or poor; like or dislike; fast or slow; often or seldom; birth order; military rank; high or low.
Continuous	**Scale**	**Interval**	Data with sequence and equal units of measurement between values but with no true zero point. Ex: Actual sea level in feet; actual degrees in Celsius; actual IQ scores.
		Ratio	Data with sequence and equal units of measurement between values with a true zero point. Ex: Age in number of years; actual number of attempts; actual number of crimes; actual number of people; actual percentage number; actual number of points.

Once the data are collected, descriptive statistical analyses need to be performed. For example, if the variables have been classified as continuous variables, then they need to be assessed in order to determine if the parametric assumptions have been satisfied. If the parametric assumptions have not been satisfied, then either the data may need to be manipulated in order to satisfy the requirements or non-parametric tests will need to be performed. In short, parametric statistics are preferred over non-parametric statistics because parametric statistics provide more detailed information (Norusis, 2008).

Research is a systematic process of collecting, analyzing, and interpreting information in order to better understand the subject of study (Leedy & Ormrod, 2005). Research attempts to resolve a problem by answering a question. Researchers communicate their thoughts, objectives, methods, and data interpretation for other people to evaluate and act upon. Researchers accomplish this by developing a hypothesis, which is an educated conjecture, and by determining if the data support the hypothesis. In short, the purpose of research is to add to the body of knowledge.

Research begins with an unanswered question and a problem. For example, suppose the public is dissatisfied (the problem). The question is, "Is there a relationship between the new police-community relations program and public satisfaction?" Research is needed to answer the question to see if the problem has been resolved. For a quantitative study, a hypothesis must be written so that it includes the variables being tested.

Sampling

In order to generalization a study's findings to the general population, the sample must represent the population as much as possible. See Table 40 for sampling designs. Furthermore, the sample size must be large enough to ensure adequate power and to produce credible information about the population (Tabachnick & Fidell, 2007). The required sample size depends on many factors, which include the number of independent variables, the statistic employed, the alpha level, and the desired power. Too small of a sample size will produce less than credible information. In short, there are statistic books and software programs that will recommend a minimum number of cases for specific factors. The researcher must determine the statistical parameters before an adequate sample size can be determined.

For example, in order to a obtain a 95% confidence level and a confidence interval of five, and in order to achieve a large enough sample size for regression analysis, an optimal resultant sample size of 384 participants needs to be targeted (Creative Research Systems, n.d.). According to Tabachnick and Fidel (2007), if N is the number of participants in the sample and k is the number of independent variables, then the minimum desirable sample size for significant results is $N \geq 50 + 8k$ or $N \geq 104 + k$, whichever is larger. If $k = 10$, then $N \geq 50 + 8k = 50 + 8(10) = 130$ and $N \geq 104 + k = 104 + 10 = 114$. As a result, the minimum desirable sample size for the study will be at least 130 participants. However, the larger sample size of 384 participants should be targeted because a larger sample size will provide more precise estimates and it will increase the likelihood of a more adequate representation of the population (Warner, 2008). If by some chance fewer than 130 participants respond to the survey, the statistical analyses can still be performed. The researcher will just have to disclose it as a limitation of the study.

In representing the population, a larger sample will provide more accurate results. However, there is a point where additional participants will add very little additional information in representing the population. For example, for a 95% confidence level with a 5% confidence interval, a population of 100 will need a sample size of 80, a population of 1,000 will need a sample size of 278, a population of 10,000 will need a sample size of 370, a population of 100,000 will need a sample size of 383, and a population of 1,000,000 will need a sample size of 384 (Creative Research Systems, n.d.). See Table 41.

Table 40

Sampling Designs (Balian, 1988; Field, 2005; Leedy & Ormrod, 2005)

Sampling Designs		
Probability Sampling	Simple random	Every member of the population has an equal chance of being selected.
	Stratified random	An equal number of participants in each group is selected and the individuals in each group have an equal chance of being selected.
	Proportional stratified	Individuals have an equal chance of being selected but in proportion to defined properties.
	Cluster	A large geographic area is divided into smaller units that are comprised of the same characteristics. All of the units are clustered together as the sample, and a subset of the cluster is randomly selected.
	Systematic	A sample is selected based on a predetermined sequence; method is accurate only if the listing is not biased in any way.
Nonprobability Sampling	Convenience	A sample that uses any participant who is willing and available to participate.
	Quota	A sample that seeks participants only until a pre-determined number is achieved.
	Purposive	A sample that is targeted according to particular criteria.
	Snow Ball	A sample in which one participant recommends other potential participants.

Table 41
Sample Size Plateau

Population	Sample Size Needed (95% confidence level, 5% confidence interval)
100	80
1,000	278
10,000	370
100,000	383
1,000,000	384

However, if the sample is not representative of the population, which may occur during the collection of large samples, then a larger sample size may produce less accurate results. For example, many undocumented persons may not be considered in the census and this will bias the results. Indeed, a smaller and more representative sample will provide better results. A larger sample will provide more solid information, but if the sample is biased then the results will be more solidly biased away from the true population.

An investigator should never accept information at face value. Indeed, there are many assumptions and limitations that need to be disclosed. Failure to disclose a study's assumptions and limitations is unethical and undermines the credibility of the study. Knowing the study's assumptions and limitations may prevent the findings from being misapplied.

As with anything of value and importance, confirmation is important. Being able to replicate a test will improve its credibility. The reason for confirmation is to assure that errors have not been made. All processes have to start somewhere. Everything that people know has started from someone who conducted an initial research (Balian, 1988). The goal is to continue research and to add to the body of knowledge.

See Table 42 for research study designs.
See Table 43 for determining the proper statistical test.
See Table 44 for types of correlational statistics.
See Table 45 for types of inferential statistics.

Table 42
Research Study Designs (Bordens & Abbott, 2008; Champion, 2006; Creswell, 2009; Leedy & Ormrod, 2005)

Research Designs			
Designs	Name	Notation	Comment
Pre-experimental	One-shot case study	N, A: X --------O	Treatment precedes observation.
	One-group pretest-posttest design	N, A: O_1 ---X---O_2	Observation before & after treatment.
	Posttest-only with nonequivalent groups design	N, A: X------O N, B: --------O	Comparing 2 groups, one group receiving treatment before observation.
	Alternative posttest-only with nonequivalent groups design	N, A: X_1---O N, B: X_2---O	Comparing 2 groups, each receiving a different treatment before observation.

Quasi-experimental	Nonequivalent (pretest and posttest) control-group design	N, A: O---X---O N, B: O---------O	Comparing 2 groups, one group receiving a treatment between observations.
	Single-group interrupted time-series design	N, A: O-O-X-O-O	Allows change to be measured as a result of treatment during lengthy period.
	Control-group interrupted time-series design	N, A: O-O-X-O-O N, B: O-O-O-O-O	Allows change to be measured as a result of treatment during lengthy period and can be compared to control group.
	Reversal time-samples design	N, A: X-O---O-X-O	To determine if a treatment consistently leads to a particular effect.
	Alternating treatment design	N, A: X_1-O---O-X_2-O	To show that different treatments have different effects.
	Multiple baseline design	N, A:--O-X-O-X-O N, B: --O---O-X-O	To indicate the effect of a treatment by administering it at different times for different groups.

Research Designs			
Designs	**Name**	**Notation**	**Comment**
Experimental	Pretest-posttest control-group design	R, A: --O--X--O R, B: --O------O	To show the effect that follows a treatment by using a control group.
	Posttest-only control-group design	R, A: ---X---O R, B: --------O	Uses 2 groups to assess the effects of a treatment when pretesting cannot be accomplished.
	Solomon four-group design	R, A: --O--X---O R, B: --O-------O R, C: ------X---O R, D: -----------O	Uses 4 different groups and a combination of treatments and observations to determine the effect of pretesting.
	Within-subjects design	N, A: X_1----O N, A: X_2----O	Uses the same group to determine the effect of 2 different treatments.
Ex post facto	Simple ex post facto	N, A: X---O N, B: -----O	To assess the effect of a condition that was experienced long ago; cannot manipulate the independent variables.

Factorial	Randomized 2-factor design	N, A: X_1--X_2--O N, B: X_1--------O N, C: ------X_2--O N, D: -----------O	Examines the effects of two or more independent variables in a single study; to assess the effects of 2 treatments along with their interaction.

N = Nonrandom sample; R = Random sample

-- = time

O = Observation

X_1 = Treatment 1; X_2 = Treatment 2

A = group 1; B = group 2; C = group 3; D = group 4

Table 43

Determining the Proper Statistical Test

(Field, 2005; Norusis, 2008; Salkind, 2007)

Number of Dependent Variables	Type of Dependent Variables	Number of Independent Variables	Type of Independent Variables	If the Independent Variable is Categorical, Number of Categories	If the Independent Variable is Categorical, Same or Different Participants in Each Category	Parametric Assumptions Satisfied	Appropriate Statistical Test
1	Continuous	1	Categorical	2	Different	Yes	Point-Biserial Correlation or Independent t-test
						No	Mann-Whitney test
					Same	Yes	Dependent *t* test
						No	Wilcoxon Matched-Pairs test
				≥ 3	Different	Yes	One Way Independent ANOVA
						No	Kruskal-Wallis Test
					Same	Yes	One Way Repeated Measures ANOVA
						No	Friedman's ANOVA
			Continuous	-	-	Yes	Regression or Pearson Correlation
						No	Spearman Correlation or Kendall's Tau
		≥ 2	Categorical	-	Different	Yes	Multiple Regression or Independent Factorial ANOVA
					Same	Yes	Factorial Repeated Measures ANOVA
					Both	Yes	Factorial Mixed ANOVA
			Continuous	-	-	Yes	Multiple Regression
			Both	-	-	Yes	Multiple Regression or ANCOVA
	Categorical	1	Categorical	-	Different	-	Pearson Chi-Square or Likelihood Ratio
			Continuous	-	-	-	Logistic Regression, Biserial Correlation, or Point-Biserial Correlation
		≥ 2	Categorical	-	Different	-	Loglinear Analysis
			Continuous	-	-	-	Logistic Regression
			Both	-	Different	-	
≥ 2	Continuous	1	Categorical	-	-	Yes	MANOVA
		≥ 2	Categorical	-	-	Yes	Factorial MANOVA
			Both	-	-	Yes	MANCOVA

Table 44

Types of Correlational Statistics

(Field, 2005; Leedy & Ormrod, 2005; Norusis, 2008)

Types of Correlational Statistics		
	Statistic	Data Description
Parametric Statistic	Pearson correlation	Both variables are continuous
	Coefficient of determination	Both variables are continuous
	Point biserial correlation	One variable = continuous One variable = discrete & dichotomous
	Biserial correlation	One variable = continuous One variable = discrete & dichotomous (with underlying continuum)
	Phi coefficient	Both variables = dichotomies
	Triserial correlation	One variable = continuous One variable = trichotomy
	Partial Correlation	Assessing the relationship between 2 variables when a 3rd variable is held statistically constant.
	Multiple regression	Predicting an outcome by a linear combination with $\geq$ 2 independent variables.
	Weibull distribution	Test-to-failure analysis; continuous probability distribution. Predicts how long a product will survive at a given confidence level. Good for very low volume.
Nonparametric Statistic	Spearman's rho	Both variables are rank-ordered.
	Kendall coefficient	Both variables are rank-ordered and the statistic assesses their degree of similarity.
	Contingency coefficient	Both variables are nominal.
	Kendall's Tau correlation	Both variables are ordinal and the statistic is useful with a small sample size.

Table 45

Types of Inferential Statistics

(Field, 2005; Leedy & Ormrod, 2005; Norusis, 2008)

Types of Inferential Statistics		
	Statistic	Purpose of Test
Parametric Statistic	Student t test	To determine difference between 2 means
	Analysis of variance (ANOVA)	To determine differences among 3 or more means by comparing variances across and within groups. If significant, may also require a post hoc test.
	Analysis of Covariance (ANCOVA)	To determine differences among means while controlling for the impact of a variable that is related to the outcome variable.
	Regression	To determine how effectively one or more variables predict the outcome variable.
	Factor analysis	To determine the correlations among many variables and to identify highly interrelated variables that reflect themes.
	Structural equation modeling (SEM)	To determine the correlations among many variables in order to determine casual relationships.

Nonparametric Statistic	Sign test	To determine if the values of one variable are larger than the values of a correlated variable.
	Mann-Whitney *U*	It is used to compare two groups when the variables are ordinal.
	Kruskal-Wallis	It is used to compare ≥ 3 groups when the variables are ordinal.
	Wilcoxon matched-pair	It is used to determine if two samples with ordinal data differ from one another when each data point in one sample is paired with a data point in the other sample
	Chi-square goodness-of-fit	It is used to compare observed values with predicted values; can be computed for nominal, ordinal, interval, or ratio data
	Odds ratio	It is used to assess whether 2 dichotomous nominal variables are correlated.
	Fisher's exact	It is used with a small sample size to assess whether 2 dichotomous nominal or ordinal variables are correlated.

If the guide for the appropriate statistical test indicates that multiple regression analysis should be used, for example, this is not good enough because there are three different analytical strategies for multiple regression analysis (Newton & Rudestam, 1999; Tabachnick & Fidell, 2007). Thus, the researcher must articulate the correct method by examining the methods and their assumptions. Blindly relying on the guide for the appropriate statistical test is insufficient. The guide may point the researcher in the right direction, but the researcher must investigate further.

Indeed, multiple regression has three major analytical strategies: standard (simultaneous entry), sequential (hierarchical), and statistical (stepwise) (Newton & Rudestam, 1999; Tabachnick & Fidell, 2007). In all three models, the relationships of the independent variables to the dependent variable and the relationships of the independent variables with one another must be assessed in order to obtain a complete picture of the function of the independent variables. The appropriate procedure that should be applied will be determined by the goal of the study (Newton & Rudestam). Furthermore, selecting the incorrect model may significantly change the interpretation of the output.

Once the data have been collected, descriptive statistical analyses will need to be performed. For example, if the variables have been classified as continuous variables, then the data will need to be assessed in order to determine if the parametric assumptions have been satisfied. If the parametric assumptions have not been satisfied, then the data may need to be manipulated (e.g., logarithmic transformations) in order to satisfy the requirements (Warner, 2008). If the requirements cannot be satisfied, then the data may need to be reconfigured into non-parametric classifications. In short, parametric statistics are preferred over non-parametric statistics because parametric statistics provide more detailed information (Norusis, 2008).

Preliminary Data Screening and Cleanup

Three situations will be discussed in order to improve the quality of a study's data. The first involves missing data values. The second involves inconsistent responses. The third involves outlying data values.

Missing Data

If surveys contain missing data that impact the statistic, then those questionnaires may need to be dismissed. If the missing data do not impact the statistic, then the data should still be included. For example, if the researcher is assessing the relationship between religion and aggression, missing data on religion or aggression will impact the statistic. If a person fails to disclose age, this will not impact the aggression and religion statistic.

Inconsistent Responses

Some scales can detect inconsistent or contradictory responses (Buss & Warren, 2000). These will detect deceitful or contradictory response values. A high inconsistent measure means that the data are suspect and should be dismissed.

Outliers

Boxplots of variable distributions can detect outliers (extreme and unusual data values). Even though including outliers in the statistical analysis may disproportionately influence the outcome of the analysis, and because removing outliers may change the outcome of the analysis, there needs to be good rationale for removing the outliers (Warner, 2008). If the outlier data values are within acceptable parameters, perhaps they should not be dismissed.

Interaction Variable

Although two independent variables may uniquely impact the dependent variable, they may also interact with one another and produce a combined impact on the output that is greater than any additive combination of their separate effects (Cohen & Cohen, 1983; Neuman, 2006; Norusis, 2008). The interaction between two independent variables may be significant if the importance of one of the independent variables varies over the range of the other independent variable (Tabachnick & Fidell, 2007).

Multicollinearity

A high multicollinearity between two independent variables poses a threat to the validity of multiple regression (Field, 2005). If two variables have a correlation above .80, then there is most likely a multicollinearity problem (Allison, 1999; Berry & Feldman, 1985; Field). Multicollinearity exists when variables overlap and explain the same thing. Thus, the contribution of each variable is not accurate. For example, living in a poor neighborhood may explain 90% of aggression and making low income may explain 90% of aggression. However, they do not explain 180% of aggression when they are considered together. If there is a multicollinearity problem between two variables, then one of the variables should be dismissed. In a puzzle, a high multicollinearity would mean that the same piece is being called by two different names.

Parametric Assumptions

Multiple regression is a parametric statistic, which requires that several assumptions be satisfied (Norusis, 2008). First, multiple regression requires that the independent variables be either continuous or categorical and that the dependent variable be continuous (Field, 2005). Second, the sample size must be adequate (Tabachnick & Fidel, 2007). Third, the observations must be independent from one another (Norusis). Fourth, the error terms must be independent from one another (Tabachnick & Fidel). Fifth, there must be sampling normality, which indicates that the samples are from populations that are approximately normally distributed and that have scores that are normally distributed (Bordens & Abbott, 2008). Sixth, the variance of the criterion variable must be the same for all values of the independent variable (Norusis). Finally, the dependent variable must have a linear relationship with the independent variables.

Scales of Measurement

The first assumption can easily be satisfied prior to the data collection. The independent variables can be defined as either continuous or categorical. The dependent variable can be defined as continuous. The format in which the survey questions are asked will dictate the scales of measurement.

Independent Observations

All observations need to be independent from one another. Pairs of values cannot be collected from the same participant (Norusis, 2008).

Sample Size

For multiple regression, Tabachnick and Fidell (2007) has recommended that the minimum sample size be the greater of either a) 8 times the number of independent variables plus 50 or b) the number of independent variables plus 104.

Independence of Error Terms

Multiple regression requires that the residual error terms be independent from one another (Tabachnick & Fidell, 2007). The Durbin-Watson statistic is useful for assessing whether error terms are independent (Field, 2005). The statistic can range from zero to four. A value of two indicates that adjacent residuals are independent; a value greater than two indicates that the adjacent residuals have a negative correlation; and a value less than two indicates that the adjacent residuals have a positive correlation.

Normally Distributed Data

Multiple regression requires that the data be approximately normally distributed (Field, 2005). The normality assumption can be evaluated via visual examination of the histograms and statistics generated by SPSS Descriptive analysis. A normal distribution has a skewness and kurtosis of zero (Warner, 2008). The skewness relates to symmetry and to the degree in which the distribution deviates from the ideal normal distribution shape (Tabachnick & Fidell, 2007). A positive value of skewness indicates that more values are on the left side of the distribution and a negative value of skewness indicates that more values on the right side of the distribution (Field). Kurtosis relates to peakedness and to the degree in which the distribution deviates from the ideal normal distribution shape (Warner). When the kurtosis is non-normal, there is an underestimate of the variable's variance (Tabachnick & Fidell). A positive value of kurtosis indicates a pointy distribution and a negative value of kurtosis indicates a flat distribution (Field). The further the skewness and kurtosis are from zero, the more likely the data are not normally distributed.

Before the skewness and kurtosis of the dependent variables are compared to zero, they must be converted into z-scores (Field, 2005). A z-score is a standardized score that has a mean of zero and a standard deviation of one. Although skewness and kurtosis values that are greater than 1.96 are significant at $p < .05$ and indicate a distribution that is skewed and has a non-normal peakedness, no such criterion should be applied to a sample that has over 200 participants. For a sample size greater than 200, it is more important to visually examine the shape of the distribution and to consider the values of skewness and kurtosis rather than to calculate their significance. When a sample size is large, a small deviance may produce significant results.

The Normal Q-Q plot is another way to assess the normality of the data. The Q-Q chart plots the observed values against the values that are expected if the distribution is normal (Field, 2005; Norusis, 2008). If the sample comes from a normal population, then all of the data values should fall along a straight line.

Homogeneity of Variance

For correlational analysis, homogeneity of variance is often evaluated via graphs (Field, 2005). The appropriate plot to use for correlational analysis is the standardized residuals versus predicted values scatterplot. When the constant variance assumption is satisfied, the variance of one variable is stable for all values of the other variable. In other words, when there is a homogeneity of variance, the standardized residuals versus predicted values scatterplot will display a random pattern of values. If the assumption is not satisfied, multiple regression analysis may still be valid (but it may be weakened) (Tabachnick & Fidell, 2007).

Linearity

Multiple regression involves predicting an outcome based on a linear equation involving two or more predictor variables (Leedy & Ormrod, 2005). Thus, there is an assumption that there is a linear relationship between the predictor and criterion variables. This assumption can be tested in two ways. First, the independent variables can be plotted against the dependent variables to see if the data form straight lines (Norusis, 2008). Second, residual scatterplots can be examined to see if the residual error values form a line (Tabachnick & Fidell, 2007). If there is nonlinearity, the standardized residuals versus predicted values scatterplot will display a curve instead of a rectangular shape. However, if the linearity assumption is not satisfied, multiple regression analysis may still be valid (but it may be weakened).

Limitations

All studies have limitations. Limitations exist in the following areas and they must be disclosed. Failure to disclose limitations may indicate incompetence or deceit.

- Theoretical orientations
- Research context
- Methodologies
- Sample and sampling designs
- Research instruments
- Data collection methods

Following are several examples of possible limitations. First, the researcher may assume that the participants will complete the surveys themselves and that they will report truthful responses. Second, in accordance with the social learning theory, pro-social and anti-social behaviors are assumed to be learned through the same cognitive and behavioral mechanisms, learning is assumed to be an on-going process, and various social learning experiences are assumed to influence one another (Hwang & Akers, 2003). Third, a correlational design does not indicate casual relationships (Bordens & Abbott, 2008). Fourth, if the sample is convenient, purposive, and non-random, then there is the possibility that the participants who choose to participate may be different in meaningful ways from those individuals who choose not to participate. Finally, a quantitative study does not provide an in-depth understanding of the meanings that the participants have associated with their lived experiences (Berg, 2007). In short, there are many assumptions and limitations in any study and the researcher is responsible for disclosing them.

Factors to Consider in Research

1) When conducting an investigation, it is important to select the method that will properly answer the research question. Will the study be a test of relationships (e.g. correlational design) or a test of difference (e.g., t-test)? Non-experimental and non-longitudinal studies do not indicate casual relationships (Bordens & Abbott, 2008).
2) Will the sample be convenient, purposive, and non-random? Are the participants who choose to participate in the study different in meaningful ways from those individuals who choose not to participate? In short, the findings cannot be generalized to populations that do not match the sample's characteristics.
3) Quantitative studies do not provide an in-depth understanding of the meanings that the participants have associated with their lived experiences (Berg, 2007). On the other hand, qualitative studies are not very effective in determining relationships and for predicting future events.
4) Non-parametric statistics are not as strong as parametric statistics (Field, 2005).
5) Finally, will a Likert-type scale be used? If so, there is a possibility that a) the participants will engage in central tendency bias by simply selecting the middle option rather than the best option, b) the participants may simply select positive responses over negative responses, and c) due to limited options, the participants may be forced to select options that do not accurately represent their realities (Antonovich, 2008).

Ethics in Research

In order to protect participants, all university researchers must obtain the approval of the Institutional Review Board (IRB) prior to gathering participant data (Berg, 2007). This is a federal law. The purpose of the Institutional Review Board (IRB) and approval process is to ensure the ethical treatment and protection of human research participants and/or their records. Researchers must comply with principles of the Belmont Report, federal guidelines, and professional societies and organizations (e.g., American Education Research Association, Academy of Management, American Counseling Association, and American Psychological Association).

The Institutional Review Board (IRB) helps guarantee that human participants are protected by requiring that all researchers associated with a university obtain IRB approval prior to any interactions with participants. This policy is important because it provides for an objective, neutral party to evaluate the research proposal and to provide unbiased recommendations, which help protect the participants. Although there may be some risk of harm in any research project, this risk must be identified and evaluated prior to the research commencing. Furthermore, the participants must be made aware of any potential risks. Indeed, if the researchers are secretive, then they will lose credibility and this may negatively impact future research. In addition, the researchers should debrief the participants after the study and make counseling available to those participants who need it (Berg, 2007).

In order to inform potential researchers of the appropriate federal guidelines involving research, universities that conduct research offer training modules on informed consent, on assessing risk, and on privacy and confidentiality. In some cases, the participants, such as pregnant women, may be vulnerable. Indeed, the fetuses within their bodies must be protected. Thus, researchers must be aware of potential concerns so that they may design their research projects appropriately.

When children are participants, there are two types of informed consent: active and passive. Active informed consent is the formal written permission of an informed parent or legal guardian who allows their children to partake in a research study (Berg, 2007). However, many times parents and legal guardians fail to return signed consent forms, resulting in poor response rates. This is not to say that the parents and legal guardians are denying the participation of their children in the studies. Many times, they just simply fail to respond.

In order to avoid excluding relevant young participants in a study, researchers often use passive informed consent (Berg, 2007). Passive informed consent assumes that the parents and legal guardians grant permission for their children to participate in a study if they do not return a refusal form after being informed about the study. Passive informed procedures often do not fully inform parents and legal guardians about a research study or give them amply opportunities to refuse. It is assumed that the parents and legal guardians are not refusing to allow their children to participate if they do not say no. However, if parents and legal guardians do not respond due to lackadaisical parental attitudes, they may not necessarily be saying yes. Thus, this is an ethical concern that must be considered.

See Table 46 for an example of an institutional review board checklist.

Table 46

Institutional Review Board – Checklist

Done	Items
	1. Research Description
	• Research hypotheses, questions, and purpose
	• Research procedures
	• Instruments
	• Adequacy of resources to protect and accommodate participants
	2. Research Setting
	• Description of research settings
	• Research sites' IRB information
	• Approval for access
	• Contact information for the research sites
	3. Participant Population and Sample
	• Number and ages of participants
	• Special groups
	• Inclusion criteria and rationale
	• Excluded populations
	4. Participant Recruitment
	• Recruitment methods
	• Recruitment incentives
	5. Risks
	• Classification of risk
	• Explanation of risk classification
	• Participant protections and risk mitigation
	6. Benefits
	7. Privacy & Confidentiality
	8. Informed Consent
	9. Conflict of Interest
	10. Supplemental Forms
	• Risk Assessment Addendum
	• Pregnant Women, Fetuses, etc.

	• Prisoners
	• Children
	• Vulnerable Population (e.g., cognitively impaired)
	• Request for a Waiver of Elements of Informed Consent Form
	• Internet-Based Research
	• Records-Based Research
	• Disclosure of Financial Interest
	• Certification of Translation
	• IRB Training Records
	• Approval Letters Granting Access to Sites and/or Participants
	• Informed Consent Document
	• Instruments, Surveys, or Other Research Documents
	• Recruitment brochures, flyers, scripts, etc.
	• Other:

Examples of Addressing Ethical Issues

Guidelines that govern how human participants should be treated in research are based on the 1979 Belmont Report, which was published by the National Commission for the Protection of Human Subjects of Biomedical and Behavioral Research (Berg, 2007; Zimmerman, 1997). The Belmont Report has established ethical principles to guide researchers' conduct when they collect data from human participants. Even if the risks for the participants in the study are minimal, the researcher needs to take measures to ensure that the participants will be protected throughout the entire study. Below are examples of ethical issues that were addressed during a correlational research study involving a) religiosity and school-sponsored contact sport participation and b) aggressive behaviors later in life (Davis, 2014).

Budget

The researcher has disclosed the cost of the study and the source of the funds to the Institutional Review Board. First, it is important to know if the study is financially feasible. Second, it is important to know that a third party is not influencing the researcher's interpretation of the study's findings via its financial support.

Researcher's Position Statement

The researcher has played contact sports from fourth grade through twelfth grade. Although the researcher believes that contact sports may teach some children anti-social behaviors, the researcher also believes that contact sports may teach some children pro-social behaviors. Consequently, the researcher will be open-minded and will interpret the study's data objectively. Furthermore, the researcher is currently a police officer who enforces laws involving aggressive behaviors. Although the researcher has no personal interest in the participants, who will be recruited from local colleges and universities, the researcher will protect the participants' anonymity by disassociating their names from the instruments.

Protection from Harm

To help ensure that the participants are not harmed, the researcher will obtain an Institutional Review Board approval prior to gathering data (Berg, 2007). Furthermore, the researcher will collect data from the participants in a comfortable and secure place. If the participants feel uneasy, especially if their responses are sensitive, then they may withhold valuable data.

Potential Negative Risks

Because the study will ask questions about aggression, there is the chance that negative emotions may be generated. Therefore, the researcher will provide the participants with counselor information so that troubled participants may seek assistance. In addition, the researcher will respect the research sites and will keep any disturbances to a minimum.

Informed Consent & Assurance of Volunteerism

Informed consent provides the participants with information on the purpose of the study, the procedures, and the potential risks (Creswell, 2009). As a result, the participants will be able to make informed decisions on whether they want to consent and to participate in the study. Because the participants' safety take precedence over all else, the researcher will make it quite clear to the participants that they may withdraw from the study at any time without consequence. Indeed, their participation is voluntary.

Confidentiality & Anonymity

The researcher will protect the confidentiality of participant information throughout the entire study. Personal information about participants will be secured to prevent the loss and misuse of data; completed surveys will only be accessible to the research team and will not be shared with anyone else. After the data from the surveys have been analyzed, the researcher will secure the data in a locked safe until it is time to be destroyed. Furthermore, the researcher will clearly claim ownership of the data in order to avoid any misunderstandings about who controls the data. Although the researcher will protect the participants' personal information, there is a risk that any collected data could be subpoenaed by a court.

The researcher will protect the anonymity of the participants. For example, in order to help protect the participants' identities, the researcher will contact professors at local colleges and universities and have them distribute a letter of invitation to potential participants. If students are willing to participate in the study, then they will respond to the letter and contact the researcher. Second, because knowing the identities of the participants is not crucial to the study, there is no need for the participants to place their names on the surveys.

Honesty with Professionalism

Ethical guidelines will be followed during the writing and dissemination of the data (Creswell, 2009). First, the paper will be written using nonbiased language. Second, the data will be complete, unadulterated, and the researcher will make a clear distinction between the evidence and the researcher's interpretation of the evidence. Third, no one will be allowed to use the data to take advantage of another person. Finally, the study's findings will be open to public review, which will enhance its credibility.

Reducing Anxiety

In order to reduce the participants' anxieties, the researcher will effectively communicate with the participants. For example, the researcher will provide a letter of introduction prior to the study as a way to promote its legitimacy (Creswell, 2009). The researcher will make the study's purpose and benefits known to all participants. In addition, the researcher will make the participants aware of the study's process so that they will know what to expect. In short, clear communication will promote the credibility of the study and reduce the participants' anxieties.

Autonomous Agents

The study will be designed so that participants are considered autonomous agents. For example, factors that may indicate that the participants are autonomous agents include a) whether the participants are at least 21 years of age, b) whether they are free to act on their own judgments on whether or not to participate, and c) whether they have previously indicated an interest in participating in the study. Furthermore, an informed consent form describes the purpose of the study, the benefits, and the potential risks (Creswell, 2003). As a result, the participants will be able to make informed decisions on whether or not they want to participate in the study. A statement will make it quite clear to the participants that they can withdraw from the study at any time without consequence. Thus, their decision to participate will be informed, will be voluntary, and will require a signature.

Implied Consent via Electronic Signature

Before electronic data are collected from a participant, the individual will be required to provide an electronic signature of consent (Post, 2008). A signature of consent may be obtained electronically by integrating it into the informed consent form.

For example, the electronic consent form may provide information on a) the researcher, b) volunteer participation, c) data storage, d) compensation, e) benefits, f) risks, g) confidentiality, h) legal rights, i) contact information, and j) how to exit the study, if so desired. In addition, if the potential participant agrees to participate in the study, then the participant will be required to click on the link that clearly indicates her consent to participate in the study. If an individual does click on the link that indicates willingness to participate in the study, then consent as a willing participant in the study will be implied. In this case, the participant will be allowed to complete the questionnaire. However, if an individual does not want to participate in the study, then the person will click on the link that clearly indicates unwillingness to participate in the study. Consequently, if the individual declines to participate in the study, then the person will be denied access to the questionnaire. Furthermore, a participant should be able to exit the study at any time before data are submitted electronically.

In short, ethical standards will be followed in three specific areas. These three areas are the data collection process, the analysis and interpretation of the data, and the writing and dissemination of the report (Creswell, 2003). See Table 47 for an ethics checklist.

Table 47

Ethics Checklist in Data Collection, Data Analysis, and Writing of Report

Ethics Checklist
Data Collection Process
__Participation is voluntary
__Purpose understood by participants, including benefits
__Process understood by participants
__Participants' privacy safeguarded – data collected confidentially
__Appropriate signatures obtained – from participants
__Appropriate permission obtained – from data collection site
__Research site respected
Analysis and Interpretation of Data
__Participants' anonymity safeguarded – names not attached to surveys
__Ownership of data declared
__Data put into storage for 7 years – only shared with study team
Writing and Dissemination of the Study
__Use of nonbiased language
__Unadulterated data
__Proper use of data
__Credibility of study confirmed by readers

University Research – Best Practices for Research

Below are **general practices** for qualitative research. These general practices are necessary in order to effectively investigate and present a qualitative study.

General Practices for Qualitative Research

1) In order to protect participants, all university researchers must obtain the approval of the Institutional Review Board (IRB) prior to gathering participant data (Berg, 2007). This is a federal law.
2) The researcher must describe the topic of the qualitative research in an interesting manner. For example, the study's aim and purpose must be clear and important in order to gain the attention of potential participants. Otherwise, many individuals may not read the study.
3) The researcher must consider the availability of the data before the researcher commits to a study. If the data are controlled by the government, for example, and the information is sensitive, then the data might not be available for analysis. Individuals may simply refuse to participate in the study.
4) The researcher must establish the need for a qualitative study (Seale, Gobo, Gubrium, & Silverman, 2004). Qualitative studies provide thorough investigations of individuals in specific social settings and include detailed behavioral and psychological descriptions of persons in those settings (Champion, 2006). These findings may not be generalized to other populations (Creswell, 2009). If predictions are needed and generalizations to larger populations are required, then quantitative techniques should be investigated.
5) The researcher must select the proper kind of qualitative research to be performed (Hatch, 2002). Each qualitative research method is designed to obtain information in a different

way. Thus, a research question may be better answered by a particular kind of qualitative research method. For example, a longitudinal case study may be better in assessing incremental changes over time than will a focus group interview. Align the method of research with the research question.

6) A researcher must have an open mind and must be willing to interpret data that are unexpected and contrary to personal beliefs (Seale et al., 2004). The participants are being studied, not the researcher.
7) The researcher must present authentic findings (Creswell, 2009). The researcher must not fudge the data; otherwise, the researcher will have no credibility and the study will be questionable. Indeed, perhaps the significance of the study will indicate that other variables exist that affect the results.
8) The researcher must make a clear distinction between the evidence and the interpretation of the evidence (Seale et al., 2004). This is important because to mix the two is misleading and less than ethical. The goal is to provide legitimate information; it is not to try to trick someone.
9) The researcher needs to select the appropriate participants for the study. For example, if police officers are the subject of study, then investigate police officers. A purposive sampling is appropriate for a difficult to reach, specialized population (Neuman, 2006).

Below are **specific practices** for qualitative research. These practices are important in carrying out a qualitative study.

Specific Practices for Qualitative Research

1) The researcher needs to record the evidence as accurately as possible. Video tape the data (i.e., interviews) if possible because this will provide a more complete visual and audio account. Always supplement the data collection process with note-taking, just in case a problem develops with the audio-visual equipment.
2) For a qualitative one-on-one interview, the researcher needs to develop a question that is open-ended and allows for in-depth answers (Creswell, 2009). Qualitative studies seek to understand the meanings, concepts, symbols, and characteristics of things. Thus, this requires narrative style answers. In addition, develop probe questions for further elaboration.
3) The researcher needs to protect the participants (Berg, 2007). The researcher needs to follow ethical guidelines and to protect the privacy and confidentiality of the participants by explaining the research process to them and by obtaining their permission to proceed.
4) The researcher needs to perform a literature review (Balian, 1988). The goal is to add to the body of knowledge. Gaps in the knowledge will not be known unless prior studies are examined. Otherwise, the study may be meaningless, especially if the topic has already been exhausted.
5) The researcher needs to use triangulation (Creswell, 2009). This will help validate the data and may provide additional insights or generate additional questions. There are several ways to use triangulation in research (Berg, 2007). These include data triangulation, investigator triangulation, theory

triangulation, and methodological triangulation. All help enhance the validity of the study.

6) The researcher needs to obtain the proper software for content (data) analysis and needs to practice using it for identifying themes (Berg, 2007). The software is only useful if it is used in the right manner. Free qualitative software packages are available on the Internet and the researchers should familiarize themselves with what is available.
7) During interviews, the researcher needs to keep the participants focused on the topic. The data sought should seek to answer the research question. Because the amount of raw data can be overwhelming, the researcher should continually evaluate whether the data are related to the question. This will allow the researcher to manage the huge amount of data. Do not get side-tracked.
8) The researcher needs to interview the participants in a comfortable and secure place (Berg, 2007). If the participants are afraid that someone may overhear their responses, especially if those responses are sensitive and may get them into trouble, then they may withhold valuable information.
9) The researcher needs to be flexible (Berg, 2007). Adjust personal schedules to meet with the participants. After all, they are going out of their way to provide data, so personal schedules may have to be adjusted to meet the participants when they are available.
10) The researcher needs to dress appropriately (Berg, 2007). If the researcher fails to dress professionally, then the participants may doubt the quality of the study and the confidentiality of the data. The image of the researcher may reflect the quality of the study.

11) For focus group interviews, use a round table so that all of the participants can be observed. Otherwise, valuable information may be missed.

Purpose of Informed Consent Form

Before data are collected from a participant, ethical standards require that the researcher obtain informed consent from the participant. The main purpose of the form is to provide information that may affect the participant's decision about whether or not the person wants to participate in the research project. The potential participant must sign the informed consent form before data are collected from the person. However, it is possible to obtain implied consent if the data are collected over the Internet. If data are collected over the Internet, the researcher will need the participant to actively click on a link that indicates that the person is willing to participate in the study.

The informed consent form will answer the following questions.

1. Who is conducting the research?
2. What does participation involve?
3. Why is the person being asked to participate?
4. What are the risks involved?
5. Will the participant realize any benefits?
6. What will happen if new information becomes available during the study that may impact the person's decision to participate?
7. How will confidentiality be protected?

8. What are the consequences if the participant withdraws from the study?
9. What is the cost to the participant?
10. Will the participant be compensated for illness or injury?
11. Will the participant show consent by providing a signature?

In addition, if any type of health or medical information is sought, a HIPPA form will be required. On the next several pages are examples of an **Invitation Letter, a HIPAA form, and an Informed Consent Form.**

Example of Electronic Invitation Letter

Invitation to Participate in Research Study

A Correlational Study of Childhood Religiosity, Childhood Sport Participation, and Sport-Learned Aggression Among African American Female Athletes

Participants are needed for a research study in order to gain insight on the relationships among childhood religiosity, childhood sport participation, and sport-learned aggression. The research cannot be performed without data. Your participation is voluntary and provides that data. Your name will not be written on the questionnaires. The survey site will be active for three weeks.

You are being invited to participate in this study because you are a member of Zoomerang and because you match the characteristics of the population. The population of interest is African American females, 21 to 40 years of age. However, in order to gain control over the study's variables, there are several other conditions that must be satisfied in order to participate in the study. You must meet the all of the qualifications listed below in order to participate in this study. If you do not meet all of the qualifications listed below, please exit the study. Because the study requires that the participants have not been medically treated for depression or diagnosed with Attention Deficit Disorder, a health information release form will be required.

Various Types of Sports (for reference)

Contact Sports	***Collision Sports***	***Non-Contact Sports***
a) Volleyball	a) Football	a) swimming
b) Basketball	b) Wrestling	b) tennis
c) Soccer	c) Boxing	c) track
d) Lacrosse		d) gymnastics
e) Water Polo		e) softball

Qualifications to Participate

a) You must be an African American female.
b) You must be 21 to 40 years of age.
c) You must have attended U.S. secondary schools.
d) You must have graduated from high school.
e) You must not have been medically treated for depression.
f) You must not have been diagnosed with Attention Deficit Disorder.
g) You must not have played collision sports in secondary school.
h) You may have been a non-athlete and may never have played sports in secondary school.

i) You may have played non-contact sports in secondary school. This will not impact the number of years that you have played contact sports.
j) If you have played contact sports in secondary school, then you must have played in 12th grade.
k) If you have played contact sports in 12th grade, then you must have not skipped a grade level of participation once you started to play. In other words, you must not have had any discontinuity in contact sport participation from grade level to grade level, starting from the time when you first engaged in school-sponsored contact sports. For example, if you first started to play school-sponsored contact sports in 7th grade, then you must have played in 7th, 8th, 9th, 10th, 11th, and 12th grades. However, if you first started to play school-sponsored contact sports in 11th grade, then you must have played only in 11th and 12th grades.

If you meet the above conditions, then please respond to this letter of invitation and take the survey. Otherwise, you cannot take the survey.

Example of Electronic HIPAA Form

CONFIDENTIAL HEALTH CARE INFORMATION (HIPAA)

Authorization to Use or Disclose Health Information

Health information is sensitive information related to a person's medical condition. Because only individuals who have not been medically treated for depression or diagnosed with Attention Deficit Disorder (ADD) will be invited to participate in the study, and because these two conditions are confirmed in the demographics section of the study, a health information release form is required. Therefore, you will need to electronically sign this document before you will be allowed to participate in the study. Otherwise, you will need to withdraw from the study. By signing this health care information form, you give permission to the researcher to use or disclose (release) your health related information as part of the research study. After the data are recorded, the data will be secured in a locked safe for seven years. After seven years, the data will be destroyed. During the seven years, the data will not be disclosed without additional participant consent or unless required by law.

By nature of the study, it will be known to all readers that all of the study's participants have not been medically treated for depression or diagnosed with ADD. Although the results of the research study will be published, your name or identity will not be revealed. The health information provided in the research study will be used by the researcher as a way to control extraneous variables. This information may be confirmed by members of the dissertation committee.

The researcher is required by law to protect your health related information. By electronically signing this document, you authorize the researcher to use and/or disclose your health related information for this research. Those individuals who receive your health related information may not be required by Federal privacy laws to protect the information and they may share it with other people without your permission, if permitted by the laws that govern them.

This authorization has no expiration date. However, you may voluntarily withdraw from the study at any time prior to electronically submitting the data. Once the data are collected, it will no longer be possible to link the data to the signed confidential health care information forms. Please click on the appropriate box below that indicates whether you would like to participate in this study or whether you want to withdraw from this study.

I have read and understand this HIPAA form and

□ I agree to participate in this study
□ I do not agree to participate in this study

Example of Electronic Informed Consent Form

INFORMED CONSENT FORM

A Correlational Study of Childhood Religiosity, Childhood Sport Participation, and Sport-Learned Aggression Among African American Female Athletes

Name of University: __________ School Address: ________________

Researcher: _________ Phone: _____________ E-mail: ___________

I am conducting a research study in order to determine the relationships among religiosity, sport participation, and aggression. I would like to invite you to participate in this study. The main purpose of this form is to provide information about the study so that you can make a good decision about whether you want to participate. If you choose to participate, please sign in the space at the end of this form.

I. Background

This study is being conducted in order to assess relationships among variables. The variables include childhood religiosity, childhood sport participation, and aggression. However, it is not necessary that you have played childhood sports. Only African Americans females are being surveyed. You must be from 21 to 40 years of age. You must not have been medically treated for depression. You must not have been diagnosed with Attention Deficit Disorder (ADD). Please read the following information before you make your decision.

II. Purpose

The purpose of this study is to determine the relationships among childhood religiosity, childhood sport participation, and sport-learned aggression. However, other variables may affect the study. Some of them will be controlled by design. Others will be assessed in the demographics part of the survey.

III. Participation

About 500 females have been invited to participate in this study. You have been selected because you represent the study's population. You are an African American female. You are 21 to 40 years of age. You have not been medically treated for depression. You have not been diagnosed with ADD.

Participation is voluntary. You do not have to participate in this study. Nothing will happen to you if you do not want to participate in this study. If you have any questions involving this study, you may call the researcher at xxx-xxx-xxxx.

IV. Procedures

The study will take a total of about 20 minutes to complete. You will mark your answers by clicking on the best response. You will then submit the completed survey online to Zoomerang.

V. Reason for Participation

You have been asked to participate in this study in order to provide data. The data will be used to gain insight on the relationships among variables. The research cannot be performed without data. Your participation provides the needed data.

VI. Research

This study is important in the human services and public safety fields. The study may provide public officials with data that is currently unavailable to them.

VII. Confidentiality

Your personal information is confidential. It will not be disclosed to persons outside of the study without your permission, unless required by law. After the data are recorded, the data will be stored in a locked safe for seven years. After seven years, the data will be destroyed. Furthermore, your name will not be recorded.

The results of the study will be published. However, your name will not be revealed. Completed surveys will only be accessible to the researcher.

All persons involved with this study will honor this agreement. The Institutional Review Board (IRB) will be allowed to inspect sections of the research records related to the study. Members of the IRB or the Human Research Protection Office (HRPO) can answer your questions and concerns about your rights as a research participant. They can be contacted at xxx-xxx-xxxx.

VIII. Risks

No study is completely risk-free. Answering questions about yourself may lead to old memories that generate undesired feelings. However, there is no collaboration or competition in this study and you may withdraw from the study at any time without consequence. The researcher does not anticipate that you will be harmed by participating in this study.

IX. Compensation for Illness or Injury

As a participant, you are not waiving any of your legal rights. However, no funds have been set aside to help you in the event of harm. If you have any questions, you may call the HRPO at xxx-xxx-xxxx.

X. Benefits & Costs

As you are aware, you may receive points, which are of nominal value, from Zoomerang. However, the researcher will not give you anything to participate in this study.

The information from the study may be useful to other people. The only cost to you will be a few moments of your time.

XI. Ownership of Data

The researcher will own the data. This will limit access to the data.

XII. Freedom to Question

You may call the researcher at any time during the study.

XIII. Freedom to Withdraw

Your participation in this study is voluntary. You are free to stop participating in the study at any time without any cost. You do not have to submit any data. However, once data are submitted, it will be too late to withdraw from the study.

XIV. If New Information Becomes Available

The researcher will contact you if he learns about new information that could change your decision about participating in this study.

XV. Voluntary Consent

By signing this form, you are saying that you have read this form. You are saying that you understand the risks and benefits of this study. You are also saying that you know what you are being asked to do. The researcher will be happy to answer any questions you have about the study. If you have any questions, please feel free to call the researcher at xxx-xxx-xxxx.

If you have questions about your rights as a research participant, you may call the HRPO. This is also true if you have any concerns about the research process, the researcher, or experience any unexpected problems with the study. Your identity, questions, and concerns will be kept confidential.

By clicking on the link below, you are saying that you have read this information. You are also saying that you understand what you are being asked to do.

If you click on the following link that indicates *you agree to participate in the study*, your consent as a willing participant will be implied. Otherwise, if you click on the link that indicates *you do not agree to participate in the study*, you will exit the study.

Please print a copy of this consent form for your records.

Choose and click on a link below.

I have read and understand this informed consent form and

□ I agree to participate in the study
□ I do not agree to participate in this study

Research Site(s) Approval

The following institution has granted the researcher access to their participants and/or facilities:

Name: Zoomerang
Approval Date: October 17, 2014
Approval Authorization: 382-7777

IRB Approval

This consent is not valid without the approval information below.

This research has been approved by xxxx University's Institutional Review Board. Approval number: _______________; Effective dates: From: __________________ to ____________________.
(*This information will be supplied by xxxx University's IRB Office upon the approval of the IRB application.*)

References

Allison, P.D. (1999). *Multiple regression: A primer.* Thousand Oaks, CA: Pine Forge.

Antonovich, M.P. (2008). *Office and SharePoint 2007 user's guide: Integrating SharePoint with Excel, Outlook, Access, and Word.* Berkeley, CA: Apress.

Balian, E.S. (1988). *How to design, analyze, and write doctoral or master's research* (2nd ed.). New York, NY: University Press of America.

Berg, B. (2007). *Qualitative research methods for the social sciences* (6th ed.). Boston, MA: Pearson Education, Inc.

Berry, W.D., & Feldman, S. (1985). *Multiple regression in practice.* Beverly Hills, CA: Sage.

Bordens, K., & Abbott, B. (2008). *Research design and methods: A process approach* (7th ed.). Boston, MA: McGraw Hill.

Buss, A.H., & Warren, W.L. (2000). *Aggression questionnaire manual.* Los Angeles, CA: Western Psychological Services.

Champion, D. (2006). *Research methods for criminal justice and criminology* (3rd ed.). Upper Saddle River, NJ: Pearson Merrill Prentice Hall.

Cohen, J, & Cohen, P. (1983). *Applied multiple regression/correlation analysis for the behavioral science* (2nd ed.). Hillsdale, NJ: Lawrence Erlbaum.

Creative Research Systems (n.d.). *The survey system: Sample size calculator.* Retrieved from http://www.surveysystem.com/sscalc.htm

Creswell, J. (2009). *Research design: Qualitative, quantitative, and mixed methods approaches* (3rd ed.). Los Angeles, CA: Sage Publications.

Davis, W.L. (2014). *Religiosity, sports, and learned aggression for Black female athletes.* Saarbrücken, Germany: Scholars.

Field, A. (2005). *Discovering statistics using SPSS* (2nd ed.). Thousand Oaks, CA: Sage.

Hatch, J. (2002). *Doing qualitative research in education settings.* Albany, NY: State University of New York Press.

Hwang, S., & Akers, R.L. (2003). Substance use by Korean adolescents: A cross-cultural test of the social learning, social bonding, and self-control theories. In R. Akers & G. Jensen (Eds.), *Social learning theory and the explanation of crime* (p. 39-63). New Brunswick, NJ: Transaction.

Leedy, P., & Ormrod, J. (2005). *Practical research: Planning and design* (8th ed.). Upper Saddle River, NJ: Pearson Merrill Prentice Hall.

Neuman, W. (2006). *Social research methods: Qualitative and quantitative approaches* (6th ed.). Boston, MA: Pearson Education, Inc.

Newton, R.P., & Rudestam, K.E. (1999). *Your statistical consultant: Answers to your data analysis question.* Thousand Oaks, CA: Sage.

Norusis, M.J. (2008). *SPSS 16.0 guide to data analysis.* Upper saddle River, NJ: Prentice Hall.

Post, M. (2008). *Impact of internal and external factors on working women's successful completion of online college level courses* (Doctoral dissertation). Retrieved from Dissertation Abstracts International-A. (AAT #3316346)

Seale, C., Gobo, G., Gubrium, J., and Silverman, D. (2004). Introduction: Inside qualitative research. In C. Seale, G. Gobo, J. Gubrium, and D. Silverman (Eds.), *Qualitative research practice* (p. 1-12). Thousand Oaks, CA: Sage Publications.

Tabachnick, B.G., & Fidell, L.S. (2007). *Using multivariate statistics* (5th ed.). Boston, MA: Pearson Education, Inc.

Warner, R.M. (2008). *Applied statistics: From bivariate through multivariate techniques.* Los Angeles, CA: Sage Publications.

Zimmerman, J.F. (1997). The Belmont report: An ethical framework for protecting research subjects. *The Monitor.*

Appendix A

ASSESSING QUALITATIVE INFORMATION

Qualitative Theme Analysis

Qualitative research studies attempt to understand **why** events happen by discovering themes in the data. There are many different techniques for identifying themes in qualitative data. Some of the techniques work better for short, open-ended responses while other techniques work better for rich, complex narratives. There is no single technique that is optimal for all situations. See Table 48 for several techniques that are used for identifying themes in qualitative data (Ryan & Bernard, n.d.).

Table 48

Several Techniques used in Qualitative Research for Identifying Themes

<table>
<tr><th>General Technique</th><th>Specific Technique</th><th>Description</th></tr>
<tr><td rowspan="4">Analysis of Words</td><td rowspan="2">Word repetitions</td><td>Informal: Note unique words (and their synonyms) that are used often because they determine important ideas.</td></tr>
<tr><td>Formal: count the number of times unique words are used to create a list of important ideas.</td></tr>
<tr><td>Indigenous categories</td><td>Experience and expertise often use specialized vocabulary. Create categories by seeking terms that sound unfamiliar or are used in unfamiliar ways.</td></tr>
<tr><td>Key-words-in-context</td><td>Look at how concepts are used. Identify key words and search the text to find all instances of how the words are used. Assess the immediate context. Themes are identified by sorting examples into piles of similar meaning.</td></tr>
</table>

Analysis of blocks of text	Compare and contrast	Conduct a line-by-line analysis to identify the idea in the current line and how the idea is similar or different from the previous line.
	Social science queries	Search for specific topics that may generate major social and cultural themes (e.g., managing interpersonal social relationships, informal methods of social control, achieving social status, etc.).
	Searching for missing information	Search for themes that are absent from the text. Silence may indicate a topic that the person is unwilling or afraid to discuss.
Intentional analysis of linguistic features	Metaphors and analogies	Look for metaphors that produce patterns of underlying principles.
	Transitions	Look for naturally occurring shifts in thematic content (new paragraphs in written text and pauses in oral speech).
	Connectors	Look for phrases that indicate relationships among topics (e.g. causal relationships, conditional relationships, time-oriented relationships, and spatial orientations).

Physical manipulation of text	Unmarked texts	Read the text several times, highlight different salient themes, and group similar themes. Then, in the remaining text, look for less obtrusive themes.
	Pawing	Read the text several times, separate the key phrases, and look for patterns in the data via the interocular percussion test.
	Cutting and sorting	Look for quotes that seem important; group similar quotes to identify themes. Good for identifying subthemes.

The Message of Music

Local residents use music to communicate. Therefore, officers need to pay attention to the music of minorities because their songs may be transmitting qualitative messages of how they perceive society. For example, there must be a reason why minorities sing songs about excessive police force. Perhaps they have experienced such events. Even if the officers do not believe these messages, the minorities may believe them. Hence, it is important for the police to listen to what the community members are saying and to understand their messages.

Example of Assessing Information in Love Songs

The lyrics for 10 love songs, which have all been ranked number one on the billboards, have been collected and examined (About.com: Country music, n.d.; AlaskaJim.com, 2007; Songfacts, n.d.; Songlyrics.com, n.d.). Five of the songs are performed by men and five are performed by women. The five songs performed by men include 1) *Pretty Woman*, by Roy Orbison, 2) *Daydream Believer*, by the Monkees, 3) *El Paso*, by Marty Robbins, 4) *Running Bear*, by Johnny Preston, and 5) *Hello, I Love You*, by the Doors. The five songs performed by women include 1) *I Will Always Love You*, by Dolly Parton, 2) *To Sir With Love*, by Lulu, 3) *Love Child*, by the Supremes, 4) *Will You Love Me Tomorrow?*, by the Shirelles, and 5) *Respect*, by Aretha Franklin. The songs performed by men will be compared to the songs performed by women by comparing themes between the lyrics. All of the lyrics performed for each sex will be combined and an overall comparison will be made.

The unit of analysis, which "is the amount of text that is assigned a code" (Neuman, 2006, p. 327), shall be the stanza. Furthermore, because the words "I love you," may actually mean, "I am infatuated with you and want sexual intercourse even though I do not know you," the theme of each stanza shall be evaluated by using latent coding. Indeed, latent coding may be more valid than manifest coding, which simply counts the number of times that the words appear. This means that the entire song must be read prior to any evaluations so that the overtone can be assessed. In addition, a stanza may include more than one theme. However, before a content analysis can commence, a list of variables needs to be developed (Sproull, 1995).

Variables:

1) Long term love – a long term commitment, perhaps as in marriage;
2) Infatuation – burning desire for immediate action;
3) Puppy Love –nonsexual and superficial;

4) Gain love – want other person to provide love;
5) Give love - willing to sacrifice oneself for love;
6) Believes superior to other person;
7) Believes subordinate to (i.e., worships) other person; and
8) Believes equal to other person.

Table 49

Summary of the 8 Variables for the Lyrics of 10 Love Songs

Variable	# of times variable appeared (Men)	# of times variable appeared (Women)
1	9	17
2	17	1
3	1	0
4	5	2
5	9	4
6	0	1
7	8	6
8	6	5

According to Table 49, the overall themes on the songs indicate that men seem to be more interested in short term love than in long term relationships as compared to women. Furthermore, men seem to want women to submit themselves in love, and they are willing to die for it. Women, on the other hand, seem to want lasting relationships. Moreover, women sometimes are willing to submit themselves to men, but they may want something in exchange (e.g., respect).

Content analysis is a useful way to assess information in everyday life. Being a police officer, it is important to analyze what is being said through both verbal and nonverbal manners. For example, if a police officer stops a pickup truck and is suspicious that there might be drugs in the vehicle, if the suspects clinch their fists (they may be preparing to fight), if they take off their hats and sunglasses (they do not want to damage them), if they start whispering to one another (they may be making a plan of attack), if they try to keep certain parts of their bodies shielded (they may be trying to conceal weapons), if they start looking around (they may be looking for witnesses, weapons, or escape routes), and if they try to position the officer between them, this may indicate a theme that violence is about to occur. Indeed, being able to recognize themes may save an officer's life.

Value of Information

The value of information is relative. What is considered important information to some individuals may be considered less important to other individuals. Police officers need to understand that certain individuals will seek out particular information. Police officers will be more effective if they understand what information certain people value.

Read the following paragraph and highlight important information.

A man entered a home. There were surveillance cameras all about the home. Inside the home, there was a strong odor of mold in the air. There was a big flat-screen TV and a laptop in the living room. In the kitchen was a backed-up sink and the pipe was leaking. Near the sink were a woman's diamond ring and a gold watch. There was a desk in a study in which there was a wad of cash; there was also a safe in one of the closets. In one of the bedrooms was the sound of someone snoring; there was also some water dripping from the bedroom's ceiling. A car then pulled into the driveway.

Now, read the following paragraph and highlight important information from a thief's point of view. Assume the man who entered the home was the thief.

A man entered a home. There were surveillance cameras all about the home. Inside the home, there was a strong odor of mold in the air. There was a big flat-screen TV and a laptop in the living room. In the kitchen was a backed-up sink and the pipe was leaking. Near the sink were a woman's diamond ring and a gold watch. There was a desk in a study in which there was a wad of cash; there was also a safe in one of the closets. In one of the bedrooms was the sound of someone snoring; there was also some water dripping from the bedroom's ceiling. A car then pulled into the driveway.

Now, read the following paragraph and highlight important information from a potential home buyer's point of view. Assume the man who entered the home was the potential home buyer.

A man entered a home. There were surveillance cameras all about the home. Inside the home, there was a strong odor of mold in the air. There was a big flat-screen TV and a laptop in the living room. In the kitchen was a backed-up sink and the pipe was leaking. Near the sink were a woman's diamond ring and a gold watch. There was a desk in a study in which there was a wad of cash; there was also a safe in one of the closets. In one of the bedrooms was the sound of someone snoring; there was also some water dripping from the bedroom's ceiling. A car then pulled into the driveway.

Summary

A thief and potential home buyer will value the same information differently. What is important to the thief may not be important to the potential home buyer. Likewise, what is important to the potential home buyer may not be important to the thief.

Police officers cannot effectively serve the community if the officers do not understand the community. Therefore, police officers need to understand the information that is transmitted by community members. Police officers only need to look around to see how people communicate. There is much information all about.

Ethnography: Assessing Information in a Natural Setting

Date: Monday, November 2013
Location: Wana Cup Restaurant in Shipshewana, Indiana
Time: 11:00 am – 11:30 am

Ethnography seeks to describe a culture from the local or indigenous people's point of view (Berg, 2007). Data collection includes participant observation, participant interviewing, and artifact examination in order "to understand the cultural knowledge that group members use to make sense of the everyday experiences" (Hatch, 2002, p. 21). Thus, I entered a local restaurant to observe customers.

Sense of Vision

As I pulled up to the restaurant, I observed one car parked in front of the restaurant and 4 horse-and-buggies parked on the side of the restaurant. All of the horses were either brown or black and all of the buggies were black. The car, on the other hand, was red. All of the lights on the outside of the restaurant were gas lanterns. The entire building was gray, even the roof top. Furthermore, there was a white wooden fence in front of the building. In short, there were no extravagant colors advertising this restaurant.

Once inside the building, I observed 8 customers: 4 men and 4 women. All of customers seemed to be between 50 and 60 years of age. The customers sat at two tables, 2 men and 2 women at each table. The men sat across from the women.

The men had some particular characteristics. First, all 4 of the men had full beards but none of them had mustaches. Second, none of them wore belts; instead, they all wore suspenders. Third, all 4 of the men wore dark blue pants, which appeared rugged, like workpants (they were not blue jeans). Fourth, all 4 of the men wore black coats, black boots, and black hats. Fifth, all 4 of the men wore eye glasses (versus contact lenses). Sixth, none of the men wore any jewelry.

The 4 women seemed to match the men that they accompanied. First, all four of the women wore black coats and white bonnets. Second, all of the women wore either black or blue dresses. In other words, the colors were conservative and they were not blue jeans.

Third, all 4 of the women wore black boots and black stockings. Fourth, all of these women wore eye glasses (versus contact lenses). Fifth, all of the women had black purses. Sixth, none of the women wore any jewelry.

As far as the environment, I noticed that there was a wooden sign on the wall with the Lord's Prayer on it. This seemed to be significant; indeed, the men and women closed their eyes and seemed to pray before they ate. Furthermore, I noticed that the advertisement signs above the cash register were made of cardboard, although they did have professional looking drawings on them. For example, a banana split sign had a very good drawing of a banana split on it. In addition, the colors in the building were simple. The walls had wood paneling halfway up on them. Above that, the walls were white. Finally, the unisex bathroom utilized a single cloth roller towel (i.e., a single towel that everyone uses). Thus, all of the clues indicate that the restaurant is low tech.

Finally, I noticed that there was some money (unknown amount of dollar bills) resting on a tray on top of the garbage can. No one seemed to care that it sat there. This indicates that the people probably trust one another not to take it. The waitress finally picked the money up about 10 minutes later.

Sense of Smell

Sitting next to the group, I was overwhelmed by their bodily odor. Thus, it seems as though the individuals may not bathe daily. However, this odor did not seem to bother them.

Sense of Hearing

Except for the talking among the individuals, the inside of the restaurant was quiet. There was no music playing and there were no cell phones. In addition, the entire group appeared to speak a combination of German and English. However, when a man dressed in a suit approached them, they started speaking English to him.

Summary

In short, this culture is quite different than my culture. They do not desire modern technology and do not fancy materialistic products. Indeed, they do not even drive motor vehicles. However, they do seem to have strong social bonds within their community. Furthermore, they do not seem to be concerned about what outsiders think (as evidence by the Lord's Prayer on the wall).

Artifact Data: Assessing Information in Cemeteries

Greenwood Cemetery (Lagrange, Indiana)

Much unobtrusive actuarial data can be obtained in cemeteries (Berg, 2007). Greenwood Cemetery in Lagrange, Indiana is a public cemetery with thousands of grave sites. This cemetery does not have a policy requiring that flat stones be used. Consequently, there are many different types of headstones used in this cemetery. All of the headstones face east, a Christian tradition, and there is an overall Christian theme at the site (other religious denominations are not obvious) (Graves, 2006).

Headstones from 200 years ago

Greenwood Cemetery, a municipality cemetery, contains headstones with dates ranging from persons who fought in the American Revolutionary War until the present day. Most of the headstones for military personnel are similar to one another. They are about three feet high, white, and contain a cross at the top. A military headstone contains the name of the deceased, the state identifying where the person came from, the rank of the person during the war, the name of the war fought in, and the dates of birth and death. In many cases, the commanding officer's name is also included on the headstone. For example, one headstone reads as follows, "Abel Mattoon, Massachusetts, PVT, Capt. T. Williams Co, Revolutionary War, 1759-1837." Next to each of these headstones for military personnel is a metal rod, about two feet high, with a five point star on top of it with the word, "Comrade," on it.

Analysis - Basically, it appears that individuals in this era wanted to advertise great accomplishments. By listing the commanders' names on the headstones, it appears that these historic headstones allow for confirmation of the facts. In addition, by having crosses near the top of the headstones, the headstones appear to indicate loyalty to God and country.

Headstones from 100 years ago

Another section of the cemetery contains family plots. In one example, there are six headstones for one family. The one on the farthest right is a 10 foot high megalith, which looks like the Washington monument (Butterfield, 2003). Near the top are decorative images of diamonds. The front of this headstone reads, "In memory, father and mother." The back side states a name, the date died, and the age in years, months, and days; no actual date of birth is listed. The other five family members' headstones are to the left of the monument and are about two feet high and attached to one another via a concrete slab. For these, only names and dates are provided (e.g., Jacob Brown, 1829-1906). Of these five headstones, a male's name appears to be on both the farthest right and on the farthest left with three female names between them. Due to their relative positions to one another, it seems as though the females are being protected by the males. Many headstones in this era seem to describe men as independent human beings, but women are depicted as attached to men.

Analysis - Basically, headstones in this era describe women by their social relationships to men. Many times, a woman's headstone lists her name, wife of [man's name], and dates of birth and death. However, the headstones of men do not describe the men's social relationships to women. Although most of these headstones have symbols on them, such as crosses, a hand holding the Bible, doves, and a variety of flowers (e.g., roses or Easter lilies), the text on them is brief.

Headstones from about 25 years ago

More recent headstones appear to be custom designed by making use of laser and digital technologies (Heller, 2008). Indeed, recent headstones in Greenwood Cemetery contain photographs, images, and text statements. For example, one young female who passed away in 1990 has her photograph in the center of the headstone, a fraternity emblem on the left side, an image of a swimmer on the right side, a Southwest Allen County Fire Department emblem at the bottom, and four statements from loved ones on the back. These statements include, "My darling Allison, God gave me the most precious gift in the world, it was you. You will always be with me in my heart, love always, Mom," and "To Allison, though lovers be lost, love shall not. Death shall have no dominion, Mike." In this section of the cemetery, headstones often have marriage dates on them with symbolic pictures (e.g., wedding rings interlocked or two hands holding one another), the name of the spouse, children names, etches of recreational activities (e.g., fishing), occupations (e.g., a tractor-trailer), and they are surrounded by urns, flowers, solar lights (which represent the eternal flame), and statues of pets, such as dogs.

Analysis - Basically, these headstones seem to describe family unity, social memberships, personal accomplishments, recreational activities, occupations, and pets. Furthermore, many of them contain colored photographs of the deceased, which can provide valuable physical characteristics. At the same time, crosses, angels, and doves indicate a Christian atmosphere.

Headstones from about 15 years ago

There is a baby section of headstones that date about the year 2000. On these headstones are words like, "our little angel," and "forever in our hearts." Moreover, surrounding these headstones is an abundance of angels, Easter bunnies, bears in the form of angels, toys, crosses, and flowers.

Analysis - The atmosphere seems to suggest a spiritual connotation where parents are trying to assure that their children are protected and cared for. In other words, the babies are not alone. Indeed, this area is heavily visited.

Eastbaren Cemetery (Shipshewana, Indiana)

Because there are many Amish in Lagrange County, Indiana, Eastbaren Cemetery, a private Amish cemetery with about 200 grave sites, was also examined. Every headstone in this cemetery is less than two feet high and all but four are white. The older headstones (in the 1800 era), simply state names and dates of birth and death. If marriages were involved, the spouse's name with the words "wife of" or "husband of" may be included on the headstones. More recent headstones (dated in the 1970s) may include the names of surviving family members on them (e.g., loving mother of James and Sara) along with bible verses on the back. For example, the back of one headstone reads, "Fear not little flock; for it is your father's good pleasure to give you the kingdom. Luke 12:32." Several headstones dated in the 1990s have both male and female names on them along with marriage dates.

About 10% of the grave markers in this cemetery simply state a name and date. In one case, there is a wooden cross made of weathered barn siding with a date of 2008. On this cross is a handwritten message made with a black marker that states, "What a great sacrifice so others can live," and "we miss you."

Analysis - Basically, this cemetery seeks simplicity and uniformity. There are no flowers, urns, photographs, solar lights, or statues. There are just headstones and crosses. Although some social statuses are indicated (e.g., wife of), significant others are listed (e.g., surviving family members' names), and significant events recorded (e.g., wedding dates), the atmosphere seems to focus on the afterlife and not on personal accomplishments in life. This is a sharp contrast to the Greenwood Cemetery.

References

About.com: Country music (n.d.). *Dolly Parton – Jolene*. Retrieved from http://countrymusic.about.com/od/cdreviewsmz/fr/Jolene.htm

AlaskaJim.com (2007). *Top songs of the 1960's*. Retrieved from http://www.alaskajim.com/polls/2002topsongs1960s_results.htm

Berg, B. (2007). *Qualitative research methods for the social sciences* (6th ed.). Boston, MA: Pearson Education, Inc.

Butterfield, A. (2003). Monuments and memorials. *New Republic*, *228*(4), 27-32.

Graves 'will be allowed to face east' (2006 September 26). *Europe Intelligence Wire*.

Hatch, J. (2002). *Doing qualitative research in education settings.* Albany, NY: State University of New York Press.

Heller, S. (2008). Death, be not staid. *Print*, 62(4), 90-95.

Neuman, W. (2006). *Social research methods: Qualitative and quantitative approaches* (6th ed.). Boston, MA: Pearson Education, Inc.

Ryan, G.W., & Bernanrd, H.R. (n.d.). *Techniques to identify themes in qualitative data.* Retrieved from http://www.analytictech.com/mb870/readings/ryan-bernard_techniques_to_identify_themes_in.htm

Songfacts (n.d.). *To sir with love*. Retrieved from http://www.songfacts.com/detail.php?id=2780

Songlyrics.com (n.d.). Retrieved from http://www.songlyrics.com/

Sproull, N. (1995). *Handbook of research methods: A guide for practitioners and students in the social sciences* (2nd ed.). Lanham, MD: The Scarecrow Press, Inc.

Appendix B

QUALITATIVE & QUANTITATIVE RESEARCH QUESTIONS

Example of the Difference between a Quantitative and Qualitative Study

Example of Quantitative Study

Quantitative study: Many more people speed at 5:00 pm than at noon (a large problem exists but we have no idea **why** people are speeding around 5:00 pm). Although a problem has been identified, we would be guessing as to **why** the problem exists. Spending a lot of resources on a guess is risky and unwise. Perhaps people should be asked **why** they were speeding.

Example of Qualitative Study

Qualitative study: People speed around 5:00 pm because they have kids at daycare and daycare closes at 5:15 pm (this is **why** a problem exists, but it is unclear if only a few people actually speed at 5:00 pm due to daycare issues; perhaps people speed for different reasons and this was a one-time event.) It would be unwise to spend a lot of resources to fix the daycare problem based on one speeder's response.

Quantitative Studies

Quantitative studies are scientific, objective, and effective in describing phenomena in terms of magnitude (Balian, 1988). Quantitative studies use numeric values and statistics to identify patterns, to objectively quantify relationships between variables, and to make predictions. In addition, because larger sample sizes are used, data can be generalized to larger populations (Creswell, 2003). However, numeric values are ineffective in describing the subjective interpretations of human emotions (Wakefield, 1995).

Examples of Quantitative Research Questions

What is the relationship among the number of years that African American girls have participated in school-sponsored contact sports prior to graduating from high school, their childhood religiosity, and their amount of aggression as young adults?

Is there a significance difference between male and female athletes and their amount of religiosity?

Is there a relationship between age and emotional intelligence?

Qualitative Studies

When studying a topic that cannot be quantitatively predicted, such as human emotions, qualitative studies are most effective. Indeed, qualitative studies are preferred for describing and interpreting experiences in context specific settings because each person's reality is construed in his or her own mind (Adams, 1999; Ponterotto, 2005). Qualitative research attempts to reveal the meanings that participants have given to various phenomena. This kind of information cannot be attained through quantitative analysis and requires probing the participants for great detail through in-depth interviews using open-ended questions. However, there are some limitations. Because the sample size is often small and the experiences have occurred in context specific settings that are unique to each participant, the results cannot be generalized to a larger population. In addition, due to depreciating memories, participants' experiences from the past may be reported less than accurate (McLeod, White, Mullins, Davey, Wakefield, & Hill, 2008).

Examples of Qualitative Research Questions

What is your perception of how negative punishment in sports has influenced you as a parent?

What are the perceptions that adolescents have of their role models in determining their smoking status?

How do you feel that company policies have affected your work performance?

Why do you believe that the riot broke out?

How do you feel about affirmative action?

Focus Group Qualitative Instrument

Example: Focus Group Study

The topic of discussion is community members' perceptions of police profiling.

Following is a statement of the basic rules (Berg, 2007). The discussion will be conducted in a polite and professional manner. Indeed, different points of view and experiences will provide an overall understanding of the issue. Therefore, all opinions are valued. A question will be asked, each participant will be asked to provide a short response, and then the question will be open for group discussion. Everyone is encouraged to respond.

Five open-ended questions will be asked during the interviews. The five questions are listed below.

- What is your perception of the relationship between the police and community?
- What is your perception of the relationship between the police and minorities?
- What is your perception of the relationship between minorities and whites?
- What is your experience with police profiling or racial discrimination?
- Do you think that the police have earned your respect? Explain.

Probe questions

Does the community support the police or is there constant conflict? Explain.

Do community members file a lot of complaints against officers? Explain.

Are there gangs in the area? Explain.

Do the police effectively serve minorities? Explain.

Are minorities adequately represented in local police? Explain.

Do minorities and whites struggle over political power? Explain.

Are minorities adequately represented in local courts? Explain.

Can you provide an example of a profiling experience? Explain.

Why do you trust the police? Explain.

Why do you not trust the police? Explain.

Have you ever had an encounter with a rude (or polite) police officer? Explain.

References

Adams, W. (1999). The interpermeation of self and world: Empirical research, existential phenomenology, and transpersonal psychology. *Journal of Phenomenological Psychology, 30* (2), 39-65.

Balian, E. (1988). *How to design, analyze, and write doctoral or master's research* (2nd ed.). New York, NY: University Press of America.

Berg, B. (2007). *Qualitative research methods for the social sciences* (6th ed.). Boston, MA: Pearson Education, Inc.

Creswell, J. (2003). *Research design: Qualitative, quantitative, and mixed methods approaches* (2nd ed.). Thousand Oaks, CA: Sage Publications.

McLeod, K., White, V., Mullins, R., Davey, C., Wakefield, M., and Hill, D. (2008). How do friends influence smoking uptake? Findings from qualitative interviews with identical twins. *Journal of Genetic Psychology, 169* (2), 117-132.

Ponterotto, J. (2005). Qualitative research in counseling psychology: A primer on research paradigms and philosophy of science. *Journal of Counseling Psychology, 52* (2), 126-136.

Wakefield, J. (1995). When an irresistible epistemology meets an immovable ontology. *Social Work Research, 19* (1).

Appendix C

ANNOTATED BIBLIOGRAPHY & ANNOTATED OUTLINE

Annotated Bibliography - Marijuana

Earleywine, M. (2002). ***Understanding marijuana: A new look at the scientific evidence.*** **New York: Oxford University Press.**

The author, who is the Director of Clinical Training in Psychology at the University of Southern California and a leading researcher in psychology and addiction, conducted a review of research on marijuana and provides a balanced view of the biological, psychological, and social impact of marijuana use (Earleywine, 2002). Through academic rigor, the author traces the medical and political debates and separates science from opinions. By providing objective information, the author provides an overall view of the current demand for marijuana. The data indicate that the War on Drugs is a failure. At a minimum, a policy change is required.

Gahlinger, P. (2004). *Illegal drugs: A complete guide to their history, chemistry, use, and abuse.* New York, NY: Plume.

The author, a physician and certified substance abuse medical review officer, has studied the effects of drugs in various settings (Gahlinger, 2004). Because the author believes that the War on Drugs has been a failure and that the best solution to the drug problem begins with education, he has written this book to provide objective information. With the input from Drug Enforcement Agency (DEA) officers, substance abuse counselors, the Department of Pharmacology and Family and Preventative Medicine, and drug users, the author collected data and has found that there are two opposing sides to the drug debate. One side believes that marijuana is a health issue and should be controlled by the government, and the other side believes that marijuana is a safe recreational drug that should not controlled by the government. The data provided by the author contributes to the understanding of marijuana's history, its chemical properties and effects, its medical uses, its recreational abuses, its associated health problems, and its impact on America's cultural and economic systems. The author also indicates how the media use their power to influence marijuana policies.

Indiana State Police (1997). [Brochure]. *Marijuana: Get straight on the facts.* New Orleans, LA: Syndistar, Inc.

The author, who is the leading law enforcement agency in the State of Indiana, has the legal authority and responsibility for enforcing marijuana laws (Indiana State Police, 1997). This agency states that it will solve problems, reduce crime, and promote public safety by openly communicating with the public and other governmental agencies. Because marijuana possession and consumption is presently illegal in Indiana, the author has created a brochure in which to educate people on the consequences of possessing and consuming marijuana. The author clearly states that marijuana laws will be enforced.

Liska, A. and Messner, S. (1999). ***Perspectives on crime and deviance*** **(3rd ed.). Upper Saddle River, NJ: Prentice Hall.**

Liska was a professor at the University of Albany, State University of New York and was considered an expert in the field of criminology and deviance and was named a Fellow of the American Society of Criminology (Liska & Messner, 1999). With Messner, who is currently a Distinguished Teaching Professor at that same university, they present case studies, historic and cotemporary illustrations, and statistics in order to apply theories to crime and deviance. Their focus is on the understanding of research strategies and how they can test theories involving deviance. In this case, the authors provide an explanation as to why marijuana is classified as contraband. What makes deviance a crime is that there are a small group of people in power who arbitrarily define it that way in order to protect their own self-interests. This puts the law on their side and creates conflict.

Annotated Bibliography: Situational Crime Prevention

All five sources listed below are credible, as evidenced by the credentials of the authors. In addition, all sources examine situational crime prevention (SCP) measures, which relate to the topic of interest.

1) LaVigne, N. (1996). Safe transport: Security by design on the Washington metro. *Crime Prevention Studies*, *6*, 163-197.

Dr. Nancy LaVigne received her doctorate degree in educational psychology from McGill University in Montreal and is a professor at the University of Delaware (LaVigne, 1996). She has numerous publications in peer-reviewed journals, book chapters, and technical reports. In this study, LaVigne investigates the implementation of SCP measures in the Washington, D.C. Metro subway system using quantitative techniques.

After implementing SCP measures in the Metro subway system, crime data that are reported to the police are collected (LaVigne, 1996). Analysis of variance (ANOVA) and F-tests are then used to compare this subway system to the subway systems in Chicago, Boston, and Atlanta, which do not employ SCP measures. The findings ($F = 8.45$, $p = 0.001$) indicate that the Metro subway system's mean rate of crime is significantly lower than the other three subway systems. Unlike the other three subway systems, the Metro subway system is designed so that the customer waiting area is free of obstructions and is highly visible, the system utilizes closed circuit televisions, the area is well lit and maintained, and the laws are stringently enforced. As a result, the Metro subway system is believed to be one of the safest subway systems in the country.

2) Beavon, D., Brantingham, P., and Brantingham, P. (1994). The influence of street networks on the patterning of property offenses. *Crime Prevention Studies*, *2*, 115-148.

Daniel Beavon, Director of Strategic Research and Analysis Directorate of Indian and Northern Affairs Canada, Patricia

Brantingham, a mathematician and Director of the Institute of Canadian Urban Research Studies, and Paul Brantingham, a lawyer and past Director of Special Reviews at the Public Service Commission of Canada, examine the relationships between accessibility of street networks, property crime, and concentration of potential victims (Newhouse, Voyager, & Beavon, 2005). A quantitative research study is conducted in two towns over a one-year time period where the official crime rate as reported to the police is examined in various street segments (Beavon, Brantingham, & Brantingham, 1994). In evaluating the relationship between street accessibility and breaking and entering, one-way ANOVA and Pearson Correlation statistical techniques are employed.

The findings ($F_{4,1570}= 9.735$, $p= 0.0000$; $r=0.97039$, $R^2=0.94149$, $p=0.00306$) indicate that the crime rate is significantly greater on streets that are more accessible to the public and that are used more often (Beavon et al., 1994). Thus, criminal opportunities vary depending upon the environment in which one lives. In these cases, potential offenders have the opportunity to search for their targets in these highly traveled areas, and opportunities seem to dominate the pattern of criminal behaviors.

3) Atlas, R., and LeBlanc, W. (1994). The impact on crime of street closures and barricades: A Florida case study. *Security Journal*, 140-145.

Dr. Robert Atlas, a national security trainer and America's only expert architect/criminologist, and Dr. William LeBlanc, who earned his doctorate degree in experimental psychology and who specializes in research design and analysis of data, study the implementation of

SCP measures to the traffic flow in a local neighborhood by using barricades (Atlas & LeBlanc, 1994; "Expert witness", 2008). Reported crime data from the City of Miami Shores, Metro Dade County, and the City of Miami are examined before and after the implementation of barricades in the City of Miami Shores. However, because changes in the crime rates within the communities are the subject of interest, statistical comparisons are only performed within each municipality and not between the municipalities.

Using a multiple range test (MRT) to compare the pre-barricade and post-barricade reported crime data, the findings indicate that burglaries, larcenies, and auto thefts had significantly decreased in Miami Shores over a 7-year time period (Atlas & LeBlanc, 1994). Thus, by implementing SCP measures, such as by changing street designs and by closing roads, vehicular traffic can be controlled. By controlling vehicular traffic in a particular area, crime in that area can be reduced. However, the findings also indicate that crime in the neighboring areas had increased during this same time period, possibly as a result of crime displacement.

4) Knutsson, J. (1996). Restoring public order in a city park. *Crime Prevention Studies*, 7, 133-151.

Johannes Knutsson, a 2004 Herman Goldstein Award finalist, is a professor of police research at the Norwegian Police University College in Norway and has published several studies on crime prevention measures (UCL Jill Dando Institute of Crime Science, 2005). In this study, Knutsson (1996) studies the implementation of SCP measures in a city park, which was considered a drug dealing hot spot. Data are collected by surveying local residents, by interviewing local businesses and park drug offenders, and by performing site observations.

Using chi-square analysis, the findings (Chi Sq. = 101.70, d.f.=4, $p<0.0001$) indicate that SCP measures reduce the perceived level of criminal activity in the area (Knutsson, 1996). However, the findings also suggest that some crime displacement does occur.

Annotated Outline – Police & Gratuities

I. Introduction to the Problem: Police officers accepting gratuities is not uncommon (Hess & Wrobleski, 1997). Because police officers have discretionary powers, and because their attitudes may be influenced by gratuities, accepting gratuities may create a problem if they impact the performance of their duties.

II. Purpose of the Study: The purpose of this study is to understand how police officers perceive their accepting of gratuities impacts public relations and job performance. Police officers accepting gratuities may be good or bad (Coleman, 2004; Prenzler & Mackay, 1995; Pozo, 2005; Ruiz & Bono, 2004).

   A. Pros of Police Officers Accepting Gratuities
   B. Cons of Police Officers Accepting Gratuities

III. Research Questions: In order to understand the reality of police officers accepting gratuities as perceived by police officers, two qualitative research questions have been developed (Adams, 1999).

A. How do State Police officers describe their perceptions that accepting gratuities may affect their enforcement of traffic laws and the quality of public services that they provide?

B. What do State Police officers believe that the public thinks about them accepting gratuities?

IV. Theoretical Framework: Officers accept gratuities because they learn from other officers that the benefits of accepting gratuities are greater than the associated costs (Siegel, 2003).

A. Rational Choice Theory

B. Social Learning Theory

V. Definition of Terms: Definition of terms may be inconsistent among different individuals (Coleman, 2004; Prenzler & Mackay, 1995). Thus, these terms need to be clarified so that a common understanding of the problem is developed.

A. Gratuities

B. Discretionary Decisions

C. Public Service

VI. Assumptions and Limitations: It is assumed that the police officers are truthful in their disclosures and that they can detect and interpret the feelings of other people. Limitations include limited applications of the findings to other populations (Leedy & Ormrod, 2005).

A. Assumptions

B. Limitations

VII. Literature Review: The literature review will investigate 1) the influence of gratuities on police officers, 2) the attitude of police officers compared to criminal justice students, 3) whether an ethics course is effective in modifying behaviors, 4) the attitude of the general public, 5) the prevalence of police officers accepting gratuities, and 6) whether officers are willing to self-police themselves in changing their ways (Ivkovic, 2004; Kirchgraber, 2004; Lord & Bjerregaard, 2003; MacIntyre & Prenzler, 1999; Prenzler & Mackay, 1995; Trautman, 2001).

A. Police Officers' Attitudes

B. Police Officers versus Criminal Justice Students

C. Criminal Justice Ethics Course

D. General Public Perceptions

E. Prevalence of Accepting Gratuities

F. Code of Silence

VIII. Methodology: The research design will employ in-depth, personal, semi-structured interviews based on a phenomenological approach. This method attempts to understand the perceptions of police officers and how these perceptions impact discretionary decisions (Hatch, 2002; Leedy & Ormrod, 2005). The sampling will be purposive, the sample size will be small (i.e., 15 participants), the instrument will consist of several open-ended questions, data will be collected via interviews and transcribed verbatim, and the data will be context analyzed (Berg, 2007; Creswell, 2003).

A. Research design
B. Sampling
C. Instruments
D. Data Collection Procedures
E. Data Analysis Procedures

IX. Significance of the Study: This study is significant because all U.S. residents are under some sort of police authority. Because proper police service requires good police-community relations and fair treatment of all persons, it is important to know if gratuities interfere with police performance (Carter, 2002). The results may provide an assessment of police management's traditional approach to managing gratuities and may indicate the need for future policy changes.

A. Findings
B. Conclusions
C. Recommendations

References

Adams, W. (1999). The interpermeation of self and world: Empirical research, existential phenomenology, and transpersonal psychology. *Journal of Phenomenological Psychology*, 30(2), 39-65.

Atlas, R., and LeBlanc, W. (1994). The impact on crime of street closures and barricades: A Florida case study. *Security Journal*, 140-145.

Beavon, D., Brantingham, P., and Brantingham, P. (1994). The influence of street networks on the patterning of property offenses. *Crime Prevention Studies, 2*, 115-148.

Berg, B. (2007). *Qualitative research methods for the social sciences* (6th ed.). Boston, MA: Pearson Education, Inc.

Carter, D. (2002). *Issues in police-community relations: Taken from The Police and the community* (7th ed.). Boston, MA: Pearson Custom Publishing.

Coleman, S. (2004). When police should say "no!" to gratuities. *Criminal Justice Ethics, 23*(1), 33-44.

Creswell, J. (2003). *Research design: Qualitative, quantitative, and mixed methods approaches* (2nd ed.). Thousand Oaks, CA: Sage Publications.

Earleywine, M. (2002). *Understanding marijuana: A new look at the scientific evidence*. New York: Oxford University Press.

Expert witness directory jurispro: Dr. Randall I. Atlas (2008). Retrieved from http://www.jurispro.com/RandallAtlas

Gahlinger, P. (2004). *Illegal drugs: A complete guide to their history, chemistry, use, and abuse*. New York, NY: Plume.

Hatch, J. (2002). *Doing qualitative research in education settings.* Albany, NY: State University of New York Press.

Hess, K., and Wrobleski, H. (1997). *Police operations: Theory and practice* (2nd ed.). St. Paul, MN: West publishing Company.

Indiana State Police (1997). [Brochure]. *Marijuana: Get straight on the facts*. New Orleans, LA: Syndistar, Inc.

Ivkovic, S. (2004). Evaluating the seriousness of police misconduct: A cross-cultural comparison of police officer and citizen views. *International Criminal Justice Review*, 14, 25-48.

Kirchgraber, T. (2004, November 1). When policy and practice collide: The mixed message on gratuities. *Sheriff.*

Knutsson, J. (1996). Restoring public order in a city park. *Crime Prevention Studies*, *7*, 133-151.

LaVigne, N. (1996). Safe transport: Security by design on the Washington metro. *Crime Prevention Studies*, *6*, 163-197.

Leedy, P., and Ormrod, J. (2005). *Practical research: Planning and design* (8th ed.). Upper Saddle River, NJ: Pearson Merrill Prentice Hall.

Liska, A. and Messner, S. (1999). *Perspectives on Crime and Deviance* (3rd ed.). Upper Saddle River, NJ: Prentice Hall.

Lord, V., and Bjerregaard, B. (2003). Ethics courses: Their impact on the values and ethical decisions on criminal justice students. *Journal of Criminal Justice Management*, *14*(2), 191-211.

MacIntyre, S., and Prenzler, T. (1999). The influence of gratuities and personal relationships on police use of discretion. *Policing and Society*, *9*(2), 181-201.

Newhouse, D., Voyager, C., and Beavon, D. (2005). Hidden in plain sight: Contributions of Aboriginal peoples to Canadian identity and culture, volume 1 (Eds.). *University of Toronto Press Inc.*

Pozo, B. (2005). One dogma of police ethics: Gratuities and the "democratic ethos" of policing. *Criminal Justice Ethics*, *24*(2), 25-46.

Prenzler, T., and Mackay, P. (1995). Police gratuities: What the public think. *Criminal Justice Ethics*, *14*(1), 15-25.

Ruiz, J., and Bono, C. (2004). At what price a "freebie'? The real cost of police gratuities. *Criminal Justice Ethics*, *23*(1), 44-54.

Siegel, L. (2003). *Criminology* (8th ed.). Belmont, CA: Thomson Wadsworth.

Trautman, N. (2001, March 1). The code of silence . . . now we know the truth. *Sheriff.*

UCL Jill Dando Institute of Crime Science (2005). Retrieved from the University College London Web site: http://www.jdi.ucl.ac.uk/ people/academic/knutsson.php

Appendix D

TENTATIVE BUDGETS

Example of Quantitative Tentative Budget

With a sample size of 384 participants, the estimated total budget is about $1,654. The $1,654 can be broken down as follows: $80 for data collection (384 surveys in 4 hours @ $20/hr), $200 for data entry and data cleaning fees ($20/hr x 10 hrs for entry and cleaning), $640 for data analysis (384 surveys x 5 minutes per survey = 32 hours x $20/hr), $200 for a statistical software program, $50 for transportation fees, $100 for supplies, and $384 for the cost of instruments ($1 per Aggression Questionnaire instrument x 384 participants). Indeed, because quantitative studies involve collecting a large amount of data in a relatively short period of time, a small increase in the sample size will only add a nominal increase to the cost of the study.

Tentative Budget (Quantitative Study of 384 participants)

Salaries = $20/hr	
Data collection (4 hours x $20/hr) =	$80
Data entry/cleaning (10 hours x $ 20.00/hr) =	$200

Time to analyze data	
(384 surveys x 5 minutes per survey = 32 hours x $20/hr) =	$640
Cost of statistical software =	$200
Transportation cost: (20 miles to collect all data) =	$50
Supplies =	$100
Cost of instruments =	$384
Total Budget =	$1,654

Example of Qualitative Tentative Budget

With a sample size of 12 participants and an average interview time of 3 hours, the estimated total budget is about $5,200. The $5,200 can be broken down as follows: $720 for data collector, $240 for the participant incentive fee, $1,440 for the transcription fee, $2,000 for the coding transcription fee, $500 for the transportation fee, $200 for data analysis software, and $100 for supplies. Because it takes time in a qualitative study to obtain in-depth information, a small increase in the sample size can significantly increase the cost of the study.

Tentative Budget (Qualitative Study of 12 participants)

Salaries = $20/hr	
Time to interview: 12 interviews x 3 hrs each = 36 hours	
Data collection (36 hrs x $20/hr) =	$720
Participant incentive (12 participants x $20/participant) =	$240
Transcription (72 hours x $20/hr) =	$1,440
Coding transcription fee (100 hrs x $20/hr) =	$2,000
Transportation fee (200 miles to collect all data) =	$500
Cost of data analysis software =	$200
Supplies =	$100
Total Budget =	$5,200

It is important to forecast what a study will cost. If the total expected cost is too high, then management may not approve the study. Although the itemized costs may not be exact, they do provide a general figure of expected expenses, which may be important for budgeting purposes.

In summary, a quantitative study can obtain much more information in a shorter time at a lower cost per participant. A qualitative study, on the other hand, can obtain more detailed information but at a much higher cost per participant. Consequently, a small increase in the sample size for a qualitative study can significantly increase the cost of the study. Furthermore, because it takes longer to obtain data in a qualitative study, the potential participants may need to be offered a greater financial incentive to motivate them to participate.

Appendix E

LITERATURE REVIEWS

Examples of How to Summarize Academic Articles

To be useful, the summary of an academic peer-reviewed study must provide certain information. At a minimum, the study should indicate the purpose of the study, who were studied, how the data were collected, how the data were analyzed, the findings, and the limitations of the study. For example, a study conducted on white elderly men in Italy may not be applicable for black female juveniles in the U.S. Do not withhold information from the readers. Provide the readers with enough information so that they may make their own educated decisions. The credibility of an argument is only as good as its references. See Table 50.

Table 50

Analogy between Choice of Police Weapon and Type of Reference

Strength of Resource	Police Weapon for Deadly Force Encounter	Level of Credibility for Argument
Strong	Gun	Scholarly, Peer-reviewed Academic Research Article
Moderate	Baton	Textbook
Weak	Fists	Personal Opinion

Winnail, Valois, McKeown, Saunders, & Pate

In an effort to assess the relationship between physical activity level (low, moderate, and high) and substance abuse, Winnail et al. (1995) used data collected from the 1993 Centers for Disease Control Youth Risk Behavior Survey. The sample included 745 African American female high school students from 26 different public school districts in South Carolina. The researchers applied multiple logistic regression analysis to assess the relationship between physical activity level and smokeless tobacco use, cigarette use, and marijuana use. Except for the smokeless tobacco, the findings indicated that there was no statistically significant relationship between physical activity level and substance abuse.

However, there are limitations in the Winnail et al. (1995) study. First, the participants were all from the state of South Carolina. Consequently, the sample may not be representative of adolescents from across the nation. Second, the researchers used a software package that eliminated participants from the study who had missing data. Third, because students were asked about their own deviant behaviors, there is the possibility that they were less than truthful in their responses. Thus, because the data may have been incomplete and less than accurate, the findings could be misleading.

Women's Sports Foundation

A similar study was conducted by the Women's Sports Foundation (2000) to quantitatively assess the relationship between sport participation and health-risk behaviors. In this case, the researchers used data collected from the 1997 Centers for Disease Control Youth Risk Behavior Survey. In order to generate a nationally representative sample, data were collected from 16,262 public and private high schools from across the nation. The sample included 1,010 African American females: 602 non-athletes and 408 athletes. The researchers used logistic regression and odds ratios to assess athletes' and non-athletes' odds of engaging in risky and anti-social behaviors. The findings indicated that African American female athletes were a) more likely to binge drink, b) more likely to drive a motor vehicle after drinking, c) less likely to use illicit drugs, although they were more likely to use steroids, d) less likely to smoke, and e) less likely to be suicidal.

There are limitations in the Women's Sports Foundation (2000) study, which may impact the value of the study's findings. First, because the data were collected at a single point in time and after the participants had already been exposed to the independent variable (i.e., athletic participation), causal relations cannot be determined. Second, because the data were collected using self-administered surveys, and because students were asked about risky and deviant behaviors, there is the possibility that they were less than truthful in their responses. Finally, the study was quantitative in nature and failed to provide the meanings and motivations behind the students' behaviors.

Polman, de Castro, and van Aken

In an effort to examine the association between a) actively playing a violent video game, passively watching the same violent video game, and actively playing a non-violent video game and b) the children's level of aggression, Polman, de Castro, and van Aken (2008) conducted a between-subjects experimental design involving 28 boys and 28 girls. The researchers recruited children in the 5th and 6th grades from four different classrooms in two different schools in The Netherlands. The children were randomly selected to either play a violent video game, to passively watch the same violent video game, or to play a similar non-violent video game. The researchers collected data through peer nomination questionnaires in which children nominated other class participants who fit particular aggressive behavioral descriptors. The non-parametric Kruskal-Wallis test was performed on the data to compare the means of the three groups. The findings indicated that boys who had played violent video game were more aggressive than boys who had passively observed. However, there was no difference for girls or for boys who had played the non-violent video game.

There are limitations in the Polman et al. (2008) study, which may impact the generalization of the study's findings to the general population. First, there were no racial demographics on the children. Perhaps because the participants were in The Netherlands, the researchers may have assumed that the readers understood this to mean Caucasian children. Second, the aggression of the participants was determined by their behaviors at recess. However, some children may have come across provocative situations during recess whereas others did not. These possible scenarios were not taken into consideration during the study. Third, playing a violent video game is not the same experience as actually engaging in physical violence. Thus, receiving physical pain may promote compliance and may result in different behaviors than playing video games where no physical pain is realized. In addition, although there was a group that passively watched the violent video game, there was no group that passively watched the non-violent video game.

Lichter and McCloskey

In an effort to determine if children's exposure to marital violence is related to dating violence later in life, Lichter and McCloskey (2004) conducted a longitudinal prospective study over a 7 to 9 year period. The researchers used public announcements, posters, and agency referrals to recruit mother-child pairs from violent and nonviolent households in low income households. Of the 208 adolescent participants, about 53% were Caucasian, 36% were Hispanic, and only about 5% were African American. The researchers collected data through personal interviews, focus group interviews, and questionnaires. Regression analyses were conducted on the data and the findings indicated that children who were exposed to domestic violence were not more likely to engage in dating violence later in life but that they were more likely to develop attitudes condoning dating violence.

There are some limitations in the Lichter and McCloskey (2004) study, which may impact the generalization of the study's findings to the general population. First, the context in which the violence occurred and the context of the romantic relationships were absent during the study. Indeed, the characteristics of romantic partners and relationships may create the social structures that reinforce or inhibit violent behaviors. Second, because the data on attitude and behavior were collected at the same time, the study does not allow for the determination of causal relationships between attitude and behavioral outcomes (i.e., dating violence). Because marital violence is illegal, harmful, and has the intent to punish whereas contact sports are legal, helpful, and has the intent to promote perfection, applying the study's findings to African American females in contact sports is questionable. In other words, the social learning environments for domestic violence and contact sports are quite different from one another and the difference may impact what is learned in each environment.

References

Lichter, E.L., & McCloskey, L.A. (2004). The effects of childhood exposure to marital violence on adolescent gender-role beliefs and dating violence. *Psychology of Women Quarterly*, *28*(4), 344-357. doi:10.1111/j.1471-6402.2004.00151.x

Polman, H., de Castro, B.O., & van Aken, A.G. (2008). Experimental study of the differential effects of playing versus watching violent video games on children's aggressive behavior. *Aggressive Behavior*, *34*(3), 256-264. doi:10.1002/ab.20245

Winnail, S.D., Valois, R.F., McKeown, R.E., Saunders, R.P., & Pate, R.R. (1995). Relationship between physical activity level and cigarette, smokeless tobacco, and marijuana use among public high school adolescents. *Journal of School Health*, *65*(10), 438-442.

Women's Sport Foundation (2000). *Health risks and the teen athlete.* Retrieved from http://www.womenssportsfoundation.org/

Appendix F

EXAMPLES OF RESEARCH PROPOSALS

EXAMPLE 1

Quantitative Study: Ex Post Facto Correlational Survey Design

Sports Participation and Aggression

One way to answer the research question, *What is the relationship between the number of years that African American boys play school-sponsored football prior to graduating from high school and aggressive behavior later in life?,* is to perform an ex post facto correlational survey study. An ex post facto correlational approach is a non-experimental design that seeks to determine the relationship between the independent and dependent variables without the attempt to manipulate the independent variable (Bordens & Abbott, 2008). Indeed, correlational ex post facto studies are effective in linking past experiences to current behaviors. Furthermore, survey studies can obtain information from a large number of people in a short amount of time and in a uniform manner (Champion, 2006). Thus, an ex post facto correlational survey design can effectively answer the research question.

There are several ways that a correlational survey study can be executed. First, the researcher must decide the manner in which the population and sample will be defined, how the variables will be classified, how the data will be collected, and how the data will be analyzed (Gelo et al., 2008). Furthermore, the benefits and costs of the study's methodology need to be considered.

Population

The population will be African Americans males from across the U.S. who are currently 21 to 30 years of age, who have attended U.S. middle schools and high schools, and who have played school-sponsored football prior to graduating from high school.

Sample

In order to obtain a 95% confidence level and a confidence interval of five, a sample size will of 384 participants will be targeted (Creative Research Systems, n.d.). The sample will be recruited on-line via an online survey generator (SurveyMonkey.com, 2009). The study will use a non-probability sampling design that is convenient and purposive because particular criteria will be used to target specific people (Creswell, 2009). Indeed, the sample will be comprised of adult African American males who have attended U.S. middle schools and high schools, who have participated in school-sponsored football prior to graduating from high school, and who are currently 21 to 30 years of age. Furthermore, the sample must have the ability to access the Internet. The sample is convenient because the potential participants who respond first to the study's invitation will be the ones recruited to participate in the study. Consequently, the study's findings may be limited and they may not necessarily apply to members of populations who do not match the sample's characteristics (Mascaro & Rosen, 2008; Mehall et al., 2009).

Classification of Variables

Both the independent variable and the dependent variable will be classified as categorical variables (Leedy & Ormrod, 2005). The independent variable is the number of years that the participants have played school-sponsored football prior to graduating from high school and will be categorized as low, moderate, or high. For example, if the participants started to play football in seventh or eighth grades, then the number of years that they participated in football will be considered high; if the participants started to play football in ninth or tenth grades, then the number of years that they participated in football will be considered moderate; if the participants started to play football in eleventh or twelfth grades, then the number of years that they participated in football will be considered low. Because the independent variable does not have an equal interval between data values, it has an ordinal scale of measurement (Leedy & Ormrod). For example, the interval between eighth grade and ninth grade is equal to the interval between seventh grade and tenth grade.

The number of years that the participants have played school-sponsored football will be defined by when the individuals started to play. In addition, there must not be any discontinuity between the years of participation once an individual started to play. In other words, once a participant started to play football, he must have continued to play every school year until he graduated from high school. Thus, the only difference in the amount of time that the participants will have played school-sponsored football will be their starting points. This will minimize the numerous combination of years that an individual may have played school-sponsored football during middle school and high school.

The dependent variable, which is aggressive behavior, will also be classified as a categorical variable. Indeed, data on aggressive behaviors will be categorized into one of four levels, which are low, low-moderate, moderate, and high (Vagg & Spielberger, 1999). Thus, like the independent variable, the dependent variable has an ordinal scale of measurement.

Collection of Data

Data will be collected on a one-time basis using an electronic form of the State-Trait Anger Expression Inventory Interpretative Report (STAXI-2) via an online survey generator (Freeman, 2004; Schibler, 2008; SurveyMonkey.com, 2009). The STAXI-2 is one of the most widely used instruments to measure expressed anger in adult populations (O'Keefe, 2004). The survey will be set up so that those individuals who complete the survey will have provided implied consent. In addition, data will be collected from the first 384 qualified adult participants who complete the online survey.

Data will be collected using the 57 question STAXI-2 (Freeman, 2004). Responses will measure anger expression, which is the overall tendency to express aggression, and will be provided in a four point

Likert-type format. The data will then be converted into an overall anger expression index score, which will be classified into one of four levels of aggression: low, low-moderate, moderate, and high (Vagg & Spielberger, 1999). The STAXI-2 takes about 15 minutes to complete and is designed for individuals 16 years of age and older.

The STAXI-2 has demonstrated to be reliable (Freeman, 2004). The STAXI-2 has internal consistency reliability alpha coefficients of .73 to .95 for the subscales. Thus, the STAXI-2 has demonstrated to have moderate to excellent internal consistency reliability. However, the STAXI-2 test-retest reliability has not been demonstrated.

The STAXI-2 has not been effectively validated (Freeman, 2004). Indeed, the validity of STAXI-2 relies upon the validity of its prior version, the STAXI. Thus, an effort must be made to help ensure that the STAXI-2 is valid.

In order to help demonstrate test-retest reliability and to help validate the STAXI-2, a pilot study of 10 to 15 individuals will be conducted (Champion, 2006; Glicken, 2003). The pilot study will be a small scale version of the proposed study. First, the instrument will be provided to several experts in the field who will be asked to evaluate whether the STAXI-2 measures the characteristics in question. Second, in order to demonstrate face validity, the STAXI-2 will be administered to a representative sample of individuals who will be asked to indicate what they believe that the questions are asking (Kennedy, Homant, & Barnes, 2008). Third, in order to demonstrate content validity, the pilot study participants will be asked to discuss their responses in order to determine if the STAXI-2 provided an accurate range of questions so that they could provide complete and accurate information about their anger and aggression. Finally, in order to demonstrate test-retest reliability, the STAXI-2 will be administered to the pilot group participants at two different times, about three months apart (Carretta, Zelenski, & Ree, 2000). If the pilot group participants answer the questions in the same manner at both times, then test-retest reliability will have be demonstrated.

Data Analysis

Using SPSS, the data will be analyzed using descriptive and inferential statistics (Norusis, 2008). First, descriptive statistics will be performed to produce various diagrams, such as scatter plots, boxplots, and histograms, so that trends and patterns can be easily recognized. However, because the independent and dependent variables have ordinal scales of measurement, the parametric assumptions have not been satisfied (Leedy & Ormrod, 2005). Therefore, the appropriate nonparametric statistic that will be used to assess the correlation between the ordinal independent variable and the ordinal dependent variable is the Spearman *r* (Schaeffer, 2007). The Spearman *r* will assess the strength between the number of years playing football and aggression level.

The Spearman *r* is a nonparametric statistic that is used to measure the strength between two ordinal variables (Warner, 2008). However, the Spearman *r* ignores some of the available information because it uses ranks instead of the actual data values (Norusis, 2008). Therefore, the statistic will not provide the same high quality information as would a parametric statistic. However, the Spearman *r* statistic can effectively be applied to answer the research question, considering the nature of the variables and data.

Benefits of Approach

There are several benefits in employing the ex post facto quantitative correlational survey study as described. First, a correlational study allows the researcher to predict the probable values of the dependent variable based upon the known values of the independent variable (Bordens & Abbott, 2008). Second, ex post facto studies are effective when the independent variable cannot be manipulated (Gelo et al., 2008). Indeed, because aggression will be measured after the completion of high school and after the participants have already played football, the independent variable cannot be manipulated. Third, because data will be collected at a single point in time, only 384 participants will need to be recruited and they will not need to be tracked (i.e., the attrition rate of a longitudinal study is not a concern). Fourth, by using an online survey generator, the data can be collected relatively quickly from participants all across the nation. Fifth, electronic surveys will allow for the collection of a great deal of information in a short amount of time. Finally, because nonparametric statistics use medians and ranks instead of actual data values, the results are not easily influenced by outliers (Norusis, 2008). In short, the Spearman r is appropriate for evaluating the strength of the relationship between the ordinal independent variable and the ordinal dependent variable (Schaeffer, 2007).

Costs of Approach

There are several costs in employing the ex post facto quantitative correlational survey study as described. First, the study's internal validity is threatened (Bordens & Abbott, 2008). Indeed, because of the variables' ambiguous temporal precedence, the findings will not indicate causal relationships. For example, other variables that are not accounted for may have affected the participants' behavioral changes. Second, the study's external validity is threatened. Because the study uses a non-probability, purposive, and convenient sampling, the findings may not be applied to other populations (Gelo et al., 2008). Indeed, individuals who decide to participate in the study may be different in meaningful ways from those individuals who cannot or choose not to participate in the study. Third, because the validity and reliability of the STAXI-2 has not been effectively demonstrated, a pilot study will need to be completed to ensure that a) the language and directions on the instrument are clear and easily understood, b) the instrument measures what it is supposed to measure, and c) the chosen statistical analyses are appropriate (Champion, 2006; Glicken, 2003; Kennedy et al., 2008). However, a pilot study will consume time and financial resources. Fourth, there will be a financial cost for using the online survey generator. However, the services for the online survey generator will only cost about two hundred dollars (SurveyMonkey.com, 2009). Finally, because the Spearman *r* uses ranks instead of actual data values, the statistical analyses will be less than optimal (Norusis, 2008).

With a sample size of 384 participants, the total estimated financial cost of the correlational study is about $1,731. The following is a breakdown of the $1,731 cost: $200 for data collection via the online survey generator, $384 for data cleaning fees (384 participants x $10/hr x 0.1 hr each for cleaning), $226 for the instrument, $500 for a statistical software program, $200 for supplies, $21 for transportation fees (50 miles x $.42/mile), and $200 for the pilot study (Spieldberger, n.d.; SurveyMonkey.com, 2009). Indeed, much online data can be collected in a short amount of time over a large geographic area with very little travel.

Conclusion

An ex post facto correlational survey design will be employed to answer the research question. The goal of the study is to recruit 384 African American adults via an online survey generator. Data will be collected at a single point in time after the participants have already been exposed to the treatment (i.e., played school-sponsored football). On the one hand, the benefits of using a Likert-type survey design are that much data can be collected quickly, inexpensively, and in a uniform manner. Surveys are very effective in providing numeric values that can be used to quantify the strength of relationships. On the other hand, correlational studies do not allow for the observation of incremental changes in behaviors and the findings do not indicate causal relationships (Bordens & Abbott, 2008). In addition, because the variables have been defined with ordinal scales of measurement, a less powerful non-parametric statistic will be required (Norusis, 2008). Finally, data collected from surveys are superficial (Champion, 2006). Although surveys allow for the collection of data from many participants in a short amount of time, numeric analyses are ineffective in describing subjective interpretations, human emotions, and the reconstruction of meanings (Berg, 2007).

References

Berg, B.L. (2007). *Qualitative research methods for the social sciences* (6th ed.). Boston, MA: Pearson Education, Inc.

Bordens, K., & Abbott, B. (2008). *Research design and methods: A process approach* (7th ed.). Boston, MA: McGraw Hill.

Carretta, T.R., Zelenski, W.E., & Ree, M.J. (2000). Basic attributes test (BAT) retest performance. *Military Psychology*, 12(3), 221-232.

Champion, D. (2006). *Research methods for criminal justice and criminology* (3rd ed.). Upper Saddle River, NJ: Pearson Merrill Prentice Hall.

Creative Research Systems (n.d.). *The survey system: Sample size calculator*. Retrieved from http://www.surveysystem.com/sscalc.htm

Creswell, J.W. (2009). *Research design: Qualitative, quantitative, and mixed methods approaches* (3rd ed.). Los Angeles, CA: Sage Publications.

Freeman, S.J. (2004). State-trait anger expression inventory-2. *Mental Health Measurements Yearbook database.*

Gelo, O., Braakmann, D., & Benetka, G. (2008). Quantitative and qualitative research: Beyond the debate. *Integrative Psychological & Behavioral Science*, *42*(3), 266-290.

Glicken, M.D. (2003). *Social research: A simple guide*. Boston, MA: Pearson Education, Inc.

Kennedy, D.B., Homant, R.J., & Barnes, E. (2008). An inside view of the sleeper cell terrorist: A face validity study. *Journal of Applied Security Research*, *3*(3/4), 325-350.

Leedy, P., & Ormrod, J. (2005). *Practical research: Planning and design* (8th ed.). Upper Saddle River, NJ: Pearson Merrill Prentice Hall.

Mascaro, N., & Rosen, D.H. (2008). Assessment of existential meaning and its longitudinal relations with depressive symptoms. *Journal of Social and Clinical Psychology*, *27*(6), 576-599.

Mehall, K.G., Spinrad, T.L., Eisenberg, N., & Gaertner, B.M. (2009). Examining the relations of infant temperament and couples' marital satisfaction to mother and father involvement: A longitudinal study. *Fathering*, *7*(1), 23-48.

Norusis, M.J. (2008). *SPSS 16.0 guide to data analysis*. Upper saddle River, NJ: Prentice Hall.

O'Keefe, K.C. (2004). Anger and aggression in hockey players. *Dissertations & Theses*. (UMI No. 3144776).

Schaeffer, C. (2007). A study of the influences of nutrition, physical activity, income, and family lifestyles choices on the overweight of elementary-age children. *Dissertations & Theses*. (UMI No. 3259721).

Schibler, K.M. (2008). A Delphi study of skills that will help first-year elementary principals in California address critical issues they will face by 2012. *Dissertations & Theses*. (UMI No. 3338011).

Spieldberger, C.D. (n.d.). State-trait anger expression inventory-2. *Mental Health Measurements Yearbook database*.

SurveyMonkey.com (2009). *Our pricing fits every budget*. Retrieved from http://www.surveymonkey.com/

Vagg, P., & Spielberger, C.D. (1999). *State-trait anger expression inventory interpretive report (STAXI-2:IR)*.

Warner, R.M. (2008). *Applied statistics from bivariate through multivariate techniques*. Los Angeles, CA: Sage Publications.

Example 2

Quantitative Study: One-group Pretest-posttest Design

Residential Burglary – Situational Crime of Opportunity

Abstract

Situational crime prevention (SCP) is a crime prevention strategy that departs radically from mainstream criminology because it does not focus on offenders or the reasons why they commit crime. Instead, SCP strategies focus on the opportunities to commit crime, the settings for crime, and on the prevention of crime. By enhancing home defense mechanisms that increase the effort, increase the perceived risks, and reduce the anticipated rewards in committing residential burglary, this crime can be diminished. Furthermore, because deadly force may sometimes be used against residential burglars, and because homeowners are not likely to ask the offenders how old they are when they are committing their crimes, prevention is the key to saving lives, especially of children who may not understand the law.

Because residential burglary is a situational crime of opportunity, there are several ways to address this crime. Indeed, authorities have a choice of how they will allocate public funds: they may harden the targets or they may reduce the opportunities to commit the crime. At a minimum, lawmakers should write use-of-force laws to require homeowners to show signs of hardening their targets before they are authorized to use deadly force against residential burglars. This simple requirement in the law may save lives.

Table of Contents

RESIDENTIAL BURGLARY: VIOLENT CRIM E OF OPPORTUNITY

Introduction

Situational crime prevention (SCP) is a crime prevention strategy that departs radically from mainstream criminology because it does not focus on offenders or the reasons why they commit crime (Clarke, 2000). Instead, SCP strategies focus on the opportunities to commit crime, the settings for crime, and on the prevention of crime. Indeed, by employing SCP measures, which are defense mechanisms, crimes of opportunity in specific locations can be prevented.

Residential burglary is assumed to be a situational crime of opportunity that can be explained by the rational choice, deterrence, and routine activities theories (Siegel, 2003). If this is true, then SCP measures, which are also based on the rational choice, deterrence, and routine activities theories, should be effective in reducing this crime (Clarke, 2000). Therefore, the purpose of this study is to investigate the effectiveness of SCP measures in preventing residential burglary.

Background and Statement of the Problem

Residential Burglary and Indiana Law

Burglary in Indiana is defined as a violent crime (Office of Code Revision Indiana Legislative Services Agency, n.d.a, n.d.c). Indiana Code (IC) 35-50-1-2 specifically lists crimes of violence, which includes residential burglary. Furthermore, a way to measure the seriousness of the crime is to evaluate how much force that the law allows for a victim to use to stop the offense. Indeed, according to IC 35-41-3-2, homeowners may sometimes use deadly force to stop residential burglary (Office of Code Revision Indiana Legislative Services Agency, n.d.b). Thus, this is a major concern because the law does not discriminate against the age of the perpetrators. Hence, unless homeowners take preventative actions to discourage burglary, children may die. Consequently, this makes residential burglary a very serious crime.

Indiana Statistics

In 2007, there were 147 reported cases of residential burglary committed by juveniles in Indiana (Indiana Department of Correction, n.d.). Of these, 95.9% were committed by boys. However, although there were only 6 girls convicted of residential burglary in 2007, they may be killed just as easily as boy burglars. Life is precious and one death is too many. Therefore, in order to ensure that no children are killed as a result of committing burglary, their criminal acts must be prevented.

Definitions of Terms

For this study, SCP measures are home defense mechanisms that increase the effort, increase the perceived risks, and reduce the anticipated rewards of committing residential burglary (Clarke, 2000; Siegel, 2003). Home defense mechanisms may include items such as motion sensors, burglar alarms, a closed circuit surveillance system, a watch dog, increased lighting around the home, a fenced yard, increased line of sight around the home, and enhanced door locks. In addition, reducing the anticipated rewards may include keeping easily transportable valuables in a safe, marking property with identification numbers, and placing tracking devices inside items.

Variables

SCP measures seek to reduce the opportunity to successful commit a rewarding crime (Clarke, 2000). The three independent variables that will be manipulated in this study are 1) increasing the perceived effort to commit residential burglary, 2) increasing the perceived risks of committing residential burglary, and 3) reducing the anticipated rewards of committing residential burglary. The dependent variable is the likelihood of committing residential burglary.

First, SCP measures include increasing the perceived effort in successfully committing residential burglary (Clarke, 2000). These measures include a) hardening the target, such as by using heavy duty locks, b) controlling access to the property, such as by using fences, c) deflecting potential offenders, such as by closing the street, and d) controlling facilitators, such as by using caller-ID. For example, the fourth measure may be effective in determining who is calling in the situation where the potential perpetrator is calling just to see if anyone is home.

Second, SCP measures include increasing the perceived risks in successfully committing residential burglary (Clarke, 2000). These measures include a) formal surveillance, such as using burglar alarms, b) natural surveillance, such as by using street lighting, and c) neighborhood surveillance, such as by using neighborhood watch.

Finally, SCP measures include reducing the anticipated rewards in successfully committing residential burglary (Clarke, 2000). These measures include a) removing the targets, such as by placing the items in a safe, b) reducing temptation, such as by not placing expensive items out in the open, c) denying benefits, such as by requiring security codes for items to work, and d) identifying the property, such as by marking the property with identification numbers.

Research Question

It is expected that employing SCP measures will reduce adolescent residential burglary. To investigate this, the following research question has been developed, *Is there a relationship between employing SCP measures in homes and adolescents committing residential burglary against those homes in Indiana?*

Directional Hypothesis

There is a negative relationship between employing SCP measures in homes and adolescents committing residential burglary against those homes in Indiana.

Null Hypothesis

There is no relationship between employing SCP measures in homes and adolescents committing residential burglary against those homes in Indiana.

Rationale for the Study

Residential burglary is an important topic to investigate because this crime creates fear among residents, resulting in anxiety, feelings of vulnerability, posttraumatic stress disorder, and anger due to the loss of confidence in local police (Barkan, 2006; Hess & Wrobleski, 2003). Because burglary invades a family's personal place of security, it creates the threat of harm to occupants (Hess & Wrobleski). Indeed, when residents are home during a burglary, which is about 10% of the time, there is about a 30% greater chance of the homeowners being harmed (Schmalleger, 2007).

In Indiana, there were 2,010 reported residential burglaries in 2007 (Indiana Department of Correction, n.d.). Of these, 147 were committed by juveniles. Because Indiana residents are sometimes allowed to use deadly force to stop intruders, this is a serious situation, especially for young children who may not understand the law (Office of Code Revision Indiana Legislative Services Agency, n.d.b). Indeed, homeowners are not going to ask intruders how old they are before they kill them. Thus, the motives that drive residential burglary must be evaluated so that they can be eliminated. Lives depend upon it.

The motives behind residential burglary are being examined through a combined rational choice theory and routine activities theory lens (Siegel, 2003). Accordingly, residential burglary depends upon the targets, the victims, the offenders, and the locations

(Ministry of Justice, n.d.). Indeed, motivated offenders tend to operate in tightly clustered hot spots and select easy targets that appear to have minimal guardianship (Clarke, 2000). Furthermore, would-be burglars perceive that the benefits of the crime are greater than the associated sanctions. Thus, information in this study will determine if hardening the targets (i.e., employing SCP measures) effectively deters burglary. If it does, then SCP will support the assumptions that residential burglary is a crime of rational choice and opportunity. Knowing this, resources can then be effectively utilized and applied toward specific programs to reduce this problem.

The benefits of this study will provide authorities with credible data in order to address residential burglary by implementing public programs and policies to address any of the factors that lead to burglary (Ministry of Justice, n.d.). Indeed, limited resources can be applied in different ways, depending upon which variable that the authorities want to address. For example, if opportunities are necessary for burglary to occur, then limited resources can be used to create programs like the Midnight Basketball program, which will keep kids busy and reduce their opportunities to commit residential burglary (Tucker, Donovan, & Marlatt, 1999). On the other hand, if the targets are to be hardened, then local policies could be developed that require hedges in residential yards, for example, to be trimmed in order to improve visibility of the homes. Hence, social programs and policies can be developed to harden targets, to reduce the motivation for individuals to commit crime, or to reduce the opportunities for individuals to commit crime. All may be equally effective.

Literature Review

Conceptual Framework

There are three criminological theories that can be applied to the crime of burglary as a situational crime of opportunity. The three theories are the rational choice theory, the deterrence theory, and the routine activities theory. However, for SCP measures to be effective in deterring burglary, the assumptions of the theories must be in alignment with the problem.

Rational choice theory has its foundation in the classical school of criminology developed by Beccaria in 1764 (Siegel, 2003). According to this classical school of criminology, individuals freely choose their behaviors, both good and bad. It is believed that individuals calculate the potential pleasures and pains associated with each act and then chose to perform the ones that are most beneficial. This being the case, Beccaria believed that crime could be controlled by increasing costs so they are higher than the pleasures gained. In short, people rationally choose to engage in those acts that they perceived as beneficial.

In 1975, political scientist James Wilson wrote a book called, *Thinking about Crime* (Siegel, 2003). In his book, Wilson claimed that individuals are likely to engage in crime if they perceive that criminal acts are beneficial and that society will fail to effectively respond. Consequently, the U.S. government passed tough new laws with increased penalties in order to convince potential perpetrators that crime is irrational. Thus, these are the roots for the contemporary version of the rational choice theory. Indeed, according to the rational choice theory, which is based upon economic theory, people will choose to perform those acts where the gain is greater than the associated costs (Akers & Sellers, 2009). This includes gain, both extrinsic (e.g., cash) and intrinsic (e.g., thrills), and costs, both direct (e.g., legal sanctions) and indirect (e.g., humiliation) (Liska & Messner, 1999).

Conventional deterrence theory is a special case of the rational choice theory (Liska & Messner, 1999). However, unlike the rational choice theory, which was initially applied to the economy and considered all costs, the deterrence theory was applied to the field of law and only considered legal sanctions (Akers & Sellers, 2009). According to the deterrence theory, if the costs of legal sanctions are greater than the benefits of crime, then people will refrain from engaging in crime. Thus, the greater the certainty of punishment, the greater the severity of punishment, and the swifter the punishment, the greater individuals will be motivated not to engage in crime (Liska & Messner).

Deterrence can be learned in two ways (Barkan, 2006). First, specific deterrence is learned when people experience firsthand the events of being caught and punished for their crimes (Akers & Sellers, 2009). People learn through personal experience that the cost of committing crime is too high; thus, they learn to refrain from committing future acts of crime. Second, general deterrence is learned when individuals observe the punishment that the state inflicts upon other people who have been convicted of crime. Consequently, this instills fear in the public and individuals decide to refrain from crime.

According to Clarke (2000), Cohen and Felson indicate that different lifestyles are equated to different risks of being victimized.

Specifically, each person's normal and legal daily activities, known as routine activities, will affect what and whom a person will encounter. Thus, all persons will be exposed to varying degrees of illegal activities. For example, individuals who must park their cars in isolated, dark parking garages may be at greater risk of being victimized than individuals who park their cars in garages that are attached to their homes. When motivated offenders, suitable targets, and the lack of capable guardians all converge at the same place and at the same time, then the atmosphere is right for crime (Akers and Sellers, 2009). Potential perpetrators compare the rewards (i.e., what they will gain) to the risks (e.g., the chances of being seen) in determining their actions. Hence, it can be seen that the routine activities theory incorporates the rational choice theory.

Contemporary Research

If residential burglary is a situational crime of opportunity, then the crime can be effectively prevented by employing a SCP strategy, which is based on the rational choice, deterrence, and routine activities theories. Indeed, since the 1980s, there has been an increasing effort to reduce crime by reducing the opportunities to successfully commit crime (Clarke, 2000; Siegel, 2003). Instead of relying upon police officers, SCP programs redistribute crime control responsibilities to private individuals and community organizations (Kraska, 2004). Instead of focusing on the individual, SCP measures focus on the opportunities and settings for crime, attempting to reduce the opportunities to commit specific crimes at specific locations (e.g., residential burglary) by making crime more difficult to accomplish and more risky to attempt (Clarke). If residential burglary is truly a situational crime of opportunity, then SCP measures should be able to effectively prevent this crime, independent of other factors, such as unjust economic and educational opportunities. Therefore, before resources are invested into SCP programs, it is important to know if SCP measures can even work, if crime is concentrated in areas where SCP measures can effectively be implemented, and if SCP measures result in crime displacement.

It is important to know if SCP measures can even work. This question is answered by a couple of studies. First, one study is a quantitative study involving the implementation of SCP measures in the Washington, D.C. Metro subway system (LaVigne, 1996). By using analysis of variance and comparing this subway system to the subway systems in Chicago, Boston, and Atlanta, the findings indicate that, after employing SCP measures, the Metro subway system's mean rate of crime is significantly lower than the other three subway systems. Unlike the other three subway systems, the Metro subway system is designed so that the customer waiting area is free of obstructions and is highly visible, the system utilizes closed circuit televisions, the area is well lit and maintained, and the laws are stringently enforced. As a result, the Metro subway system is believed to be one of the safest subway systems in the country. Second, another study that substantiates the effectiveness of SCP practices is a meta-analysis study of 31 evaluation reports of SCP measures (Willemse, 1994). The findings of this study indicate that SCP measures are very effective if employment efforts are intensive.

It is also important to know if crime in the city is concentrated in areas where SCP measures can effectively be implemented against residential burglary. Three studies examine official law enforcement data to investigate whether reported crime is tightly clustered in micro places over extended periods of time (Sherman, Gartin, & Buerger, 1989; Weisburd, Bushway, Lum, & Yang, 2004). Two studies, one examining the 84 square mile city of Seattle for 14 years and one examining the 115,000 addresses in the city of Minneapolis for one year, indicate that most of the reported crimes are concentrated in relatively few hot spots. For example, in Minneapolis, half of the 323,979 calls to police occurred in 3% of the area. Thus, because crime consistently occurs in micro areas, SCP measures may be very effective in addressing residential burglary. A third study, using *cleared crime* data, indicates that prolific offenders often repeat crimes against the same households (Everson & Pease, 2001). Thus, crime appears to stay in tightly clustered areas.

Two additional studies indicate that crime is likely to occur and reoccur in highly traveled areas. First, an ex post facto research study in two towns examines the crime in various street segments (Beavon, Brantingham, & Brantingham, 1994). The findings indicate that the crime rate is greater on streets that are more accessible to the public and that are used more often. Thus, criminal opportunities vary depending upon the environment in which one lives. In these cases, potential offenders have the opportunity to search for their targets in these highly traveled areas and opportunities seem to dominate the pattern of criminal behaviors. Second, an empirical research study indicates that repeat victimization is more likely to occur in high-crime areas than in low-crime areas (Kleemans, 2001). Thus, once residential burglary occurs in an area, it is likely to re-occur in the same area. This indicates that SCP measures should be concentrated in homes that have been burgled before. Indeed, being victimized is a good predictor of being re-victimized.

SCP measures have been employed to the traffic flow in a highly traveled local neighborhood to reduce crime (Atlas & LeBlanc, 1994). The SCP measures included closing roads and changing street designs. The quantitative findings indicate that burglaries, larcenies, and auto thefts had significantly decreased over a 7-year period. However, the findings also indicate that crime in the neighboring areas had increased during this same time period, possibly as a result of crime displacement.

Therefore, to evaluate SCP effectiveness, it is important to know if SCP programs displace crime to other times, places, and targets (Hesseling, 1994). One study, for example, employed SCP practices in a city park, which was considered a drug dealing hot spot (Knutsson, 1996). By surveying local residents, by interviewing local businesses and park drug offenders, and by performing site observations, the findings indicate that the implementation of SCP measures through park redesign, which increased the general visibility of the area and increased the number of capable guardians in the area, reduced illegal drug activity. However, the findings also suggest that some crime displacement did occur.

It must be remembered that employing SCP measures involves three variables, which are a) increasing effort, b) increasing perceived risks, and c) reducing anticipated rewards. Thus, all three variables need to be considered when employing SCP measures.

This was done during an analysis of 55 published articles on SCP measures (Hesseling, 1994). The study's findings indicate that crime displacement depends upon on the particular crime committed and the particular SCP measures that have been implemented to combat that crime. According to Hesseling, employing tactics that a) solely increase the effort to commit the crime, such as by hardening the target, b) solely increase the risk of successfully committing the crime, such as by increasing formal surveillance, or c) solely reduce the rewards of the crime, such as by marking the property, have sometimes displaced crime and have sometimes not displaced crime. However, for residential burglary, when all three SCP measures are implemented simultaneously, the results indicate that it is possible to reduce residential burglary without displacing crime.

Finally, a very important study was conducted with 11 to 16 year old adolescents in order to determine if SCP measures are effective in preventing juvenile crime (Smith, 2003). By administering 461 self-report surveys and by providing the children with situational scenarios, and after performing multivariate analysis of variation, the findings indicate that SCP measures are effective in deterring adolescent crime. In other words, the children have indicated that they are significantly less likely to attack hardened targets. This is essential because this means that SCP measures may be effective in deterring juveniles from committing residential burglary. This is very important because, in Indiana, an 11 year old child may not understand that deadly force may be used against him or her for breaking into someone's home (Office of Code Revision Indiana Legislative Services Agency, n.d.b). Thus, prevention is the key to saving lives.

Proposed Research Methodology

Participants

This study will utilize a non-probability sampling design based on convenience and purposive sampling (Leedy & Ormrod, 2005). The criteria for the sample will be adolescents who live in burglary hot spots in Indiana and who are on probation due to property crime convictions. This is a convenient and non-probability sample because the participants who respond first via their probation officers will be the ones selected to participate in the study. A sample of 384 participants is required in order to achieve a 95% confidence level with a confidence interval of 5 (Creative Research Systems, n.d.).

Research Design

This quantitative research design is a pre-experimental one-group pretest-posttest design (Creswell, 2003). A single group of adolescents will be administered a survey, the independent variables (i.e., measures that increase effort, increase perceived risks, and reduce anticipated rewards) will be manipulated, and then the participants will be administered a second survey. The dependent variable (i.e., the likelihood of committing residential burglary) will be assessed. Indeed, this within-subjects design is appropriate because it is very sensitive to the manipulation of independent variables (Bordens & Abbott, 2008). Below is the research design.

Group A O_1---------X-------------$O_{2;}$ X = Treatment, O = Observation

The participants will be provided with situational scenarios (Smith, 2003). The participants will be shown 50 computer-generated colored photographs of homes having various levels of SCP measures. Using the following 5 point Likert-type scale, the participants will be asked to rate how likely that they would be to commit residential burglary: (1) definitely would not, (2) probably would not, (3) 50/50 chance, (4) probably would, and (5) definitely would. The second time that this survey is administered, 75% of the homes will have had some level of crime prevention measures added.

There are advantages in using this research methodology. First, the independent variables can be manipulated and the significance of their impact on the dependent variable can be statistically and objectively determined (Bordens & Abbott, 2008). In addition, the Likert-type scales are easy to construct and interpret, they are very popular in the criminal justice field, they are flexible and can include as many statements as desired, they lend themselves to numerous ordinal-level statistical procedures, and they produce results similar to other scales, such as the Thurstone and Guttman scales, thus enhancing their validity (Champion, 2006).

There are several disadvantages in using this research methodology. First, because the study utilizes a non-probability sampling design based on convenience and purposive sampling, this limits the findings so that they may not be applied to other populations (Leedy & Ormrod, 2005). Second, for the Likert-type scale, there is no consistent meaning in the raw data, it is assumed that each item on the scale has identical weight (which may not be true), and individuals receiving the same scores do not necessarily possess the same degree of the trait being measured. Finally, due to time and effort, a within-subjects design is very demanding on the participants and attrition may occur (Bordens & Abbott, 2008).

Statistical Analysis

Because the variables are categorical and rank ordered and do not satisfy the parametric assumptions, the nonparametric Spearman's rho test will be used (Bordens & Abbott, 2008). The Spearman's rho test will measure the relationship between the independent and dependent variables in terms of rank and will yield a coefficient value and an associated significance level (Balian, 1988). The Spearman's rho test will effectively indicate whether increasing SCP measures will reduce the likelihood of adolescents committing residential burglary.

Conclusion

SCP is an effective way to reduce residential burglary at specific locations with limited resources (Taylor & Harrell, 2000). Studies have shown that crime is tightly clustered in particular areas, is stable over time, and that prior victimization is a good indicator of future victimization (Sherman, Gartin, & Buerger, 1989; Weisburd, Bushway, Lum, & Yang, 2004). Therefore, tightly clustered areas that have a history of being burgled are prime areas to implement SCP measures. If SCP measures are implemented in these areas, and if residential burglary is displaced, then other measures will need to be addressed at a later date.

Although there are many studies involving the implementation of SCP measures, only a few of them involve children. Overall, it appears that SCP measures are effective in preventing specific crimes at specific locations, so it makes sense that this strategy will be effective in preventing residential burglary committed by adolescents. Because no studies found to date have measured the relationship between SCP measures and children's attitude toward committing residential burglary, this study will provide valuable data. In addition, this study may indicate that different SCP measures as employed by homeowners may not be perceived by adolescents to be symmetrical (Smith, 2003). In other words, having a fenced yard may not have the same preventative weight as having security cameras. However, this study will indicate that children do readily comprehend the meaning behind hardened targets and that the level of deterrence will be directly related to the amount and intensity of SCP measures employed.

Implication for Practice

The results of this study may have an impact on social policies. Because crime is tightly clustered in hot spots, limited resources can effectively be used in specific areas that do the most good. Indeed, there are limited public funds so policymakers need to decide how to allocate the resources (Taylor & Harrell, 2000). For example, because residential burglary is a situational crime of opportunity, authorities could allocate resources in an effort to harden the target, such as by spending money on more street lights, or they could allocate the resources to develop after school recreational programs for kids, thus keeping adolescents busy and reducing the opportunities for them to commit residential burglary (Clarke, 2000; Tucker et al., 1999). Moreover, because economic, social, and political conditions change over time, the reasons for crime may also change. Thus, SCP is an effective crime prevention technique because it does not require local authorities to resolve all of the many reasons why individuals may commit crime. Finally, in order to save lives, especially of children who may not understand the law, the law may be changed to require that homeowners provide signs that their homes have been hardened before they will be allowed to legally use deadly force simply to prevent the unlawful entry into a dwelling.

References

Akers, R., and Sellers, C. (2009). *Criminological theories: Introduction, evaluation, and application* (5th ed.). New York, NY: Oxford University Press.

Atlas, R., and LeBlanc, W. (1994). The impact on crime of street closures and barricades: A Florida case study. *Security Journal*, 140-145.

Balian, E. (1988). *How to design, analyze, and write doctoral or master's research* (2nd ed.). New York, NY: University Press of America.

Barkan, S. (2006). *Criminology: A sociological understanding* (3rd ed.). Upper Saddle River, NJ: Pearson Prentice Hall.

Beavon, D., Brantingham, P., and Brantingham, P. (1994). The influence of street networks on the patterning of property offenses. *Crime Prevention Studies*, 2, 115-148.

Bordens, K., and Abbott, B. (2008). *Research design and methods: A process approach* (7th ed.). Boston, MA: McGraw Hill.

Champion, D. (2006). *Research methods for criminal justice and criminology* (3rd ed.). Upper Saddle River, NJ: Pearson Merrill Prentice Hall.

Clarke, R. (2000). Situational crime prevention: Successful studies. In R. Glensor, M. Correia, & K. Peak (Eds.), *Policing communities: Understanding crime and solving problems, an anthology* (p. 182-225). Los Angeles, CA: Roxbury Publishing Company.

Creative Research Systems (n.d.). *The survey system: Sample size calculator.* Retrieved from http://www.surveysystem.com/sscalc.htm

Creswell, J. (2003). *Research design: Qualitative, quantitative, and mixed methods approaches* (2nd ed.). Thousand Oaks, CA: Sage Publications.

Everson, S., and Pease, K. (2001). Crime against the same person and place: Detection opportunity and offender targeting. *Crime Prevention Studies*, 12, 199-220.

Hess, K., and Wrobleski, H. (2003). *Police operations: Theory and practice* (3rd ed.). Belmont, CA: Thomson-Wadsworth.

Hesseling, R. (1994). Displacement: A review of the empirical literature. *Crime Prevention Studies*, 3, 197-230.

Indiana Department of Correction (n.d.). *Offender population statistical report: Calendar year 2007.* Retrieved from http://www.in.gov/idoc/files/CY07OffenderPopulation.pdf

Kleemans, E. (2001). Repeat burglary victimization: Results of empirical research in the Netherlands. *Crime Prevention Studies*, 11, 53-68.

Knutsson, J. (1996). Restoring public order in a city park. *Crime Prevention Studies*, 7, 133-151.

Kraska, P. (2004). *Theorizing criminal justice: Eight essential orientations*. Long Grove, IL: Waveland Press, Inc.

LaVigne, N. (1996). Safe transport: Security by design on the Washington metro. *Crime Prevention Studies*, 6, 163-197.

Leedy, P., and Ormrod, J. (2005). *Practical research: Planning and design* (8th ed.). Upper Saddle River, NJ: Pearson Merrill Prentice Hall.

Liska, A. and Messner, S. (1999). *Perspectives on Crime and Deviance* (3rd ed.). Upper Saddle River, NJ: Prentice Hall.

Ministry of Justice (n.d.). *Reducing residential burglary: What can police do?* Retrieved from http://www.justice.govt.nz/

Office of Code Revision Indiana Legislative Services Agency (n.d.a). *IC 35-50-1-2. Consecutive and concurrent terms.* Retrieved from https://iga.in.gov/legislative/laws/2014/ic/

Office of Code Revision Indiana Legislative Services Agency (n.d.b). *IC 35-41-3-2. Use of force to protect person or property.* Retrieved from https://iga.in.gov/legislative/laws/2014/ic/

Office of Code Revision Indiana Legislative Services Agency (n.d.c). *IC 35-43-2-1. Burglary.* Retrieved from https://iga.in.gov/legislative/laws/2014/ic/

Schmalleger, F. (2007). *Criminal justice today: An introductory text for the 21st century* (9th ed.). Upper Saddle River, NJ: Pearson Prentice Hall.

Sherman, L., Gartin, P., and Buerger, M. (1989). Hot spots of predatory crime: Routine activities and the criminology of place. *Criminology,* 27(1), 27-55.

Siegel, L. (2003). *Criminology* (8th ed.). Belmont, CA: Wadsworth – Thomson Publishing Company.

Smith, M. (2003). Exploring target attractiveness in vandalism: An experimental approach. *Crime Prevention Studies*, 16, 197-236.

Taylor, R., and Harrell, A. (2000). Physical environment and crime. In R. Glensor, M. Correia, & K. Peak (Eds.), *Policing communities: Understanding crime and solving problems, an anthology* (p. 167-181). Los Angeles, CA: Roxbury Publishing Company.

Tucker, J., Donovan, D., and Marlatt, G. (Eds.). (1999). *Changing additive behavior: Bridging clinical and public health strategies.* New York, NY: Guilford Press.

Weisburd, D., Bushway, S., Lum, C., and Yang, S. (2004). Trajectories of crime at places: A longitudinal study of street segments in the city of Seattle. *Criminology*, 42(2), 283-321.

Willemse, H. (1994). Developments in Dutch crime prevention. *Crime Prevention Studies*, 2, 33-47.

Example 3

Qualitative Study: Case Study

Police Officers Accepting Gratuities

Abstract

Police officers accepting gratuities is not uncommon. Because police officers have discretionary powers, and because their attitudes may be influenced by accepting gratuities, this may create a problem if this impacts the performance of their duties. Thus, in order to learn more about this poorly understood problem from the police officers' perspective, a qualitative longitudinal case study involving five Indiana State Police cadets will be performed, following the officers for two years after they graduate from the police academy. This study will allow incremental behavioral changes to be measured at specific points in time.

Purpose of the Study

The purpose of this study is to understand how police officers perceive their accepting of gratuities impacts public relations and their job performance.

Qualitative Research Question

In order to understand the nature of police officers accepting gratuities as perceived by police officers, the following qualitative research question has been developed. *How do police officers perceive the accepting of gratuities impacts personal relationships and their discretionary decisions?*

Theoretical Framework: Rational Choice and Social Learning Theories

The rational choice theory, based on Beccaria's classical school of criminology, claims that people freely choose their behaviors (Siegel, 2003). It is believed that people calculate the potential benefits and costs associated with each behavior and then they choose to perform those acts that are profitable.

The social learning theory, as developed by Albert Bandura, combines operant conditioning and cognitive psychology (Siegel, 2003). According to this theory, behaviors can be learned and reinforced through personal rewards and punishments and by observing the rewards and punishments of other people.

Assumptions and Limitations

It is assumed that the police officers are truthful in their disclosures and that they can detect and interpret the feelings of other people. In addition, limitations include limited applications of the findings to other populations (Leedy & Ormrod, 2005).

Literature Review

There are several research studies involving police gratuities. First, an Australian ex post facto quantitative descriptive study measured police officers' attitudes toward accepting gratuities by providing them with various hospitality scenarios (MacIntyre & Prenzler, 1999). The findings indicate that police officers' attitudes may be influenced by accepting gratuities. Second, a cross-cultural quantitative study of police officers and college students indicate that police officers are significantly less tolerant than college students of accepting gratuities (Ivkovic, 2004). Third, a quasi-experiment pretest-posttest study indicates that one college course in ethics is not enough to develop values or behavioral changes in college students (Lord & Bjerregaard, 2003). Fourth, an ex post facto quantitative descriptive study indicates that there is strong community support that favors police officers not accepting gratuities (Prenzler & Mackay, 1995). Fifth, an ex post facto quantitative descriptive study investigates city, county, and state law enforcement agencies in Florida (Kirchgraber, 2004). The findings indicate that police officers do regularly accept gratuities. Finally, a mixed methods ex post facto study was performed examining the code of silence (Trautman, 2001). The findings indicate that the code of silence is common and that police officers do not readily inform management about each other's questionable behaviors, such as accepting gratuities.

Proposal for Research Design

To capture the participants' points of view involving their beliefs, attitudes, and behaviors surrounding the event of accepting gratuities, a qualitative case study is appropriate (Creswell, 2003). In this study, five cadets (i.e., participants) will be assessed while at the police academy before they are sworn police officers and before they are provided gratuities, and then they will be followed for two years after graduation. Interviews will be conducted with each participant once a month and other pertinent information about the topic, including department policies, disciplinary postings, and newspaper articles, will be gathered to supplement and substantiate the interviews.

Methodology

Research Design

Different research designs have different strengths and weaknesses. First, ex post facto quantitative descriptive studies, where data are collected after the fact, are effective in determining the impact of the independent variable (e.g., accepting gratuities) on the dependent variable (e.g., behaviors), but the independent variable cannot be manipulated (Leedy & Ormrod, 2005). Thus, definite conclusions about cause and effect cannot be established. Second, focus group interviews, where individuals who share common traits and experiences interact and provide data beyond what any single participant could provide, are most appropriate for studies that are explanatory in nature (Hatch, 2002). However, a weakness in this technique is that the group consensus may overshadow a particular individual's perspective (Berg, 2007; Hatch). Third, phenomenology, which explores the essence of experience, gains a deeper understanding of an experience and uncovers hidden phenomena (Hatch). However, these studies are based on interviews that may take place long after the fact and may be influenced by forgetfulness and exaggeration. Fourth, unobtrusive ethnography seeks to describe a culture from the local or indigenous people's point of view through participant observation and artifact examination in order "to understand the cultural knowledge that group members use to make sense of the everyday experiences" (Hatch, p. 21). However, the weaknesses in unobtrusive data are 1) the data presents a distorted view of the events and social context, 2) the data are gathered piecemeal, presenting an incomplete picture, and 3) those individuals initially presenting documented records may have done so in a biased fashion. Finally, a case study is a type of qualitative research where in-depth data are collected on a single event, program, or individual bound by time and activity for the purpose of learning more about a poorly understood problem (Creswell, 2003; Hatch; Leedy & Ormrod, 2005). Indeed, a case study, which focuses on few participants, will be most effective in understanding how police officers develop their attitudes about accepting gratuities (Berg, 2007).

There are four advantages in performing case studies (Champion, 2006). First, case studies are flexible and they allow the researcher to collect data in multiple ways, such as by interviewing people and by examining records. Second, this flexibility can be extended to virtually any dimension of the gratuities topic. Third, case studies can be performed in many types of social environments. Finally, a longitudinal case study will allow incremental behavioral changes to be measured at specific points in time.

There are three disadvantages in performing case studies (Champion, 2006). First, case study findings are unique to particular individuals and settings and may not be generalized to other populations. Second, attrition is a concern; participants may simply lose interest and stop participating. Third, findings from individual case studies may not always support theories. Therefore, an accumulation of case studies is important.

Sampling

The sampling will employ a non-probability sampling design based on purposive criterion sampling. Five Indiana State Police cadets will be selected based on who responds first to the study's invitation.

Instrument

The following are five open-ended questions that will allow for narrative style responses. *"What is the police department's position on accepting gratuities?" "What does the public think about you accepting gratuities?" "What are the advantages and disadvantages of accepting gratuities?" "How does a police officer accepting gratuities differ from doctors, politicians, or restaurant employees accepting gratuities (free perks) in their respective trades?"* And, *"How has accepting gratuities created personal relationships with store owners, which have affected your discretionary enforcement of minor violations of the law or the delivering of public services?"*

Data

This qualitative research design will employ in-depth, personal, semi-structured interviews utilizing a multiple subject longitudinal case study (Champion, 2006). One-hour interviews will be conducted once a month, tape recorded, and transcribed verbatim. Furthermore, department policies, disciplinary postings, and newspaper articles will be gathered to supplement and substantiate the interviews (Berg, 2007).

The data will be context analyzed (Berg, 2007; Creswell, 2003). Content analysis "is a systematic technique for categorizing words into content categories using special coding rules" (Churyk, Lee, & Clinton, 2008, p. 52). Groupings of words will reflect themes, and the evaluation of themes will provide answers to the research question.

Philosophical, Political, and Ethical Issues

There are philosophical, political, and ethical issues when police officers accept gratuities. These issues are important because law and order depend upon residents submitting themselves to the government in order to be governed (Carter, 2002). This requires faith that officers will be just; and faith is influenced by image. Indeed, if the public becomes dissatisfied with police and breaks the agreement, then chaos will result.

Because proper police service requires good police-community relations and fair treatment of all persons, it is important to know if gratuities interfere with police officer performance (Carter, 2002). Indeed, the results of this study may provide an assessment of police management's traditional approach to managing gratuities and may indicate the need for future policy changes.

The police officer code of ethics does not necessarily disapprove of police officers accepting gratuities (Hess & Wrobleski, 1997). However, the concern is that accepting gratuities may negatively affect a police officer's discretionary decisions. Because accepting gratuities may be good, such as in developing positive social relationships, or bad, such as in leading to corruption, this study is essential in determining which is true.

Strategies to Help Facilitate Study

In order to protect participants, ethical guidelines will be followed throughout the research process. First, the purpose of the study and its benefits will be effectively communicated to the participants (Creswell, 2003). Second, because participation is voluntary, it will be made clear to the participants that they can withdraw from the study at any time without consequence. Third, to help protect anonymity, names will not be attached to the data collection instruments. Fourth, to protect the confidentiality of the data, a Certificate of Confidentiality will be sought (Berg, 2007). Fifth, member checking will be employed to ensure accurate interpretations of the data (Creswell).

References

Berg, B. (2007). *Qualitative research methods for the social sciences* (6th ed.). Boston, MA: Pearson Education, Inc.

Carter, D. (2002). *Issues in police-community relations: Taken from The Police and the community* (7th ed.). Boston, MA: Pearson Custom Publishing.

Champion, D. (2006). *Research methods for criminal justice and criminology* (3rd ed.). Upper Saddle River, NJ: Pearson Merrill Prentice Hall.

Churyk, N., Lee, C., and Clinton, D. (2008). Can we detect fraud earlier? *Strategic Finance*, *90*(4), 51-54.

Creswell, J. (2003). *Research design: Qualitative, quantitative, and mixed methods approaches* (2nd ed.). Thousand Oaks, CA: Sage Publications.

Hatch, J. (2002). *Doing qualitative research in education settings.* Albany, NY: State University of New York Press.

Hess, K., and Wrobleski, H. (1997). *Police operations: Theory and practice* (2nd ed.). St. Paul, MN: West publishing Company.

Ivkovic, S. (2004). Evaluating the seriousness of police misconduct: A cross-cultural comparison of police officer and citizen views. *International Criminal Justice Review*, *14*, 25-48.

Kirchgraber, T. (2004, November 1). When policy and practice collide: The mixed message on gratuities. *Sheriff.* Retrieved from http://www.highbeam.com/doc/1P3-750878951.html

Leedy, P., and Ormrod, J. (2005). *Practical research: Planning and design* (8th ed.). Upper Saddle River, NJ: Pearson Merrill Prentice Hall.

Lord, V., and Bjerregaard, B. (2003). *Ethics courses: Their impact on the values and ethical decisions on criminal justice students. Journal of Criminal Justice Management, 14(2), 191-211.*

MacIntyre, S., and Prenzler, T. (1999). The influence of gratuities and personal relationships on police use of discretion. *Policing and Society, 9*(2), 181-201.

Prenzler, T., and Mackay, P. (1995). Police gratuities: What the public think. *Criminal Justice Ethics, 14*(1), 15-25.

Siegel, L. (2003). *Criminology* (8th ed.). Belmont, CA: Thomson Wadsworth.

Trautman, N.E. (2001, March 1). The code of silence . . . now we know the truth. *Sheriff.* Retrieved from http://www.highbeam.com/doc/1P3-69904278.html

Appendix G

DISCUSSION QUESTIONS/EXERCISES

1) Explain how a feminist, an Afrocentrist, a logical positivist, and a postmodernist would respond to a complaint made by an African American female who states that she has been treated unjustly by a male police officer, who is Caucasian. She claims that she was profiled, which lead to a traffic stop. How would the different perspectives explain or assess the complaint?
2) What is meant by the comment that citizens must develop ownership of their community in order to maintain peace? Should civil commitment be endorsed? Support your position.
3) Describe the American culture. Why might residents not want to become involved in community policing efforts?
4) Describe 3 attributes that make a job candidate a good fit for a police department that is committed to community policing. Select a community problem you feel is important and describe the partners who might collaborate to address the problem.
5) What are the main reasons why individuals join gangs? How does a street gang member differ from other juvenile delinquents? What efforts exist in your community to combat the gang problem? Discuss community ambivalence toward gangs. What risks exist for children who are exposed to violence?

6) Discuss the conceptual similarities and operational differences between 5 different community policing projects (e.g., TIPS, GREAT, DARE, etc.).
7) Community members must take responsibility for making a healthy society. Discuss the Alcoholics Anonymous 12-Step program and critique its effectiveness. Discuss how applied and clinical sociologists would assess the program.
8) Discuss the relationships between news media, entertainment media, and violence. Why are police sometimes reluctant to disclose information to the media? Do you feel that when cases of police misconduct are publicized, citizens view this as a generalization of all officers or as an exception to the rule?
9) From your own community, provide some specific examples of negative perceptions between the police and community members that have caused or may cause poor police-community relations. Suggest ways to modify these negative perceptions.
10) What are the main complaints of minorities against the police? Discuss why the view of minorities toward the police may be different than that of Caucasians. Describe how a resident's experience with the police may shape the resident's image of all officers. What is the main complaint of police officers?
11) A controversial issue is related to how a police officer's performance review is determined. Discuss the pros and cons for the traditional quantitative evaluation of performance (i.e.., quotas) and the qualitative evaluation of performance, which may be preferred for community policing.
12) Perform a literature review on community policing and summarize three scholarly, peer-reviewed research studies. When you summarize each study, answer the following questions in the order listed. 1) What was the purpose of the

study? 2) Who were studied? 3) How were data collected? 4) What inferential statistic or qualitative analysis was used? 5) What were the findings? 6) What were the limitations of the study?

13) Discuss how a citizens' review board works in dealing with complaints. Discuss strengths and weaknesses. In addition, discuss how individuals' may never come to trust the police if they perceive that they have been treated unjustly and there is no forum in which to explore their claims.
14) What is the image of the police in your community? What factors are responsible for this image? Can the police image be made more positive? What expectations do you have of law enforcement agencies? Discuss the conflict between the right to dissent and the need to maintain order.
15) Researchers are required to use ethical procedures when performing studies. Discuss the ethical procedures.
16) The Institutional Review Board (IRB) is required to approve all university affiliated studies. Why did the IRB come about? What should be presented on an **informed consent form** before any research is conducted**?** Why?
17) Find a website that provides a service to a particular group of people. Provide that link. Describe the company that provides the services. Describe the services provided. How are the services related to peace and order? Are all social problems law enforcement related? How can the police serve people who have the particular problem?
18) Discuss the reasons behind the Benton Harbor (MI) riot. You are a police chief. Discuss ways that you can prevent future riots.
19) **Ethical systems.** Explain whether the police deceiving suspects via lies is acceptable practice (i.e., deemed good) according to

the following ethical systems: ethical formalism, utilitarianism, act utilitarianism, rule utilitarianism, religious, natural law, ethics of virtue, ethics of care, egoism, enlightened egoism, ethical relativism, cultural relativism, and situational ethics. Provide an example of each situation to support your position. In other words, convince the reader to agree with you.

Ethical System	Good Behavior	Explain if acceptable to lie to public (justify response)
Ethical Formalism		
Utilitarianism		
Act Utilitarianism		
Rule Utilitarianism		
Religious		
Natural Law		
Ethics of Virtue		
Ethics of Care		
Egoism		
Enlightened Egoism		
Ethical Relativism		
Cultural Relativism		
Situational Ethics		

20) **Police Department Orientations**

Select an ethical system to represent your beliefs (does not have to be true). Define your ethical system. Now apply your ethical system to the 9 different police department orientations (define each of the police department orientations). If a police department operates under each of the orientations, how well will you fit into the department?

Your Ethical System	Police Department Orientation	Definition of Police Department Orientation	Good Fit between your Ethical System and the Police Department Orientation? (Explain)
	Rational		
	Crime Control		
	Due Process		
	System		
	Politics		
	Growth Complex		
	Social Constructionist		
	Late Modernity		
	Oppression		

21) Compare and contrast a) Tough Cops, b) Clean-Beat Crime Fighting Cops, c) Problem Solving Cops, and d) Professional Cops. Describe which one best matches your local police department. Provide an example.
22) Compare and contrast Authoritarian Leadership Style to Participatory Leadership Style. Describe which one best matches your local police department. Provide an example.
23) Compare and contrast a) Traditional Policing, b) Community Policing, and c) Problem-Oriented Policing. Describe which one best matches your local police department. Provide an example.
24) **Team Assumptions – Class Activity**

Individuals make assumptions about other people. We draw conclusions about other people based on experiences, rumors, and personal filters. Without knowing it, these assumptions are often displayed by how we communicate with one another.

Class Activity

1) Write words on 3" x 5" cards that describe human qualities/behaviors (e.g., clown, idiot, genius, happy, grumpy, love sick, feminist, etc.).
2) Have group members sit at a table and tape the unique word on a stick above and behind each individual. Do not let the individual see the word that will represent that particular person. Each individual will see every word that describes all the other individuals. The only word that each person cannot see will be the one that describes himself/herself.
3) Have the group play a game of cards.
4) Without saying the word behind each person, individuals are to treat all other individuals according to the word that describes each person. Assumptions will be made about one another based on the description written on each person's card.
5) The rest of the class will take notes on what they observe.